Invisible Families

Invisible Families

Gay Identities, Relationships, and Motherhood among Black Women

Mignon R. Moore

UNIVERSITY OF CALIFORNIA PRESS
Berkeley · *Los Angeles* · *London*

University of California Press, one of the most
distinguished university presses in the United States,
enriches lives around the world by advancing
scholarship in the humanities, social sciences, and
natural sciences. Its activities are supported by the UC
Press Foundation and by philanthropic contributions
from individuals and institutions. For more information, visit www.ucpress.edu.

A portion of chapter 2 appeared previously in "Lipstick
or Timberlands? Meanings of Gender Presentation in
Black Lesbian Communities," *Signs: Journal of Women
in Culture and Society* 32, no. 1 (2006): 113–39.
Portions of chapter 5 appeared earlier in "Gendered
Power Relations among Women: A Study of Household
Decision-Making in Lesbian Stepfamilies," *American
Sociological Review* 73, no. 2 (2008): 335–56.

University of California Press
Berkeley and Los Angeles, California

University of California Press, Ltd.
London, England

Library of Congress Cataloging-in-Publication Data

Moore, Mignon R.
    Invisible families : gay identities, relationships, and
motherhood among Black women / Mignon R. Moore.
—1st ed.
        p. cm.
    Includes bibliographical references and index.
    ISBN 978-0-520-26951-4 (cloth : alk. paper) —
ISBN 978-0-520-26952-1 (pbk. : alk. paper)
    1. African American lesbians—United States.
2. African American lesbians—Identity.   3. Same-sex
marriage—United States.   4. Gay rights—United
States.   5. Puerto Rican lesbians—Identity.   I. Title.
HQ75.6.U5M66 2011
306.84'80899607307471—dc23

                                        2011024085

Manufactured in the United States of America

20   19   18   17   16   15   14   13   12   11
10   9   8   7   6   5   4   3   2   1

This book is printed on Cascades Enviro 100, a 100%
post consumer waste, recycled, de-inked fiber. FSC
recycled certified and processed chlorine free. It is acid
free, Ecologo certified, and manufactured by BioGas
energy.

For Black and Brown lesbians, and for Black and Brown women everywhere – may your voices be heard and your stories be told

Contents

Acknowledgments   *ix*

Introduction: Two Sides of the Same Coin: Revising
Analyses of Lesbian Sexuality and Family Formation
through the Study of Black Women   *1*

1. Coming into the Life: Entrance into Gay Sexuality for
   Black Women   *21*

2. Gender Presentation in Black Lesbian Communities   *65*

3. Marginalized Social Identities: Self-Understandings
   and Group Membership   *92*

4. Lesbian Motherhood and Discourses of Respectability   *113*

5. Family Life and Gendered Relations between Women   *153*

6. Openly Gay Families and the Negotiation of Black
   Community and Religious Life   *180*

   Conclusion: Intersections, Extensions, and Implications   *215*

Appendix A: A Roadmap for the Study of Marginalized
and Invisible Populations   *223*
Appendix B: Selected Questions from Invisible
Families Survey   *239*
Appendix C: Questions from In-Depth Interview on
Self-Definitions of Sexuality   *249*
Notes   *251*
References   *269*
Index   *289*

Photographs follow page 152

Acknowledgments

I want to thank the many people and organizations who have helped guide this book from inception to completion. Elaine Harley introduced me to the Black and Latina women's communities of New York. Prior to meeting her I was similar to many other social science researchers of lesbian populations, in that I was not aware of the history, depth, and breadth of gay life for women of color. During my time as a faculty member at Columbia University, a group of colleagues in New York City encouraged me to pursue this work and I appreciate their support. They include Farah Jasmine Griffin, the late Manning Marable, Sam Roberts, Steven Gregory, Nicole Marwell, Debra Minkoff, Sudhir Venkatesh, Peter Bearman, Priscilla Ferguson, Florencia Torche, Lydia English, and my NY "Sister Scholars," especially Farah, Leith Mullings, Monica Miller, Dana-Ain Davis, Kim Hall, Jennifer Morgan and Diane Harriford.

Several organizations provided financial resources and time-off from teaching that allowed me to collect the data and begin my analyses. Sabbatical fellowships supported by the Andrew W. Mellon Foundation and the Woodrow Wilson Foundation were critical, as was my year-in-residence as a Visiting Scholar at the Russell Sage Foundation, where conversations with my colleagues in the 2004-2005 cohort, particularly Chas Camic, Dina Okamoto, Ingrid Banks, and the late Kenneth Sokoloff helped me develop critical components of this work. The Columbia University Institute for Research in African-American Studies and Institute for Economic Social Research and Policy also provided support in the way of funding for research assistance and equipment. Shawn Mendoza and Sharon Harris were more than generous with their administrative support. While at Columbia, I had excellent graduate students who traversed Long Island, New Jersey and all five boroughs of New York with me throughout the fall and cold winter to conduct interviews. They helped enter, code and transcribe the survey and interview data, and willingly did everything I asked of them (or at least that is how I'd like to remember it). Thank you Patrice Bradshaw, Kellee Terrell, Tara Spencer, Felicia Rector, and Amanda Gilliam. Other students during that time who participated in discussions that were part of the ideas in this book include Marcus Anthony Hunter and Mikaela Rabinowitz.

Many people I met in the field taught me so many things about so many things! First of all I thank the New York Women's community and particularly the more than 100 women who are the subjects of this book for generously opening their homes and sharing their thoughts and experiences, inspiring me to write about their lives. Kate, Monique, Lisa S., Madison, Knowings, Ms. Bess, Judi, Rose, Ife, Myrna, Cheryl, Mimi, Glisa and Beverly gave advice and showed me how to put on social events that bring women together, and I continue to draw from their insights today. During the course of my work I met many people who became good friends. Thank you Sohad, Eva, Sandy, Zola, Rebecca, Tonya, Deborah, Andrea, Marta and Staceyann for stimulating conversations, good meals and great times. My long-time friends in New York have shown me unconditional love and support throughout my research period, and I thank Maati, Galia, LaTonya, Corlisse, Kenya, Martha J. and Nicole for their friendship.

Naomi Schneider, my editor at the University of California Press, has been supportive of this book throughout the publication process. Thanks also to Stacey Eisenstark and Brian Desmond for keeping the book on track throughout the production process. Do Mi Stauber was an excellent indexer for the manuscript, and I am appreciative of the editorial assistance Ruth Homrighaus has provided.

The majority of the writing for this book took place in Southern California. From my very first visit until today, my colleagues in the UCLA departments of sociology and African American studies have remained enthusiastic and supportive of this work. In particular I thank Abigail Saguy, Darnell Hunt, Mark Sawyer, Walter Allen, Judy Seltzer, Stefan Timmermans, Belinda Tucker, Ruth Milkman, Brenda Stevenson, Megan Sweeney, Bill Roy, Toni Yancey, Vilma Ortiz, Rebecca Emigh, Min Zhou, Russell Robinson, Arthur Little, Chandra Ford, Grace Hong,

Maylei Blackwell, Scot Brown, Aisha Finch, Lorrie Frasure, Chris Littleton, Sandra Harding, Lisbeth Gant-Britton and Kathleen McHugh for conversations and correspondence that kept the work moving forward and kept me moving forward as a member of the faculty. The UCLA Center for the Study of Women, Institute for American Cultures, Ralph J. Bunche Center for African American Studies and Center for the Study of Race, Ethnicity and Politics supported this work with research and travel funds, and I am thankful. Carol Mangione, Ron Andersen and Carole Nagy at the UCLA Resource Centers for Minority Aging Research/Center for the Health Improvement of Minority Elders supported me on other projects that indirectly contributed to the completion of this work. I am indebted to the members of the Women of Color Writing Group in Southern California (the LOUD Collective) and in particular Maylei, Tiffany Willoughby-Herard, Aisha, Erica Edwards, Grace, Jayna Brown, Deb Vargas, Caroline Streeter, Arlene Keizer, and Kara Keeling for great meals, stimulating exchanges of ideas, and lots of warmth, laughter and support. Research assistants that helped with this manuscript in LA include Danielle Wondra, Walter Tucker and Jessica Kizer.

There were colleagues and friends across the country who read and listened to drafts of this book in its many forms. These include the audiences at many colloquia and conferences where I have presented this work. They also include Cathy Cohen, Barbara Risman, Paula England, Ellen Lewin, Juan Battle, Kathy Edin, Michael Rosenfeld, Dina, Prudence Carter, Karolyn Tyson, Karyn Lacy, Kerry Ann Rockquemore, Celeste Watkins, Arlene Stein, Myra Marx Ferree, Lindsay Chase-Lansdale, Zsuzsa Berend, France Winddance Twine, Judy Stacey and Irv Garfinkel. The Council on Contemporary Families has been a wonderful source of professional socialization and friendship. The relationships I have developed as a CCF board member with Stephanie Coontz, Pepper Schwartz, Barbara, Kerry Ann, Paula, Kathleen Gerson, Jennifer Glass, Waldo Johnson, Josh Coleman and others have sustained me and will continue to grow throughout the course of my career. Together, all of the criticisms and suggestions I received from these and other people have made this a substantially better book.

Many friends and loved ones cheered me to the finish line in Los Angeles. A special thank you to Tajamika, Diane, Flora, Deborah, Lynora, Yemi, Carneka, Sinaa, Shelbie, Chris, Camille, Chaun, Dana, Delena, Chonsie, the late NaaMeka White and the women of Chocolate & Wine Upscale Events. The LGBT community in Los Angeles has supported me in all of my research efforts, and I sincerely thank them. I conclude with a special acknowledgement to my parents James and Carolyn Moore, my siblings Deirdre, Melanie, Rebecca, LaToya, Marquise and Andrew, and my other family members for their never-ending support and love. Last but not least, I thank Elaine "DJ One" Harley for taking this journey with me, reading and listening to many, many drafts of the work in its various forms, sharing her brilliant insights and perspectives, helping me see my own biases, encouraging me to be brave, providing me with unconditional love, and showing me how to dig deep within myself to finish this book and give voice to the lives of so many women.

Two Sides of the Same Coin

*Revising Analyses of Lesbian Sexuality and Family
Formation through the Study of Black Women*

As dusk falls, I pull up to the house feeling embarrassed at my lateness. The e-mail invitation said to come any time after 4 P.M., but I am arriving slightly after eight, and the sun has already set. I have been here before. The first time was to interview Ruthie Erickson[1] about the family she has created with her three-year-old adopted son, Lawrence. Ruthie is a thirty-six-year-old accountant for a large financial institution. During the interview, she talked a great deal about Lawrence's godmothers, Dana and Angie Russell, who live on the second floor of the two-family house that Ruthie owns. Angie was recently promoted to sergeant in the New York City Police Department, and Dana works for the post office. This evening I am at their home for a purely social event: an end-of-summer/back-to-school barbeque. Dana's only child, whom she had in a prior heterosexual relationship, is headed off to college in a few weeks, and the invitation asks that we bring something her daughter can use for school. I forget to do this but manage to follow the other instruction, which is to bring "a dish or bottle to share." I've made a jerk chicken pasta salad and am hoping everyone will like it.

The Ericksons and the Russells share a large two-family house in a Black middle-class neighborhood in Queens, a short distance from a well-known shopping mall. It is a warm night and lots of folks are sitting on the front porch. A few people are smoking, and some children are tossing a ball outside. The family dog playfully chases other kids as they run in and out of the house. Rhythm and blues music floats into the yard and a few people are casually doing a two-step, though at this point no one is actually dancing. Most are standing around laughing, talking, eating, and drinking. The scene looks and feels very familiar and reminds me of countless summer barbeques I have attended in my family throughout the years, with one exception: almost everyone here is gay. While walking up the front stoop I pass two men together on the stairs. One sits on the lower step between the legs of the second. He leans back into the other's chest, and they laugh at something they have just shared. As they talk, I detect a West Indian accent but cannot decide if it is Jamaican or Trinidadian. At the top of the steps, two women stand underneath the porch light; one takes the other's hand, playing with her fingers as they talk. On a bench near the front door a woman sits on another's lap feeding her a burger. From the entrance to the front yard it is difficult to see that the couples are of the same sex. Others who are not coupled are scattered throughout, so a casual observer might not notice the same-gender pairings. At this point I have been in the field for more than a year, but this scene still slightly throws me off. I expect to see gay people openly expressing their sexuality at bars or in nightclubs, but a lesbian outdoor barbeque in this Black neighborhood creates a subtle dissonance in my mind, because everything else about the setting suggests Black heterosexual life. In a context like this one it quickly becomes apparent that the family life of gay women of color has for many years been largely invisible to African Americans, myself included.

Scholarly research on lesbian identity, gay and lesbian family formation, and Black family life have also paid scant attention to these "invisible families." While a maturing field of study examines gender and sexuality in the construction and maintenance of families headed by gay people, particularly lesbian women, those scholars who deal with race at all tend to do so by including the experiences of very few racial minorities. Their overarching theme is gay sexuality, not sexuality and race. In fact, few scholars and hardly any sociologists have made race or ethnicity the focus of analysis of lesbian families. Past research has also taken for granted the middle-class and upper-middle-class status of its subjects, with less consideration of how middle-class experience helps produce particular ideological understandings of family. Yet if we allow "lesbian families" to mean "White middle-class lesbian families," and if we do not fully "race" ourselves and our subjects, we cannot de-center the White gay subject as the norm, and we reify the myth that "Black people aren't like that." We also continue to perpetuate unidimensional understandings of the experience of creating and maintaining openly lesbian families and relationships.

Invisible Families offers a corrective, building on past work by asserting the fundamental importance of race, class, and gender in organizing lesbian sexuality and lesbian-headed families. It shows the ways in which Black cultures, ideologies, and the historical experiences of Black women structure lesbian identities, as well as how Black lesbians' participation in and enactment of their intersecting identities as Black, as women, and as gay people influence family formation, mate selection, expectations for partners in committed relationships, and other aspects of family life. The structural positions Black women have historically occupied in the labor market, in their families, and in cultural institutions, I argue, are critical to how Black lesbians define themselves and use those definitions to construct families (Moore 2011).

Both the inclusion of Black women in the study of lesbian identity and family formation and the inclusion of homosexual women in the study of Black families challenge some of the theoretical and empirical approaches that scholars have previously taken. In living as openly gay people raising families, the women I studied make their homosexuality a salient component of the selves they project to others in predominantly Black social spaces. These are spaces that have historically asked for allegiance to a social group whose boundaries are drawn around Blackness. Because gay people of color have to deal with the perception by some racial group members that lesbian sexuality challenges their race consciousness, their experiences may differ qualitatively from those of their White peers, whose racial identities may not be as salient to their sense of self. Including women of color in the study of lesbian practice and lesbian family formation reveals how these women structure their lives and approach family formation and identities of all kinds, including sexual identities, from a perspective that has at its foundation not lesbian feminism but Black feminist ideologies, discourses of Black respectability, racial socialization, race consciousness, and structural experiences with racism and racial discrimination. These alternative foundations lead Black women to approach lesbian sexuality and the structuring of lesbian-led families with different goals and objectives than previous theories of lesbian sexuality might predict.

This is not a story of oppression and victimization, though racism and discrimination are important parts of the histories and current experiences of these women and their forbearers. Instead, I attempt to simultaneously deconstruct and claim marginalized and intersectional identity statuses for Black American and West Indian women who are gay and creating families. Moreover, I analyze race, class, gender, and sexuality not just as identity statuses but structural locations that influence the life chances of my respondents and the ways they experience their social worlds. I followed one hundred women for three years and gathered survey, in-depth interview, participant-observation, and focus group data to gain insight into how they negotiate their lives and form and raise families as openly gay people in predominantly Black and Latino neighborhoods in New York.[2] Given the structural inequalities that have historically been associated with race, gender, and sexuality for this population, my subjects cannot entirely stop thinking about or escape from categories. Therefore, I pay attention to—and sometimes (but not always) reconcile—the fractured, problematic aspects of identity. *Identity* is represented in this work not as a settled status but as a lived, continuous project.

The broader framework for the study of Black lesbians in this work is the examination of the intersections of race, sexuality, and socioeconomic status as they shape the construction and experience of identities, behavior, and social relationships.[3] The intersectional approach taken in this study offers two modifications to traditional intersectionality paradigms. First, this approach derives its strength from what McCall terms an "intracategorical" approach to intersectionality (2005, 1774), because rather than compare respondents across race or gender categories it analyzes the experiences of individuals who lie at the intersection of single dimensions of multiple categories (in this case race, gender, and sexuality). These respondents are revealed to vary within-group and to reflect multiple dimensions of those and other categories (i.e., ethnicity, class, gender presentation, motherhood status). It is the intersection of race, class, and gender presentation within a *single group*—in this case, Black lesbians—that is of interest in this work.

Second, while the intersectional perspective ultimately ties together the book's chapters, and while Black lesbians are the perfect embodiment of an intersectional existence and agency, this work specifically recognizes the significance of race in structuring Black women's lives and in defining their identities. Both Higginbotham (1992) and Dill (1983) have shown that political, religious, and other identities of African American women have historically been framed around and are embedded within the context of race. A close scrutiny of the ways Black women in this study experience these multiple statuses suggests something similar.

Age cohort, region, racial socialization, and racial hierarchies in society work together for the respondents to produce particular understandings of gender and other identification categories through a racial lens that reflects a given sociohistorical period. Although the women presented here are multiply positioned, racial ideologies, racial identities, racialized social systems, and racial inequalities together create a framework for understanding and articulating their other statuses as women, as gay people, and as mothers. The lens of race does not negate the intersectional experience; rather, it guides these respondents' interpretations of how gender, sexuality, social class, and other axes shape their lives.

Black lesbians and their families have historically crossed the boundaries of traditionally constructed groups, and this work reveals the complexity of lived experiences within this population. My approach to the study of Black lesbian identities and their relationship to family formation explicitly uses categories to define the subjects of the analysis and to articulate the broader structural dynamics that are present in the lives of the respondents.[4] It simultaneously acknowledges the stable and durable relationships that social categories represent at any given point in time, while interrogating the boundary-making and boundary-defining process itself.

This work offers a counterpoint to postmodern theorists who understand identity categories to be so inconsistent, transient, and unstable that they are virtually meaningless. While the shifting nature of sexuality is certainly apparent in the lives of Black lesbians, I find some aspects of anti-categorical approaches to identity problematic as frameworks for explaining how people who have had their entire lives structured around race experience identity categories. Race remains a relatively stable and slowly changing power system in the way it structures the life chances of Black Americans. For this group, the idea of categories being meaningless is largely a theoretical one, with little application to their experiences of being in the world or to their experiences of the domination and subordination that Alexander and Mohanty (1997) argue are named and articulated through the processes of racism and racialization.

The answer of one respondent, Jackie Roberts, to the question "Where are you from?" is illustrative:

I: *Where you are from? Where did you grow up?*
JACKIE ROBERTS: Harlem, born and raised.
I: *Which part of Harlem?*

JACKIE: Upper Harlem, Upper West Side; 150th and Broadway, right on the end of Harlem.

I: Isn't that the beginning of Washington Heights?

JACKIE: No! Washington Heights starts on 155th Street. I make it clear to people when they ask me that. [They say,] "That's Washington Heights." No, it's *not* Washington Heights. Washington Heights starts on 155th on the other side of the cemetery. So, I am very clear about that.

I: How was Washington Heights different from Harlem when you were growing up?

JACKIE: Basically, Washington Heights was considered more of an upper-echelon type of neighborhood, whereas Harlem has always been seen as something that had to do with poverty and the ghetto and that type of thing. I'm from the 'hood, but if you lived in Washington Heights when I was growing up, it was like, "Oh, I live in Washington Heights." It sounded better.

From the very beginning of the interview, Jackie Roberts makes it clear that she is from Harlem and that this information is important to her identity. In answering a simple question, she establishes categories to clarify where she sees herself and where she wants others to place her. Her father's Portuguese ancestry has given her fair skin and long, wavy hair, so she could be mistaken for part of Washington Heights' predominantly Latino population. But she wears her hair in dreadlocks to help others identify the group to which she belongs. She claims all that a Harlem identity has to offer a Black woman raised in New York City in the 1960s and 1970s: the poverty, the toughness, the history of the streets, and the inequalities that have constrained the life chances of many in her generation. Jackie's statements offer a glimpse into how she sees the world and the meaning-making that goes into it. The way she introduces herself in her interview and the categories she uses to frame her identity and experiences not only include sexuality and motherhood but also race, class, gender presentation, and other statuses that, when taken together, offer a corrective to those who theorize social categories as social fictions. For Jackie, to treat these categories as fictions would be to disintegrate her sense of self.

Moreover, the structural position of Jackie as a young, Black, poor woman whose family life has been one of struggle amid a neighborhood of struggling Black and Brown people typifies the structural nature of racial inequality. Rather than try to dismantle categories, I aim to understand how people whose lives have historically been structured by categories make sense of them and use them in different ways to explain who they are and how they fit in the world.

RACE AND CLASS IN THE STUDY OF LESBIAN SEXUALITY AND FAMILIES

In order to understand how lesbian-headed families are organized and function, we have to first understand lesbian sexual identity and its origins. The research on lesbian identity once framed it as a subculture of the dominant society, with some similarities but also some important differences in how lesbian values are demonstrated—particularly in terms of monogamy, future orientation, feminist ideologies, and family structure. This division was assumed to be based in or driven by sexuality, with the homosexual group suffering isolation from the larger heterosexual society and turning to one another, thereby increasing solidarity within the sexuality-based subculture (Lisagor 1980). For members of groups whose primary feelings of group identification lie elsewhere, however, there may be reason to question the assumption that boundaries in lesbian communities are primarily drawn along the axis of sexuality. That is to say, it may be the case that race rather than—or in addition to—sexuality is a primary organizing identity for some Black lesbians, with ramifications for how we understand the ways memberships in the "Black" and "gay" identity categories affect the daily lives of gay women and their participation in communities organized around just one of these statuses.

Race as an identity status or as a social location has not been well analyzed in the lesbian identity literature. Esterberg argues, for example, that lesbians' understanding of race has been limited to seeing race as "an invisible backdrop" used in constructing one's own identity, as a source of guilt and shame (viewed through the lens of Whiteness), as racism or a subject around which to rally, and as a force that creates hierarchies in society (1997, 99–100). Work like this fails to consider how "Whiteness" as a racial experience, or race/ethnicity more generally, affects the creation, enactment, maintenance, and reception of the individual identities and group identities that gay people take on or choose to ignore. The experiences of women whose biology, cultures, and structural positions in society have produced similar same-sex desires but different ways of identifying with those desires have not been fully recognizable in past research. This study references a particular set of lived experiences that fall outside of much of what is currently represented in this field.[5]

In order to understand how Black lesbian families function, we must draw from previous understandings of the roles, experiences, and ideologies of Black women in heterosexual African American households. Both the literature on family process and functioning and the research theorizing Black feminist ideologies have emphasized several distinctive characteristics of Black heterosexual households. Two features that have attracted considerable discussion, research, and analysis have been the mother-centered nature of family relationships within Black nuclear and extended family structures and the long history of women's employment and economic contributions to the survival and stability of poor, working-class, and middle-class Black households. Some have pointed to these characteristics as evidence of cultural deviance and as an explanation for the economic uncertainties and conditions that Black women's poor and working-class male partners face (Rainwater and Yancy 1967). Others view the central position of women in Black families and their financial contributions to the home as adaptive compensations for the structural limitations of racism and inequality, and as key features of the intersectional nature of Black women's oppression in the social, economic, and political realms of society (Collins 2000; Dill 1983). Still others see the strong participation of Black women in the economic and occupational spheres as evidence of their greater autonomy and self-reliance across social class (Kessler-Harris 2003; Wolcott 2001) and as a route to greater egalitarianism, self-actualization, and fulfillment that Black middle-class women have had more success in following relative to their White middle-class peers (Landry 2000; Moore 2009; Shaw 1996).

My point is not to support or refute these perspectives but to show how the vulnerability of Blackness makes the vulnerability of sexual and familial intimacy more burdensome for African Americans, creating a double jeopardy.[6] One must examine the experiences of prior generations of Black women who lived through the major racial struggles of American history in order to understand family processes and expectations of autonomy in Black lesbian households.[7] A volume edited by Honey (1999), for example, contrasts how White and Black America understood the experience of female blue-collar workers who became welders, riveters, and line workers during World War II. Honey argues that White women in dominant-culture magazine stories and advertising were featured as leaving behind or sacrificing their homemaking desires and activities so they could take "temporary" industrial jobs and by doing so help the country win the war. These mothers and wives were shown in static roles, waiting for the return of soldiers so they could "resume" their lives as homemakers. Women workers in Black magazines, by contrast, were shown as trailblazers able to escape low-wage domestic work. The blue-collar jobs they now held were depicted as better alternatives to domestic work because of the higher wages and greater autonomy they brought to Black women and, by extension, to Black families. Labor recruiters noted the war's disruption of Black women's historic confinement to domestic work and assumed they would continue in this new line of work even after the war ended (Honey 1999, 12). This contrast suggests that differences in White and Black perceptions of women's labor run deep and are likely to affect how Black women perceive labor and its place in their lives today.

The centrality of the Black church and African American religions more generally, provides a different example of how prior experiences in Black social environments frame the expectations lesbians have for how to structure their lives. Religious institutions both react to and shape local sexual attitudes and behavior (Ellingson, Tebbe, Van Haitsma, and Laumann 2001), and this is particularly the case in African American communities.[8] The body of research on the functions of Black religious organizations as *cultural* institutions has highlighted the integral role they play not only as places of worship but as direct actors in secular organizations, financial and educational institutions, and political movements (Lincoln and Mamiya 1990; Taylor, Mattis, and Chatters 1999). The church and mosque act simultaneously as a school, bank, benevolent society, political organization, social hall, and spiritual base. Pattillo-McCoy's 1998 research on the South Side of Chicago suggests that the rituals, beliefs, ideologies, and practices of the Black church in African American communities become part of the cultural repertoire of its members. If this is true, church rules and rituals are something that residents in predominantly Black communities believe in, even if they do not attend services regularly or have no particular religious affiliation (Moore 2010a). The involvement of churches and other religious institutions in so many aspects of Black community life means that the teachings of the church or mosque indirectly infiltrate and influence nonreligious components of life, including how people who live in Black communities go about expressing their sexuality.

BLACK WOMEN'S SEXUALITY AND DISCOURSES OF RESPECTABILITY

When trying to understand how Black lesbians interpret and portray their own sexuality, it is also critical to draw from the literature on discourses of respectability in Black communities. This literature takes two forms. The first dates back to the response of middle-class Black women to the ideology of the cult of true womanhood, which defined the boundaries of acceptable female behavior in the South from the 1820s through the Civil War and well into the twentieth century. The second draws from Black feminist arguments responding to this field, criticizing the absence of analysis of the sexual agency of Black women. When taken together, the silence surrounding Black women's sexuality that emerged as a middle-class response to accusations of immorality as well as the active defense of sexual autonomy and exploration of pleasure expressed by the working class are simultaneously competing and complimentary forces at work in the open expression of Black lesbian sexuality.

True womanhood was presented by elite women's magazines and religious literature of the nineteenth century as an ideal by which a (White) woman judged herself and was judged by her husband, her neighbors, and middle- and upper-class society (Welter 1966). The attributes of this ideal were divided into four cardinal virtues: piety, purity, submissiveness, and domesticity. They were understood to represent a certain type of womanhood to the world. Regardless of social class, Blacks were seen as lacking virtue, an essential characteristic of true womanhood. Indeed, true womanhood was often defined in opposition to Black and working-class women. Darlene Clark Hine, Paula Giddings, and other Black feminist historians have shown that in the generations after emancipation and throughout the first half of the twentieth century, Black middle-class women collectively sought to create alternative self-images in order to shield themselves from pervasive stereotypes about and negative estimations of their sexuality.[9] In *Righteous Discontent* (1993), Higginbotham defines a "politics of respectability" through which turn of the Century Black women sought to gain status in the minds of Whites by reforming Black working-class behavior. A vulnerability around intimacy developed within Black communities because Black bodies were "assumed to be excessively proximate and desirous bodies, too readily revealed or exposed, too willing to reveal and expose others" (Jenkins 2007, 19–20).[10]

A crucial difference between Black and White women in their quest for true womanhood is that the model of Black respectability and virtuous Black womanhood was one of achievement in *both* private and public spheres. Research on women raised in Black middle-class families during the Jim Crow era shows that Black women not only had to maintain a certain image of womanhood in their day-to-day lives, but these images were also critical to their ability to obtain work (Shaw 1996). In order to take advantage of the best work opportunities available, Black women had to be "extremely circumspect and never give even the slightest hint of impropriety" lest they be "negatively typecast" and raise doubts about "their abilities and fitness to serve in professional, educational, or other public settings" (Shaw 1996, 14). Black women's strategies of cultivating respectability included formal schooling, moral behavior, self-assurance, self-discipline, and social responsibility.

Not only did Black women have to be concerned about how their portrayals of self would impact potential work and educational opportunities, they also had to be concerned about how the way they carried themselves would affect their acceptance by the larger Black community, which could reject them for being ineffectual or for being improper role models. Members of the Black middle class were taught from an early age the importance of collective consciousness, of setting an example for others in the community, and of being competent. Those with lower socioeconomic statuses also held the Black middle class to these standards, seeing community leaders as vehicles for their own and their children's advancement.

Moving forward into the new millennium, Jenkins argues that Black women have been "scripted out of narratives of American national belonging" because of their alleged sexual and domestic character—their intimate lives (2007, 5). Black women's high rates of nonmarital childbearing and disproportionate representation among the poor have fueled a need for their ongoing self-defense of respectability. This is the case for Black women in the Caribbean as well, where changing economic conditions in Jamaica, to take one example, have had the consequence of increasing the rigidity with which social status, and Black middle-class behavior in particular, is policed. Black women emigrating from the Caribbean bring these understandings with them to the United States.[11] The emphasis on respectability for the Black middle class today goes beyond a general concern about images that are portrayed to Whites or the enhancement of employment opportunities. It is equally important for Black women to be seen by other members of the racial community as "people of good character," meaning that they show respect toward others, commitment and responsibility to the group through the demonstration of loyalty, and accountability to themselves and to others for their actions. An openly gay sexuality, however, complicates this image.

Black women choosing to live openly as lesbians—expressed through behavior, gender presentation, styles of dress, display of gay-affirming symbols, and other such actions—offer an active expression of Black women's sexual autonomy. This expression of sexual pleasure and desire flouts the type of respectability championed by Black middle-class leadership. Carby's article "It Jus Be's Dat Way Sometime" (1986) and Davis's book *Blues Legacies and Black Feminism* (1998) analyze the sexual agency expressed in Black working-class communities through popular music culture of the 1920s, 1930s, and 1940s. Carby says women Blues singers appear as liminal figures who explore the various possibilities of a sexual existence. They are "representations of women who attempt to manipulate and control their own construction as sexual subjects" (12). Davis also locates a Black feminist consciousness in the type of lyrics and tonality of the Blues and jazz music sung by Black women, a consciousness that was expressed through the open dialogue in song text about desire, heartache, violence, infidelity, and sexual intimacy. The singers and performers themselves embodied sexualities that were associated with working-class Black life in their styles of dress, hair, make-up, ways of walking, and ways of communicating with their audiences. The performances, the lyrics and arrangement of the music, and the dances that accompanied the music were open representations of sexuality and pleasure that were at odds with the type of Black respectability that educated and other higher-status Black women struggled to teach. Davis locates in social class these differences in expressions of Black feminist consciousness, finding that working-class women preferred and often embraced a space for the expression of feelings, behaviors, and experiences that contradicted the prevailing standards of femininity. The Blues women and the music they created provided "emphatic examples of black female independence" (1998, 20). They offered an alternative way to understand the autonomy of Black women, a way of being that was not in alignment with middle-class discourses of respectability.

In a different analysis of working-class Black women's consciousness, Wolcott (2001) shows how the extremely limited job market in the decades following the 1920s required Black women to participate in the illicit economy through sex work, selling liquor, and other jobs that placed them in opposition to the "respectable" roles of mother, homemaker, and worker. This, combined with their engagement in less wholesome leisure activities like suggestive dancing in dance halls, public drinking, and even ecstatic styles of worship in storefront churches, blurred the distinction between respectable and disreputable women (103). Working women needed to survive, and they were involved in various, sometimes sordid social activities to escape from the economic realities of their lives. Their participation in the informal economy and in urban nightlife as employers, employees, and consumers transformed certain behaviors from disreputable to acceptable, expanding the boundaries of respectability for women and making visible the autonomy of Black women.

Openly gay Black women today are positioned at the juncture of middle-class respectability and working-class sexual agency. Many lesbians across the socioeconomic stratum who are forming families are concerned about whether and how much they should conform to "acceptable" images of motherhood, but they also stand in defense of their own sexual agency and their right to define and declare a sexual freedom. Black lesbian couples reclaim sexuality, and through activities like weddings and commitment ceremonies, simultaneously affirm their own representations of Black respectability. They are at the forefront of a new era of Black female sexuality and offer a visible representation of female sexual expression.

When evaluating family formation and the development of a gay sexuality among Black lesbians, then, we must consider the economic, political, and socioemotional positions Black women have historically occupied in heterosexual families. We must also consider the racial socialization these women and their parents and grandparents experienced in order to understand how the structural and cultural experiences of race influence lesbian practice. In this work, I show how Black lesbians, socialized in Black families and communities, incorporate and navigate notions of Black respectability into their identity construction simultaneously with their behavioral expression of sexual autonomy and sexual freedom. This is particularly the case for middle-class lesbians and women trying to achieve middle-class status. Relative to working-class women and women who are not mothers, the upwardly mobile and women who were mothers before taking on an openly lesbian identity use the framework of Black respectability as a guide for how to enact a gay sexuality.[12] Their use of this framework affects when they publicly claim a lesbian identity, how they approach lesbian motherhood, and their more general self-presentation as lesbians.

THE WOMEN OF THE INVISIBLE FAMILIES STUDY

New York is the best place to study gay populations of color. During the time of my fieldwork, from 2003 through 2006, it offered several public social events each week that specifically catered to Black lesbians.[13] Information about these activities is not readily available through the usual outlets of gay-themed periodicals, which showcase a city's lesbian and gay-themed parties and social groups, however. It was only once I was introduced to several gatekeepers in New York's Black gay community that I began to receive party flyers and hear through word of mouth about these types of events. I began this research by spending time at a variety of public events, including after-work networking cocktail hours, karaoke socials, church meetings, book clubs, art salons, shared meals, poetry readings, parties, and workshops on parenting and adoption. I also attended gay pride and Black gay pride events in Brooklyn, Manhattan, Philadelphia, Washington, DC, Atlanta, and Orlando, all of which draw large crowds of Black women from New York.[14]

At the start of this fieldwork, I was not sure how the study would evolve. I was meeting working-class and low-income Black lesbians in the South Bronx, middle- and upper-middle-class gay women in Brooklyn's Park Slope neighborhood, older lesbians in Harlem, and African American adolescents with lesbian, gay, bisexual, or transgender (LGBT) identities at the pier off of Christopher Street in Greenwich Village. As I began to delve further into these women's lives, I discovered their participation in intricate, multilayered, expansive networks with other Black lesbians who occasionally intermingled socially with Whites but who tended to remain with other Black people for their primary social interactions. Drawing on my past research experiences with African American heterosexual families, I decided to focus my efforts for this study on how Black gay women formed families.

When I began my fieldwork, I was not familiar with Black lesbian communities in New York and had had very few experiences with Black gay social groups more generally. I had spent the majority of my adult life in graduate school and doing postdoctoral work outside of New York, where my social networks consisted primarily of colleagues and students. Hardly any were Black gay women, and to my knowledge none were significantly involved in New York's public Black gay life. McCorkel and Myers (2003) write about the ways in which the multiple dimensions of the researcher's identity take shape when relating to subjects in the field. They and other feminist ethnographers argue that the researcher's status as both an outsider and an insider shifts throughout her time in the field as she negotiates and renegotiates relationships.[15] I write from the perspective of someone who was an insider by virtue of my race and sexuality, but also as an outsider, having no prior knowledge of the norms and practices of Black lesbian social spaces. The shifting contexts where my fieldwork took place at times made some of my identity statuses less visible and at other times heightened their visibility. During the time I was collecting data I did not have children, which particularly cast me as learner, rather than expert, when respondents would describe childrearing issues and household dynamics related to parenting. I am Black American, and some Caribbean-born women saw me as culturally different from themselves. I was a professor at Columbia University while conducting this research, and my social class made middle- and upper-class women feel connected to me and willing to share their lives. I believe it made some working-class women proud of my accomplishments. It is also possible that other working-class women thought of me as having significantly different life experiences than themselves. Despite this difference, I was able to successfully gain a rapport with working-class women, who represent 42 percent of my sample.

Once I was invited into the friendship groups of gay Black women in New York, I was introduced to others who did not participate as frequently in lesbian public events. These more private women hosted parties and other activities in their own homes, and many of these events bore a striking resemblance to the vibrant portraits painted by Lorde (1995) of 1950s Black lesbian life. I began taking field notes approximately four months after learning about these activities, and soon after began talking informally with my contacts about their potential involvement in other forms of data collection.

There are populations that traditional methods of data gathering will not capture, and the Black lesbian community is one such group. Public advertisements, notices, flyers at lesbian nightclubs, or postings at LGBT community centers largely go unnoticed or unanswered by gay populations of color, and studies that use these methods of getting in touch with research subjects are not successful in recruiting significant numbers of non-Whites in their samples.[16] By spending time at social events attended by Black women, I was able to recruit respondents who are not part of predominantly White social groups. They are understudied in part because of the tendency of researchers who study gay families to be White and to recruit participants from their own networks. I drew from more traditional Black social spaces to recruit individuals for the more formal methods of data collection in the study. For *Invisible Families*, I targeted women living in New York and the surrounding metropolitan area who identify as lesbian, gay, bisexual, "in the life," and/or same-gender-loving and who are forming families. These women are either in committed relationships with other women or are gay mothers. To be eligible for the study, one person in the relationship had to identify as Black.

I collected four types of data: (1) participant-observation fieldwork gathered over a period of approximately thirty months; (2) focus groups on Black lesbian identity, family life in households with children, gender presentation in relationships, and the influence of religious background on individual sexuality; (3) a fourteen-page mail-in survey of one hundred women who provided demographic and family background information and answered questions about the methods they have used or considered to obtain children, the division of household and economic labor in the home, relationship quality, changes in the respondents' sexuality over time, physical representations of gender, experiences with female and male partners, and the extent and nature of their friendship groups and social interactions in Black communities, gay communities, and predominantly White communities; and (4) in-depth, semistructured interviews with fifty-eight of the respondents who participated in the mail-in survey. The more process-oriented, detailed information provided by the interviews complemented the broader data of the survey.[17] I used a variety of collection strategies to create a multidimensional portrait that would help me evaluate behavioral patterns over time and allow me to capture not only how respondents said they behaved but also their actual behavior, which I observed repeatedly over a three year period.

The women who have shared their lives with me and who are represented in this book are those who in some way participate in public or private social groups organized around gay sexuality. To some extent, they see themselves as part of or interested in some aspect of a lesbian community, and they interact with people who see themselves in this way. There are others with same-sex desire who do not identify as a member of a sexual minority group or who do not interact with others who self-identify around these categories. While they may share some similarities and experiences with the women in this work, their voices are not directly incorporated here. Lesbians who do not ever spend time in predominantly Black gay social spaces or who do not have an understanding of themselves as having a Black ethnic or cultural group membership are also not well-represented in this book, though they may also find some commonalities with the women who are the focus of this study.

My work draws loosely from Cornell and Hartmann's definition of a "race frame," which conceives race as "an organizing principle that is deeply embedded in culture and social structure and has profoundly shaped both intergroup relationships and society as a whole" (2007, 105). My discussion of *Black lesbians* throughout this work in no way describes an essential Black gay woman with certain inherent or natural traits. I use the term, rather, to refer to women who participate in same-gender-loving relationships and social or political communities, and who also participate in Black heterosexual families, social groups, and institutions. I realize that my definition may not adequately capture the ideologies, experiences, and ethos of some Black women who predominantly participate in social worlds that contain few Black people, women who experience a social distance from Black communities, or women with same-sex desire who do not identify as lesbian or gay.

In this work, I categorize my respondents as "lesbians" and as "gay women." I use both of these descriptors to be consistent with the terms the respondents use to describe themselves and the larger women's community. *Lesbian* is a term not uniformly embraced by the women in this work and by many Black women born before 1970. As a label and identity, "lesbian" is at times politicized in a way that some Black women do not appreciate. These women prefer "gay," "gay woman," or "in the life" as descriptors for their sexuality, so throughout this work I also use "gay woman" to identify members of this population. While the term *queer* is used by some scholars and activists to describe the LGBT community, as well as in reference to queer theory, it has not been embraced by the women in my study, and I do not use it in this work. Throughout the book, I also use the term *Black* to refer to people of the African Diaspora and to such populations that reside within the United States. In New York, approximately 30 percent of Blacks are foreign-born, first- or second-generation American, or identify as members of Caribbean and African ethnic groups (Kent 2007). Because some of them are first-generation immigrants or for other reasons do not identify as African American, I tend to use *Black* rather than *African American* to describe the women in the study.

As suggested above, "Black" is not a monolithic racial category and the diversity of my respondents reflects this point. Almost two-thirds (64 percent) of the study participants are Black Americans, while 26 percent identify as Caribbean or African, 5 percent are Latina from non-Caribbean countries, and 5 percent are the White partners of Black respondents. Twenty-two percent of my respondents are foreign-born. The women in this book range in age from twenty-one to sixty-one years old, with a mean age of thirty-six. Ninety-two percent live in neighborhoods with substantial Black and Latino populations. Thirty-six percent completed their education with high school, 29 percent hold a bachelor's degree, and one-third hold a master's degree or higher. The respondents' occupations vary considerably and include physician, exotic dancer, professional football player (for the New York Sharks, a Tier I team in the Independent Women's Football League), electrician, secretary, police sergeant, elementary school teacher, nonprofit organization director, and attorney.

Education, income, and occupation were taken together to create a composite measure of socioeconomic status: 45 percent of the respondents are categorized as working class, 42 percent as middle class, and 13 percent as upper middle class. There are three types of households in the study: partnered with children (40 percent of respondents), partnered without children (34 percent), and single-mother families (26 percent of respondents). During the survey and interview data collection period (October 2003– June 2004), 74 percent of respondents were cohabiting with a partner, and those relationships had a mean length of 3.7 years ($SD = 3.1$). Sixty-four percent were parenting or co-parenting at least one child, and 45 percent were biological mothers. Please see the methodological appendix for additional information about data collection and methods.

OVERVIEW

The central six chapters of this volume explore, through different analytic lenses, concepts of gender, power, class, and identity in processes of lesbian family formation and family life. Chapter 1 offers a process analysis of the spectrum of affect and choices that individuals make as they come to recognize and act on their same-sex desire in Black racial and ethnic contexts. The majority of Black lesbians born before 1975 have a sense of themselves as Black that was formed before they accepted a gay sexuality. Even if they felt same-sex attraction or a sense of "difference" at early ages, they tended not to name those feelings or link them to a particular identity until much later. This chapter reveals four dominant pathways by which these women have come to accept a lesbian sexuality, and it emphasizes the importance of race, class, and geographic dislocation in the initial move from private to public presentations of gay sexuality. Chapter 2 analyzes processes of gender presentation and mate selection in racially segregated lesbian social environments, showing how race, class, and notions of authenticity through style influence the presentation of lesbian sexuality. It introduces three categories of gender presentation that organize interactions in Black gay social environments and shows how gender complementarity is used to express the eroticism of difference.

Chapter 3 looks at race, gender, and sexuality as multiple stigmatized social identities as well as structural positions for Black lesbians. It analyzes how reception by outside forces (i.e., mainstream society, family members) and from within the self (i.e., self-assignment of some identities as primary) influence the differential importance lesbians assign to race, gender, and sexuality as identity statuses. These evaluations have critical relationships to the ways they express a gay sexuality and create families. These statuses are not only markers of identity but representations of positions these women occupy in the larger social structure. Chapter 4 examines the different constructions, pathways, and timing of motherhood for Black lesbians. It compares the ways Black women view motherhood and lesbian identity when they become mothers in a heterosexual context before they take on a self-definition as gay, to the ways they view motherhood and lesbian identity when they identify as lesbians before becoming parents. It also shows how discourses of respectability and differences in social class permeate those experiences. Chapter 5 concentrates on family life and the division of labor among couples with and without children. It reexamines lesbian-feminist assumptions of greater egalitarianism in lesbian relationships and presents a provocative argument for alternative conceptions of "gendered" power between women drawn from Black feminist frameworks.

Chapter 6, the final analytical chapter, shifts away from specific processes of family life to explain how the move from private to public expressions of gay sexuality has affected the quality of the relationships Black lesbians cultivate with their families and with others in their larger racial communities. It also explores the contradictions of Black religions and religious ideologies as organizing features of Black community contexts, analyzing how Black lesbians' experiences with religion as a simultaneous source of condemnation and support influences how they interact with others in the racial group and how they interpret their own sexuality. Finally, the concluding chapter situates the findings of this book in contemporary debates on same-sex marriage and the future of identity group politics. The appendices detail the process by which this study evolved, the methods used to recruit subjects, and the instruments used to collect data.

Taken as a whole, *Invisible Families* offers at least three important correctives to disparate literatures and fields. First, it speaks directly to the sociology of the family and study of household divisions of labor through its examination and rethinking of how gender structures familial relationships and organizes labor in the home. It will help others rethink definitions of egalitarianism as a feminist ideology by bringing in alternative foundations upon which lesbians build a sense of self and use those foundations in the creation of families. It also extends the literature on Black families to sexual minority populations and draws conclusions about the ways cultural experiences of Black American and Caribbean families work with structural experiences and understandings of racism and discrimination to influence the ways Black lesbians "do" family.

This book also contributes to the study of sexuality and identity construction by showing how lesbian family formation and lesbian sexual identities are shaped by racial differences in norms, culture, historical understandings of women in families and the labor force, and historical interpretations of women's sexuality. It simultaneously explores how people with multiple stigmatized identities imagine, construct, and reconstruct an individual and a collective sense of self, negotiating the maintenance of boundaries around various identities according to social context. It looks at how individual agency works with structural conditions and social stratification on the basis of identity categories like race and gender to reify these categories and individuals' memberships in them.

Finally, this volume contributes to a growing sociological literature interrogating intersectionality using the intra-categorical approach by offering a nuanced understanding of how social class interacts with race and sexuality to affect the experiences of Black lesbians. It does this by looking not only at economic disadvantage but also at how class privilege and diversity within this group mediate the stigma of gay sexuality. Race and class status are often conflated in ways that inadvertently construct images of "the Black woman" from the experiences of those who are poor. Those images are then compared to images of middle-class White women to illustrate difference. I highlight and analyze the significance of class diversity and even class advantage among Blacks in shaping ideologies about lesbian sexuality, pathways to lesbian motherhood, gender presentation, notions of respectability, and the lived experiences of being openly gay in Black social contexts.

CHAPTER I

Coming into the Life

Entrance into Gay Sexuality for Black Women

COMING INTO THE LIFE VERSUS COMING OUT

Psychologists and psychotherapists have portrayed coming out of the closet, or acknowledging one's same-sex attractions, acting upon them, disclosing them to others, and accepting them as part of a sexual identity, as a developmental process that most homosexuals share.[1] Variations on a core model describe six stages of this process. First, individuals have a subjective sense of feeling "different" from others of their same gender. Subsequently, they identify these feelings as homosexual, disclose the feelings to others, come to accept the feelings as part of an identity, and search for a community of like persons. They complete the transition when they become involved in a relationship with someone of the same sex.[2] "Coming out" is understood as a process that ends in its subject's acceptance of a "modern" gay identity, in which the subject has merged her private self-understandings with the public self she reveals to others.

Several scholars of lesbian and bisexual identity have criticized this model for its failure to consider alternative, often nonlinear paths by which many gay women construct a sexual identity.[3] Drawing on my fieldwork with Black lesbians in New York City, I have found that the linear five-stage model of coming out does not fully capture the complex ways in which individuals construct a personal and sexual identity based not just on sexual orientation and gender but on race and class as well. The development of women's sexual orientation follows diverse pathways shaped by multiple social and cultural influences.

To begin with, the concept of "coming out" does not accurately capture the experience of acting on same-sex attraction by entering and participating in Black gay social life. Instead, this experience, broadly understood, is best conceptualized as "coming into" a life and community with particular norms and expectations for its members. The phrase "coming into the life" not only better describes the experience of same-sex desire for Black people who learn how to "be" gay in Black social settings, it also captures the essence of how they learn to label that desire and reveal it to others. The concept of "coming into the life" more completely represents the experiences of my respondents, then, because it describes coming into an understanding of a particular subculture—of learning about and adjusting to the patterns of interaction expected in lesbian communities and in Black lesbian social environments specifically. "Coming into the life" also encompasses coming into a greater acknowledgment and acceptance of one's gay sexuality and beginning the process of negotiating and managing this identity status as it relates to race and to other established identities. The set of processes, range of possibilities, and spectrum of choices Black lesbians encounter as they come to recognize and become comfortable acting on their same-sex desire in Black communities and various Black American and West Indian social contexts are described in this chapter.

There are different ways of coming into the life (or not). To understand these processes, I drew from a variety of sources of data. During the in-depth interviews I asked my respondents questions about how they defined their sexuality (i.e., their relationship experiences with women and with men), and I asked them to tell me the story of how they came into "the life" (the exact wording of these questions can be found in Appendix C). I conducted a focus group on respondents' experiences in the gay social worlds of New York that raised questions about the contexts in which they came to understand their same-sex desires. The survey also contained questions that I used to identify patterns in the ways women came to take on a gay sexuality. I asked the extent to which respondents agreed or disagreed with the following two statements: "Being gay is something that is completely beyond one's control" and "Being gay is a conscious choice I have made." Responses ranged from *strongly agree* to *strongly disagree*, and no opinion. There were other survey questions that were analyzed to identify differences in women's pathways into a gay sexuality, including questions that asked the respondent to describe her sexuality now, at age 15, and at age 21. Possible choices were "Exclusively lesbian," "Predominantly lesbian, only slightly heterosexual,"

"Predominantly lesbian, but significantly heterosexual," "Equally lesbian and heterosexual," "Predominantly heterosexual, but significantly lesbian," "Predominantly heterosexual, only slightly lesbian," and "Exclusively heterosexual." I asked whether there was a term other than "lesbian" that better described their sexuality, what was the longest amount of time they have spent in committed relationships with men and with women, and what have been their experiences with heterosexual marriage.

Ultimately, all the women I studied came to recognize and act on their attraction to women. One group named it, acted on it, or both in their adolescent years, while a second group felt this attraction but conformed to societal gender norms in their early years, turning to a gay sexuality in adulthood. For a third group, same-sex desire did not emerge until adulthood, after which they confirmed a lesbian rather than a bisexuality. For a fourth group, there is a persistent and ongoing fluidity in their desire for women and men. I organize the analysis that follows around these four groups, each of whose members came into the life in a distinct way. In the process, I distinguish carefully between having a first experience of same-sex desire, acting on that desire, and claiming an identity based in a sexuality. In later chapters I suggest that the pathways women take in coming to terms with and openly practicing a gay sexuality have important associations with the types of women they partner with, the processes by which they enter motherhood, and the types of families they create.

As scholars of Black sexuality have shown, American- and Caribbean-born Black women often must negotiate a complex set of demands for gender "respectability" and racial uplift.[4] Black lesbians, in order to live openly gay lives, must negotiate this terrain while simultaneously engaging in an active expression of sexual agency. Women who have followed different pathways into a gay sexuality share various tropes common to coming out stories, such as an unnamed attraction to members of the same sex, feelings of difference, and fear of retribution from family and community members when coming to terms with same-sex desire, and these tropes are discussed in this chapter. The chapter also shows how different race and economic contexts influence the ways individuals come to understand a gay sexuality and portray it to others.

STRAIGHT-UP GAY WOMEN

Carlie Lewis, a hairstylist born in 1962, explained how she defines her sexuality: "I'm a lesbian without, you know, having a reason behind it.

It's just, there's no reason. I've always liked women. Didn't realize what my attraction was when I was younger, 'cause I had boyfriends, but to me they were never really boyfriends, they were just like boys that were my friends—you know what I'm saying? It was like I never really treated them like boyfriends, and I was more attracted to women, so to me I've always been a lesbian. . . . Once I realized there were women, ahh, forget about the men!"

Carlie belongs to a category that I have labeled "straight-up gay." There were twenty straight-up gay women in my interview group of fifty-eight women, making up 34 percent of the sample. Those who followed this first pathway into a gay sexuality either self-identified as gay at an early age or deemphasized any sexuality until adulthood. All but two of them have a history of nonfeminine gender presentation and an interest in stereotypically male activities. The members of this group tend to link their same-sex desire and feelings of difference regarding masculinity and femininity to their self-understandings of gay sexuality. For them, gay sexuality is not merely behavior they engage in: rather, it is an identity category, something they experience as part of an essentialized sense of self.

Feelings of Difference: Gender Presentation and Growing Up as a Tomboy

In my survey, I asked, "If you had to select only one, which of these definitions would describe your sexuality?" There were seven responses available, ranging from 1 (exclusively lesbian)" to 7(exclusively heterosexual). All but one of the women in the straight-up gay category defined herself as exclusively lesbian.[5] When asked during the in-depth interviews how they would define their sexuality, the respondents said things like "I am strictly homosexual," "Straight-up gay," and "I'm a lesbian without having a reason behind it." In the interviews, 90 percent (18 of the straight-up gay group) reported having romantic same-sex attractions before the age of eighteen, and on the survey, 90 percent said they considered themselves predominantly or exclusively lesbian by age twenty-one.[6]

Most respondents in this group found it difficult to pinpoint the particular moment when they first felt same-sex attraction. They said things like "I've always known I was different," "I've always known I was a lesbian," "I was born gay, it has been in me forever," and "Everyone already knew—[I] didn't have to make no grand announcement." Before they took on a gay identity or even knew what it meant to have same-sex desire, these women felt different from other girls. Earlier research has found a similar category of lesbian women; Ponse's 1978 study of lesbian identity and community, for example, identified as "primary lesbians" those who reported feeling a sense of difference from other girls and women at early ages.

It was Corey James, a union organizer born in 1966 and raised by her grandmother in a Bronx housing project, who used the words "straight-up gay" to describe her sexuality to me. She said: "There's no ifs, ands or buts about it. And I've know it since I was about—since seven." When I asked her what it was in her experiences with women and men that prompted her to reply in this way, she answered: "I've just always known. I didn't experience, have any [sexual] experience with men until I was almost eighteen. And that was only because I didn't have any references to acknowledge how I was feeling. I didn't have—I was the only gay person around me. I was the only gay person that I knew of in my family. I mean, I had uncles who were kind of feminine, but they never were openly gay. So I kinda kept how I felt in the background. And then I got to college and said, 'To heck with it.' "

In addition to feeling different but not specifically being able to name that difference, straight-up gay women reported that when they were younger they behaved in ways that did not conform to gendered expectations. All but two identified as tomboys in childhood and adolescence. Trina Adams, a hotel associate born in 1969 and raised in a lower-middle-class neighborhood in Queens, referred back to her childhood interest in boys' activities and her inability to perform simple tasks and play games associated with African American girls' leisure as evidence of her sexual orientation: "I was always a tomboy. I never could jump double-dutch, I can't braid hair. I never liked skirts—even when I was in first grade, I would cry if I had to wear a skirt. I always liked to play boy things like 'kick the can.' I remember climbing trees, wrestling, and I could play basketball, but I could *really* play, not like girls. I was good like the boys. They'd pick teams, I would be the first one they picked." For Trina, her athleticism and the way it was expressed—through her desire to compete with boys and play on boys' teams—was evidence not just of divergent interests from girls but of a future gay self.

Like Trina, straight-up gay women tend to label certain childhood behaviors as male-identified and to link those activities to the same-sex attraction they felt as children, teenagers, or young adults. They reported preferring a clothing style that was "very casual" and never too feminine, and almost all had a similar story about how they hated wearing dresses in their youth or had an embarrassing and awkward experience when they were forced to wear a dress. Social historian Robin D. G. Kelley argues that our sense of gender is made and developed in childhood, and "the limits, boundaries, and contestations in the world of play constitute key moments in the creation and shaping of gender identity" (1997, 205). Sports like football or jump rope are forms of play that are central to the construction of masculinity and femininity, and children as well as authority figures often erect strict gender boundaries to control access and keep boys and girls separate in their forms of play.

In their historical account of lesbian identity formation, Kennedy and Davis (1993) found that many women who adopted masculine gender presentations as adults had experienced an early appropriation of masculine behavior, and for them this gender nonconformity was an indicator of difference at an early age. It was difficult for the women in Kennedy and Davis' study to separate their interest in women from the masculinity they enacted. Rather, they saw sexuality as firmly embedded in gender, so that masculine behavior was closely entwined with same-sex attraction. Bullough (2008) cautions against assuming that gender nonconformity in childhood *always* leads to homosexuality in adulthood. It does not. However, several studies have found that lesbians are more likely than are heterosexual women to report being a tomboy or preferring boys' games and toys to those of girls in childhood.[7]

When describing how they came to think of themselves as gay, twelve of the twenty women I interviewed (60 percent) specifically mentioned that as a young child they wished they were a boy, wished they could have the freedoms of a boy, or wanted to engage in the types of activities that boys participated in. There was a sense that they did not want to be male physically, but were aware that they did not look or act in ways that were consistent with how girls were supposed to act, and did not share the interests that girls were supposed to have. They viewed their childhood desire to participate in experiences reserved for boys as an essential part of their realization of a gay identity as adults.

Zoe Ferron, for example, a telephone linesman born in 1960 to lower-middle-class Black American parents, said of her gender identity, "I would have made a better boy than a girl." When I asked her why, she replied:

I never felt like a girl. Never really understood what it felt like to feel like a girl in terms of roles on television. I think roles for me were always skewed, especially what we saw environmentally, what we saw visually. There weren't even Black people on TV when I was growing up. The White people were

Barbie, and I am not Barbie. I didn't even feel like a Barbie, and I didn't even feel—I would probably say that I never viewed myself really as a girl. . . . Um, there was a time when I thought I would consider gender reassignment. I actually thought about that. I saw a therapist, even met some transgender people and decided that I would rather be a healthy woman than an unhealthy man . . . and also I think my religious upbringing had something to do with that. I figured at some point 'God would fix it,' whatever that means. I never had any kind of sexual attraction to men. I think much more like a man. I appreciate women. I don't know how men appreciate women—sometimes I don't think they do appreciate them—but I appreciate women.

At an early age, Zoe had a keen awareness of how she differed from the ideal gender type and of how her race as well as her physical mannerisms played a role in her inability to ever achieve the ideal type. She was also aware that her interests deviated from those expected of girls and were more similar to those given to boys. She felt a mismatch that stayed with her throughout childhood and even into adulthood, and she contemplated gender reassignment as a strategy to align her with the sex that matched her interests and desires. While others have written about the inarticulate gender conflicts of masculine-identified lesbians who, from a young age had feelings of perplexity about their gender differences (i.e., Hiestand and Levitt 2005), racial difference was importantly implicated in the mismatch described by Zoe. Race as well as gender expression made it difficult for her to see how her experience as a Black girl related to the image of Barbie as the ideal expression of female gender.

The pressures of gender conformity were equally strong for Nilda Flores, though she responded to them in a different way. Nilda's account of her adolescent understanding of gender and how it related to her sexuality suggests the importance of gender complementarity, which made it possible for her to envision herself in a same-sex romantic encounter. Born in South America in 1963 to parents who were both physicians, she and her family left a repressive dictatorship and immigrated to the United States in 1974. While growing up, she says she was "very out of touch" with herself and "living in denial" about her sexuality. As a result, from the time she was a teenager in the late 1970s until her mid-to-late twenties, she operationalized her desires for women in daydreams in which she retreated into a male body. Experiencing her desires as a boy and as a fantasy allowed her to avoid having to see herself as gay or think concretely about sexuality at all:

I think what I did is kind of live in a fantasy world, and this is going to sound crazy, but I created this persona who was a boy—but I realize now that that was really me! And so I would live in this fantasy world, whenever I had a free minute that's what I would do, think about that, but I never really lived as a lesbian in those years, and I never even thought of my own [sexuality]. . . . I had a *mad* crush on this guy . . . who was a drag queen, I guess you would say, and I just loved him when he dressed up, and we would go out to dinner and I would open the doors for him, so I don't know how I didn't know this about myself, but at the time I didn't know it. I know it sounds crazy, but I didn't. I always had fantasies about women from very young, kissing, but I was always in this persona that I invented and I never, like, saw *myself*. I had these mad crushes on girls.

When Nilda was asked: "When you sort of created this persona, were there other women around you who were lesbians? Did you know what that was?" she replied: "I don't think I ever—I mean, now when I look back, I think about some people in high school, and I am like, 'Yeah, they were lesbians.' But at the time I was just not aware. I was in my own world." Here, we see an interest in occupying a male body as a way to appropriately enact a desire to be with women. For Nilda, gender complementarity was necessary to romantic interaction, and since she was interested in women, she had to think of herself as a male in order to engage that fantasy. Research suggests that extreme patterns of gender nonconforming behavior in youth, combined with a strong desire to be a boy, are associated with a greater likelihood of having a homosexual orientation in adulthood (Zucker 2004). However, rather than reflecting ingrained masculine dispositions, these feelings may reflect respondents' *cultural beliefs* about sexual orientation. That is to say, women who believe in an essentialist lesbian identity may interpret tomboy behaviors in childhood as a sign of masculinity. Gottschalk (2003) makes this point, and it is emphasized in the work of Peplau and Huppin (2008).

Experiences with Men and Transitions into Lesbian Sexuality

The responses of straight-up gay women clearly reveal a lack of visible models of lesbian sexuality for young women of color coming of age in the 1960s and 1970s. The majority in this group say they were not aware of the possibility of a lesbian sexuality, what that might actually mean for their lives, or how to process feelings of same-sex attraction. For many, the lack of models delayed their open acknowledgement and acceptance of their same-sex desires until adulthood.

Straight-up gay women say they like men and enjoy their company but see women rather than men as objects of desire. Many report close friendships with men, but any romantic relationships they had with men were short, shallow, and primarily nonsexual. Shaunte Austin's account was typical for this group: she had a close male friend who she called her "fake boyfriend" and who eventually became like a brother to her. Their relationship was never sexual, and she says she only brought him home "to make an appearance" because her mother threatened to disown her if she ever found out Shaunte was gay. Other women in the group said they tried to date boys in their teenage years because that was what was expected of them and because they had not identified their lack of interest in boys and feelings for girls as specifically lesbian.

Twelve (60 percent) of the straight-up gay respondents reported acting on their romantic interest in girls before age eighteen and seeing those experiences as evidence of same-sex desire. They described hand-holding, "going with" or "going steady" with a girl, and having someone in their lives they considered a romantic girlfriend. These relationships tended not to be explicitly sexual, though they did involve intimate kissing and fondling, and the women distinguished them from the more adult female sexual activity they experienced as grown women. Ruthie Erickson, born in 1966, says the same-sex attraction she felt in her earlier teen years was different from the sexual relationships she had later on, and when she finally did have her first sexual experience, "The desire was not new, but actually going out in public was new." She felt she was "taking it to the next level." So it was the open expression of her same-sex desires that made her finally define herself as gay.

Class Differences in the Expression of Gay Sexuality for Straight-Up Gay Women

For all of the women in this group, feelings of shame and stigma accompanied their early recognition of same-sex desire. Social class seems, however, to have influenced whether the women expressed that desire in adolescence or in adulthood. Those women who completed college and entered high-status occupations tended not to have relationships with other women until adulthood, while those who entered working-class occupations often began romantic relationships in adolescence. The former group delayed acting on their lesbian desires because they wanted to acquire additional schooling and build their careers first, and saw the open expression of same-sex desire as inconsistent with those goals. This was the case not only for women who were raised middle class but also for women who were raised working class or poor but achieved middle- and upper-middle-class status in adulthood. While 60 percent of straight-up gay women had romantic female involvements in adolescence, the other 40 percent, all of whom now hold high-status occupations, reported having had no serious romantic or sexual experiences with women until adulthood. They also did not have any serious romantic involvements with boys during that time. While many of their heterosexual peers had their first sexual experiences with boys at age fifteen or sixteen, straight-up gay women felt unusual because they were not having sex with anyone.

High-status women had difficulty acknowledging a gay sexuality in their younger years because being gay carried such a stigma, and they had a strong interest in portraying a Black middle-class respectability to the outside world. Lynn Witherspoon's experience suggests a desire to be seen as "respectable" in three different areas of her life. Lynn is a corporate attorney born in a small town in Pennsylvania in 1971. Her father was a physician and her college-educated mother did not work outside the home. When asked how she defines her sexuality, she responded, "I usually say that I am gay." When I asked what it is about her experiences with women or men that makes her say she is gay, she told me she used to date men in high school and in college but has never had intercourse with a man and was never "super emotionally attracted to guys." The first way she tries to embody a sense of respectability that is linked to class and race is in her discussion of why she could not acknowledge her attraction to women as a teenager. In her community, strangers would recognize her as "Dr. Witherspoon's daughter" because there were so few Blacks and because she looks like her father. This made her sensitive to how she behaved in public.

Lynn says her friends in high school were "pretty conservative" and very White: out of 600 students, she and her brother were the only African Americans. When she realized she was interested in women she did not know any gay people in her town. She remembers that "Everybody sort of had to fit a mold there," and the people she knew only ever discussed gay issues in a negative context. So school was a second area where conformity was expected. She did not want to bring down the reputation of her family by questioning or experimenting with her feelings, and went away to college and law school in California where she was finally able to live a gay life.

A third arena where Lynn continues to feel pressure to remain consistent with norms of respectability is in the workplace. But at her law firm, she is more concerned about how race, rather than sexuality, influences the ways her colleagues and supervisors evaluate her performance. One of the firm's partners is openly lesbian, which has made Lynn feel more comfortable bringing her mate Diana to business social functions. But Lynn is one of very few Black associates, and although she has established herself at work, she continues to worry that her peers will think she's "just an affirmative action baby" or "affirmative action candidate" for promotions. The way she carries herself, even the way she talks about and interacts with her mate at Christmas parties and firm sporting events, all reflect her continuous efforts to portray a particular Black, middle-class respectability.

Angie Russell, a police sergeant born in 1967, is an only child. Her family was one of the first to racially integrate Starrett City, a series of apartment complexes designed for the middle class that became a Brooklyn neighborhood in 1974. Angie was also one of the first Blacks to attend the predominantly White elementary school nearby. Race and racial group membership were a salient part of her identity. In looking back on her teenage years, Angie says she did not have or was not aware of any feelings of attraction to girls before adulthood. She refused to believe she was gay and became angry when as a teenager a relative suggested she might be gay. For her, being gay was equated with something negative and with behavior that fell outside of a strong racial identity. The two were not compatible. She came into her gay sexuality while in college "down South," where she was a member of the Division I women's basketball team at her school in North Carolina. Angie did not want her teammates to know she was interested in women, and traveled great distances from campus to go to African American lesbian clubs and parties. She did not feel comfortable speaking freely about her same-sex desire even to other Blacks whom she thought shared those feelings. She also kept her gay sexuality from Black heterosexuals in order to remain connected to the Black community on campus.

Upwardly mobile straight-up gays believed they had something concrete to lose in taking on an openly gay identity as they entered adulthood. These women were on a path from working-class or lower-middle-class status to joining the ranks of the middle class, and they had an added interest in conforming to expectations of heterosexuality as they entered this new world. The type of upward mobility they were striving for required conformity in all areas of their lives (i.e., in whom they partnered with as well as their clothing, dress, hairstyle, and language). Coming to terms with their sexuality would have required accepting that they were failing to meet society's expectations: they saw the enactment of a gay identity as inserting an unnecessary obstacle into what was an already difficult path because of race.[8] The majority of the straight-up gays in this study were also coming to terms with their sexuality during a time of forced racial integration of schools and neighborhoods throughout New York, and the visibility of race as an identity category influenced how they thought about and prioritized other identities based on other statuses.

Women in the straight-up gay cohort who were not college educated pursued same-sex desires in their teen years by having girlfriends and dating girls in high school and in late adolescence, though not openly. The working-class women in this category were not prevented from pursuing romantic attractions by the stigma surrounding homosexuality, but it did affect the way they viewed themselves, when and how they revealed a lesbian sexuality, and how they interacted with others whom they knew were also pursuing same-sex desire. From 1983 through 1987, for example, Trina Adams attended Andrew Jackson High School, a working-class, predominantly Black public school in Queens. She says that lots of girls at her school and many of her basketball teammates dated girls, but no one was openly gay or spoke about it among themselves or with other students: "I think for a lot of women who grew up in New York City back then in the early 1980s it was 'cliquey,' it was like a secret life. When I was in the ninth grade a lot of the students were gay. It was so funny—I don't know what we said to each other to let each other out of the closet, but we'd go in locker rooms, we would watch each other while we kissed. My team played August Martin [another public high school in Queens], and everyone was lesbians on that team every year. . . . So, when we would play high school games, going home on the bus with August Martin girls, we would match up. It was like a secret society." When I asked Trina, "So, did you hang out with a lot of gay girls in the classes in high school, or was it pretty much confined to the team?" she replied: "No, it's funny, because we would never really hang out because also it was also like a stigma. They looked at girls on the basketball team like 'They're butches, they're dykes.' They didn't know a name for it—that is what they would call us. So really we would not hang around each other because no one really liked that stigma. All my friends in high school were straight, so when I wasn't on the court, I really, really tried to hang with them [straight friends] because I didn't like the stigma of that word 'lesbian.' So they figured, 'Oh, Trina is not like them because she hangs with straight people,' but I really was like them."

Even though Trina admitted to having been a tomboy in adolescence, she was very uncomfortable with having her gay identity exposed to her Black heterosexual peers. She acknowledged the intense same-sex relationships that were taking place on her sports team, noting that her teammates took great care not to spend time together outside of the team for fear that they would be labeled "lesbians" and be perceived by their classmates in a negative way. The stigma attached to a lesbian sexuality in high school was significant and severe. Women who "looked gay" or who did not conform to traditional notions of femininity in adolescence were in danger of being singled out and ridiculed, so those who acted on their same-sex attractions did so in very secretive ways and outside of the purview of their straight friends. They also made great efforts to prevent being labeled as part of a group of "lesbians," which carried a very derogatory meaning.

For both classes of straight-up gay women, nonconforming gender presentation and social activities during childhood are mirrored in the types of jobs they pursue in adulthood: they tend to work in male-dominated blue-collar industries or high-status white-collar occupations that are disproportionately occupied by men. Their occupations include police sergeant, security guard, construction worker, corrections officer, licensed electrician, retired military officer, financial consultant, telephone company lineman, union organizer, attorney, and psychiatrist.

Geographic Distance from Family to Come into the Life

Regardless of class, as teenagers and young adults, straight-up gay women used the substantial freedom of movement children raised in cities often have, to explore their sexuality. Children in large urban areas travel by public transportation without adult supervision, and many are involved in sports, dance, or other activities that require time out of the house and away from parents. This lower level of supervision may facilitate an early exploration of their sexuality. But despite these freedoms, many straight-up gay women still had to physically distance themselves from their families by moving out of their neighborhoods in order to fully come into a gay sexuality. They needed distance to pursue identities and emotional and sexual fulfillment that were inconsistent with the desires of their families.[9] They remained in predominantly Black social settings, however. The straight-up gay women in this study learned what it meant to be gay in Black social environments—house parties, clubs, and bars that had a Black and Latina clientele.

Ruthie Erickson, for example, used to travel from her home in Brooklyn to Lower Manhattan to sneak into lesbian clubs as a teenager, and she had her first girlfriend at the age of seventeen. Her girlfriend spent lots of time at Ruthie's home, but Ruthie emphatically says she was not openly gay at that time and wanted her family to think of the girl as her platonic friend only. "[As a teenager] I definitely wasn't out to my family, the people that I grew up with and my friends—none of them really knew. So it was like living two totally different lives, you know? My take on that was if I wanted to be who I wanted to be, then I had to leave, and that's when I moved." Ruthie elaborated: "I moved to Manhattan, because at home it's like you're living two lives, and I wasn't really ready to tackle the whole thing of telling my parents and all that, so I just kinda separated it."

Corey James says that even though she's known since she was seven that she is gay, she never had any references to acknowledge or explain her feelings. It was not until she left home for college in upstate New York that she began to figure it all out. Although Corey lived away from home in the dormitory, her entrance into a lesbian life took place on the weekends, when she would return to the city to go to lesbian nightclubs and parties. She did not come out as a lesbian on her college campus until her senior year. This suggests that it was not the campus environment that facilitated her coming out process but the freedom and lack of family surveillance that being away from home gave her. The geographical and mental distance from her family allowed her to comfortably explore her sexuality and begin to live an openly gay life.

Regardless of whether their transition into a lesbian sexuality was smooth or rocky, the first experiences straight-up gay women in this study had in specifically gay environments were at bars and dance parties that were predominantly Black or that had significant numbers of African Americans. Even college-educated lesbians had their first experiences with the gay life and came into an understanding of lesbian culture through the bar and party scenes, which were mixed by social class. Marissa Dillard, born in 1964, attended a predominantly White women's college in New York and had her first lesbian relationship with a Black student whom she met her first year on campus. She learned about the life of lesbians, however, through private parties and clubs in Manhattan that catered to Black lesbian populations. Angie Russell, as we have seen, was on her college basketball team with other women she knew were having lesbian relationships, yet she would still drive forty minutes away from campus to go to Black lesbian parties in a different city. As subsequent chapters will show, these experiences of coming into the life in racially segregated settings would have important consequences for how straight-up gay women expressed their lesbian identities as adults.

Essentialist Understandings of Sexuality and Race

Straight-up gay women say that now that they have come to accept or embrace their gay sexual identity as a salient part of their being, this identity feels natural and normal, and they find the pursuit of same-sex relationships to be a satisfying experience. They report that their identity as gay women is an expression of their "true selves." Ninety percent of the straight-up gay women I surveyed agreed or strongly agreed with the statement, "Being gay is something that is completely beyond one's control," though the majority (63 percent) also agreed or strongly agreed that "One can be gay and never act on those feelings." This suggests that straight-up gay women construe their gay sexuality as pervasive and unchangeable, and they experience it as an identity based on what Katz referred to as an "essence," an inherent quality "which may be manifested, reflected, indicated or represented by, but [do] not exist in, conduct" (1975, 1371). It also suggests agency or choice in the decision to express feelings of same-sex attraction.

Essential identities are experienced as more than just an embodiment of attributes: they are a state of being rather than a consequence of any behavior. Straight-up gay women see their sexuality as part of an essentialized self, and they often create a strong visual presentation of this identity that strengthens the permanence of their commitment to it. Sociologist Wayne Brekhus (2003) labels women and men in this category as "gay lifestylers" because they have an "authentic" gay presentation, are highly visible as gay, and are perceived to organize their lives around the gay aspect of their identities. Like the "primary lesbians" Arlene Stein identifies in her 1997 work, straight-up gay women experience the process of coming to identify as gay as one of coming to terms with an authentic self.

All but two of the straight-up gay women I interviewed have a very visible nonfeminine gender presentation that is crafted not merely to reveal an authentic self to others but also to enact an authentic inner self that is at odds with dominant cultural expectations. The majority believe that an individual can be gay and never act on those feelings because at one time they followed that path. Eventually, however, circumstances allowed them to make their gay identities visible, and as a result, outsiders interpret their gay sexuality as a dominant identity category. That is, they are immediately categorized by others as gay. In their minds, however, some other status may be the more dominant, or they may integrate any combination of marked statuses into a hyphenated identity. Straight-up gay women also interpreted their racial identities in an essentialist way and had strong commitments to their racial/ethnic groups.

When straight-up gay women form families, their patterns of mate selection are strongly based on gender presentation: they actively seek out gender complementarity in a partner. They seek partners who look feminine, and they also tend to enter motherhood through routes other than heterosexual intercourse, such as adoption or partnering with a woman who already has children. I analyze the links between coming into the life and the expression of gender presentation more fully in the next chapter.

THE CONFORMISTS

Anita Adams, a receptionist born in 1970, described her path into the life to me in this way: "I've always had feelings from young for women. I've always had that *want*—to be with them, . . . to walk down the street together—I've always wanted to do that. It was in the back of my mind. But due to the fact of how things are supposed to look to family and friends, I never did that until my twenties when I started venturing off mentally. I still took my time, 'cause I guess I wanted to have children first. But I finally decided to take that next step in life."

Women like Anita who took what I call a "conformist" path to actualizing their lesbian sexuality experienced same-sex desire at an early age but had a major sexual relationship with a man before coming to terms with their gay sexuality. Despite having participated in heterosexual love relationships, conformists are similar to straight-up gay women in that they tend to be essentialist in their understanding of their gay sexuality, seeing that desire as something they have always had but were unable to fully experience due to various outside pressures to conform. They also experience sexual orientation as a state of being rather than a behavior in which they engage. For this reason, their decision to pursue same-sex desire was also a decision to permanently enact a gay identity, and they consider that identity the manifestation of their true inner selves. Now that they have transitioned into a gay identity, conformists present their stories as narratives of finding a path to self-acceptance. They often express their gay identity through regular participation and membership in gay-oriented Black activities, the raising of children within lesbian-headed families, and the establishment of social networks of Black gay friends.

Eighteen of the fifty-eight women I interviewed (31 percent) are part of the conformist group. Their gender presentation is a mixture of feminine and gender-blending, with only one person having a self-identified masculine gender style. This is in stark contrast to straight-up gay respondents, who almost all have a gender presentation that is nonfeminine. The majority of West Indian women in this study also fell into the conformist category.

Conformists Coming into the Life

Like straight-up gay women, conformists also said they had crushes on girls at early ages, and expressed those feelings physically by touching and kissing in elementary or junior high school. They did not label these attractions as "gay" at the time, though they felt a stigma around those desires when they occurred during adolescence. Like straight-up gay women, conformists also see their lesbian sexuality as a significant identity trait. However, two factors most significantly distinguish conformists from those who are straight-up gay. First, they tend not to link their early attractions to women to a sense of feeling "different" from other girls in childhood, and they do not uniformly report having stereotypically male interests or being a tomboy while growing up. Second, conformists were more responsive to cues from the racial community and from the larger society discouraging the open and public expression of a gay sexuality. Conformists were much more affected by social, cultural, and religious messages such as "If you do this you are going to hell," "Live your life decently and in order," "Do not embarrass your grandmother back on the island," "You already have three strikes against you, why make things any worse for yourself?" or "You've achieved what so few of us have been able to accomplish, why tarnish that with this kind of behavior in public?" Conformists felt a more acute pressure to conform than did straight-up gay women, and they responded by acquiescing to the demands of family, culture, and community. Instead of outwardly exploring their initial same-sex attractions, they suppressed their interest in women, avoided analyzing what these feelings of interest might mean, settled for close platonic or ambiguous friendships with women, or engaged in same-sex relationships in secret. Many of them shielded their same-sex interest by making a public show of dating or having serious cohabiting relationships with men.

At the time of the survey, all of the conformists defined their sexuality as exclusively or predominantly lesbian. This represents a significant change from how they thought about their sexuality in earlier periods in their lives. Only half of them described themselves as exclusively or predominantly lesbian by age twenty-one. (Recall that 90 percent of straight-up lesbians described themselves in this way by age twenty-one.) This suggests the greater extent to which conformists masked or ignored their feelings of same-sex attraction as younger women. For those growing up outside of the United States, that pressure was cultural: in Caribbean countries, women were expected to have close relationships with one another, but publicly acting on same-sex attraction was strongly discouraged. As a result, a long period of time passed between when foreign-born women first felt same-sex desire and when they first considered themselves lesbians.

Toni Hernandez, a public school teacher born in 1969, was raised with her grandmother and three sisters in a small country in the Spanish-speaking Caribbean. She has been attracted to girls since the age of five, but that attraction was strictly forbidden in her culture, and she was extremely afraid to express or act upon those feelings. This trepidation made her reluctant to show even platonic love for her friends: she says she was frightened to hug her friends for fear that "it" would come out and her attractions would be exposed. Toni immigrated to the United States at the age of seventeen to join her mother, who had arrived years earlier. Soon after her arrival, she entered a cohabiting heterosexual relationship and bore two children. It was not until the age of twenty-five, after firmly settling into her life in the United States, that she began to openly explore the feelings she had always had toward women. She did that by going to the New York City Gay and Lesbian Community Center and meeting other women in a group called African Ancestral Lesbians United for Societal Change.[10]

Rochelle Fitzwilliam, a business executive born in 1973, spent the first eighteen years of her life in the countryside of Trinidad. She describes the place where she grew up as a "very small village, rural by any standards" and "communal," where everyone knew each other's names and families and everyone knew one another's business and reported each other's "news," be it good or bad. Rochelle first acted on her attraction to women at age eight but it was not until the age of twenty-two, however, that she thought of herself as lesbian. She says that in Trinidad, "there was a part of [her] life [she] didn't express," and she thought that by moving to New York she would be able to more fully explore "that side" of herself. When I asked for clarification, she said: "I am really talking about my relationships with women, because coming from a small Caribbean country, there is a lot of homophobia. It's a sort of culture where there are gay people and everybody knows that they are gay, but no one ever mentions it, and no one ever says the word 'gay.' But at that point in time [right after she finished college in 1994 at age twenty-one], I had not identified that was the problem, that that was the conflict I had, but I knew that there was some point of confusion or turmoil in my life and I felt that going into a different environment might help me to address that problem."

Rochelle remembers that in the late 1980s and early 1990s in Trinidad, if a woman had an interest in women, it was not directly spoken about. Rochelle found that the process of finding a same-sex partner in Trinidad was less like romantically dating women and "more like developing a friendship that eventually leads to something . . . I don't think up front you have an agenda, where here [in the United States or in New York] I think you can have an agenda up front because people are much more open, and we sort of know what they are talking about. Over there, it's like you have a best friend and . . . you'll do a lot of things together, you know, go to the movies or just spend more time together than two best friends would normally spend, and then I guess from there you can develop an intimate relationship. So that has been sort of my experience. It wasn't going to a club or gay group or anything."

Rochelle's experience in Trinidad followed a pattern common in societies where same-sex desire is openly disparaged or legally sanctioned: individuals who want to act on that desire often do so under socially ambiguous conditions, keeping their intentions veiled and following a more obscure and longer path. This is the case for lesbians and gay men in many areas of the world, as emerging research on gay populations in rural and suburban parts of the country and in other regions has shown.[11] Others who grew up in the Caribbean describe a similar vagueness when referring to how they would enact same-sex attractions back home. Those experiences made them less likely to name their feelings as those of same-sex attraction and less likely to take on an identity as gay or lesbian.

There is a small literature on relocation to the United States as a strategy for foreign-born gay people to move their sexual desires from behavior enacted in the private realm to an identity status that encompasses part of a larger self-definition. While much of this work has been dominated by the experiences of men (see, for example, Cantú 2001), Acosta (2008) writes about Mexican lesbians distancing themselves from their families of origin through migration in order to create spaces for themselves where they feel freer to express a gay sexuality. This process is shaped by many factors, including the sexuality politics in one's country of origin, cultural expressions of sexuality and desire, as well as the reception of the receiving country toward one's racial and ethnic group. Upon arrival, the process is facilitated by the immigrant's connection with lesbian-oriented social groups and organizations. The experience of Black immigrant lesbians resonates with this work, particularly in reference to their eventual participation in Westernized understandings of identities organized around sexual desire. Black immigrant women in the United States must also contend with the lower social status of Black women as a group, and this also affects processes of incorporation into communities organized around race and sexuality.

Transitions into a Lesbian Identity: Crisis in Coming to Terms with Same-Sex Desire

In a private letter dated November 1975, the well-known Black feminist Barbara Smith wrote to noted activist Cheryl Clarke that when some women come out, they feel "scared, sick, abnormal, while others feel normal for the first time in their lives." Smith said that the latter had been her experience.[12] I found that for most of the straight-up gay women I spoke to, their feelings of taking on an openly gay identity resembled Smith's, while the majority of conformists report going through some type of crisis or fear during the process of deciding to be openly gay. Caroline Tate, born in 1966, says that at age nineteen or twenty, her daughter's father told her he thought she was gay. She had grown up in Florence, a small town in South Carolina with conservative southern values. The turmoil for Caroline surrounded whether and how to embrace a gay sexuality despite the negative associations she had with people in that category:

> He said, "You're gay, you're a lesbian, you like women." And I was like, "What are you talking about? That's not true." But in my heart I knew it was. I can't tell you why he said it. I never asked him why he said it, but I

know it was almost cutting me with a knife when he did say it, because I was feeling that way inside. But like I said, I was afraid to be that person. I was afraid for a number of reasons. One of them was because we do care what people say about us. I grew up with people saying bad things about gay women, and I didn't want to be that person that I heard about all my life— "That's sad," "They have a problem," "It's nasty." Even though I was feeling like a gay woman, I just didn't want for people to think that I was. I didn't want to be called those names. But I always knew.

Caroline says that she remembers being hurt by what he said because "It was the truth." She explains, "I just hadn't acted on it yet, but I was feeling that way in my heart."

The most important factor leading to the participation of conformists in a gay sexuality was opportunity—opportunity that they purposefully sought out or that they happened upon. Asa Bambir is a Ghanaian woman born in 1971. She says she has always been attracted to girls from the time she was young, but she was also committed to leading a respectable life, one that her Ghanaian mother would approve of. Throughout high school and into college, she dated men, and her last relationship with a man occurred over a period of two years while in college. They became engaged, and it was at that crossroads in her life that she began to share with him her interest in "experimenting with women." Her desire to act on her attraction toward women grew, and he tried several strategies to keep their relationship moving forward, including arranging for couples therapy and bringing a third person, a woman, into their sexual relationship. Eventually, Asa cheated on him with another woman, after which she says "things just fell apart."

Soon after that, Asa says she and a gay male friend "stumbled upon a gay and lesbian parade," and when they passed a section of women in the parade, she found herself "in awe." It was here that she first began to concretely consider what it would be like to take on a gay identity. She described that experience in the following way: "There was this one particular woman that was part of the crowd, and I don't know what it was about her because, to be honest, to this day if I saw her I would not look twice at her, but there was something about her. Maybe it was her toughness or the fact that she had her hair dyed platinum blonde and it was cut in a boyish cut. I was completely drawn to her—I don't know if I was projecting something of me that I saw in her, a little bit of toughness or whatever. But I was like, 'Oh my god, she is so cool!' . . . So my coming out process was basically pursuing this woman, because after the parade I needed to know who she was." Asa began searching for the woman at gay men's bars and parties with a White gay male friend. At first she avoided women-only venues because she still felt "squeamish" about lesbianism, but after a while, she began to drag her friend to the women's parties, and in the process she began to integrate herself into the public sphere of lesbian life.

Men and Heterosexual Marriage

Unlike straight-up gay women, conformists more directly report having had past attractions and love relationships with men. Looking back on these heterosexual experiences, however, conformists interpret them as "default" relationships they entered because they could not understand their desire for women, they did not want others to know they were attracted to women, or they could not see how it would be possible to act on their feelings for women. Conformists say that any feelings of love they have had for men do not compare to the depth and intensity of love, closeness, and connectedness they are able to experience with women. The greater intensity of their feelings for women are evidence for this group of their true lesbian identity. They point to barriers in their social environments that prevented them from initially acting on their same-sex desire until much later in their lives. They also mention wanting to live up to the expectations of heterosexuality imposed on them by others.

Conformists tend to agree that being gay is something that is completely beyond one's control: 83 percent of them agreed or strongly agreed with this statement on the survey. They also feel strongly that one chooses whether to enact a gay sexuality: 80 percent agreed or strongly agreed with the statement, "One can be gay at one period of time and then be heterosexual at another point in time." So they think their desires are innate within themselves (beyond their control), but they can decide when to act on those desires. This implies an essentialist understanding of their own sexualities, but it also suggests a freedom of action in how they live their lives.

Caroline, for example, said "I'm gay, I'm a lesbian. It's something I always knew. But I think some of us who have children or who have had experiences with men or who say that they don't dislike men . . . you're saying, 'I'm not against being with a man, I have been with a man, but now I'm with a woman.' Growing up, before I came into my sexuality, I knew I liked women. But because of the way I grew up and where I'm from, and it was always bad to be that way, I had to suppress those feelings. I suppressed those feelings, and I would always wonder why I was attracted to women or wonder why I wanted to kiss my best friend instead of going to a party with her and hang out. But because of my environment, I pretended that it wasn't happening to me." Some women like Caroline look back on their time with men and say that the driving force behind the feelings they had for men was a craving for attention that men gave them. This is what she says about her relationship with the father of her daughter: "I was in love with the idea of being in love I guess, because he was this good-looking guy. And I was just so happy that he paid little me some attention. And I just looked at him and went, 'Wow, he is good looking and he wants to be with *me*?' So I think at that time, I think it was enough for me, and I fell in love with that. . . . When I was with him, I think I was looking for someone to pay attention to me, someone who didn't mind being with me in public, someone who didn't mind calling me their girlfriend. At that time, that was enough, because where I came from, I didn't have that. So there's this good-looking guy, this is love for me right now."

This feeling of craving love and being open to accepting it from a man who had traits that are socially valued—she mentions that he is good looking and is surprised someone with his qualities would pay attention to her—was enough to move her forward into the relationship. His attention, in the context of her belief that the feelings she had for women were wrong and a sign of being a bad person, made her feel that being with him was the best she could do. Caroline and other conformists said they entered relationships with men because they had not sufficiently dealt with their attraction to women or were confused about the feelings they had for women and did not know what to do about them. Given this uncertainty, they found it easier to go along with the attraction they had for men. Caroline came into the life as a self-identified "fag hag" by first spending time with her best friend, a Black gay man, and his friends, going out socially with them. She met her first female lover at a gay club party. They were together for two years, and after that experience, Caroline says, "I just never looked back. I just continued my journey."

Women born in the Caribbean repeatedly told me that if they were able to recognize their own feelings of same-sex desire, they did not see how they could ever act on them in any public way or how they themselves could see a gay relationship as a legitimate relationship. They had not been able to imagine even the possibility of forming something defined as "family" with another woman. The people they knew who acted on same-sex desire did so in secret, in relationships that were fleeting, because it was difficult to have a long-term relationship without having a public gay identity. Sifa Brody, an entrepreneur born in 1964 and raised in Jamaica, West Indies, says she first acted on her same-sex attraction in 1976 at age twelve, but she did not consider herself a lesbian until age twenty. While she was attracted to girls at an early age, it was not until she grew older that she began to more fully understand and act on those feelings.

Before Sifa moved to the United States at the age of twenty-seven, she spent her young adulthood going out to private gay social events in secluded areas of the island that mainly drew gay men. She and a few other women would attend those parties, and occasionally she met women to date. She says Jamaican society during the 1980s had a "very low tolerance for gays, so it's very very very harsh. Very harsh." But the punitive nature of the culture did not stop individuals from having gay relations—it only made them more secretive in their sexual behavior. She says that in Jamaica "there is a whole community there that's gay, and it's so quiet and hidden that if you are not gay, you wouldn't know. Only if you are in that community—then you will [know]." Sifa found that people did not normally confront women about having gay relationships as long as they maintained a façade of heterosexuality: "For the most part, they don't confront you. They whisper, or they look at you, or they say stuff to make you feel bad. But they wouldn't confront you, or they didn't confront me. And a lot of the guys in my neighborhood, they knew. I didn't tell them, but they knew." While Sifa did not know of any women who had been physically assaulted as a result of their relations with other women, she knew of and had witnessed attacks on several male friends accused of being effeminate or believed to be gay, including one incident that involved a stranger drawing a gun on her friend outside of a gay men's party.

While Sifa's experiences did not stop her from spending time in gay social settings, they did make her cautious about enacting her same-sex desire publicly. She found her first lesbian relationship at age seventeen very frustrating. It began as a platonic friendship that involved phone calls every night (which was expensive, because she and her friend lived on different parts of the island) and visits every weekend. She and the woman had such a deep fear of admitting their attraction to one another and acting on it that it took four years of "constant hanging out, being in contact, and then developing feelings for her" before they did so. Cultural norms prevented her from fully acting on her own feelings and "being herself." She remembers: "You couldn't hold hands, you couldn't hug. You couldn't be yourself, because it's not accepted. That's what made it hard. And considering that it's, as I said, against the law, you don't want to put your life in jeopardy for a relationship. You would if people were more tolerant, but people in Jamaica are extremely ignorant as far as gay relationships are concerned." Even when they went to gay parties together, Sifa was reluctant to be open about the relationship. She says that gay life in Jamaica "is so quiet, so secret," that she "didn't want anybody to know that she was my girlfriend," so she would tell everyone her girlfriend was just "a friend from out of town." She says that having relationships with women in Jamaica was "really hard. Very, very hard."

Another thing Sifa did to maintain the secrecy of her relationships with women was pursue public relationships with men. Her last boyfriend was a man whom she dated for more than five years and whom she intended to marry. Sifa eventually ended the relationship, but she said the break up had less to do with her interest in women and everything to do with his controlling and abusive ways. Had he been a better person, she says, she would have married him, because it would have spared her from having to think through and deal with her feelings for women. Her relationships with women would have continued to be enacted on the sideline of her life, as secondary, discrete dalliances.

Conformists do not label themselves "bisexual," despite having had prior romantic feelings for men. They say their interests are in women, who are the source of their greatest emotional fulfillment. Daphne Competello, a Puerto Rican woman born in 1969, says that once she had a relationship with a woman, she never turned back: "I mean for me, [coming out] was very hard, because I was married before. I had a child. So for me to come out, it was *very* hard, and I did it instantly. My mother thought, 'You just did this—how are you going to say you're a lesbian?' I was like, 'No! I know I'm not going to go back to that, because I can't.' You know what I'm saying? I think that bisexual people are just greedy!" Other conformists said something similar, expressing how difficult the decision to embrace a gay sexuality was for them but how, once they had acted on their same-sex desire, they "never looked back." Anita, who has had cohabiting relationships with the fathers of her two daughters, says she knows she will not have romantic feelings for men in the future: "I just don't have it in me. It won't come back. It's not going to come back, because I already see what I can establish and what I can get and how I can grow with a woman." The narrative they tell themselves is that they are moving from one group (men) to another group (women) or taking steps to enact the desires they have always had.

Despite having had prior romantic relationships with men, conformists do not see bisexuality as a viable alternative to heterosexuality. Because they have experienced relationships with men as less fulfilling substitutes for relationships with women, they are reluctant to return to men, despite their greater interest (relative to straight-up gay women) in conforming to societal expectations. For conformists, being in long-term lesbian relationships and participating in a community with other Black gay people are primary ways they maintain a commitment to an openly gay sexuality.

Social Class and Conformity

Women with working-class and middle-class family backgrounds were equally distributed among straight-up gay and conformist pathways. Indeed, they were equally distributed among all four pathways identified in this chapter. Among conformists, however, women who were raised in high-poverty households had to deal with so many levels of family disorganization and such great economic pressure that living as openly gay was not often at the forefront of their minds. It was viewed almost as a luxury to be able to focus so intently on their personal lives.[13] Social scientists Linda Burton and Belinda Tucker (2009) observed something similar in their research on low-income heterosexual women raising families: they found that the amount of time and energy that goes into sustaining a romantic or marital union can be burdensome and overwhelming when added to the multiple demands and stressors that exist in the often chaotic lives of these women, who may find it difficult to devote the emotional and psychological resources to such an endeavor.

Elizabeth Bennett, born in 1970 in Brooklyn, was attracted to girls in high school but did not see how she could ever have a relationship with a woman. Her abusive, drug-addicted father controlled her every move and those of everyone else in her household, which included her mother and five siblings. She feels that the conditions she has lived in and the experiences she has had coming into adulthood narrowed the possibilities for who she could strive to be in life, limiting not only the types of jobs she could hold and the amount of education she could attain but whom she could love. When Elizabeth's oldest sister attended college at a private university in New York, she earned good grades. However, continuous problems with financial aid were compounded by her father making her return her books to the bookstore to give him money he would use to support his long-term drug habit. When he found the check she had received for student financial aid, which she had tried to hide under a floorboard in her room, and cashed it for his own use, Elizabeth's sister gave up on getting a college education.

Elizabeth says this event affected her decision making when she was accepted to Fordham University a few years later. When her father told her in no uncertain terms that she would not be allowed to live on campus, she worried that living at home would prevent her from doing well in school. She decided instead to forego the college route and continue full-time in the cooperative education job as an office aide that she had held since high school. At least that way, she figured, she would be able to live on her own and independently support herself. She stayed in that job for the next fifteen years, helping to support her youngest brother through college and taking occasional classes herself at a local community college.

When Elizabeth first began dating at age nineteen, it was with a man much older than she was, and she quickly left home to live with him. They married and had a child together in 1995 when she was twenty-five. Around the time of her child's birth she and her husband bought a computer, and through the "birth" of the Internet she began to meet women secretly in an online chat room. She answered a few women seeking women ads in the Village Voice newspaper and at age twenty-eight summoned the courage to leave her husband, more fully establish her own independence, and pursue life as a gay woman.

Growing up in a very poor and unstable household left its mark on Elizabeth. It took her until the age of twenty-seven before she felt confident enough to begin to pursue her personal desires. After she left her husband, she changed careers, moving from her secretarial job to work in the field of accounting and to pursue other interests. Elizabeth views her move toward embracing the gay sexuality she has always felt as part of the luxury that comes with charting one's own life course.

Conformists raised in middle- and upper-middle-class families, as well as upwardly mobile conformists raised in working-class families, by contrast, pursued relationships with men despite their same-sex desires in an effort to defend or create a self-presentation of Black female respectability. Nyla Ransom was born in 1961 to parents who migrated from the South to a city in New England. She says she "experimented with girls" when she was fourteen but did not define those experiences as gay or lesbian, only that she knew that she "might like the feelings that I was having from girls." In 1979, she met and fell in love with her best friend, Zora, while in college, but their relationship came to an end because of their mutual belief that same-sex relationships were wrong. While Zora dated a few women after the breakup, Nyla became seriously involved with a male student in the business school. After about two and a half years of this life, Nyla changed course and made the decision to return to Zora because, she said, that's "where my heart was . . . I just knew with Zora that I enjoyed the sex, my heart was there. The guy was wonderful, I mean just really no problems and all of my friends were like, 'Wow!' And it was a great relationship, but I knew that Zora was who I wanted to be with." They have been together for eleven years.

Nyla's hesitation in deciding whether or not to be with Zora had to do with her interest in fulfilling the desires of her family and the expectations that came along with being a young Black women educated at an elite institution: expectations that she move forward and "lead the race." She had overcome the obstacles that went along with being raised in a northeastern housing project, that she says was "just a little step above the ghetto," by an alcoholic mother and a father who was "in and out" of the household and living with "his other family." Despite these disadvantages, her parents had taken great pains to send her to private school through a special program for gifted minority students living in inner-city areas. Choosing a lesbian life might have upset the track Nyla was on and disrupted the image of respectability she had spent so many years perfecting. Nevertheless, she left a life of heterosexuality to be with Zora and says she has never looked back. She remains geographically distant from most of her family, only seeing them on holidays and special occasions. She says they are generally tolerant of her sexuality, and though at times she senses feelings of disapproval from them, her relationship with them is satisfactory.

The desire to present a respectable portrait of self and of Black womanhood was critically important for upwardly mobile conformists deciding whether to enact a gay sexuality. These women wanted to be seen as "good girls" and to live up to the expectations of previous generations of African Americans who had high hopes for their success. Some felt pressure to continue on the path of upward mobility that their middle-class parents had laid out for them, to use the educational opportunities that existed in their generation to do better than their parents had done, or to come to the United States to seek a better set of economic circumstances than those offered in their country of origin. Within all of these demands lies the expectation to conform to particular notions of respectability within Black American and Afro-Caribbean communities. Early efforts to conform, however, were eventually outweighed by their greater desire to actively express a sexual agency by participating in gay intimate relationships.

HETERO-IDENTIFIED LESBIANS

Santasha Andrews, a magazine editor born in 1975, was explaining to me how she met her very first girlfriend, Denise. She said it started out as a friendship and then evolved into something else. I asked Santasha at what point did she acknowledge to herself that she was attracted to Denise. She said they met at a home-buying seminar. She was a graphic artist and Denise was looking for someone to design party invitations for an event she was going to host. They agreed to get together to discuss business over dinner:

> During dinner, she asked me the question "Do you like men?" She didn't tell me what her sexuality was off the bat, so I was thinking, "Why are you asking me what do I like?" And from that point on I knew she was a lesbian. Then it was little things. She was like "Do you like flowers?" And I was thinking "This chick is not going to buy me flowers," so I'm like "No." And then she walks me to the subway station, she pays my fare, she waits for the train to come. She lives in the Bronx and we were on Bergen near the F train [in Brooklyn] so I knew it was going to take her two hours to get home. And then she calls me when I get home to make sure I get home safe. And it's just like it clicked. I think the following Saturday, she invited me to the movies and I liked her style, I liked things about her. So I started questioning myself, wondering "Am I attracted to this girl?" But that day when she invited me to the movies, I was by myself in my closet trying to find the perfect outfit to wear and I never, ever do that, not even if it was a man! (laughs) I literally had clothes *everywhere* trying them on. So that day I knew that I was attracted to her in another sense.

The eight hetero-identified lesbians I interviewed are women who report never having had any same-sex attractions in childhood or adolescence. Like Santasha, they first initiated a gay sexuality in adulthood after being attracted to or having a romantic encounter with an openly gay woman. After that relationship, they remained attracted to women and continued to pursue a gay sexuality. Unlike straight-up gay women, all of the hetero-identified lesbians once had concrete, if not completely conscious, identities as heterosexual, and they had their first experiences with same-sex desire when they were well into adulthood after serious relationships with men. Hetero-identified lesbians expressed these past heterosexual relationships as more meaningful to them than did conformists, and they all say they were in love with their male partners.

At some point in their adult lives, however, they formed a friendship with a gay woman that developed into an intimate relationship, or they sought out a lesbian social environment where they saw a woman they were attracted to and decided to further explore these newfound romantic feelings. After those experiences, they began to live out a gay identity.

For hetero-identified lesbians, gay sexuality is based primarily on current feelings of attachment and desire. They use a language of individual agency to speak about their sexuality, a language of "discovering" a possibility of female attraction and making a decision to pursue or to be receptive to it. Once they have made this decision, hetero-identified lesbians solidify their commitment to this way of life by becoming active participants in gay communities. Although they currently identify as gay and engage in same-sex romantic relationships, they may or may not see their gay sexuality as a firm component of their identities, or as an *identity status*. In other words, of all four ways of coming into the life identified in this chapter, hetero-identified lesbians are the least likely to view their sexuality through an essentialist lens, as an identity that is real and firm in their minds but that was not arrived at through an innate feeling of difference. However, they rely on the combined statuses of race and gender to create an essentialist construction of self, believing they are lesbians *right now* but will always be Black and female. Eight of the women who were interviewed fit into this group: six of them have a feminine gender presentation and the other two are gender-blenders.

Although hetero-identified lesbians comprise only 14 percent of the interview sample, they are an analytically important group because of the many ways they do not fit into the stereotypical image of lesbians held by some outsiders. They are almost always the objects of desire of less feminine women and men, and they can easily "pass" as heterosexual, giving them a particular advantage in society. Because of the way they come into a gay sexuality, other lesbians worry about this group's commitment to the gay community. Hetero-identified lesbians do not identify as bisexual. When they first pursue same-sex desire, they may be reluctant to take on any identity related to sexuality, saying they "just happened" to fall in love with a woman but do not see themselves as lesbian. They do eventually come to identify as gay/lesbian and not bisexual, however. Indeed, they are particularly sensitive to the label "bisexual" and want to distinguish themselves from this group.

Gay Sexuality: A Newfound Desire

The hetero-identified women I interviewed tended to report being exclusively or predominantly lesbian on their surveys, but they uniformly said they were exclusively heterosexual at ages fifteen and twenty-one. The age at which hetero-identified lesbians decided they were "definitely lesbian" was older than what was reported by the straight-up gay and conformist groups, ranging from twenty-eight to forty-one years old. For hetero-identified lesbians, contact with the lesbian community was critical to opening their interest in having a gay sexuality. About half actively sought out this contact, while the others fell into it by forming a friendship with an openly gay woman that later developed into a romantic relationship. Lisagor finds that public lesbian meeting places and bars in particular have historically served a particular socializing function by helping gay people to define themselves as gay (1980, 158). Gay bars also help individuals identify who is gay, and this is particularly important for individuals seeking out members of what can be an invisible, hard-to-reach group.

Unlike the women I call straight-up gay, hetero-identified lesbians are able to pinpoint the particular moment they first felt same-sex attraction. Rather than talking about having same-sex desires that they could not or would not express at an early age, hetero-identified lesbians often mention a specific woman they found themselves attracted to and making the decision to see where that attraction would lead. Berit Fontaine (b. 1967), for example, describes her foray into a lesbian life in the following way: "I was working at an organization, and there were a lot of gay and lesbian people in this particular organization. . . . And at that time I guess I was curious. I wanted to know what it would be like to be with a woman. But not even sexually, just as a friend, as a companion to hang out with and just to find out about the lifestyle. I just wanted to know about it. . . . One particular woman I was really, really interested in. I was really turned on by her, and we did get together. And, I mean, it was good for me." Berit says she was surprised to find herself desiring women and would "tingle all over" when she would see a nonfeminine woman. Eventually, she had a liaison with someone and shortly thereafter began to more fully explore her feelings of same-sex attraction.

Whereas the straight-up gay respondents tended to understand their lesbian sexualities as strong and permanent, hetero-identified women's lesbian sexualities were contingent on their having met a particular person with whom they wanted to partner. Had they not had such an encounter, they are not certain when and whether they would ever have experienced a same-sex relationship. All of the hetero-identified women were in casual or committed relationships with other women at the time of interview, and their connection to the label lesbian or gay was largely based on that relationship combined with the one immediately preceding it.

Constructionist Understandings of Sexuality

In defining her own sexuality, Adrienne Taylor, born in 1970, said the following: "As you know, sexuality is fluid, or in some people it's temporal, it depends on not the moment but the time in your life, because I dated men for most of my life. But, I am in this relationship with Nilda, and I feel like I have . . . come into myself or this is who I am, and I know I feel very strongly about that. . . . I claim a lesbian identity because I think that best describes me and my life right now and the way that I look at the world and the way that I experience the world, but it doesn't define my entire life, if that makes any sense. So it's interesting. Unlike my Black identity—I don't feel like it's [my Black identity is] fluid. I don't relate to it in that way, it's very fixed."

The trajectories of hetero-identified lesbians violate what Diamond and Savin-Williams (2000) refer to as the "master narrative" of traditional coming out models in important ways. These women do not think of themselves as being different from heterosexual women, nor do they express this difference physically: as noted, six of the eight women in this group have a feminine gender presentation, and the other two have what I define in the next chapter as a gender-blender presentation of self. They have no recollections of same-sex attraction in their pre-adult years, but once they had the experience of forming a romantic relationship or participating in a same-sex liaison, they decided to pursue it and began to insert themselves into existing lesbian communities. This pattern suggests, as other studies of lesbian sexuality have found, that homosexual identity formation is not always linear or predictable.[14]

As with some of the conformists, society's punitive response to gay sexuality made several of the women repress the possibility until they were able to move away from their families of origin. It was then that they felt safe to explore any dormant or other unexpressed romantic feelings for women. For Adrienne, director of a nonprofit organization, coming into the life was a very long process involving an awareness of lesbian desire that she did not feel she could pursue until she moved away from family and friends in the Northeast to Northern California. Prior to attending graduate school out West, Adrienne had not known or spent time around many lesbians. The Black gay people she knew in college back home had experienced harassment from other African Americans on her Ivy League campus: "I didn't know that many lesbians, and I didn't know what it was like. . . . I just didn't know the range of lesbians and what they did. I didn't have ideas, I didn't have thoughts, I didn't have images. But there were so many straight women that I could emulate or relate to on some levels, which is kind of like a default. So, I guess coming into the life was about reflecting on that and going away to school and just meeting different people and reading a lot. And just learning about different experiences."

The key to the ongoing lesbian identity of hetero-identified women is their continued participation in the gay community through intimate relationships with women or through regular engagement with other gay people. Unlike the majority of straight-up gay women, hetero-identified women do not see their gay identity as an organic part of who they are, nor do they link it to gender presentation or notions of masculinity and femininity. They tend to avoid essentialist language about lesbian identity.

SEXUALLY FLUID WOMEN

When I asked Sonjee Montag, born in 1971, how she would define her sexuality, she replied: "How would I define it? [long pause] Um, to give you an honest, honest answer to that, I consider myself a woman. I don't label myself. I do love women, but I have nothing against men. I would still consider myself bisexual only because I still have feelings for men, but I do not sleep with men. If I wasn't in a relationship with a woman and depending on the situation, who I met, I can't say that I wouldn't date men." Sonjee's refusal to label herself is typical of women in the group I call "sexually fluid," borrowing the term from a line of previous work on this topic, including a 2008 book with a similar title. As others have found at different points in time and with different cohorts of women, the majority of women who are gay report having had previous relationships and attractions to men as well as women.[15] My interviews suggest, however, that some portion of gay women have more fluid sexual desires than others, and women who eschew labels like lesbian, gay, women loving woman, same-gender-loving, or other such descriptors experience their sexuality as continuously fluid. This, in turn, affects how they are perceived by others in lesbian communities. They may be labeled "opportunists" because they are perceived as being willing to have sexual liaisons with whomever is attracted to or notices them at a given moment. These women say they are unsure whether they will remain in relationships with women; they often report that they are struggling with their sexuality.[16]

Unlike straight-up gay women or conformists, whose lesbian sexuality has become a significant component of their self-definition, sexually fluid women tend to say that sexuality is something one does or enacts and should not be considered a defining component of their identity. Instead, they build a primary sense of self around other categories, like gender and race. For sexually fluid women, whether they are gay or straight depends on who they are loving or are attracted to at a particular moment. Like hetero-identified lesbians, they understand "gay" as an identity category dictated by setting and circumstance, not by a sense of fundamental difference. Twenty percent of the interview sample (twelve women) fit into this group, and they tend to have a feminine gender presentation.

While straight-up gay, conformist, and hetero-identified lesbians all reported themselves to be exclusively or predominantly lesbian, sexually fluid women were the most likely to say they used no sexuality label to define themselves. In response to the question at what age they first decided they were definitely lesbian, eight of the twelve sexually fluid women selected "I do not consider myself exclusively or predominantly lesbian." These respondents either had no label for their sexuality or described their sexuality using terms like "open," "fluid," and "woman." Take, for example, Naja Rhodes, who was born in 1976. She has a degree in social work and is the executive director of a nonprofit organization. She says people have different definitions of bisexuality, so she just tells them that she loves whomever she is dating at the time. In high school, she realized she could care for women in the way women (and she) also cared for men, and it was then that she learned to explore the part of herself that felt desire for women. Unlike those in the conformist group, Naja did not have feelings of desire that she could not name, but rather saw herself as having a *new understanding* that she could be attracted to a woman. She did not always desire women: instead, it was a matter of discovering the possibility of having same-sex desire and following up on that interest. When she dated men, she was attracted to "feminine" men or men who "balance both the masculine and the feminine."

Alexandra DuBois, a social worker and therapist born in 1963, describes her sexuality in a similar way. In her interview, she identified herself as "bisexual with a 70-30 split leaning more towards women."

She has dated men and women, though not both at the same time; she enjoys sex more with women than with men; and she is more sexually attracted to women. Beverly Howard, a physician born in 1968, says she identifies as bisexual "for right now" because she is attracted to men and to women. At the time of interview, she was in the process of getting a divorce after a seven-year heterosexual marriage and was simultaneously experiencing her first committed relationship with a woman. Prior to meeting her partner, Adina Montenay, Beverly said she always knew women she admired and wanted to be friends with, but she had never felt anything romantic or sexual for women.

What began as a sexual liaison quickly morphed into deeper feelings of desire and wanting to share a life with Adina. Beverly was pleasantly surprised to realize that she feels a greater emotional connection in this relationship, and she attributed this to Adina's being female. She said she had never experienced with men the closeness and connection she has with women, telling me, "I don't know if there's a man out there who can have the same sensuality and a more emotional connection [with me] than I have had with this woman. . . . The relationship I'm in with this woman has afforded me way more feelings of freedom and sharing and comfort in our relationship that I just didn't have with him [her husband]." Initially, Beverly's husband did not find her interest in women threatening to their relationship, and he encouraged her to explore herself sexually. He thought Beverly's interest in women was purely sexual, but as she shared all of the feelings she was having for Adina with him, he began to worry.

Beverly's experience with her husband is similar to what other sexually fluid women in the study reported. At first, their male partners were intrigued by their mate's interest in women and allowed them to explore sexually, sometimes wanting to be part of that sexual exploration. The men began to feel threatened when their partners' interests took a more serious turn and when those interests began to manifest themselves as a desire to be only with women or to be only with one particular woman. One difference between sexually fluid women and the women who have been on other pathways to a lesbian identity, however, is that they are still open to dating men in the future. Beverly says that if she and Adina ended their relationship, she would date men again because she finds them attractive.

In comparing lesbian and bisexual women, Rust (1992) finds that both similarly report prior sexual experiences with men. However, lesbians locate these relationships firmly in the past, and current *behavior* is more important in determining sexual identity. Bisexuals report continuous and present-day attractions to men and place a greater emphasis on the *sexual feelings* they currently have when naming their sexual identity. Diamond (2008) builds on Rust's work to argue that for women with nonexclusive attractions to women and men, fixed identities do not represent the complicated, situation-specific nature of their sexuality. Bisexual or sexually fluid women also experienced gaps between the relative sexual and emotional attractions they had toward women, with some having strong physical but weak emotional attractions to women, and vice versa. These inconsistencies and gaps caused them to avoid labeling a particular identity around their sexual desires.

Five of the twelve women in the sexually fluid category (and more in this category than any other) told me that they were sexually molested or sexually abused in childhood and early adolescence by other adults, both male and female.[17] Shaniqua Banner, born in 1978, became pregnant at the age of thirteen by an adult who her mother allowed to move in with them as Shaniqua's boyfriend. The adult was physically and emotionally abusive to Shaniqua, who could not be protected by her mother, who was battling a drug addiction. While Shaniqua does not specifically label her relationship with the father of her child as sexual abuse, their age difference suggests an inappropriate and illegal relationship between adult and child. Now, at age twenty-five, despite being in a six-year cohabiting relationship with her partner, she does not want to choose a label to define her sexuality. She explained: "I don't consider myself gay, I don't consider myself straight. It is whoever catches my eye and if they are good to me, that is who I am going to be with, it doesn't matter what sex you are. So if you want to call that 'bisexual,' fine, but I choose not to even label it." She said she is still trying to define herself and has not figured it out yet.

There seems to be more than one path toward a gay sexuality for sexually fluid women. Some refuse to label their sexuality because they have no language to describe their experiences with women and men in way that would be consistent with the expectations of the larger lesbian community. Others are hesitant to apply a label because they do not have one preference and base their decisions about whom to sleep with on factors other than sexual identity. Karen Jabar, born in 1961, for example, suffered through a traumatic childhood. She moved to a group home away from her ten siblings at the age of thirteen after her mother went to prison for killing her father in self-defense during a fight that began when they were both drinking heavily. (Both of her parents were alcoholics.) She eventually married a man and stayed with him for twenty-one years before they separated and she began dating women. Karen says her first same-sex sexual experience was to "accommodate" a young woman who was in love with her when she lived in the group home as a teenager. Even though she did not come into a gay sexuality until twenty-five years later after a long-term heterosexual marriage, she links her lesbian desires to the early experience she had in adolescence. When I spoke to her, she was forty-two years old, and she identified herself as "predominantly lesbian" because her relationships in the previous five years were with women and as "slightly heterosexual" because she is still attracted to men and open to dating them in the future if she is not able to "settle down in an immediate relationship [serious committed relationship with a woman] by [age] forty-five." She said that men are still a romantic possibility for her: "I'm attracted to both sexes, and they are to me." She is also open to being with men because she says she is looking for someone who is financially secure, and she believes men are more economically stable than the women she has been meeting and dating. Notice that Karen does not base her decision regarding whether to date women or men on her identity as either heterosexual or gay, nor does she base it on particular feelings or desires for one sex or the other. It seems that Karen's sexuality responds, rather, to her perceptions of what women compared to men can provide—the perceived economic costs and benefits of heterosexual versus lesbian relationships. Her opinions reflect societal norms about men as providers of economic security.

For some sexually fluid women, Beverly Howard among them, time reveals that a stated attraction to both women and men is a stage in the transition from a heterosexual to a lesbian identity. When I met with Dr. Howard again three years after our first interview, she was still in a committed cohabiting relationship with Adina, and she claimed a lesbian rather than a bisexual identity. For others, however, past and current experiences with men as well as with women indicate an enduring fluidity in sexual orientation.

In Black lesbian communities in New York there is an unwritten taboo against self-labeling as bisexual. Women who participate in lesbian communities, who seek out female partners, and who want to be considered part of lesbian social groups are expected to choose whether they are lesbian or straight and to stick to those categories, much as many biracial and multiracial individuals experience pressure from African

Americans within their social groups to choose a racial category as their dominant identity status. Those who are thought of as "straight with bisexual tendencies" are talked about in a negative way.

Women who have committed themselves to the gay community use words like "greedy" or "selfish" to describe bisexual or sexually fluid women. This group is perceived by some to be untrustworthy in their commitment to lesbian relationships because they are thought to enjoy fulfilling sexual encounters with women while leaving the hard work and stigma of being openly and consistently gay, to others. As Elizabeth put it, "Bisexuals want to benefit from our struggle without actually going through the struggle. They can just 'dip out' and leave 'the life' when things get tough." Self-identified gay women who engage in relationships with self-identified bisexuals (also sometimes referred to in the communities I studied as "bi-curious") feel particularly vulnerable to having their relationships end with the bisexual partner returning to a hidden boyfriend or other male sexual partner. In my study, the partnered, cohabiting women who identified as "free," bisexual, or other statuses consistent with sexual fluidity remained in lesbian relationships throughout the time of the study. The unpartnered sexually fluid women dated men within the three years of my fieldwork. This suggests that the sexually fluid women in this work who defined themselves as creating a family with a cohabiting female partner retained some type of similarity with self-identified gay women, despite assigning themselves a label other than lesbian or gay. The unpartnered sexually fluid women (also single mothers), may have had a weaker commitment to a specifically lesbian way of life.

COMMONALITIES ACROSS PATHWAYS

One commonality across all four of the categories I have identified concerns the ways respondents describe their feelings for women, the reasons why they want to be in relationships with women, and how they see relationships with women as different from those with men. Desire, physical pleasure, and intimacy are the primary explanations they give for why they prefer women as romantic partners. Evangelina Tarcel, a paralegal born in 1966 and part of the conformist group, says she enjoyed dating men in the past and was once in love with the father of her child. She explains, however, that "with women it is something totally different. . . . I mean the passion is stronger, the connection for me is stronger. We relate more, we share a lot of the same experiences, a lot of the same feelings. We communicate more. Men tend not to want to communicate or they don't know how, and for me, physically it is the passion [between women] that is much more intense." Nilda Flores, a straight-up gay woman, says she prefers lesbian relationships because she feels a commonality with women in general. She says she really enjoys women, feels part of a community and a solidarity with them. Santasha Andrews, a hetero-identified woman, maintains that there is a greater expectation of closeness in relationships with women than in those with men. She says: "I think a relationship with a man and a relationship with a woman are totally two different things . . . with a woman, I think the emotion is more sensual, it's cultured, it's just different. You build the relationship differently. Like say you were dating this guy and he didn't call one night. You kind of expect that, as opposed to if you were seeing this woman, [you would say], 'Why you ain't called me!' (laughs) It's really different. That's one thing with lesbian women that really gets me is how emotional it is."

Women across all four groups also had a similar need to physically distance themselves from their families of origin before they were able to openly share their gay identities with parents and parental figures. While straight-up gay women and conformists experienced and often acted on same-sex attraction while living at home, they needed to separate themselves from parents, siblings, and others to fully express a gay sexuality before they could acknowledge it to others. Having left close family and heterosexual friends temporarily behind, they sought out racially similar lesbian and gay social environments and came into their sexuality through socialization with older, racially similar gay people. Even when these women attended predominantly White or racially integrated colleges, they still relied on settings that were culturally comfortable when learning how they would express their same-sex desire.

Sociologist Arlene Stein found that of the lesbians who came into their sexuality through lesbian feminism, some had same-sex desire, while others were "catapulted by sexual experimentation and rebellion" (1997, 154). For this group, lesbianism was a way to bond with women and gain strength and confidence. They were socialized into lesbian worlds that contained women's consciousness-raising groups, lesbian-feminist groups, and groups that identified and tried to cultivate a particular "lesbian consciousness" (55). Stein argued that the old gay world conceptualized lesbianism as desire, while the new gay world sees it as woman identification (see also Esterberg 1997). I have found, however, that the existing literature on lesbian and gay identities has not adequately looked beyond the lesbian-feminist experience when trying to create a framework for understanding and interpreting various understandings of lesbian sexuality that lesbians have created for themselves. The Black women I spoke to still link their lesbian sexuality with desire. Indeed, in all four categories, the women I interviewed tended not to ascribe their motivations for entering their relationships in lesbian-feminist or political language. Even those who came of age during the 1970s women's movement did not specifically mention feminism or make the types of feminist arguments that subjects in other recent work have presented as factors directly influencing whether and how women enact a gay sexuality.

When directly asked whether their interest in women was in any way connected to their understanding of feminism, the overwhelming majority said no. A few, like conformist Luz Rivera (b. 1972) and straight-up gay woman Corey James (introduced earlier), said yes, but neither of these women linked their development of a gay sexuality to feminism. Similarly, the women I interviewed did not expressly conceive of lesbianism as a way to dismantle the patriarchy that exists in relationships between men and women. For these women, gay identity is more about feelings of desire for women. To be sure, the threat and experience of female subordination imposed by men exists in their life histories. Many have suffered from spousal abuse, poverty, drug use, sexual abuse, controlling relationships, disruptions in household finances, and expectations of heteronormative behavior. All of these directly or indirectly involve patriarchal and oppressive relationships with men as husbands, boyfriends, or fathers. In their stories of how they came to be interested in pursuing a gay sexuality, however, these women conveyed that the relationships they had with men were not the strongest barriers to their coming to identify with a lesbian sexuality. In other words, men did not push them into enacting a lesbian sexuality. Instead, it was the quality of the relationships they had or were able to achieve with women that pulled them in that direction.

CONCLUSION

This chapter provides support for the theoretical foundations of Black queer studies, which argue that racial identity importantly contributes to the creation (some would say invention) of a total homosexual body (Johnson and Henderson 2005). An analysis of the structural positions of race and class in the process of coming into a gay sexuality adds an important dimension to what is already known about this process.

First, we see that the standard model for how an individual comes to understand her lesbian sexual orientation is incomplete. The six stages (subjective sense of being different, identifying those feelings as homosexual, telling others, accepting those feelings as part of an identity, seeking a community of like persons, and entering a lesbian relationship) at best only account for one particular pathway into a gay sexuality: that of straight-up gays, or women whom previous scholars have labeled "primary" lesbians. These are women who base their gay sexuality in feelings of difference—in an essentialist understanding of sexuality—who experience sexual orientation as a concrete identity status, and who arrive at this status at an early enough age that they have little or no romantic intimacy with men. But even when this process adequately captures the experiences of Black lesbians, it remains incomplete because it neglects the formation of other important identity statuses that are occurring simultaneously, such as those based in race and gender. The salience of race and gender cannot be ignored as it relates to the formation of an understanding of one's sexuality.

Also importantly, the sexual identities formed by the women I interviewed have a distinctive character relative to those of their heterosexual peers and their non-Black lesbian peers. Black lesbians enter into a gay sexuality with previously formed identity statuses based in race, gender, and class that are shaped by structural forces, cultural and historical experiences, and individual daily life experiences. I did not find differences by class background in my four routes into a gay identity: middle-class women, for example, were no more or less likely to have a straight-up gay, conformist, hetero-identified, or fluid sexuality. Social class did figure importantly into how women came to understand and express a gay sexuality, however. Economic conditions make the primary focus of poor people one of physical survival, so the freedom to develop and implement a gay sexual orientation becomes a luxury that is not always available, as the life story of conformist Elizabeth Bennett illustrates. For upwardly mobile women negotiating multiple stigmas of race and gender in the labor market, the decision to adopt an open, public gay identity poses specific risks to economic stability that may be too great to bear, and this may have the effect of delaying the age at which they accept an openly gay identity or the ways in which they live out a lesbian sexuality.

The work of psychologist Beverly Greene (1997, 2002) shows the ways in which the lives of women of color are influenced by their cultural histories and communities, as well as by the attitudes of the dominant society. Black women face particular challenges in integrating more than one identity, particularly when those identities are stigmatized. An analysis of coming out processes for Black lesbians reveals that Black bodies become racialized before they are "homosexualized" (to use Marlon Ross's 2005 terminology), and the multiple identity statuses they occupy become visible at different times. These things influence the formation of sexual identity and have implications for many aspects of individual and collective identity, as Chapter 3 will reveal.

In studying sexual identity processes in Black lesbians, the consequences of racial social and residential segregation become quite salient. The majority of the women in this work both "came out" by having a discussion about their sexual orientation with an important family member and "came into" a gay sexuality by learning about the social norms and expectations of Black lesbian communities. As Greene and others have shown, the dominant model omits the cultural element of sexual orientation in its description. Indeed, it omits both the cultural element of lesbian communities and the culture that individuals bring to self-understandings of multiple identities. The development of gay identities in specific racial contexts was taken for granted in previous studies of White men and women. The insular characteristics of racially segregated social spaces have historically kept separate lesbian-feminist political ideologies or other theoretical ideologies that determine what constitutes "appropriate" or "developed" sexual identity. The absence of these perspectives as active agents of socialization opened up a space for other interpretations to manifest themselves and persist over time.

Other research, like that of Hawkeswood (1996), Johnson (2008), and Peña (2004) on same-gender-loving men of color, has found that they do not always have this coming out conversation with family members in order to live fulfilled lives. All but two of the women I spoke with have told a parent or parental figure about their gay sexuality; this may be because I am specifically studying people who are forming families. People engaged in this project may have a particular understanding of their sexuality and a public enactment of it that encourages disclosure to close loved ones. As women, they may also receive greater acceptance as homosexuals relative to Black men.[18] There are other women with same-sex desire or who live in partnerships with other women who are not present in this work. They do not acknowledge having a same-sex attraction to anyone, and do not name themselves as gay, lesbian, in the life, same-gender-loving, women loving women, or any other identity status.

I find that the U.S. context and the particular environment of New York is the deciding factor for foreign-born women in their willingness and opportunity to enact a lesbian sexuality. So what is it about the United States, and New York specifically, that facilitates Caribbean women's entry into a sexuality that is specifically lesbian? First, there is a more public social life for gays and lesbians in the United States than in their countries of origin, and it provides a more open context for the exploration of an openly gay sexuality. Moreover, New York has historically provided social spaces that are racially and ethnically singular, allowing for an understanding of one's gay sexuality in a context that is culturally similar to one's own ethnic identity. Significant populations of Caribbeans and Africans and second-generation Afro-Caribbean groups in New York City participate in lesbian and gay male social events. These activities are satisfying because they allow individuals to engage their ethnic cultures in gay-identified spaces. Gay sexuality under these circumstances is not seen as White or Western, and these contexts allow gay Caribbeans to integrate multiple aspects of their identities.

How women's accounts of their lives resonate with social science theories of identity, group membership, sexual agency, and community has been the focus of this chapter. Social constructionist approaches say identities are multiple and contingent. They are created within the context of specific communities and within specific relationships. Identities are ways of sorting through experiences of desires and attractions, relationships and politics, and the meanings of identities change over time. Social constructionism distinguishes between homosexual *acts*, which can occur in many different contexts, and homosexual *actors,* whose identities and lifestyles are organized around their erotic desires for people of the same gender. The women in my study are interesting, because while the majority (81 percent) of the 100 survey respondents agree that being gay is beyond one's control, they are sharply divided on whether being gay is a conscious choice they have personally made. Half agree that it is a choice they have made, supporting a constructionist view of sexual orientation, while half disagree, suggesting an essentialist interpretation of sexual orientation. Indeed, the majority (79 percent) agree that one can be gay and never act on those feelings. This suggests a set of decision-making processes around three areas: having the feeling of same-sex desire, which the majority sees as something out of their control; participating in a homosexual act, which the majority see as within their control because they can decide whether to act on their feelings; and becoming a homosexual actor, or taking on an identity and living an "out" life as a gay person.

We can see the fluidity in how gay sexuality is perceived and enacted even among those who say they have always had same-sex desire or who have had no serious relationships with men. They view this desire in an essentialized way, but they still describe a process of *accomplishing* a gay identity, of arriving at a fixed identity. Each group's discussion of gay sexuality shows the constructed and at times flexible nature of identity that is based in sexuality. Straight-up gay women, who have never had serious romantic relationships with men, tend to have a gender presentation that is nonfeminine. Conformists, or women who dated men early on despite early feelings of same-sex desire and subsequently took on a gay identity, tend to have a gender presentation that is either feminine or a blend of feminine and nonfeminine. Hetero-identified women, who dated men exclusively and never desired women until adulthood, mostly take on a feminine gender display. Sexually fluid women also have a feminine gender presentation. These relationships between pathways to a gay identity and gender presentation in lesbian communities are further explored and developed in the following chapter on gender presentation.

CHAPTER 2

Gender Presentation in Black Lesbian Communities

Consider the way that Asa Bambir, Lynn Witherspoon, and Trina Adams explained gender presentation in New York's Black lesbian community to me:

ASA BAMBIR (AGE 34, EXECUTIVE ASSISTANT):

In New York I saw more of this butch-femme thing and I was a little floored by it, a little shocked, like why do people have to play these roles? . . . But at the same time I looked at it in awe, because there was a part of my childhood when I really liked wearing boyish clothes, but I never did. . . . So, I was very intrigued by it, and I think over the years I've just been allowing that to surface. I really do like wearing boyish clothes. . . . I was definitely drawn to women who were feminine looking, very feminine looking.

LYNN WITHERSPOON (AGE 33, CORPORATE ATTORNEY):

When I first started to come out . . . it was interesting, because I had this type that I was attracted to, and yet when I was going out I was always attracting the more butch-looking women. And I was like, "Oh, I'm carrying this purse," and all of these other things, you know, all these things you do in the straight community. So I had to change the way I dressed, and I stopped carrying a purse, and I was able to find women who I was more attracted to to go out with. When I first came out I was wearing makeup; I stopped wearing makeup.

TRINA ADAMS (AGE 32, HOTEL ASSOCIATE):

In most [Black lesbian] relationships there is one that is more feminine than the other. For some reason that is just the way it is. I've never seen two aggressives together.[1] I've seen two feminine women living together, but one is always more aggressive. As you talk to them and you are around them more, you realize that one woman is more aggressive. I don't like the labels, but they exist. Because, I mean, we are just gay, and I don't know who started the labels, but it is what it is.

These excerpts show that there are various physical representations of gender in Black lesbian communities, and suggest that portrayals of gender are not arbitrary—rather, in some salient way they structure women's expectations for and within relationships. My respondents' comments imply that in the lesbian social worlds they know, feminine-looking women are attracted to and partner with women who are not as feminine in their physical style and mannerisms, and vice versa. Even when lesbians have a preference for a particular gendered display, they may not like to acknowledge the significance of categories and their meanings for their personal preferences. At least some women exhibit a contradiction between the significance of gender display for their private desires and their wish to downplay or dismiss the categorization of gender presentation among Black lesbians.

Gender presentation among lesbians is a fraught subject that has long been a topic of interest.[2] In the early 1990s, feminist scholars began to document what was framed as a "resurgence of gendered fashion" (Stein 1992, 434), or a revival of butch and femme presentations of self within lesbian communities.[3] Whereas butch and femme styles had been understood prior to the 1970s as expressions of intensely personal experiences around sexual identity, these scholars interpreted gender display as a less serious form of sexual amusement. Categories of gender display were said to be more ambiguous than in past generations, and researchers saw more choice in the types of gender presentation lesbians created. Relative to previous eras, women were now thought to frivolously play on cultural representations of gender: "It's all a game," they found, and gender display was no longer strongly linked to a personal identity or the structure of norms for a community (Faderman 1992; Weston 1993).[4]

Weston's and other's perspectives on contemporary gender display are actually consistent with 1970s lesbian-feminist interpretations of gender presentation that reduced the significance of those aspects of women's experience that related to maleness or masculinity, particularly masculine physical presentations in women. By labeling these presentations of self as "play" or "performance" rather than considering a more serious meaning of their representation and function within lesbian social groups, scholars began to conclude that gender presentation no longer organized lesbian life in any concrete pattern (Eves 2004).

Theoretical challenges to this perspective began to emerge in the late 1990s. Butler (1999) problematized aspects of feminist theory that questioned the legitimacy of gendered behavior within any particular gender group. Halberstam's (1998) work on female masculinity began to concretely examine definitions of gender identity and changes in them through an exploration of race and gender in film. Blackman and Perry (1990) called attention to this debate between "lipstick lesbians," who create an edgy femininity to attract women rather than men, bringing greater attention to the sexuality in lesbian identity and "revolutionary lesbian feminists" who continue to eschew feminine presentations of gender. Nevertheless, the field continues to lack empirical analyses of whether and how gender presentation relates to other identities, such as those connected to race, that structure relationships in contemporary lesbian communities.[5]

The existence and meanings of gender presentation for Black lesbians in New York at the start of the twenty-first century are critically examined in this chapter. The terms *physical presentation of gender*, *gender presentation*, and *gender display* are used interchangeably throughout this work following Judith Lorber's definition of "presentation of self" as "a certain kind of gendered norm through dress, cosmetics, adornments, and permanent and reversible body marks" (1994, 31). This gender display may be represented through clothing, physical markers, such as hairstyle, body language (e.g., way of walking or sitting), mannerisms (e.g., way of talking or gesturing), and other expressions of self. The chapter's first section defines three categories of gender display that I have found in Black lesbian communities: femme, gender-blender, and transgressive.

The second section considers the impact—or rather, the lack of impact—of 1970s lesbian-feminism on Black lesbians' presentations of gender. Whereas one influential legacy of 1970s lesbian-feminism has been White middle-class lesbians' rejection of the use of gendered physical presentation, and particularly lesbian butch/femme presentation, as a way of organizing relationships and lesbian community life, I find that many Black gay women are not influenced by this legacy.[6] Instead, they have modified the older butch and femme identities into three fairly distinct categories of gender presentation. Women choose a style for the public and private performance of gender which, once formed, tends to remain consistent over time.

Context is essential to the way in which gender presentation is received. A woman walking down 125th Street in Harlem or Flatbush
Avenue in Brooklyn wearing an athletic jersey and baggy jeans will not
be immediately identified as a gay just because of the way she is dressed,
but when she steps into a convention center or nightclub filled with other
lesbians, these same clothes will reveal her membership in a distinct gender display category. The categories of femme, gender-blender, and transgressive, in other words, have the most meaning when they are presented
in a context in which Black lesbians are present; it is in this context that
the subtleties that often accompany a femme or gender-blending presentation of self become clear. Black lesbians' gender presentation choices
are influenced, moreover, by cultural norms dictated by race and class,
which structure lesbian sexuality and the enactment of gay identity. New
York contains many distinct, well-developed sexual communities, and
women can become socialized into lesbian communities that are not explicitly based on specific feminist principles, which might be the case if
the primary gay public social groups had a political focus.[7] Many of these
groups are segregated by race and ethnicity, moreover, facilitating the
development of gay identity in racially homogeneous environments. As a
result, being gay is not experienced as an identity in and of itself that creates social distance from one's racial group or that is associated with a
particular political ideology. In New York, one can be gay and still remain connected to one's own ethnic and cultural groups.[8]

The women who participated in this study are actively engaged in the
public social worlds of New York gay life, and the lesbian spaces they
frequent are predominantly Black or contain significant numbers of Black
people in them. Sixty-one percent of the women I surveyed go to a lesbian
or gay bar or dance club at least once a month; 35 percent go less than
once a month. Only 4 percent say they never go to lesbian or gay bars or
dance clubs. The gay social spaces they frequent are predominantly racially integrated or mostly Black and Latina; just 5 percent spend time at
bars and clubs that are predominantly White. The women I studied are
entrenched in social networks that are racially diverse but that also have
plenty of Black LGBT people in them. Seventy-two percent said at least
half of their friends are Black, while 57 percent said most or all of their
friends are Black. The survey also showed that when the Black lesbians in
this study spend time with gay people, those people are usually racially
similar. Seventy-four percent said at least half of their gay friends are
Black, while 64 percent said most or all of their gay friends are Black. Just
7 percent said half or most of their gay friends are White.[9]

As the excerpts that open this chapter suggest, in the Black lesbian communities of New York, physical representations of gender indicated by clothing, hair, physical stance, the presence or absence of makeup, and various other symbols are extremely important markers of identification. An individual's style of clothing broadcasts to the community how she chooses to represent her race and gender, as well as the type of physical representation she is attracted to. The expression of gender presentation attempts to authentically capture other distinctions that characterize larger Black communities: style is used to represent not only gender but social class, ethnicity, culture, and finer group memberships.[10] The modes of gender expression inform and shape social contexts and importantly organize intimate and other social relationships. It takes hard work to represent a particular raced, classed, and gendered sense of self that is deemed authentic by others in the racial and sexual communities that define the social worlds of New York's Black gay women.

In the latter sections of this chapter, I consider how gender presentation functions in Black lesbian communities today. First I show how complementarity in gender display grants lesbians the freedom to create a physical presentation of their sexual identity at the same time that it imposes restrictions on whom individuals can partner with. I then look at class differences in attitudes about nonfeminine or "transgressive" gender display. Middle-class lesbians avoid transgressive gender presentation because it interferes with their attempts to erect moral and symbolic boundaries that signify their class status and facilitate their assimilation into larger society. Working-class lesbians embrace nonfeminine gender display and use it as an act of resistance to social norms. Asserting a transgressive gender presentation is one way they express feelings of difference from larger society based on the multiple marginalized statuses they occupy. Race has important consequences for the expression of masculinity, and I consider how presentations of masculinity expressed in the Black female body relate to broader notions of hegemonic masculinity and feminist analyses of sexual autonomy. The chapter's conclusion offers four reasons for the persistence of distinct forms of gender presentation among Black lesbians at the start of the twenty-first century.

PHYSICAL PRESENTATIONS OF GENDER

I measured physical presentation of gender in three ways. First, I asked women who responded to the survey to rate their own physical attributes, the physical attributes of their current mates, and the physical attributes of their ideal mates on a scale of one to ten, with one being very feminine and ten being very masculine. These categories represent physical style and mannerisms and are separate from items measuring personality traits and interaction styles (appendix B).[11] I also measured physical presentation of gender by asking a series of open-ended questions in the in-depth interviews about how the respondent perceives her own gender display, whether the type of person she is attracted to influences how she dresses, how she came to decide on a style that was comfortable for her, and how she feels about the labels that exist for different presentations of lesbian gender (see appendix C).

In addition, my fieldwork provided three years of observations of the interview and survey respondents as well as other Black lesbians in a variety of social contexts: restaurants, religious meetings, lesbian and straight bars and dance clubs, house parties and backyard barbecues, book clubs, and black-tie and other formal events. Seeing my respondents repeatedly in a variety of locales allowed me to get a clear sense of how they chose to represent their gender when they were in social settings with other gay people and when they were in predominantly heterosexual spaces. Observing unpartnered women in these settings also allowed me to see the physical presentations of gender of women they were attracted to or chose to date. Observing couples gave me a multidimensional picture of how each dressed relative to the other so I could see, for example, how someone who assigned herself a score of 2 (*very feminine* on the scale) looked next to her partner whom she assigned a score of 4 (*gender-blender*). I examined style in relation to that of a partner and in relation to the styles of other lesbians in the social environment.

I recoded the survey results to create three categories of gender display: "femmes" score between one and three, "gender-blenders" score between four and six, and "transgressives" score between seven and ten. The femme, gender-blender, and transgressive categories of gender presentation are classes of ascription and identification used not just by me as the researcher but by lesbian community members themselves, though the *terms* used by community members to describe these categories vary across age, class, and geographic region.

Femmes

About half of the respondents (48 percent) are femmes, or feminine women. When asked "How do you feel about labels like 'femme' or 'aggressive' or 'butch?'" "Where do you think you would fit in if you had to choose a label?" and "What is it about your style of dress or personality that makes you answer in that way?" the women in this category referred to themselves as "femme," "fem-looking," "femme, sort of" and sometimes "aggressive femme," which indicates a feminine style of dress combined with an assertive or outspoken personality. Women who were attracted to feminine-looking women referred to them as "femme," "feminine," "pretty," and "a real lady." Some middle-class women were reluctant to give themselves a label: they mentioned not liking the labels that exist and not liking the act of labeling someone else's gender presentation. Everyone who turned in a survey, however, assigned herself a score between one and ten on the scale as a way to measure her own gender presentation.

In one sense, the style of Black femme women is consistent with what researchers have found for other feminine lesbians: they wear dresses or skirts, form-fitting jeans, tops that are low cut or that show cleavage, makeup, jewelry, and accessories such as purses. When going out socially, they take care to wear clothes that show this gender presentation. But even in more casual settings with other lesbians, they wear clothing that lets others know they want to be seen as feminine, such as makeup and high-heeled shoes. The hairstyles of femme women include long and short relaxed or straightened styles; dreadlocked hair, twists, braids and other "natural"-styles; and head wraps made from African-inspired cloths. Femmes with very short hair or bald heads still exude a feminine image by wearing makeup, large earrings, and other markers of femininity. These styles are consistent with the range of fashions seen on other Black women in New York at the turn of the twenty-first century, and represent a link between lesbian style and Black culture. Blackman and Perry (1990), writing about the strong African- and culturally-inspired looks worn by Black lesbians in the late 1980s, say their presentation of self reflects an effort to bring a particular racial and cultural visibility to their lesbian identities in the White-dominated, public lesbian communities of that time. The styles they portrayed represent the tension of belonging to Black as well as gay cultures and a refusal to give up either one.[12]

A feminine gender presentation is not necessarily connected to any specific personality traits or ideologies about gender or gender display. Women who scored between one and three on the gender presentation scale were no more likely to report a personality or interaction style that was laid-back or assertive than were other women. In this sense, they did not conform to stereotypes of feminine women as soft-spoken, submissive, or indirect.

Femmes were the least likely to have entered into a gay sexuality through the pathway I define in Chapter 1 as straight-up gay. They were most likely to be hetero-identified lesbians, having grown up with little or no sense of difference from other Black women; conformists, who experienced same-sex desire in their younger years but did not act on it until much later; or sexually fluid women, who reported ongoing attractions to both men and women. Historically, femme lesbian identity has not been based in strongly internalized feelings of difference, but rather in commitment to a gay life through socializing in the gay world and having intimate and sexual relationships with women. Researchers Kennedy and Davis (1993) and Ponse (1978) found that the gay sexuality of femme women is dictated more by setting and circumstance than by feelings of difference. Harris and Crocker (1997) argued that femme gender presentation is a "sustained gender identity," or a model of critical reshaped femininity and assertive sexuality that is neither biologically assigned nor a mere representation of costumes and play.

Black feminine women have a presentation of self that is consistent with what scholars of the African American experience have identified as the dual character of African American culture. Black lesbians with a femme gender presentation are less affected than are White lesbians by what Harris and Crocker (1997) term "patriarchially imposed femininity" because historically, femininity has been viewed differently by the dominant society and by African Americans themselves when enacted by Black women. Second-wave feminists saw femininity as oppressive, but Black women may not experience it in the same way, because while the social position of Black women has certainly exposed them to gendered oppression, it has left little room for that oppression to be based in characteristics associated with the type of patriarchy experienced by White women, who are depicted as frail, dainty, submissive, dependent, and weak. These stereotypes have not been consistent with Black women's self-created, self-imposed femininity.

The femininity achieved by Black women is associated instead with power, independence, and leadership. Historian Shirley Carlson (1992), writing about Black community expectations of Black women during the late Victorian era (around the turn of the twentieth century), describes "Black Victoria" as a woman who simultaneously embraced the social expectations of the larger society and emphasized and performed the different expectations for women that emanated from the Black community. This model of Black femininity stressed virtue and modesty alongside intelligence, outspokenness, race consciousness, and work in the public domain. Carlson writes: "The ideal Black woman's domain, then, was both the private and the public spheres. She was wife and mother, but she could also assume other roles, such as schoolteacher, social activist, businesswoman, among others. And she was intelligent" (62). Likewise, Shaw's (1996) historical account of Black womanhood for the middle class during the Jim Crow era (1880s–1950s) persuasively shows that Black femininity encompassed traditional notions of beauty along with intelligence, independence, and commitment to the uplift of the racial community. Today, Black gay women who are femme apply this historical understanding of the role of women in African American communities as the model from which they develop and interpret their gender presentation and sexuality.

Gender-Blenders

Gender-blender is a style related to, but distinct from, an androgynous presentation of self. Thirty-four percent of the respondents fit into this category. None of them came into a gay sexuality as hetero-identified lesbians or sexually fluid women. Rather, gender-blenders followed the pathways associated with conformists and straight-up gay women. Rather than de-emphasize femininity or masculinity, gender-blenders combine specific aspects of both to create a unique look. They usually wear certain items of men's clothing, like men's pants or shoes, combined with something less masculine, like a form-fitting shirt or a little makeup. Sometimes their clothes are not specifically men's clothes but are tailored, conservative women's items worn in a less feminine style. Some of the labels used in the community to express this gender presentation style included "soft butch," "futch" (suggesting a combination of "feminine" and "butch"), "sporty," "casual," and "fem-aggressive," which indicates a combination of feminine and masculine gender display.[13] Women attracted to gender-blenders referred to them as "soft butch," "pretty and boyish," "not too hard looking," and as women who are "less feminine . . . but who still look like women."

What struck me most about the women in this category was the creativity with which they presented themselves. They almost never wore skirts or dresses, and yet they never looked completely like boys. While androgynous women are often stereotyped as looking very similar to one another—wearing plaid men's shirts, buzz cuts or short hair, no makeup, and comfortable shoes or boots—Black gender-blending women encompassed many different styles. Younger gender-blenders who hung out in the East Village might wear t-shirts underneath button-down men's shirts layered over cargo shorts, with flat 1970s-style Pro-Keds sneakers, in a look similar to that worn by male skateboarders. Gender-blenders from Brooklyn might pair brightly colored dashiki tops with jeans and wear their hair in twists or some other natural style. Or you might see the standard urban uniform of a crisp white t-shirt, baggy blue jeans, fresh white uptown sneakers, and a long ponytail underneath a fitted Yankees baseball cap sported by Puerto Rican gender-blenders from Harlem or the Bronx.

What unites these different fashions as a group is that the style is specifically nonfeminine. The clothes are worn in a loose-fitting masculine presentation, though hips, hair, and breasts signal that the bodies are women's, and the look is softened with lip gloss, eyeliner, or a feminine hairstyle. Because there is so much variation in women's styles of dress, gender-blenders are not necessarily labeled as lesbians in the heterosexual world. In this context, they may appear as straight women who do not dress in an overtly feminine way. It is mainly in lesbian environments that the gendered identity of gender-blenders becomes apparent. Gender-blenders tend to partner with more feminine-looking women.

Transgressives

Eighteen percent of respondents have a non-gender conforming presentation of self. They scored themselves between seven and ten on the gender presentation scale and expressed gender in ways that are considered masculine. The majority would be considered straight-up gay according to the categories in Chapter 1, although a few came into the life as conformists. None are hetero-identified lesbians or sexually fluid women.

Transgressive women usually wear men's shirts, pants, and shoes and coordinate these outfits with heavy jewelry, belts with large, masculine buckles, ties, and suspenders (the use of these items varies with age and sense of fashion). Unlike women with a gender-blender style, their clothes are never form-fitting—a clear way to distinguish between a femme and a transgressive who are both dressed casually in jeans and a t-shirt. Their hair might be dreadlocked, braided in a cornrow style that is close to the head, or worn very short and not accompanied by makeup, earrings, or other accessories that would soften the look. In their interviews, transgressive women said they leaned toward being boyish in their clothing and mannerisms. When asked what label they would use to define themselves, many of them readily identified with a specifically nonfeminine or masculine style, calling themselves "boyish" and saying things like "I was always a tomboy from the time I could remember," "I dress aggressive—I don't put on a front for nobody," and "They would call me a butch. I prefer stud, dom, aggressive."

Over and over, transgressive women described themselves as dressing in a way that makes them feel "comfortable." This statement has several meanings. On the one hand, dressing comfortably means wearing casual clothes that allow the body to move freely. On the other hand, dressing comfortably is also associated with feeling good or having a sense of authenticity in their self-expression that is conveyed through their clothing and overall comportment. These women could have chosen larger-sized women's clothes, such as women's jeans that have a loose fit but still complement or help construct a feminine silhouette. They could have worn "sensible" women's shoes. But in seeking out clothes that made them feel comfortable, they specifically and repeatedly chose men's styles and clothes that were structured to portray a more masculine silhouette. Ro Gaul, for example, a licensed electrician born in Jamaica, West Indies in 1963, gave herself a score of seven on the scale. She is tall and thin, with long dreadlocked hair. She says she does not need a label to define herself, but she "could put on a ball gown and [would] still walk like a boy." She dresses fashionably in men's clothes, wearing button-down shirts with a white t-shirt underneath, square-toed men's boots with an animal print, and a large, masculine belt buckle on her jeans. She has to be proactive in creating this look because her slim build makes it difficult to find men's clothes that fit her frame.

Ro says that often when she walks down the street, "guys and girls" look at her like she's "peculiar." Nevertheless, I have seen African American men come over to Ro and to other gender-blending and transgressive women to compliment them on their sense of style in ways that are not hostile but that suggest admiration. They have said things like, "I just wanna tell you I like the way you put that all together; much respect to you," "Excuse me, I like those sneakers and the way you hook them up with those shorts. You have a nice style. Where'd you buy those shorts?" or "I just wanted to tell you I like your look, Ma." The way Black transgressive women present themselves suggests an attempt to incorporate Black social and cultural markers and Black aesthetic style with Black masculinity on their bodies—to display multiple identities while openly acknowledging their gay identity. The responses of some men suggest they have successfully accomplished this goal.

Researchers writing about non-gender conforming lesbians often argue that transgressive identity is based in internal feelings of difference, masculine inclination, and sexual interest in women consistent with my "straight-up gay" pathway into lesbian sexuality.[14] And indeed, the majority of the transgressive women I studied report having the feelings of internal difference consistent with this pathway. I have defined this gender presentation as "transgressive" because women in this group transgress notions of femininity, because many do not like or use the label "butch," and because transgressive is linguistically similar to the term *aggressive*, which many Black lesbians in New York use to denote a woman with a masculine gender display.[15] Transgressive women might have been called studs in a previous generation or butch in the predominantly White women's community, in that they use the female body as the site for signifying masculinity (Halberstam 1998). Most Black lesbians I spoke with were not comfortable calling themselves or the women they desired butch or stud, however. Some did not want to label them at all, while others (mostly working-class women) used "aggressive" to indicate a woman who does not look feminine.

Consider the example of Morgan Banner (born in 1962), a former military officer from Staten Island. When asked, "How do you feel about labels like femme, or aggressive, or butch?" she said: "I hate 'butch,' I hate 'butch.' I don't mind 'aggressive,' and I don't mind 'femme' because I think those categories fit. I mean people at my job, they don't know my lifestyle, but they tell me all the time, 'You're very aggressive,' because it is a standpoint you take. I don't take no shit, I do what I gotta do, and as an aggressive person, I feel like there is nothing I can't do if I put my mind to it." When I asked her how she would label herself if she had to choose a label, Morgan replied, "As being very aggressive." To the question, "What is it about your style of dress or personality that makes you say that?" Morgan responded, "Well, I shop—I wear men's clothes." When asked, "Oh, you only wear men's clothes. Do you shop at men's stores?" she affirmed, "Only men's stores."

While some women identify a masculine style as well as an assertive, dominant personality as components of a transgressive presentation of self, the relationship between physical presentation and interaction style is not at all clear. Many women who report a nonfeminine presentation of self declare they also have an assertive personality, but sheepishly admit that their partners might not agree. Morgan later noted that although she thinks of herself as having an aggressive, dominant personality, her mate calls her "girly" because she has certain emotional responses and other qualities stereotypically associated with femininity: "Sometimes she [partner Shaniqua Banner] teases me and says I'm kind of girly.[16] She says I'm kind of feminine because sometimes I pluck my eyebrows or because of how I used to wear my hair. She says that I'm kindhearted and I'm so soft. . . . In the house I'm one person and outside, she says, 'You put on a front outside, you try to act all hard and then you are all soft here.' I mean, I 'water up' [cry], I'm sensitive. My eyes tear when I'm real emotional, so she says 'Oh, that makes you femme. You're femme.'"

Morgan's comments juxtapose two images of the transgressive as assertive and masculine, with an undercover sensitive, emotional, and therefore feminine expression as well. Her partner's comment—"You put on a front outside, you try to act all hard and then you are all soft here"—implies that Morgan's willingness to show a more vulnerable side of herself only takes place in certain physical locations ("here" meaning inside the home) as well as in private emotional spheres ("here" meaning within the relationship). It suggests that there are limited places where Morgan feels comfortable expressing these types of feelings and implies their association with a traditionally feminine demeanor.

The majority of respondents distinguished between having an aggressive style of dress and a dominant or forceful personality, saying the two are separate. Evangelina Tarcel, a feminine woman, for example, said the following: "I have an aggressive nature, but I love my high heels and my lipstick and my eye makeup and my cleavage showing. But if I see something I like, you'd better believe I am going over there to ask her her name [chuckles]." Transgressive women were no more likely than were femme or gender-blending women to report a very assertive or aggressive interaction style, measured as a score of seven or higher on the personality scale (Appendix B). Traits traditionally thought of as masculine, such as straightforwardness, assertiveness, or being a particularly rational thinker, did not reveal themselves in any consistent way within the three gender display categories. Likewise, gender-blenders and transgressive women often joked about their more feminine partner having the more aggressive sexual appetite, or they admitted wanting not only to give sexual pleasure to their partners but also to receive it. These sexually aggressive behaviors in the more feminine partner contradict the expectations created by studies of butch-femme relationships in previous generations, which suggested that the more masculine-identified partner had to be the more aggressive pursuer sexually.[17]

The three gender display categories contain some overlap. Women who scored a seven out of ten on the physical presentation of gender scale might be considered gender-blenders or transgressives depending on the relationship between their style, the symbols they used to express gender, and their mannerisms. And while in most cases my assessment and my respondents' assessments of their gender display category matched, in 20 percent of the cases I assigned the respondent a category that was different from her self-assignment. This discrepancy was mainly found for middle-class and upper-middle-class lesbians, who, as I explain later in the chapter, were the least likely to report a nonfeminine presentation of self, despite their own responses in the in-depth interviews that suggested otherwise.

My gender display categories are not fixed: women may move further to the left or right on the scale or modify their gender presentation over time as their tastes change. Changes in gender display are not random, however, and gender display does not vary from day to day. When women do shift categories, it is usually for one of four reasons: they have recently come to identify as gay and are negotiating the type of gender display that feels most comfortable, they have moved from one geographic lesbian community to another and adopted new styles or variations consistent with the new locale, they have entered a new relationship and taken on a gender presentation that is oppositional to the new partner's gender display, or they have exited gay communities and taken on a heterosexual (and more feminine) presentation of self.

SEPARATE SPHERES: 1970S LESBIAN-FEMINISM AND BLACK LESBIAN IDENTITY

In the 1970s, the association between lesbian identity and the women's liberation movement became so powerful that lesbian-feminist perspectives on gay identity began to overshadow the experiences of lesbians who were unconnected to that movement, gay women whose lives were primarily being shaped by other events in their social worlds. Most research on that era has not done a good job of documenting whether and how lesbian-feminist ideologies influenced racial and ethnic minority gay communities of that time, though work by Audre Lorde (1995), Barbara Smith (1983), and Anita Cornwell (1983) offer important exceptions. Nevertheless, we do have some historical accounts of the conflicted feelings shared by Black and White lesbians as they struggled with whether and how Black women would participate in the lesbian-feminist subgroup of the women's liberation movement.[18] These accounts suggest that Black women were never fully indoctrinated into the particular type of feminism espoused by White women during the 1960s and 1970s.

The persistence and meanings of gendered presentations of self among Black gay women offer additional evidence that Black lesbian communities remained largely outside of White lesbian-feminist influence. In their efforts to assimilate into the larger women's movement, 1970s lesbian-feminists took a stance that was disparaging of feminine/masculine gender display among lesbians and encouraged women to move toward androgynous gender presentations in their everyday fashions (Brown 1972). Butch and femme roles were said to have been silenced in all but the toughest lesbian communities, which were most visible in the bar culture (Loulan 1990). As a group, however, Black lesbians were less engaged in the public bar culture that defined many White working-class women's experiences; instead, they primarily socialized with one another at private house parties in their own racially segregated neighborhoods (Thorpe 1996).[19] Furthermore, Black lesbians maintained a physical distance from White lesbian-feminists and had less exposure to the assaults directed at gender presentation in their relationships. Since many Black women were never fully part of White lesbian-feminist leadership or on board with their goals, they were less influenced by these efforts to replace butch and femme identities with androgynous presentations of self.

Anita Cornwell's writings as a Black lesbian-feminist in the early 1970s help to make this point. Cornwell recounts the time when her friend referred to her as a "stud," a term used in Black lesbian communities to denote a lesbian with masculine-identified style and mannerisms. Cornwell was critical of the label, did not like it used to identify her, and was frustrated that her group of friends were relating to other lesbians with that terminology. She credited the persistence of gendered categories to Black women's distance from the feminist movement: "Not surprisingly, fear of encountering racism seems to be one of the main reasons that so many Black womyn [feminist alternative spelling of woman that removes "man" from the word] refuse to join the Womyn's Movement. This is especially unfortunate for the Black Lesbians because, unless they have come across Feminist ideas from somewhere, they are apt to remain in the old rut of sexual role-playing that apparently affects all traditional Lesbian circles" (1983, 12). It is clear from Cornwell's writing that she believed that 1970s Black lesbians were not being sufficiently influenced by lesbian-feminist ideologies toward gender identities, and as a feminist she found this problematic.

I have found very little published research analyzing gender presentation in Black lesbian communities during and after the 1970s women's movement. Shockley writes more generally about the dearth of scholarship by and about Black lesbians, saying they are not analyzed as literary subjects because White female writers are concerned with making their own voices and experiences heard, because Black female writers give priority to writing about racism, and because those who have written about lesbian themes have had difficulty getting those works published. One major issue for Black women writing about lesbians has been the fear of being identified by other Blacks as "gay, queer, funny, or a bulldagger" (1983, 84). Shockley says these names are "embedded deeply within the overall homophobic attitude of the Black community, a phenomenon stemming from social, religious, and 'biological' convictions" (84).

Silvera (1992) reports experiences as a lesbian in Toronto's Afro-Caribbean communities that are similar to what Shockley found nearly a decade earlier. The harshest, most critical language about Black lesbians was reserved for women with a nonfeminine presentation of self. These women have always been the face of lesbian identity, bearing the brunt of the hostility and misunderstanding for the group. The fear of being stigmatized by one's own group members can be paralyzing, particularly when those whose opinions matter most, those to whom one feels closest, and those to whom one turns for support and protection from outsiders become one's harshest critics. Clarke agrees, saying that because Black gay people have always contributed significantly to the well-being of Black communities, "it is exceedingly painful for us to face public denunciation from Black folk—the very group who should be championing our liberation" (1983, 207). The double transgression of acting on same-sex desires and defying societal norms of femininity has rarely been publicly acknowledged or analyzed in research on Black lesbians, perhaps in an effort to protect Black women from having their behaviors categorized as deviant or nonnormative.

Historically, raced notions of women's sexuality, morality, tempera-ment, beauty, and behavior have portrayed Black womanhood as the in-ferior "other" relative to the normative status of White womanhood.[20] Cahn's (1994) argument that racially polarized axes have historically imparted greater masculinity to Black women athletes based on their work history as slaves, sharecroppers, domestics, and laborers also ex-plains the reluctance of researchers to consider the significance of gen-dered categories among Black sexual minorities. Some fear that racist ideology will be validated and used to marginalize and debase the behav-iors and experiences that Black women record. Even in the broader con-text of lesbian identity and experience, where gendered presentations of self exist among women of all racial groups, there is a fear that calling attention to and analyzing the experience of Black gay women will result in their actions being interpreted as opposed or inferior to those of White lesbians.

USES OF GENDERED CATEGORIES IN CONTEMPORARY BLACK LESBIAN LIFE

Elizabeth Bennett, a gender-blender, shared how her gender display has changed over time. She thinks lesbians develop a gender presentation af-ter spending time in lesbian social settings. She says that when one first comes into the life, "You're just 'being gay,' you don't realize how the community is." In the newness of spending time in gay social circles, what she noticed first were the masculine-identified women: "You might think that everybody looks like a boy and you're the only one who looks like a girl. But then you see that some people look like girls, some people look like boys, and some people are in the middle. So you will pick something that you are comfortable with."[21]

Elizabeth said that when she first came out, she wore feminine clothes to lesbian bars and nightclubs because that is how she used to dress for social occasions in the heterosexual world. With a feminine gender dis-play, however, she attracted mostly nonfeminine women. Because she wanted to attract feminine-looking women, she learned to change her clothing and adopt a more masculine style: "Feminine girls are usually not attracted to other feminine girls, so you've got to be a little more aggressive-looking to get the feminine girls." Elizabeth said she also found the gender-blending style to more closely reflect the way she feels inside. She is hetero-sexually divorced but says that even when she was married to her ex-husband she never had a very feminine style. Pictures she shared with me from a photo album of her married life support this recollection. She concludes that participating in the Black lesbian social world gave her the freedom to "be herself," as she put it, by dressing in a nonfeminine way. It also rewarded her with the attention of feminine women, who found her gender display desirable.

During the period of my research, it was very unusual to see both lesbians in a Black couple dress in a masculine style. Indeed, in the eight years I have spent studying Black lesbian groups, I have not consciously come across a Black couple in which both partners have a strong non-feminine gender display.[22] As Trina Adams commented, "In most relationships there is one that is more feminine than the other. For some reason that is just the way it is. I've never seen two aggressives together. I've seen two feminine woman living together, but one is always more aggressive." Sometimes, both partners in a relationship have a feminine presentation of self—often when one is just entering into a gay identity and still developing her own sense of style, when one or both partners do not want people to know they are involved in a lesbian relationship, or when one or both partners claim a bisexual identity and are not committed to being perceived as a lesbian.[23]

Black lesbians in New York use gender display to organize social interactions. In order to attract a person with a certain gendered style, one must possess a complementary gender display. While the structure imposed by these norms maintains order in the community, it also grants women the sexual agency and freedom to present themselves in a gendered way if they so desire; this differs from the expectations in many lesbian-feminist social circles that encourage lesbians to present in ways that are not overtly feminine or masculine. In Black lesbian environments, lesbians feel liberated by the categories of gender display—especially the gender-blender identity—because the categories allow them to express nonfeminine gendered selves in ways that are valued by other gay women. Kennedy and Davis (1993) argue that gender complementarity in lesbian couples of the 1940s and 1950s both imitated and transformed heterosexual relationships. They imitated heterosexual patterns because they were structured around gender polarity, with femininity representing the object of desire. They transformed heterosexual patterns in that they were rooted in the similarity of two female bodies and did not conform to society's dominant gendered pattern of men being the dominant receiver of pleasure.[24] Instead, masculine-identified women were primarily the givers of sexual pleasure. I find Kennedy and Davis's analysis relevant to contemporary presentations of gender in Black lesbian relationships. While Black lesbian culture draws on heterosexual models, it also transforms them in specifically lesbian interactions that define and affirm women's sexual desire and embody women's sexual autonomy.

I have seen transgressive women spend an inordinate amount of time selecting just the right men's shirt or blazer or having a jacket tailored to fit their bodies in a specific way while still retaining the clothing's masculine look. These experiences call up images of Kennedy and Davis's 1950s butch women dressing to go out to the bars in Buffalo. Styles that appear tough or cool among certain groups, however, can also draw negative responses when they become associated with a particular classed stereotype of Black masculinity. Black women's sense of sexuality is structured as much by raced cultural norms as by lesbian standards, and the types of clothing that femmes, gender-blenders, and transgressives choose represent definitions of femininity and masculinity that become raced when racial/ethnic women participate in them. When Black lesbians take on non-gender conforming presentations of self, then, they not only visually affirm their sexual freedom, but in the process run the risk of confirming negative stereotypes about Black women's sexuality. They subject themselves to dangerous confrontations with a larger society that devalues any raced expression of sexuality and particularly denounces and denigrates images of masculinity in Black women. Transgressive presentations of self also reify stereotypes of Black women as mannish and are particularly threatening to the male possession of masculinity. Many nongender conforming women face hostility from conformists in mainstream society—and from middle-class Black lesbians as well.

SOCIAL CLASS AND RACIALIZED NOTIONS OF GENDER

There are important differences by socioeconomic status in how lesbians relate these categories of gender presentation to their own lives. While middle- and upper-middle-class women in this study also chose femme and gender-blending displays, they did not self-identify as transgressive, they were less likely to acknowledge the types of pairings that exist between feminine and nonfeminine women, and they were reluctant to support a transgressive gender presentation in other lesbians.

Consider the perspective of Josephine Owens (b. 1963), an attorney. She defines her style as "pretty casual," saying, "I wouldn't call myself really feminine." She does not like to wear makeup or dresses, says she has never carried a pocketbook, and shows other signs that suggest a gender-blender sense of style. When I asked Josephine how she feels about labels like femme or butch, she gave a long pause, then said: "I don't like people to label folks—I mean, people are who they are. Unfortunately we do [label] everything, but I don't like the labels at all. People are who they are, and that's just it. As long as they're nice and decent people, that's all that really matters to me." When I asked if she would be able to choose a label for herself, she had difficulty answering the question. "For myself?" she asked, and I responded, "For yourself. Where would you fit in if you had to choose a label, or is it that you just don't think any of them apply to you?" Josephine paused, then asked in a defensive tone, "What are the labels?" "Well, I don't know," I said, "There are all of these different ways to—" "Yeah, I don't think—" she interrupted, "I wouldn't want to be labeled anything. I wouldn't want to, I couldn't choose one for myself."

Josephine's partner of ten years is Marissa Dillard, who has a very feminine gender display. The day we met Marissa wore a black and white form-fitting wrap dress, red lipstick, and long curly hair. Earlier in the interview, I had asked Josephine about the types of women she was attracted to when she was single and if there were particular characteristics, such as race, education, style of dress, or other such things, that she looked for in a partner. She said: "I guess the way she looked. I mean, education really doesn't matter to me. It was the way she looked. I liked a more, I guess I should say I don't like the 'butchy' kind. I like the feminine, semi-feminine kind of woman. So, it's more of the way she looked. The way she dressed, I mean, I'm not a great dresser myself, so that doesn't really matter." Josephine was able to think of labels when describing the type of gender display she was attracted to, but she became defensive when I asked her to label her own gender presentation. While she admitted that she would not refer to herself as particularly feminine, she avoided having to name her own nonfeminine gender display, actively resisting a construction of herself as falling outside of mainstream gender ideologies.

American Studies professor Chad Heap, writing about sexuality and race in 1930s Harlem and Chicago, provides an important historical analysis of class differences in African American attitudes about gender presentation and the open and public display of homosexuality. He notes:

> Many middle-class blacks shunned the highly gendered performances of the mannish woman and the fairy—or, the "bulldagger" and the "faggot," as these two types were more commonly known in black urban culture—by refashioning themselves as normatively gendered homosexuals, whose con-

servative comportment and public discretion won them a level of respect and toleration among their heterosexual peers. But among the working-class blacks of Harlem and Bronzeville, the earlier sexual framework of marginalized fairies and mannish women continued to predominate, as was easily seen when such women and men interacted with prospective sexual partners on the streets and in the queer resorts of the cities' black entertainment districts (2009, 260).[25]

Josephine's response is also consistent with Crawley's (2001) analysis of Black and White middle-class lesbians as tending to have assimilationist attitudes toward gender presentation. I would argue that working-class lesbians are more likely than more advantaged women to perform their resistance to societal norms through nonconforming gender presentation. They see this resistance as a representation of a sense of difference they have always felt. Many Black, highly educated lesbians are reluctant to claim labels or membership in categories that are marked in the larger society as deviant or are perceived in a negative way. Some Black feminist scholars have argued that Black women, in an effort to retaliate against the pathological image of Black women's sexuality, have historically promoted a public silence about sexuality and proper morality.[26] In this sense, cultural stereotypes of Black women as hypersexual inhibit lesbians' freedom of gender expression and disrupt the image of respectability that middle-class women have been able to achieve through high-status occupations and home ownership. As Black women, many feel they have to work hard to be accepted in mainstream society, and a nonfeminine gender display would mark them as "other" by confirming pejorative conceptualizations of "the Black bulldagger" and other stereotypes of Black lesbian sexuality.

Sociologist Karyn Lacy (2007), who studied identity construction among middle- and upper-middle-class heterosexual Blacks, argues that members of this group work hard at making their middle-class status known by erecting symbolic boundaries that signify and sustain a Black middle-class identity to other Blacks, to middle-class Whites, and to the larger society. She says that the middle-class draw on moral boundaries to reinforce and strengthen their already confident hold on a higher social standing (11). I find that in Black lesbian social spaces middle-class lesbians differentiate themselves from less advantaged women by enacting boundaries around clothing and style, creating hierarchies of respectability through social class distinctions.

Black middle-class lesbians were the harshest critics of transgressive gender presentation. They were the least likely to report a transgressive gender presentation, even when their clothing, jewelry, and other markers of style were consistent with a nonfeminine display. At parties, middle-class women said that lesbians wearing athletic jerseys, do-rags on their heads, or baseball caps lowered the quality or status of events, and often reacted negatively to women wearing these types of fashions. Flyers announcing the latest party tried to discourage this style of dress by including the warning, "No caps, do-rags, or athletic wear: Dress to impress." As part of my data collection, I hosted a weekly party for women of color at a lounge in Greenwich Village. A few of the women who attended each week wore athletic jerseys and fitted caps. Other than their style of dress, they did not stand out or behave in ways that were different from the other guests. Each time, however, a few patrons would invariably complain that I had "let those type of people" into the party. They would say things like "They bring the party down" and "We work so hard to get away from them, only to have them turn up at a classy event like this one." The harshest critics were usually middle-class gender-blending lesbians who wanted to be distinguished from more working-class or urban expressions of Black masculinity.

DANGERS OF REPRESENTING BLACK MASCULINITY

When transgressive lesbians appropriate certain representations of masculinity owned by Black and Latino men, they portray images that are raced, classed, and stereotypically associated with violence and menace.[27] Some lesbians resent this presentation of self in other women because it is associated with an image of men who are disrespectful to women. Others seek to distance themselves from a style that signifies identification with lower-class life. But many women are attracted to this type of masculinity on a female body, finding the image of a "hip-hop bad boy" alluring or cool when modified and transplanted on a woman.

There are dangers, however, in representing masculinity, particularly through the female form. Transgressive women are rebelling against strong conventional norms. Their emphasis on self-expression and resistance to gender conformity attacks the core of male dominance and invites openly punitive responses from others. But more than that, a nonfeminine gender presentation in women may cause men to question the meaning of their own masculinity. Lexington (Lex), a thirty-nine-year-old, working-class straight-up gay woman, said that on an almost daily basis she and other non gender-conforming women are discriminated against and denied their basic human rights: "People call us out [of] our names, threaten us, all because of who we are and what we look like, what we represent." When I asked Lex why she thinks men respond to her and other transgressives in such a negative way, she paused, then said, "Because they've spent their whole lives with one idea of who they are, and then they look at us with our men's shirts, our men's shoes, and realize *gender is something that is taught*" (emphasis in original).

That Black transgressives consistently partner with women who are more feminine and whose style is consistent with heterosexual standards of beauty also endangers the relationships and expectations that go along with male ownership of masculinity. Heap argues that historically, the uncertain economic circumstances of Black men caused them to perceive the visibility of masculine-identified women in Black neighborhoods as a direct threat to their manhood. He says these women "presumably had the power to undermine black men's strongest remaining claims to masculinity—their sexual prowess and ability to pleasure women. As a result, while black popular culture portrayed faggots as abnormal but relatively harmless buffoons, it generally presented mannish women as dangerous interlopers" (2009, 262). Lex says that lesbians are threatening to men. She explains: "We are a threat to them because we are not supposed to be able to get what they have. Not just aggressives, but other [lesbian] women out there, too. How dare we own our own homes, have cars, raise families, and pull a woman that looks as good as theirs!" Lex sees transgressive women as contesting male hegemony by pursuing masculine status at the expense of heterosexual men.

Race has important consequences for female masculinity. White masculinity in butch women—women whose gender presentation is reminiscent of rockers, motorcycle riders, and the like—gives them an outsider status relative to traditional notions of White femininity and White respectability.[28] The masculinity portrayed by Black women, however, is particularly feared in society and tends to be associated with violence, so transgressive women become problematized and feared by others because of the masculinity they portray. This raced and classed gender nonconformity can be dangerous for the women who appropriate it: Black masculinity is disproportionately punished in American society,[29] and the enactment of dress and mannerisms consistent with Black male masculinity can lead to police harassment, distrust from strangers, and alienation from the Black middle class. In this sense, transgressives bear the cross of Black lesbian sexuality. Transgressive women keep Black lesbian sexuality and women's sexual autonomy visible to the larger society by their continuous presence in the Black community. Theirs is an act of resistance not just to dominant societal expectations of gender conformity but also to feminist ideologies who call for the suppression of gendered behaviors and mannerisms.

GENDER PRESENTATION AND GENDER IDEOLOGIES

In trying to understand how Black lesbians negotiate the organization and meanings of gender display, I find that it is desire, not lesbian feminism or a particular politics, that takes center stage. As we have seen, most of the women I spoke to, when asked if their sexuality was tied to feminism, did not consciously link the two.[30] Some women have a masculine presentation of self, are primarily attracted to feminine women, and also hold feminist beliefs about eradicating gender inequality. There are also transgressive, gender-blender, and femme women who would like their partners to take on some of the more stereotypically female or male roles in relationships.

The lesbians I studied make a distinction, moreover, between styles or mannerisms that represent masculinity and the gendered privileges and dominance that men tend to benefit from. That transgressives and gender-blenders appreciate and emulate a masculine way of dressing does not preclude them from experiencing the world as women in a society where men still have economic, social, and other advantages. Men are granted greater status and authority because society continues to privilege male leadership of important societal institutions and awards men an earnings advantage. Gender-blending and transgressive lesbians do not benefit from these gendered structural advantages, so relationships organized around gender display do not provide a gendered economic benefit for the less feminine partner. Transgressives also do not view their nonfeminine state as a higher or more powerful status relative to other women. They do not, to borrow Crawley's language, "pursue status at the expense of more feminine women" (2001, 192), nor do they perceive their gender nonconformity as carrying greater authority than the gendered femininity portrayed by femme Black women in lesbian communities.

Black femininity, when represented in particularly middle-class ways, represents authority and power. Black social environments value feminine women who are assertive, educated, and economically independent.

Kennedy and Davis (1993) found that in Black lesbian communities, femmes often took on leadership roles by desegregating predominantly White bars and by organizing house parties, the primary arena of Black lesbian social life.

In the past, butch-femme roles eroticized and structured sexual interactions around the principle of gender difference. In the twenty-first century, however, gender presentation has come to be defined more broadly and is no longer primarily a means of structuring sexual interactions. Nevertheless, it does continue to structure membership in and organization of lesbian social worlds, and it continues to be a visible expression of a distinctive lesbian eroticism. The majority of Black lesbian women I have met take pains to present a particular type of gender display when they participate in lesbian social life because they are looking to create a particular aesthetic self, and the norms of the community require consistency in gender presentation. The structure imposed by community social norms becomes problematic when it impedes a person's freedom to partner with someone who has the "wrong" gender display. It also liberates lesbians, however, by allowing them a sense of freedom in their ability to express their sexuality in a way that is feminine or nonfeminine.

Black lesbians use boundaries to create complementarity in gender presentation, to show social class distinctions, and to communicate status. At parties, nightclubs, and other public settings, many middle- and upper-middle-class lesbians communicate their status position by avoiding transgressive gender presentations and clothing associated with urban hip-hop styles. Some also criticize or refuse to directly acknowledge the gender categories constructed by the community, even as they participate in them.

UNDERSTANDING THE PERSISTENCE OF GENDER PRESENTATION IN BLACK COMMUNITY LIFE

Black lesbians who regularly participate in Black gay spaces have carefully maintained and modified the culture of lesbian gender presentation, with its class and geographic distinctions, as a form of sexual and personal expression for at least four reasons. First, historically, Black lesbians as a group have been less influenced by lesbian feminist ideologies that discourage or stigmatize gender categories. From the 1960s onward, Black women have been less likely than White women to interpret the *expression* of a gendered self as the most important component of their oppression as women. Consequently, Black women have been less likely to view the elimination of a gendered self as a requirement for their own liberation. This stands in contrast to feminist arguments that call for the suppression of gender differences as a strategy for achieving gender equality.

Second, gender complementarity also continues to structure lesbian relationships because it helps define the erotic "other." An important part of gay sexuality is the pursuit of same-sex desire, and many find that clothing and mannerisms help create an attraction through a sense of difference within the context of two women's bodies. Gender presentation serves to maintain lesbian identity as a *sexual* identity, and the eroticism engendered by complementary gender display makes visible the expression of women's sexuality. Lesbians feel empowered when they are able to move away from societal constructions of gender. Gender-blenders and transgressive women liberate themselves from the constraints of hegemonic femininity by drawing from other sources to create a sense of self.

Third, gender presentation style helps to create and perpetuate identity and cultural expression for Black lesbians. Mahon (2004) writes about the links between music and style in nontraditionally Black cultural spaces in which the authenticity of Black culture is expressed through music, clothing, and style; these are also important means by which to express other identity categories. Ralph Ellison, in a collection of essays first published in 1964, wrote about the complexities of Black identity and the public presentation of the Black body to communicate meaning and portray a sense of self: "We recognized and were proud of our group's own style wherever we discerned it—in jazzmen and prize fighters, ballplayers and tap dancers; in gesture, inflection, intonation, timbre and phrasing. Indeed, in all those nuances of expression and attitude which reveal a culture. We did not fully understand the cost of that style but we recognized within it an affirmation of life beyond all question of our difficulties as Negroes" (Ellison, 1964, 54). In Black lesbian communities, gender presentation is simultaneously an articulation of African American expressive culture and lesbian group membership. It fuses Black and lesbian cultures to create and express a distinctive cultural identity.

Finally, Black lesbian community norms police behavior and encourage conformity to group expectations of identity representation. The gender displays that are portrayed by femme, gender-blender, and transgressive lesbians, and the complementarity that is produced in Black lesbian couples, make the categories they represent particularly visible

markers of sexual freedom as well as group affiliation. Gender presentation is used by communities to create social space, identification categories in gay and lesbian settings, and sexual selves. The distinctions made
in gender presentation and in class and cultural portrayals of gender presentation have as their foundation and require for their existence *interaction* within a social system, which in this case is Black lesbian social
space.[31] The integration of these spaces by lesbians who do not adhere to
the meanings of gender presentation Black women have created would
change the social organization of these environments.

CHAPTER 3

Marginalized Social Identities

Self-Understandings and Group Membership

As Black people, as women, and as lesbians, the women in this book possess multiple social identities that are marginalized in society. People use identity as a "category of practice" to make sense of themselves, their activities, what they share with and how they differ from others (Brubaker and Cooper 2000, 4), and to construct meaning about who they are and how they fit in the world. All people experience identity-formation processes, but they have a particular complexity and nuance for those who occupy multiple marginalized social statuses. Many of the women I interviewed were the children or grandchildren of former sharecroppers who moved north during the Great Migration, or were themselves immigrants to the northeastern United States. Their understandings of the meanings of Blackness and femaleness have been shaped as much by the particular historical contexts and structural conditions in which they and their parents came of age as by their present-day experiences. Their sense of what race represents to them was formed early on in their lives, before they began to define themselves as gay. A combination of past experiences, present-day self-understandings, and more general social hierarchies in society work together to shape self-perceptions of identity group membership.

In this chapter, I investigate Black lesbians' self-understandings of race, gender, and sexuality and analyze the ways these social positions affect a sense of group identification. The primary identity statuses I examine are Blackness as a race, femaleness as a gender, and gay sexuality.

92

These categories are not homogeneous and do not have absolute boundaries. The racial category "Black" includes individuals who self-identify as Black American, as foreign-born ethnic Blacks, and as multiracial. The gender category "female" includes women with a variety of gender presentations. And the sexuality category "gay" includes not only women with a firm and consistent view of themselves as gay or lesbian, but also those who report having continuous attractions to women and men, those who may have had more relationships with men than with women, and those who may not view their sexual preference as an identity status but rather as a sexual behavior in which they participate (see Chapter 1). Individuals who recognize that these categories exist and who see themselves—or believe others see them—as members of these groups may or may not have feelings of group belonging or social identity associated with these statuses. Indeed, as I will show in this chapter, the identity status that some consider most important to how they define themselves as *individuals* is not necessarily the one for which they have the strongest feelings of *group* belonging.

During the fifty-eight in-depth, in-person interviews gathered for this study, respondents were asked two questions about identity. First, I inquired, "Which identity would you say is most important to you: your identity as a Black person, as a lesbian, or as a woman? Or are you unable to rank them in any particular way?" This question required the respondents to evaluate the importance they place on race, gender, and sexuality identity statuses as categories of analysis for self-definition or self-identity, and to consider these statuses in relation to one another as *personal traits* or micro-level characteristics that represent their private lived experiences. Next, they were asked, "Who do you think you would have the most in common with: a Black straight woman, a White lesbian, or a Black man?" This is a relative question about *collective identity*, or the types of people the respondent perceives herself to share common ground with.[1] It inquires about identity statuses as social groupings. I purposely did not ask my subjects how close they felt to the category "Black lesbian," hoping instead to learn more about what it is that makes individuals feel that they share similarities with groups whose members do not simultaneously share their sexual, racial, and gender identity. My respondents' answers to these two questions invite this chapter's simultaneous consideration of identities as fundamental elements of self-conception, and identities as ties that either bind or create distance in our relationships with others.

When these questions were asked in the in-depth interviews, I expected respondents to say that race was the most important status around which they form social identities. That is, based on my observations of their participation in predominantly Black social environments and their largely Black friendship groups, I hypothesized that the majority would name race as a primary identity category for their self-definition. I also assumed that those who said that race was the identity status most important in their self-definition would also perceive themselves to have more in common with Black heterosexual women than with White lesbians or Black men.

The responses I received suggest, however, that marginalized social identities are more complex, and identity generally more dynamic, than I expected. I found that race is most often a primary status for Black lesbians who are "The Firsts," meaning those who have racially integrated neighborhoods, schools, and workplaces. These are usually (but not always) women with high-status jobs whose experiences navigating power structures at work and in predominantly White environments have made race a particularly salient social identity for them. I also learned that among working-class women with feminine gender presentations, race and gender are simultaneous primary statuses that cannot be separated because of how the outside world sees and interacts with these women and because they are firmly guided by norms of respectability in Black communities that dictate how they should represent themselves to others. Lastly, women whose gender is performed more ambiguously or who have a masculine gender presentation are the most likely to say they cannot rank the importance of race, gender, and sexuality as identities. For reasons tied to their gender expression, transgressive women (the majority of whom are working-class), express and experience a distance from each of these identities, depending on the social context. I explore each of these findings in the first three sections of this chapter.

I also found that the ways Black gay women conceptualize the importance of an identity status as a *self*-definition is not always consistent with how they think about their membership in a *group* organized around that same social identity. In other words, a significant percentage of the women I interviewed value a particular identity as part of their self-definition *even if they do not perceive themselves to have much in common with the members of that group*. This finding, in the chapter's final section, has important implications for our understanding of the situational nature of identity and the ways statuses change in salience when the social context is altered.

RACE AS PRIMARY SOCIAL IDENTITY

Zoe Ferron installs and maintains telephone lines and network optics for a major communications company. She stands about five feet, eight inches tall, weighs roughly 180 pounds, and at the time of interview wore her hair in dreadlocks that hung all the way down her back. Zoe was born in 1960 and raised in a predominantly White housing development in Canarsie, Brooklyn, during a time when African Americans were just beginning to integrate this tough White ethnic neighborhood.[2] Hers was one of only a few Black families in a housing project dominated by working-class Italians and Jews. It is not easy to be the first Black person to integrate an all-White institution where you are not wanted, and such experiences are particularly formative when they occur during the early years of a child's life.[3]

Asked to rank her identities, Zoe ranked Black identity as most important because race and racism more overtly shaped her earliest and most fully formed self-understandings: "If I had to number them one, two, three? Probably Black and lesbian—real close, to be honest with you. I don't know which would come up as one. Probably Black. Woman last." When I asked, "What makes you say that?" she replied: "Because that is just what it is. People see your Blackness, and the world has affected me by my Blackness since the very inception of my life. . . . Coming into a sexuality and recognizing a sexuality I think is something that is secondary to the color of your skin, at least for African Americans in this country. So, you know, my sexuality is something that developed later on, or I became *aware* of later on, [because] I think it's always been what it's been, but I think that it was just something that developed in my psyche. But being Black is something that I've always had to deal with: racism since day one and recognizing how to navigate through this world as a Black person, and even as a Black woman" (emphasis in original).

From kindergarten through fourth grade, Zoe was the only African American in her classes for gifted children. She describes her years in elementary, junior high, and high school as a "volatile" time because of the protests around neighborhood integration that were taking place. During her first year in junior high and periodically throughout that period of her education, a bodyguard had to escort her to the newly integrated school each day to protect her from protesters in the neighborhood who shouted racial epithets at her, such as "Nigger, go home!" Race was continually salient for Zoe during her childhood, an identity on the basis of which she and other family members were forced to interact with others outside of the racial group. For example, her older brother had to over-come significant racial discrimination to attain the rank of battalion chief in the New York City Fire Department.

Many Blacks who have direct experiences with racism understand race in the sense that Higginbotham defines it, as a "social construction predicated upon the recognition of difference and signifying the simulta-neous distinguishing and positioning of groups vis-à-vis one another" (1992, 253). That is to say, conceptions of race are a way of dividing people into groups on the basis of some real or perceived difference be-tween them, and these groups represent the "relations of power between social categories by which individuals are identified and identify them-selves" (253). Societies in which racial demarcation is endemic to the sociocultural fabric, epistemologies, and everyday customs particularly shape race as a social identity. Zoe Ferron's childhood experiences reveal, for instance, how racial categories are strategically necessary for the func-tioning of power. Her responses to my questions suggest, in turn, how such experiences with racial discrimination influence identity formation. The context in which Zoe grew up and her experiences as a young person limited some of her choices in regard to self-representation, meaning even if she herself felt socially distant from Blacks as a group, or preferred to have social networks and friendship groups that were predominantly White, the society she lived in would have made these interests difficult to pursue. The racial inequality that structured the lives of African Ameri-cans during that historical period tells us race is not just an imagined re-lationship individuals like Zoe perceive themselves as having with other Blacks. In Zoe's youth, race was far from being an imaginary category: she was taunted with racial slurs on her way to school, and she had a strong sense of being a racial Other in her all-White classes. These were concrete societal forces at work creating boundaries around which Zoe formed her racial identity.

Zoe understands her sexuality as an identity that is second to the one she has formed around race, because her lesbian self is something she developed "later on"—this even though she felt "different" from others from the time she was a young girl because she was never attracted to boys. Throughout her childhood, she had crushes on girls but did not discuss these feelings with anyone, including her parents (saying she knew such a discussion would "wreak havoc" in her house). Her first romantic relationship with a woman occurred when she was sixteen, an experience she describes as "coming into the light." But she did not pro-cess her feelings of same-sex desire until early adulthood, so her gay sexuality remained the source of an individual but not a collective identity—an identity that was not a basis for group identification.

When Zoe did experience sexuality as a marker of difference, it was combined with a masculine-identified gender presentation. Growing up, she says, she never felt like a girl and did not relate to the ways television depicted the experiences and interests of girls. When asked which group she has the most in common with, White lesbians, Black heterosexual women, or Black heterosexual men, Zoe again identified with her racial identity but chose Black men over heterosexual Black women because she says she understands men, thinks like them, shares the same interests that they have, and feels the same type of desire for Black women that they feel: "I don't know what White men feel about Black women, but I know what Black men feel about Black women, and that is how I feel about Black women. And I have been known to translate [that] to women of various colors (chuckles), but in my heart lies a Black man. Absolutely. Unequivocally."

Both the relational and the structural nature of identity categories are exemplified in Zoe's life story. She was forced to relate to the outside world through the structural inequalities of a racially ordered society, which cemented her group membership around Blackness. It was not until much later that she came to understand how her same-sex desires played a role in how she fit into the world, and when this happened those desires were accompanied by a gender presentation that was different from what was expected of women. Sexuality and gender presentation together served to create a social identity for her as lesbian. So both Zoe's individual and her collective identities have race at their core: her identity is structural as well as relational.

Dr. Beverly Howard is twelve years younger than Zoe. She was raised in a different region of the country and has a different occupational status, but, like Zoe, her sense of individual and collective identity revolves around race, largely for structural reasons. Beverly was born in 1972 to middle-class parents in a small city in southwest Louisiana. Her neighborhood was African American and middle-class, and most of the adults were teachers, as are her parents, who each hold master's degrees in education. She says that in the South, "Growing up there is a little different than growing up here. As far as racially, things are pretty much split down the middle. You're either Black or you're White. No matter what you are, you have to choose. If you're Black, you have no choice. If you're White, you pretty much can say what you want to say. If you're Vietnamese, you need to choose one [race]. So that's a little different than I find my experiences have been up here in New York." Beverly's comments reveal the salience and structural nature of racial categories in the Louisiana city where she was raised.

Her parents expected and encouraged her to do well in all of her endeavors. They took a leadership role in various aspects of community life, serving as mentors to some of the children in the neighborhood and opening their home to other families for barbeques and other social activities. Beverly was raised in and bound tightly to a tradition of Black womanhood that expects both high achievement and social responsibility. Shaw (1996) refers to this as "socially responsible individualism" and says that historically, the Black middle class has made great efforts to socialize their children into a collective consciousness around race.

Today, Beverly is a physician in the male-dominated field of emergency medicine. She is a gender-blender with light skin and shoulder-length relaxed hair, stands about five feet, seven inches tall, and weighs approximately 175 pounds. When I asked Beverly to rank the importance of race, gender, and sexuality as identity statuses for herself, she responded that her experiences growing up and attending universities in the South have heightened her sense of difference around race: "I think it's just the way I've lived the majority of my life, where I had to be proud of being Black, possibly the only Black person. I didn't really even feel the effects, I guess the disadvantage, of being a woman until I got to medical school, where there were so many men and very few women. And they kind of pointed it out to me, whether it was [through] harassing jokes or whatever. But even still, it was an issue of being Black. I guess in New York it's not as big of an issue because there are just so many different ethnicities. And my work puts me as being the boss, so I never have to deal with some of the stressors of race and sexuality that others may have to deal with."

When I asked Beverly whether she had most in common with a Black straight woman, a White lesbian, or a Black man, she answered, "Ooh. That's a tough question. I guess I would say a Black male." Beverly elaborated: "Just relating to my work, the majority of the people there are men. I don't know. It's hard to say. I would identify mainly with a Black woman, period. [But] to say with a *straight* Black woman, I don't know. I could see how I could identify with a Black man just because of the positions that I hold and the way my household is. But it's hard for me to categorize it. . . . I think if other people would look at me, they would put me in the Black man role, so that's why I'll make that choice."

Beverly's responses reveal several important aspects of the importance of context when evaluating race, gender, and sexuality as identity
statuses. First, in the context of the neighborhood in which she was
raised, race was the salient identity status for everyone. When she entered
medical school, gender inequalities became more relevant for her.[4] Once
she attained a high-ranking status within the medical profession, many of
the inequalities she once experienced because of race and gender were
reduced. In the context of her professional life, she is a leader despite her
race and gender. She told me she has always been "a bit tomboyish," and
it has served her well: "To get ahead in my field, to be a female doctor,"
she said, "you have to have some masculinity about you." Nevertheless,
her racial identity remains salient for her in the context of the predominantly White leadership of the hospital, even if it does not limit her occupational mobility. Beverly's example highlights both the situational
nature of group identity and the ability of high occupational status to
mitigate some of the structural inequalities individuals with marginalized
identities might experience.

Also important in understanding how race, sexuality, and gender
operate for Beverly is that she bases her collective identity on how others
perceive her rather than on whom she feels closest to. She says she can
identify with Black men not just because of her work life but also because
of the way her household is structured. Beverly is newly divorced. When
she was married, she earned much more than her husband. Currently,
Beverly owns a large house in a suburb of New Jersey that she shares
with her partner, Adina. Adina is an artist who stays home full time to
care for Beverly's two-year-old daughter from her previous marriage.
Beverly is the sole financial provider for their family, and in many respects their household is structured in the traditional breadwinner-
homemaker style of responsibility allocation.

Beverly's experience of upward mobility from the middle class to the
upper middle class, and the change in power that accompanied this transformation, suggests the ways social class and education affect how one
experiences and interprets race. Prager defines the genealogy of identity as
"the process by which individuals vertically place or imagine themselves
into ongoing social categories of experience and construct their own understanding of themselves in relation to these categories" (2009, 142). He
emphasizes the ongoing nature of social categories and their ability to
change their relationship to those who occupy them. We see in Beverly's
case, and in others as well, how social class filters the experience of being

Black, female, and lesbian, as well as how respondents portray these statuses and how others view and interpret these individuals as Black women.

When asked about the relative importance of race, gender, and sexuality for their own lives, high-status respondents (meaning those who have advanced degrees and personal incomes greater than $75,000 per year in 2005 dollars) were more likely to name race or the experience of being Black as a primary identity status. Historically, race has been important both as a collective identity and as an individual social identity for the Black middle class, and one reason for that is the more frequent contact Black middle- and upper middle-class people have with Whites. Such interactions reify the salience of race and can cause them to experience a sense of difference around this identity. Naja Rhodes, for example, offered the most common response for middle-class lesbians to the question about identity status, linking her experience of being Black with having a responsibility to represent herself in a certain way to others, particularly when she is in the minority: "When I think about having to represent myself in a particular way, most of my life I've felt the Black part as being the most important because of the environments I've been in where I've been—when there's [only] like five Black people. So Blackness is definitely what I've had to stand up for the most."

Similarly, Katrice Webster, a gender-blender and corporate attorney at one of the top law firms in Manhattan, says her identity as a Black person is most important because it has the greatest effect on how others in her upper-middle-class social world perceive and relate to her:

> I think more adversity comes to me because of being Black. The negative things that happen to me have happened because I'm Black. When I go to work every day I have to work a little harder, not so much because I'm a woman, not so much because I'm gay (because they don't know), but because I'm Black. When I go shopping and a person is following me around the store—like I went, we went into Tiffany's the other day. I wanted to get a bracelet. And this woman is like, "Oh, here's a bracelet, but it's $240." I wanted to say, "Who cares. Give me twenty." I felt like she didn't know anything about me, but because I was Black she just made a lot of assumptions. People don't necessarily make—I mean, they make some assumptions because you're a woman, but not as many assumptions.

Such responses suggest that on the route toward upward mobility, middle- and upper-middle-class Blacks are more likely to have thought about how being Black, female, and gay measurably effect the quality of social relationships they engage in with non-Blacks. While they believe they have not suffered as many derailments because of gender and have been able to selectively shield their gay sexuality from the knowledge of their colleagues and peers, race has noticeably threatened their success. In the process of training for professional occupations and in these positions, moreover, members of the Black middle class interact in social contexts that require them to navigate largely White middle- and upper-class cultures; furthermore, relative to poor Blacks, middle-class Blacks generally find themselves in more contexts that require interaction with Whites.[5] The workplace and other settings like restaurants or museums may call for the continued negotiation of boundaries around race. These experiences reinforce a sense of difference around racial identity.

Highly educated lesbians in my study are also more likely than working-class women to view the politics of personal identity and the politics of collective identity as inextricably linked. Beverly's comments regarding the shifting power that she possessed as she transitioned from college to medical school, and then to work as an emergency room doctor, illustrate this point. They have competed successfully with Whites to gain prominent placements in prestigious careers. As a result, they discuss identity statuses like race and gender as power relationships in a social system that influences how resources are allocated, rather than just representations of different lifestyle preferences, beliefs, or practices. When comparing across socioeconomic groups, I have found that high-status Black lesbians are the least likely to be openly gay in the workplace. Many of these women felt same-sex desire during late adolescence or early adulthood but either chose not to act on it or kept their feelings hidden until they had finished their educations or moved into secure jobs. Among high-status survey respondents (those with a bachelor's degree or greater and earning more than $75,000 per year), the average age at which they first acted on same-sex attraction was 20.6 years, around the time they were completing college. They did not accept a lesbian identity until five years later, however, at 25.7 years old, when they tended to be finished with advanced degree programs and settled into professional jobs. Lesbians in the lowest-status category (those with less than a bachelor's degree and earning less than $50,000 per year), by contrast, first acted on their same-sex desire three years earlier than the high-status women on average, at age 17.5 years old—right at the end of high school. Working-class women accepted an identity as lesbian about three years earlier, at 22.8 years old, and entered into the social world of lesbian life earlier as well, spending more time at parties and other events that made it easier for them to become comfortable with a gay sexuality. Although the working and middle-class groups both took about five years between having a first same-sex experience and coming to identify as lesbian, the later timing of same-sex desire and acceptance of lesbian identity for the middle and upper middle class suggests that, consciously or unconsciously, higher-status lesbians delayed coming into the life until they were more established in their careers or more securely on the path toward upward social mobility.[6]

Responses from the in-depth interviews support this interpretation. For example, Josephine Owens is an attorney who told me she has always been attracted to women "from a young age" but did not "get into the life" until after she finished law school. When I asked if there was a particular incident that brought her into a gay sexuality, she said it was "just an attraction to women, I guess." She does not know if the delay was because she was just too busy to explore her feelings or if it was because she wanted to wait until she "was more sure of [herself] and more sure of [her] sexuality." Katrice said she was drawn to women in high school and college but only acted on those interests in secret by occasionally sneaking out to lesbian bars to admire or dance with women. It was not until she finished school and became successful in her career that she let her family and friends know about her interest in women. Even today, she is discreet about her sexuality at work because she does not want her gay identity to influence how her colleagues perceive her.

Other high-status respondents like the psychologist Nilda Flores told me they avoided thinking consciously about their sexuality during college or graduate school because they were not ready to deal with the consequences of what a gay sexuality might mean for them. It was not until they had begun to advance in their occupations that their focus turned more directly to the open expression of a gay sexuality. Rather than confront early on family conflicts and the possibility of societal prejudices that might limit professional opportunities, these women shelved their feelings of lesbian attraction until they had accumulated enough social status to reduce the liability of having a lesbian identity.

Once they acknowledge their gay sexuality, middle- and upper-middle-class lesbians can and do utilize class as a privileged status to move in and out of the marginalized aspects of stigmatized identities. They can select into neighborhoods where lesbian and gay people experience more comfort in showing open affection with one another. They can also display their incomes in a way that calls less attention to any undesirability associated with a status as lesbian, and women like Dr. Howard can use their high occupational status to gain authority and power.

RACE AND GENDER AS SIMULTANEOUS PRIMARY SOCIAL IDENTITIES

Lower-middle-class and working-class women with a feminine gender presentation are the most likely to say that race and gender cannot be separated as primary statuses for understanding their individual identities. They are also the most likely to report that their collective identity with Black heterosexual women is the strongest and most important group relationship they have. The rationale they give for this ranking is tied to how others in society perceive and interpret who they are.

Berit Fontaine's responses to the questions about identity offer one example. Berit was born in Panama in 1967 and immigrated to the United States in 1980. She looks and racially identifies as Black, stands five feet, ten inches tall, is approximately 130 pounds, and has a medium-brown complexion. Berit attended college but did not complete a four-year degree. When she goes out socially, people often remark upon her exceptional beauty, and in addition to managing a women's boutique on the Upper East Side of Manhattan, she is also a part-time runway model. Prior to her current five-year lesbian relationship, she only dated men.

Berit's response to the interview questions measuring individual and collective social identities reveal her efforts to create what Jenkins (2007) calls an "inviolable respectability." When asked "Which identity is most important to you: your identity as a Black person, a lesbian, or as a woman?" she replied "Just a woman." Berit elaborated: "Although those other things make me the woman that I am, they don't define me. I was born in Panama. That is part of me. I'm a Black woman and that is just part of me. That [race] right there, [along] with being a woman, is one of the most important things as well, but all of those things are just part of the woman that I am. . . . Being the *right type* of woman is important to me" (emphasis in original). Berit stressed the importance of representing womanhood in a way that is consistent with Black norms of respectability. She defined the "right type" of woman as someone who has "respect for herself and carries herself with dignity and won't compromise" herself. She said she wants to be "a woman who carries herself with dignity, class, who has goals and ambitions and dreams and who cares about people."

Berit perceives herself to have the most in common with Black straight women rather than White lesbians or Black men, saying that she can better relate to them and that she and they have more of the same experiences. Referring to White lesbians, she explained, "All I can say is that you sleep with a woman and I sleep with a woman. That is the only thing that we can have in common." Berit considers her engagement in lesbian practice as a behavior that should be distinguished from an identity status. Race and gender are identity markers she has in common with others in a way that sexuality is not. Unlike Zoe, Berit does not interpret her same-sex attraction as being similar to the way men desire women. Instead, she understands herself as the *object* of that type of desire. She does not mention having any similarities with men, nor does she feel strong lesbian group membership.

Santasha, who also has a feminine gender presentation, similarly identified both race and gender as the most important components of her self-definition and collective identity. Santasha is a junior editor for a women's magazine and single mother of two. She stands five feet, seven inches tall and weighs approximately 220 pounds. She is medium complexioned, with long dreadlocks. When I asked her about the relative importance of her identities as a Black person, a woman, and a lesbian, she responded: "Can I say both? Black and a woman, because when I look at my milestones and what I've accomplished throughout my life, I feel better about accomplishing those things because, one, I'm Black, and two, I'm a woman. And it brings me back to something my father said when I was pregnant with my first child. I told him I'm having a child. [He said,] 'Well, you're not gonna ever finish high school, you're gonna end up on welfare and not be shit.' So I appreciate both of those things [race and gender], and I kinda can 'X' things like what my father said out." Santasha's comments suggest that she makes continual efforts to prove—not just to society but even to her own family members—that just because she had a child at a young age does not mean she is headed down a road of sexual deviance and pathology. She proudly told me that after the birth of her first child she completed high school at a special school for teenage mothers and subsequently attended and completed college.

When I posed the same question to Venus Giles (b. 1965), an army veteran with a slight build and short, relaxed hair, she replied: "Hmm. That's a good one. Well, the man is not—that's out. But now I have a hard choice between a Black straight woman or a White lesbian. I would say a Black straight woman!" When I asked her to elaborate, she said: "Because before sexuality comes into play I am looked at as a Black woman. I am not looked at as a lesbian, because you don't know where I am coming from. So when I walk down the street I am representing Black women." Venus, who has a gender-blender style of presentation, dismissed out of hand the idea that she might identify with Black men, but she had difficulty deciding whether race or sexuality is the status around which her group membership is strongest. She finally chose race and gender, selecting Black straight women as the group with whom she has the most in common. She based this choice, again, not on her feelings of connectedness to Black heterosexual woman but rather on how outsiders perceive and respond to her: because her race and gender are the most visible categories to others, they become the more important group identity categories for Venus. Within this context, she evoked a rhetoric of Black female representation. Venus believes that when she walks down the street, she is calling attention not just to herself as an individual but to Black women as a collective.

I have referred in earlier chapters to the historical origins of the search for respectability within Black communities, as well the continued efforts of Black women in the United States and Caribbean to portray a particular image of Black womanhood. Jenkins argues that today, Black women not only struggle for respectability, but also fight against the consequences of stigmatization that threaten to script Blacks "out of narratives of American national belonging because of their alleged sexual and domestic character" (2007, 5). Middle- and working-class Black lesbians like Berit, Santasha, and Venus not only participate in this struggle but also shape their self-definition and collective identity around it: their primary personal and collective identity statuses depend in part upon their understanding of how others see them and their desire to shape how they are seen.

INABILITY TO RANK STATUSES AND GAPS BETWEEN INDIVIDUAL AND GROUP IDENTITY

Women with a nonfeminine gender presentation had the greatest difficulty answering my questions about identity and were the most likely to say that they were unable to rank race, gender, and sexuality in their importance as identities. They said things like "I'm just a human being, it doesn't matter," "I'm just me, just Trina, that's all," "I embody all three of them," and "Hmm . . . which one? I don't know. Let's see. I'm all three of those, so which one am I more of? I can't really say."

Angie Russell was born in Brooklyn, New York, in 1967 and is a police officer. She is straight-up gay and her gender presentation is transgressive: she wears men's clothing, no makeup or jewelry, never carries a purse, and her hair is cut very close to her head, making her appear almost bald. She is five feet, six inches tall and the color of dark chocolate, and has a smooth, round face with almond-shaped eyes. Angie is the child of lower-middle-class parents. (Her mother is a telephone operator, and her father had a vision disability; she described him as a being a stay-at-home parent throughout her childhood.) Shortly after her interview, she was promoted to the position of sergeant in the New York City Police Department. With this promotion, Angie joins the ranks of the Black middle class.

When asked how she would order her identities, Angie said her most important identity is not as a Black person or a woman or a lesbian, but "just as a person, just as me." She could not put her race, gender, and gay sexuality in any kind of order and explained that she is "all of them evenly, so to speak." Her response might suggest that because she identifies with these three statuses as personal traits, she also sees herself as equally part of Black communities, gay communities, and communities that are organized around gender. When I asked with whom she has the most in common, a Black straight woman, a White lesbian, or a Black man, however, she immediately said, "Ooh. Definitely not the White lesbian," because Whites are "very different" from Blacks and have a "different view of the world." Angie told me she feels very different from White lesbian women despite having gay sexuality in common with them. "The lesbian part is such a small part, as far as I'm concerned," she said, "So I'll probably think more about her being White as opposed to being lesbian." When asked to choose between the remaining two categories, Angie chose the Black man (assuming he is heterosexual), saying, "Well, I'm athletic and I love women. And that's probably what all Black men think about, sports and women! (laughs)." She also shared with me her belief that Black straight women think about men in a very different way than she does: like Zoe, Angie said she thinks about and is attracted to women in the same way men think about women.

Once again, we see in Angie's comments a distinction being made between personal and group identities, as well as a classic example of the relational nature of identity statuses. While Angie does not have a stronger tie to any one of her identity statuses when they are used to describe her as an individual, she is able to sort them when they define her relationship to different collectivities of people: racial identity is important to her sense of group membership, explaining her rejection of group identification with White lesbians. What she has in common with White lesbians—sexual identity—is not sufficient to create a strong sense of group membership for Angie, or at least not one that is stronger than her racial group membership. When race is held constant, however, Angie understands herself to have more in common with Black heterosexual men than with Black heterosexual women. This commonality is influenced by the erotic desire for women that she shares with Black men. While Berit sees herself as the object of lesbian women's desires, Angie, like Zoe, presents herself as the person who is the pursuer of this "object." Angie's connected interests with Black men extend outside of sexuality: she also mentions athleticism as something she shares with them. Her sense of racial group membership invites her to notice areas of common interest with Black men, whereas her weaker sense of shared sexual identity creates no such comparisons to White lesbians.

Angie's use of comparisons points to an important way that social identities operate: identity categories work by distinguishing individuals and collectivities from one another, but they simultaneously establish relationships using notions of similarity. The construction of external difference generates internal solidarity (Jenkins 2008, 102). In his influential essay "The Stranger," social theorist Georg Simmel observes that the stranger or outsider helps others to create social identities by allowing the group to define what its members have in common and who they are in terms of who they are not. The characteristics of the stranger are defined as "the Other," which then clarifies who the "we" of the group are (Simmel 1964). Social anthropologist Fredrik Barth argues that by dichotomizing other people as "strangers" or members of other ethnicities, we implicitly recognize "limitations on shared understandings, differences in criteria for judgment of value and performance, and a restriction of interaction to sectors of assumed common understanding and mutual interest" (1969, 15). One's membership in an identity group, then, is determined by criteria of both similarity to other group members and difference between oneself and others defined as out-group members. In order to hold on to the significance of a group membership based in race, individuals must perceive a tangible difference in behavior and other characteristics between themselves and the racial out group.

We see this process at work in the concept of race through the responses of Angie, Berit, and others I interviewed who see themselves as different from Whites. Its operation is less obvious and less consistent, however, when it comes to social identities based in sexuality, particularly when the reference group coheres around race. Angie's comments about the difference between herself and White lesbians and the similarity between herself and Black men have at their core an understanding of the primacy of race over sexuality and gender as the status around which she coheres with others. This is a key point in understanding how race is understood by African Americans born and raised in earlier time periods. For my respondents, the cohesion around race is so strong and has such a deep history and importance that it is difficult for them to imagine feeling commonality with Whites even when they share with them other social identities outside of race.

The relational nature of identity is expressed a different way for Joi Jamison. Joi was born in 1968 and raised in low-income housing projects in Harlem. She was the only girl and the youngest of her parents' four children. Her mother attended college but dropped out two semesters before graduation to have a child and marry Joi's father. After her parents divorced when Joi was six, her mother raised all of the children as a single parent, and Joi proudly tells me how her mother sacrificed by not working while she was growing up. Through the help of public assistance, she remained at home, and the family made do with less money so that Joi and her brothers would be "raised right." Far from seeing her mother's decision not to work as lazy or irresponsible, Joi says she has a great deal of respect for her mother for having chosen this more difficult path to ensure that Joi and her brothers would not fall prey to the negative aspects of the high-poverty neighborhood where they lived.

Today, Joi is part-owner of a three-story brownstone with several other family members and is employed as a construction worker for the City of New York, repairing potholes and performing various other types of labor. She is about five feet, ten inches tall and weighs around 225 pounds. She has a gender presentation that I identify as on the cusp of gender-blender and transgressive because she styles her hair in a long, straightened manner that reveals her female gender, but wears men's clothes and shoes with little jewelry and no purse.

When I asked Joi which identity status is more important to her as an individual, she said her status as a woman is most important: "I am a woman first. In order for me to be a lesbian I would definitely have to be—my gender would have to be female. So I guess that presides over everything. I'm woman; after a woman, I'm a lesbian." When Joi is asked about the group she feels she has the most in common with, she responded: "My initial response is a Black [straight] woman. A Black woman—what would we have in common? Well, we are both Black, and because she is straight doesn't mean that she is not open-minded, right? Doesn't mean that is she is not open-minded or anything like that. We would be able to talk about, I don't know, I think there would be some kind of connection. She is Black, I am Black. With a White gay woman, yeah, we could talk about having intimacy with other women, but that is all there is."

Unlike Angie, Joi was able to rank the importance of the three identity statuses. Even though Joi has an everyday gender presentation that is relatively masculine, when asked about identity as an *individual* characteristic she ranked her status as a woman as the one most important to her, most likely because she was raised as the only girl in a house full of brothers, and because she repairs potholes on the city streets, an occupation that also makes her gender quite salient. When asked about which *group* she has the most in common with, however, Joi chose Black heterosexual women over White lesbians. While her answer to the first question suggested that she would identify with women over men, one might also have expected her to choose White lesbians over Black heterosexual women since she had just ranked her gay sexuality as more important to her individual identity than her race. However, the blackness Joi shares with heterosexual Black women outweighs any differences in sexual preference they may have, because it is her race that is the basis for the sense of commonality she has with others, not her sexuality. "There would be some kind of connection," Joi said, because "she is Black, I am Black."

Joi's statements suggest that she feels a sense of bounded solidarity in race—a solidarity that persists despite the fact that she and straight Black women do not share a common sexual identity. Joi sees a possibility of identifying with Black heterosexual women despite their differences in sexual preference, but she, like Angie, does not similarly see the possibility of identifying with White lesbian women despite their racial differences. Joi experiences lesbian sexuality as a behavior she may have in common with others, which is important to how she defines herself personally, but it is not a status around which she connects to others as a group. Rather, race is the foundation for group status for Joi, because she feels that she shares with other Black people a common history and understanding that facilitates the construction of social relationships.

Waters (1999) says racial identities are social identities that can only be understood in context as people relate to one another, and the in-group that contributes to one's social identity varies depending on context. Twine (1996) also argues that master-status is not fixed and that, depending on the environment, people will choose different identities as primary according to how others in that context perceive them. While these points are true, both Angie's and Joi's responses to questions about group membership and sense of connectedness reveal how the permeability of feelings of group membership plays out for some Black lesbians. Angie says race, sexuality, and gender are all ranked equally as parts of her *individual* identity, while Joi contends that for her, sexuality and gender are tied in importance and are more important than race. Nonetheless, Angie and Joi both form their *collective* identity around race. Race is the foundation of the relationships they have with others and of the difference they perceive between themselves and White lesbians. The majority of the Black lesbians I spoke to do not experience their gay sexuality as a status around which to unite with White lesbians, because Whites very clearly and consistently play the role of the Other in their group identity construction. The lack of lesbian group cohesion across race has important consequences for the types of boundaries Black lesbians design as they construct a collective group membership.

CONCLUSION

Just as boundaries exist *within* the Black community, they also work on its *outside* to contain its members within a community of solidarity (Pattillo 2007). These boundaries may shift and bend and sometimes even buckle as individuals move in and out of various social environments, but they persist. What ties people together in a particular group is not just the shared experience of being identified by others or by group members as part of a collectivity, but also each member's own evaluation of what the characteristics of that collectivity are and assessment of the extent to which he or she fits with those group characteristics. Most of the Black lesbians I interviewed reported that race is the foundation of a persistently salient and powerful collective relationship they have with others—as I had hypothesized they would. Not one of the respondents said sexuality was the primary identity around which she formed her most important collective relationships with others, particularly when that group membership would have required her to cross Black-White racial boundaries. The dominance of race as an identity revealed its influence in various ways according to the visibility of other social identities, however, and to the varying social contexts in which identity statuses were made salient.

Gender presentation as an expression of race, gender, and sexuality importantly shapes gay women's connectedness to identity statuses. For lesbians with a feminine gender presentation, race operates simultaneously with gender as a primary status that organizes the way they see themselves and believe that others see them. These women's connections to race and gender as identity statuses are enacted through their presentation of Black female respectability in an effort to overcome the image of sexual pathology and deviancy that has historically been associated with Black women and lesbian women. Women with a transgressive gender presentation were least likely to be able to rank their identities, and they tended to understand the identity that is most important for them as *individuals* to be different from the identity *group* with which they had the most in common.

In addition to gender presentation, class is important to how race is experienced as a social identity. High-status women were most often women who integrated neighborhoods, schools, and work departments or offices. They repeatedly learned what it meant to be "the only one" or "one of a few" African Americans in predominantly White contexts that required them to prove their worthiness to occupy a particular space in which they were treated as the Other. Thus, they were the most likely to experience race as a status around which they understood both an individual and a collective identity.

My interviews revealed the extent to which identity statuses are both relational and structural. They are simultaneously imagined relationships individuals form with others through active, interdependent, dynamic processes, and power relationships in a social system that influence our relative positions in society and affect the ways resources are allocated. Black gay women experience marginalized identity statuses simultaneously as personal and political projects. At times they distinguish among an identity status as a personal trait or micro-level characteristic that represents their private lived experiences; an identity status as a collective identity or representation of membership in a particular social grouping; and an identity status as a location in the larger social system that has a structural foundation. Different social contexts allow them the possibility of perceiving one identity category as primary for their own self-definition and a different identity category as a status around which to cohere with others as a group.

CHAPTER 4

Lesbian Motherhood and Discourses of Respectability

In June 2004, I attended a backyard barbeque for a birthday celebration, and among the guests were two Black lesbians who had adopted a child. Soon after, another Black lesbian couple arrived with their newly adopted daughter, who was about nine months old. Everyone oohed and ahhed at the babies. I listened as the mothers complained good-naturedly about sleepless nights and the speed at which young children can crawl. The group of women at the gathering celebrated these children, in part because they represented proof of the two couple's link (and by extension, other lesbian mothers' link) to the broader, societal community of mothers. The couples' experience served as proof to the other women that they too could "have it all": they could express a public lesbian identity and be mothers.

The version of motherhood in evidence at this barbeque is one to which scholars have devoted quite a bit of attention over the past few decades—albeit with a focus on White women. A body of research emerged over the past fifteen years that has defined as "lesbian motherhood" the experiences of women who begin parenting after taking on a gay identity. This body of work frames the issue as "lesbians choosing motherhood," and it has initiated a sustained dialogue around the extent to which parenting lesbians are transforming the institution of motherhood or assimilating into heterosexual understandings and assumptions that surround motherhood. The empirical research that has dominated this area of study tends to exclude from study participation those women who became mothers prior to enacting a gay sexuality, and in so doing has written into the discourse a particular definition of lesbian family.[1]

Many researchers have framed past studies of lesbian motherhood to make their results comparable to those of other empirical research on family structure and family process in heterosexual two-parent families. Such an analogous study design makes it easier to address central assumptions in the literature regarding the division of household labor and the distribution of child care and childrearing tasks.[2] Research on lesbian-headed families also tends to be framed around long-held assumptions about lesbian identity, particularly the idea that lesbians as a group are more egalitarian in their distribution of paid work, housework, and childcare, and that they organize their households and interact with each other in ways that support this principle. Unfortunately, restricting samples so that they only include women who take on a lesbian identity before becoming parents biases research studies, and the literature more generally, toward the experiences of White middle- and upper-income lesbians, who are better able to afford costly insemination procedures and who are more likely to support the ideological principles of egalitarian feminism.[3] Mezey (2008), who studied lesbian women's views of motherhood, noted in a discussion of her research methodology that she had considerable difficulty recruiting working-class and Black women for her study, yet this is not surprising when one evaluates the criteria she used to define who is a lesbian mother. Her criteria excluded not only women who gave birth in the context of prior heterosexual relationships but also lesbians who had become parental figures through live-in relationships with female partners and their biological children.

Maintaining such a narrow definition of who is a lesbian parent does a disservice to our understanding of the complexities of lesbian motherhood because it implicitly overrepresents the less common route to a lesbian sexuality and identity status. That is, the majority of today's mothers who identify as gay became parents by bearing a child in the context of a marital or cohabiting union. For example, a 2002 national survey of lesbians found that just 5.6 percent of White mothers and 2.8 percent of Black mothers had their children using alternative insemination techniques, while an additional 6.5 percent of White mothers and 12.3 percent of Black mothers had adopted. The vast majority of White mothers (84.4 percent) and Black mothers (84.9 percent) became parents through sex with a husband or male partner (Morris, Balsam, and Rothblum 2002). These figures suggest not only that our understanding of who counts as a lesbian mother must be expanded but also that the experience of motherhood may be transformed or influenced by the timing of when one begins to identify as lesbian. The question of how women understand and experience motherhood in the context of changing social circumstances, such as changing sexual orientation, deserves attention in its own right.

Expanding our definition of lesbian motherhood will particularly offer insight into a population that has received little attention from scholars: lesbian stepparents. We know about some of the issues and conflicts that arise when a grandmother or other adult relative shares a household and parenting responsibilities with her adult daughter and her children, and we are learning more about lesbian co-parents, who are the nonbiological but legal parents to their partners' children via alternative insemination.[4] We know very little, however, about women who act as parental figures in the context of intimate relationships with women who are already mothers through birth or adoption.

The experiences of a variety of Black lesbian mothers are presented in this chapter, including those who had their children while in heterosexual relationships, those who adopted, who experienced childbirth as a lesbian through alternative insemination, and lesbian stepparents. In my survey sample of one hundred respondents, fifty-five women are mothers through birth or adoption, and thirteen are nonbiological mothers who are parenting a partner's child in a stepfamily household. Of the sixty-eight women engaged in some form of parenting, 46 percent, or thirty-one women, entered into motherhood in a heterosexual relationship prior to coming out as gay, and all of them had their children through a biological birth. Forty-five percent of these thirty-one women became mothers in the context of a heterosexual marriage, and the rest had children in a heterosexual dating relationship. On average, these women first became mothers at age twenty-one and took on a lesbian identity at age twenty-eight.[5] In terms of education, 26 percent, or eight of the thirty-one respondents who had children in a heterosexual marriage, completed school with a four-year college degree, and 19 percent (six women) have an advanced degree beyond the bachelor's. With regard to gender presentation, 61 percent are femme, 26 percent are genderblenders, and 13 percent are transgressive. In this chapter I consider these women's experiences with coming to accept a lesbian identity and with motherhood, paying particular attention to how the interaction of these two identities are shaped by Black women's histories and current experiences with race, class, and sexuality.

After they come out as gay, many women who become mothers in the context of prior heterosexual unions continue to make a concentrated effort to satisfy the societal definition of a "good mother" that is implicitly linked to heterosexuality. Through family members, media messages, and religious messages, society tells women that good mothers are responsible not only for nurturing their children and protecting them from harm, but also for representing a particular standard of heterosexuality. This expectation produces a conflict for mothers who want to identify as lesbians. This conflict is similar to the one that single heterosexual mothers face, though it is compounded by lesbian mothers' openly gay sexuality. The types of issues that mothers face for being lesbians are compounded when they not only have a sexual orientation that is considered deviant, but must also contend with negative stereotypes around race. This is the case for Black lesbian mothers. In choosing to live an openly gay life, they battle negative images that surround their multiple marginalized statuses, and must balance societal expectations of good motherhood and respectable womanhood, while also expressing sexual freedom and autonomy.

The role of mother has been emphasized as women's true purpose and main focus in life (Collins 2000; Thorne 1992). In African American communities, the status of mother is especially revered, and for much of U.S. history motherhood was the primary means by which Black women could achieve any status at all. Historically, Black women's sexuality has been subject to particular visibility, scrutiny, and judgment. Hammonds argues that the sexuality of Black women has primarily been evaluated in opposition to the experiences of White women, and in dominant discourses it has been simultaneously rendered "invisible, visible (exposed), hypervisible, and pathologized" (1997, 170).

Certain discourses[6] around Black women's respectability emerged as a political response to negative images of Black women's sexuality that were propagated after Reconstruction as a basis for denying full citizenship (Giddings 1984). African American communities relied on discourses of respectability and the politics of silence to counteract images of Black mothers as sexually deviant and less capable of nurturing children and rearing them properly.[7] The ideologies behind these discourses remain a driving force in today's Black environments, both among the Black middle class and among Black working-class mothers. They encourage individuals to overemphasize positive images of themselves in order to reflect affirmingly on Blacks as a collective group. Black women who have been socialized in predominantly Black contexts bring these ideologies and practices with them as they enter into a gay sexuality, and they use them to organize their lives.

Openly gay Black women must negotiate the process of mothering through discourses of Black respectability, while also affirming their own sexual autonomy. Their sexual orientation forces a sexual self into visibility in the context of motherhood, which frightens some and goes against a politics of silence in this arena.[8] This chapter asks a number of questions about how they accomplish this: What are the family, neighborhood, and social contexts in which Black lesbians make decisions about whether and how to have children, and how does a gay sexuality matter for the way women conceive of motherhood? How does the timing of motherhood and taking on a gay sexuality shape how lesbians come to understand the meanings of these statuses and what they imply for their own sense of self? How do discourses of respectability shape the definitions and understandings of motherhood for Black lesbians, and how are these discourses shaped by the affirmation of sexual agency implied in living a lesbian life? And how are these issues understood and enacted for single versus partnered lesbians, middle-class versus working-class mothers, and lesbians with feminine versus nonfeminine gender presentations? I address these questions by examining in detail how women in five different families entered lesbian motherhood. These case studies reflect the range of experiences of families with children in this study. Through them, I offer an analysis of how race, class, social context, and the timing of motherhood and accepting a lesbian sexuality matter for the experience of lesbian parenting. I compare the ways women understand motherhood and their lesbian identities when they become mothers in heterosexual relationships before they take on a self-definition as gay ("mothers becoming lesbians") with the differing experiences they have when they publicly identify as lesbian before becoming a parent ("lesbians becoming mothers"). I examine these experiences through the lives of Black lesbians, who evaluate their own abilities to parent using past and current discourses on race, class, respectability, and womanhood.

Mothers who "become" gay tend to have entered into a gay identity as hetero-identified lesbians who did not experience same-sex attraction until adulthood, or as conformists who experienced same-sex desire in their younger years but did not act on that desire until adulthood (see Chapter 1). For mothers who have lived much of their childbearing years as heterosexual or as closeted lesbians, taking on an active and open lesbian identity is a separate and distinct behavior from engaging in same-sex liaisons. These women are continuing to parent their children at the same time they are experiencing a changing sexual orientation, and embrace a lesbian sexuality after first experiencing motherhood in a heterosexual framework. Lynch suggests that previously married women who commit to gay sexuality as a permanent way of life assume a "disapproved-of identity" (2004, 94). To now parent as gay women, they must disinvest in the heterosexual privilege that accompanies their previous identity as mothers. I argue that they must also be willing to reveal themselves as sexual beings, and the experience of this transformation can be harrowing.

African American lesbians from low-income and working-class families have not amassed much privilege or authority through family background, education, or employment, so for these women, the recognition, reverence, and respect that is associated with being a heterosexual mother in Black communities—and indeed in most communities—is sometimes the only source of status they have. The acceptance and support they receive from others for being an upstanding mother can be disrupted when they reveal themselves as gay. The potential for this to happen significantly influences whether and how Black mothers go about publicly asserting a lesbian identity, and expressing their sexuality.

Women who come out as lesbian *before* entering motherhood—lesbians who become mothers—experience a different set of processes in this transition. Relative to mothers becoming lesbians, these women have the reverse experience: they assume a gay sexuality at an earlier age (in their late teens and early twenties) and first enter motherhood much later, in their late twenties or early thirties and beyond. In delaying childbearing, they are able to achieve higher levels of education and accrue more experience in the labor market. When they do become parents they have greater social resources and access to additional capital to better provide economically for their children. Because they became gay at the onset of adulthood, they have lived more of their adult lives on the margins of Black respectability. By the time they enter motherhood, therefore, they have resolved much of the uncertainty and shame associated with having a public lesbian sexuality and may have also learned to rely on other statuses, such as occupation, social class, or home ownership to garner privilege in society.

Social class, reflected not merely through education and income but also through type of college education, occupational status, and other subtle distinctions, bears an important relationship to processes of motherhood for Black lesbians. In my study, women who came out as gay before having children are more likely to have attained middle- and upper-middle-class status by completing college, attaining degrees beyond the bachelor's, and working in high-status occupations. The most educated and most economically advantaged have the greatest choice in how to become mothers because they have more access to information about alternative insemination technologies, greater knowledge about how to effectively utilize those technologies, jobs that facilitate their use through superior insurance coverage, and extra income to pay for medical treatments. These women are more likely to have what some scholars refer to as the "choice of motherhood," meaning the ability to decide whether and when to become mothers.

Like mothers becoming lesbians, however, African American lesbians becoming mothers similarly employ discourses of Black respectability when they speak of their motherhood, and must simultaneously negotiate these expectations with the evidence of their own sexual freedom that a lesbian identity makes visible. Regardless of social class and timing of motherhood, the parenting lesbians I interviewed want to be perceived as "good mothers" despite having an open lesbian sexuality. They struggle to enact a public lesbian identity in predominantly Black social environments that discourage openly gay behavior. I proceed in this chapter with five case studies. In the first family, the respondent became a mother while in an upwardly mobile but working-class, heterosexual marital relationship. The second household involves a middle-class single mother who emigrated from Jamaica and had a child in a heterosexual dating relationship. The third case study examines the adoption process for a working-class, single mother. The fourth family is an upper-middle-class couple who had children together using alternative insemination, and the fifth family is a working-class lesbian stepfamily household. Together, these case studies reveal how intersections of race, ethnicity, class, sexuality, and gender presentation differentially affect parenting experiences in Black lesbian families.

MOTHERHOOD PRIOR TO TAKING ON A LESBIAN SEXUALITY

Respectability through Upward Mobility and Virtuous Black Womanhood

Jocelyn Barnum presents herself as the epitome of the successful Black woman. She describes herself as attractive, feminine, and strong, and recently purchased a home in South Jersey with her partner, Joi Jamison.

Recall that she was born in 1962 to working-class parents in the Bronx, and married her high school sweetheart in 1985 at age twenty-three, right around the time her first and only child, Issim, was born. She entered college much later, in her early thirties, going part-time for many years to complete a bachelor's degree and then received her MBA through an online university in her forties. Jocelyn describes herself as being the child whom her family thought would be most likely to make it in the way African American communities have traditionally defined success for women: the sibling who would complete her education, have a successful marriage, become a loving mother in the context of that marriage, and have a fulfilling, income-producing career. She would then use these experiences to gain entry into the world of Black middle-class life and serve as a respectable model for others to follow.

Given these expectations, it is not surprising that divorcing her husband and entering into a committed relationship with another woman were not part of the equation. Jocelyn made the decision to be openly gay rather late in life. Her pathway into a lesbian sexuality was consistent with that of hetero-identified women, as she had her first experience with same-sex desire when she was well into adulthood. She first acted on her attraction to women at age thirty while in her marriage, but it took two more years before she came to identify as a lesbian. There were several competing issues that she had to confront; all of them were interwoven with the heterosexual privilege she had amassed and would jeopardize by acting on her desires.

First, she risked losing the high status she had in her family as the role model her siblings should emulate. As the child of a Baptist minister, she knew that if she were to claim a lesbian identity it would lessen her father's authority over his congregation and bring shame to their family. Jocelyn was therefore concerned about how the public nature of her sexual identity would affect the social status her family had worked hard to build. She came into adulthood in the 1970s when rates of non-marital childbearing were rising in large urban centers like New York. The sexual behavior of low-income racial minority women like Jocelyn was under a heightened scrutiny, so this was not an ideal time for Black women and particularly Black mothers to be claiming sexual autonomy. In the context of this discourse, Jocelyn could not decide to live an openly gay life without a cost to her reputation.

Jocelyn also worried about how her relationship with her family would change after she came out. More than once, she mentioned that her family had her "on a pedestal," saying she was "always the one who was very slim, model-like, very adventurous, very studious." She told me, "I had a lot of things I wanted to do in life and accomplish in life." In Jocelyn's mind, her family's expectations and positive beliefs about her were tied to her heterosexuality. Neither her physical features nor her level of schooling would change by virtue of her assuming a lesbian identity, but they would lose value, she felt, when stripped of their heterosexual context. And indeed, Jocelyn's father's response when he learned of her interest in women was a strong and negative one. He found out from a relative, and first tried to warn Jocelyn about lesbians, saying he knew women who were "like that" when he was a numbers runner,[9] and telling her that they "push up very, very hard [come on strong], so be careful." But she says eventually it sunk in for him that she was romantically interested in a woman, and when the nature of their relationship was confirmed, her father became extremely hostile and threatening.[10]

Heterosexuality is critically important for Jocelyn's image and self-presentation as a mother. When she was first considering whether she would take on a gay identity her son Issim was eight years old, and the fact that she was a mother made her especially careful in thinking through this decision. When her father found out she was dating a woman, one of the arguments he made against her behavior was that she was not being a good mother. For example, when Jocelyn spent a weekend at her lover's home, she asked her sister to watch her son. Her father "tried to turn the tables and say 'Because you're with this woman now you can't take care of your child.' And it just wasn't like that at all." Jocelyn's father's comments suggest that her decision to acknowledge a gay sexuality would inevitably make her a worse mother, conjuring up an image of a hedonistic woman out to fulfill her own desires rather than her parental responsibilities. Her father's reaction is consistent with the belief that a mother who asserts sexual autonomy and who seeks self-fulfillment through avenues other than child rearing does so at a cost to her children, whose needs she fails to meet.

I expected to find that respondents who had been heterosexually married had ended their unions specifically because they wanted to be openly gay. It turned out, however, that the majority of previously married women in my research said they ended their marriages for reasons that were not directly related to their interest in women. Jocelyn was with her husband for eight years before they married and seven years after they wed. Over that time her husband's behavior toward her grew more violent and disrespectful. When I asked her why her marriage ended, her response suggested that the marital breakup was the result of her husband's infidelity, domestic violence, and other negative behaviors.

After she left her marriage, Jocelyn still wanted Issim to have a relationship with his father. The fact that her experience of motherhood occurred in the context of a long-term marital relationship influenced both her expectation and her ex-husband's expectation that he would continue to be involved in Issim's life. It is noteworthy that her "fitness" for motherhood was not presented by her ex-husband as an important issue in determining custody after the separation. The assumption that Jocelyn would continue to be the primary parent did not change once Issim's father discovered that Jocelyn was in a lesbian relationship. Issim's father did not contribute very much in the way of child support, and this may be one reason why there was never a custody battle. He was not pleased about her new gay status, however, and during the first years of their separation he made his disapproval overt, constantly disparaging her to their son.

Jocelyn's transition into a gay sexuality occurred during a rough period for Issim, who was about seven years old when his parents first separated. He had to contend not only with his parents' breakup but also with the death of his paternal grandfather, to whom he was extremely close, as well as his mother's new cohabiting lesbian relationship. His mother sought counseling for him to help him through the series of family transitions they were both experiencing. Throughout this time, her relationship with Issim's father continued to be combative. She remembers: "He would say things to Issim that were just so inappropriate, that he and I should discuss, not him and Issim. His father would basically put little things in Issim's head. I mean it was like I was fighting with two people, you know, I had to deal with the father who was saying things like 'I don't know what's wrong with your mother. Is she crazy?'"

She says it was tough because her child was trying to be understanding about Jocelyn's emerging sexuality while at the same time "someone as forceful as the father was saying things to him that were so condescending about his mother." Issim, she feels, was "caught in a catch-22." Today, Jocelyn and her ex-husband are on better terms, though the relationship continues to be conflictual. Jocelyn thinks it is very important that Issim continue to have a positive relationship with his father. Issim, who is now 18 years old, talks to his father regularly and sees him on weekends. The relationship between Issim and his mother's partner grew to be solid and accepting.

Women like Jocelyn who bear children in heterosexual relationships before initiating a lesbian-identified life must make a series of choices that may appear on the surface to contradict broader societal messages about motherhood and self-sacrifice. In deciding to be openly gay, these mothers declare to the world that they are going to seek to create a life that is personally fulfilling. In making this decision, however, they alter not just their own lives but also the worlds they have constructed for their children, who have known them only as heterosexual. The mother's transition from openly heterosexual to openly homosexual also alters the family's status to one that is often stigmatized. Mothers who become lesbians must do the work of changing their identity status from heterosexual to gay while they continue to parent. Jocelyn's childhood in the church and her attempts to pursue upward mobility shaped her understanding of herself as a woman. The image she wants to portray to the world is one of a person striving for middle-class respectability, and the decision to take on a lesbian sexuality disrupts the heterosexual privilege she has managed to amass. This experience is also exemplified in Althea Payne's story, if somewhat differently.

Single-Mother Management of Motherhood and Lesbian Status

Althea Payne holds a master's degree in education administration and is an assistant dean at a Catholic high school. She was born in Jamaica, West Indies, in 1964 and lived there with her grandmother until age eight, when she moved to New York to live with her mother and stepfather. In her family, people tend not to have open discussions about their lives. Althea never discussed with her mother or any family members why her mother and biological father never married, for example, nor why she has never had a relationship with her father. When her mother married her stepfather, Althea was not invited to the wedding. No one ever told her why she was not invited, and the circumstances around the wedding remained "very hush hush." Growing up in her family, she learned that certain behaviors and activities were not to be discussed, even among close relatives.

These experiences profoundly shaped the way Althea presents herself to the outside world. She has a feminine gender presentation and came into a gay sexuality as a hetero-identified woman who developed same-sex attraction in adulthood after having serious relationships with men. She is a single mother raising a teenage daughter whom she bore in the context of a heterosexual dating relationship. Althea says of her daughter's father, "He loved me like a woman, but I loved him like a brother. Well, not quite. But it wasn't that passionate love. It was the type of love that allowed me to see him as someone that I would like to father my child." Throughout the time they were together, she made it clear that she did not want to marry him, because although she loved him and knew that he loved her, "something wasn't enough." Althea explained: "I felt this emptiness that I couldn't name. Maybe I could name it but I was afraid to." When I asked what she would have named it, she replied: "I would have named it a need to be with a woman. And I had never been with a woman before, never been intimate. So I didn't really have any kind of frame of reference, you know. I just had that feeling. . . . We really tried to make the relationship work, and we had gone through a lot . . . but it just wasn't there, and that's why I felt imprisoned. I needed to get out. . . . Eventually I realized that I was just doing him and myself a disservice by trying to stay in something that was not fulfilling for me and therefore could not be fulfilling for him."

Althea says that her first sexual experience with a woman felt different from anything she had ever experienced with men: "It was more comfortable. That's the best way I can put it. It was like putting on a glove that fit as opposed to one that was too big or too small. And I felt just this sense of belonging." While she has had relations with women for more than ten years and has integrated her gay sexuality into her sense of self, she is very cautious about revealing her lesbian desires to members of her family of origin and to other people who have a place in her social world. Unlike all of the partnered women in this study, Althea has not openly shared with her family the fact that she only dates women. She is currently living as a single mother, but when she had a cohabiting relationship with another woman in the past, she presented the woman to her family as her roommate and best friend. When I asked Althea how she decided not to be open about her sexuality, she paused for a long time, then said: "I don't even know if it was a conscious choice or just something that I felt was better left as it was. Just looking at how society reacts to us, how family reacts, how even some friends react, that was kind of enough to keep me back. In terms of my family, they're very rooted in Christianity, so right there it's like a no-no. I mean, they may know, but it's one thing to come out and tell them and another for them to suspect. So, just the way I was brought up and how society looks at us, and also even being a mother, you know, that has a lot to do with it. So it's not just about me."

Noted scholar Makeda Silvera writes about her experiences as a Jamaican woman who is a lesbian mother raising teenage daughters. She says the costs of being openly lesbian are great, and thinks back on the times when she was heterosexual – the closeness and connection she experienced with her ethnic community. She says that in her early days as a "young lesbian Black mother" she was "shut out" by "both my Black sisters and my Black brothers," and experienced "the silence and whispers, the homophobic remarks, the sucking of the teeth when we passed by, the sudden breaks into a degrading song about my sexuality" (1992, 313). In a different work she notes, "The presence of an 'out' Afro-Caribbean lesbian in our community is dealt with by suspicion and fear from both men and our heterosexual Black sisters. It brings into question the assumption of heterosexuality as the only 'normal' way. It forces them to acknowledge something that has always been covered up" (2008, 353).

Althea is aware of the ways openly gay and lesbian practice are received in Caribbean communities, and says this is an important factor in her decision not to be openly gay with her family members. She has felt conflicted having lesbian relationships as an adult, because she is worried about how she would be perceived by others if they were to find out. Even though she believes her mother and grandmother would still love her if she told them she is gay, she "doesn't want to put them through that." Instead, she adopts the relatively common strategy of "just allowing them to figure it out" by bringing the partner to family functions and other events without labeling their relationship. She says this approach is particularly common with Blacks and with Caribbeans, who believe: "Just be what you want to be but don't walk around waving a flag or anything else like that. Just keep it to yourself, in a sense. I do get the sense that most people would be more comfortable with that."

Althea identifies her religion and her Jamaican culture as particular barriers preventing her from leading an openly gay life. She was raised in a conservative Pentecostal church that views homosexuality as a sin. She said that Jamaicans consider gay sexuality to be "extremely taboo," and the language they use to define homosexual activity is also negative. Just to be called "lesbian" is disparaging, and she says, "In Patois it sounds so much worse, you know, the word 'lesbian,' and maybe that's their intention for it to sound, you know, really twisted." Althea and her daughter live in a section of Brooklyn that is predominantly West Indian. She finds that being gay in Caribbean communities is "quite difficult. Probably more difficult than in any other community," and she believes the reason has to do with the fact that most Caribbeans are brought up in the church with a belief system "that does not include and is quite against homosexuality."[11]

Existing discourses about homosexuality and lesbian motherhood not only affect a person's decision to take on a public identity as gay but also significantly impact their approach to parenting. One of Althea's many concerns in integrating a public lesbian identity into her existing presentation of herself as a middle-class, virtuous mother is the negative effects she thinks living an openly gay life would have on her daughter, Ophelia, and on their relationship. She explained: "I was concerned about how it would impact my daughter. I didn't want her to feel different. I didn't want her to feel like an outcast. I just didn't want her to have to go through anything other than what I knew that she would go through as a child, as a Black girl growing up. I knew that she would have enough to contend with, and I really did not want to add to that. If there was any way that I could make it easy on her, I was going to. And my keeping this to myself was, I thought, one way to avoid additional pain."

Ulysse (1999), in her discussion of class and color in Jamaica, points to the rigid policing of social status there, particularly for those who are upwardly mobile. The middle-class standard of gendered behavior among Jamaican woman is strongly linked historically to skin color and occupational status. While Althea's dark-complexion might be perceived as a liability in her country of origin, here in the United States she has achieved middle-class status through her education and employment. She has the "look" that is valued by the middle class in New York: she wears her hair short and relaxed, and she dresses stylishly in tailored suits and high-heeled shoes that tastefully flatter her slender frame.

Though Althea keeps her sexuality private, her daughter did eventually discover it. Althea describes with some pain the way in which this happened. In Althea's mind, the problems that ensued stemmed from her own reluctance to confront the situation head-on by letting her child know the circumstances of her relationship. When Ophelia was thirteen years old, Althea's partner, Pamela, moved into their home. This was not Althea's first cohabiting relationship. When Ophelia was much younger, they had lived for several years with a man who was "like a father" to Ophelia. And after that, when Ophelia was still young, they shared an apartment with a different female partner. Althea says that neither of those relationships had a negative impact on Ophelia because "she was younger, so there was still all that innocence going on." Ophelia had not been aware of the nature of her mother's lesbian sexuality, and the cohabiting experiences were positive ones.

When Pamela moved in, by contrast, Ophelia had just begun adolescence. At this time, Althea and Pamela had been dating for about a year and a half. Pamela was friendly with Ophelia, tutoring her in math and spending some evenings at their home. When Pamela formally moved into the household, Althea followed her accustomed pattern of silence around personal matters. She did not let her daughter know about her gay sexuality and did not share with her the nature of her relationship with Pamela. Althea did not see the problems brewing as a result of this decision: "Maybe I didn't realize just how much of my attention she [Ophelia] needed, and maybe Ophelia realized that she wanted it when she saw it going elsewhere. You know, there were a lot of things going on, but the point is we were all living together here, and I did not make it a point to sit down with my daughter and talk to her about what was going on. And so she became resentful, started acting out, started cutting school. Staying away, running away practically, not coming home at night. And that was a major problem. A *major* problem." One evening, the situation reached a breaking point. Althea had come home from work and Ophelia was nowhere to be found. She went around the neighborhood to her friends' houses and to a local restaurant to see if she could find her. Althea remembers:

> And it's funny how it happened, because we were in the street not far from here, and I think I must have just tracked her down one evening because I was looking for her. And we were walking on the street and she's crying, and I'm trying to get her to calm down and come home. And then she said something. She was referring to one of her friends, and she made some reference to her friend saying that she thought that I was gay. . . . I guess in talking to her friends and telling them, "Oh she's living with so and so," her friends put two and two together, and at that point I said, "I am gay, but that doesn't mean that I don't love you. And I'm sorry that you're going through all this pain." And I tried to smooth it over as much as I could at that moment, at that time, but I see that the damage had been done. And just looking back, I would have done it differently.

The circumstances under which Althea shared the news of her sexuality and the nature of her cohabiting relationship with her daughter were fraught with emotion, confusion, and disbelief. Althea also had strong feelings of guilt, seeing her lesbian sexuality as something that caused her daughter much inner turmoil. She acknowledges that a large part of the problem was her silence around the nature of her relationship, her refusal to be forthright with her daughter and her reluctance to talk openly with Ophelia about how their relationship might be affected by Pamela's presence in the home. Althea also felt guilty, however, because she had not foreseen the problems that would erupt. As a good mother, she felt she should have anticipated her daughter's feelings and been able to provide an acceptable remedy. When I asked Althea how Ophelia responded to learning about her mother's sexuality, she answered: "She didn't accept it right away. She may have known in her own little mind before her friend even said anything but was unable or unwilling to grasp it." Our conversation continued:

I: *Did Ophelia's behavior toward [Pamela] change after you shared that with her?*

Althea: Yeah, she seemed to dislike [Pamela] even more. More resentful.

I: *That's common with teenage girls. At that time it's very hard.*

Althea: I guess I didn't see it. I didn't see it coming for whatever reason.

I: *Well how would you know? You hadn't had that experience before with a teenager.*

Althea: I know, but as a mother you're kind of expected to know these things *before* they happen.

Research shows that parent relationship transitions are particularly challenging for adolescents (Bray 1999). Even when there is full disclosure about the nature of parents' relationships with new partners, there is often a rough period of transition, and children—particularly teenagers—tend to respond with acts of rebellion (Bray and Kelly 1998; Hetherington 1989; Nicholson et al. 2008). Some work suggests that marital transitions are especially difficult on the mother-daughter relationship when the expectations of closeness are compromised by the presence of the mother's new female partner (Coleman, Troilo, and Jamison 2008). Daughters in single-parent households may also be used to having more of a peer relationship with their mothers, which can be disrupted by the mother's new partner. Research on heterosexual re-partnered mothers reports some of the same conflicts that Althea experienced. Papernow (2008) finds, for example, that the mother-child relationship competes with the mother's new marital relationship in ways that force her to choose one bond over the other. Similarly, Weaver and Coleman (2010) describe heterosexual mothers in re-partnered households as feeling split, pulled in more than one direction, or confused as to where their loyalties should lie.

Gay parents do not necessarily see the connection between their experiences and the experiences of heterosexual stepfamilies, however. And Althea, who already felt guilty about having a relationship that would force her concentration away from her daughter, felt doubly bad because the relationship was with a woman, and therefore stigmatizing for herself and her daughter. Silvera, writing about her own experiences of lesbian motherhood as a Jamaican woman, says her two daughters changed the way they felt about her sexuality once they became teenagers. While the parenting she and her partner gave was warmly received when the children were younger, once they entered adolescence it seemed as though "all the bonding, all the warm comfort, love, security, never was" (1992, 317). Silvera poignantly describes the hurt felt by her daughters' changed feelings toward her, saying "Dealing with the culture's hatred towards lesbianism and lesbian parenting is frustrating, tiring, but dealing with one's children's unspoken homophobia is painful" (318).

After Althea told her daughter about her relationship with Pamela, Althea became intensely focused on how that experience was affecting her bond with Ophelia. She says her daughter still had a lot of anger toward her and toward Pamela, and Althea was not able to think about anything other than mending her relationship with Ophelia: "As a matter of fact I had to just kind of like push everything aside and focus on her, to just repair the damage that had been done. And that actually meant not giving my attention to anyone else." When I noted how difficult it must have been for Althea to focus entirely on her daughter's needs to the detriment of her own, she responded: "It was difficult, but I saw it as something that I needed to do. I saw it as just having messed up, so now damage control was on my agenda." Althea asked Pamela to move out of the home because she thought that would be the best way to repair her relationship with Ophelia. Soon after, the relationship between Althea and Pamela dissolved.

Althea's response to her daughter's difficulty in coming to terms with her lesbian union was to end her relationship. In her mind, her lesbian relationship was an attempt to seek pleasure for herself, whereas her understanding of motherhood is that it requires altruism and selflessness. Lewin (1993) says this is a common dilemma for lesbian mothers and that the separation between "mother" and "lesbian" as elements of one's identity can be sharply drawn for women who want to maintain secrecy about their sexual orientation. What is also clearly present here is Althea's understanding of the expectations within Black communities that sexuality, and particularly behavior labeled as deviant, be invisible and submerged into private spaces only. Black feminist scholars illuminate this point. Evelynn Hammonds, for example, states that public discourse on Black motherhood has historically been shaped by processes that pathologize Black women, and these also help to produce the submersion and silence of their sexuality (2004, 303). I argue that lesbian mothers must combat ideological contestations that deny Black women's sexuality altogether, as well as contestations that pathologize specific forms of sexuality. Althea's example suggests that women who have entered motherhood before coming out as gay evaluate their performance as mothers through a heterosexual lens and absorb cultural understandings of good motherhood in ways that make it difficult for them to view their lesbian sexuality in a positive light.

Reaching what one study refers to as "developmental milestones" in the coming out process while parenting offers a qualitatively different experience for the woman who already has children (Morris, Balsam, and Rothblum 2002). The parent must not only work through any feelings of negative self-worth around the possibility that she might be gay and any fear about what a lesbian identity will mean for herself, she must also consider how this shift in her sexual identity will affect her child. She may experiment with gender presentation, go on dates with women, and experience her first same-sex cohabiting relationship. All of these transitions take place in the home, and the child experiences them on some level with the parent. The multiple transitions can be problematic, particularly when there are few resources to help families process these changes.

Jocelyn's and Althea's stories tell us several things about how mothers come to terms with a new lesbian identity. First, mothers who experience this transition are likely to be concerned about taking on a status that is perceived to be shameful by members of their families and communities, particularly because this shift disrupts the definition of "good mother" and "respectable behavior" they currently have. Hays (1996) says a logic of "unselfish nurturing" guides the behavior of middle-class mothers, even while a logic of "self-interested gain" guides our behavior in so many other areas of life, and this is the cultural contradiction of contemporary motherhood.[12] Others studying marginalized mothers would add that the history of denigration around Black women's sexuality makes African American mothers particularly sensitive about how they are perceived and whether they are conforming to society's standards of acceptable behavior.[13]

Women who become mothers in a heterosexual context and who are middle class or striving to achieve middle-class status are particularly sensitive to the possibility that their decision to live openly as lesbians will be interpreted as a selfish one. Althea continues to believe that to be a good parent she must distance herself from any public identification with lesbian sexuality. She extends this reasoning to other areas of her life, believing that to be close to her family, to be treated with respect at work, and to be a good Christian woman, she must keep her sexuality quiet, treating it as a behavior discretely enacted rather than as a visible component of who she is as a person. Lewin argues that for lesbians, "demanding the right to be a mother suggests a repudiation of gender conventions that define 'mother' and 'lesbian' as inherently incompatible identities, the former natural and intrinsic to women, organized around altruism, the latter unnatural and organized around self-indulgence" (1994, 350). As Lewin suggests, taking on a lesbian identity, particularly for women who are already mothers, is a movement toward personal autonomy. But to place motherhood at the center of one's identity often involves simultaneously placing other aspects of the self, most notably lesbianism, at the margins.

In other ways, however, some mothers who become lesbians are able to break away from essentialist expectations of motherhood through their experiences of living an openly gay life. Jocelyn Barnum married her first lesbian partner and had an elaborate wedding in the 1990s, though gay marriage was not legally recognized in New York at that time. She recently remarried, and has joined a social networking organization of professional Black women in her neighborhood. She proudly refers to Joi as her "wife," and the group of mostly heterosexual women to which she belongs is enthusiastic about Jocelyn's participation in various aspects of community life. Jocelyn actively sought to strike a balance between the self-interest required to claim her lesbian sexuality and the selflessness expected of mothers. In doing so, she forges a space for lesbian motherhood in her Black community—one more often occupied by Black women who become mothers after their identity as lesbians has been already comfortably established.

INTENTIONAL VERSUS SITUATIONAL MOTHERING
FOR LESBIANS WHO BECOME MOTHERS

Twenty-nine of the sixty-six parenting women began parenting after coming out as gay, and children entered their families in a wider range of ways than did the children of mothers who "became" lesbians. Thirteen are lesbian stepparents, meaning they live in households with a partner and her biological child, and the remaining sixteen became mothers through adoption, alternative insemination, co-parenting with a partner, or heterosexual intercourse after taking on a lesbian identity. Whereas mothers who became lesbians had children at an average age of twenty-one and decided they were "exclusively or predominantly lesbian" much later, at twenty-eight, the pattern is almost reversed for lesbians who became mothers: this group of women first became mothers much later, at age thirty-three, but came out much earlier, at nineteen years old on average.

Women who began to parent after taking on a lesbian sexuality did so after becoming established in their careers and were more likely to be middle- or upper-middle-class. Those with advanced degrees and high status jobs are the most likely to have used alternative insemination techniques to have children and to parent as legal co-mothers through adoption. Those with bachelor's degrees or some college but no degree tended to be in lower-middle-class or working-class occupations and became mothers in more varied ways. Taking on the status of mother as a lesbian is a very different process than taking on the status of lesbian as a mother. The cases in the next section identify three experiences of motherhood for the women in this study: intentional mothering through adoption of kin, intentional mothering through alternative insemination in a lesbian relationship, and situational mothering as a stepparent. The cases show how race, class, gender presentation, and ideologies about parenthood influence these experiences.

Intentional Mothering and Norms of
Responsibility in Motherhood

When Jackie Roberts responded to my request for an interview, I was intrigued. Jackie said she was the mother of a seven-year-old boy named Andrew, and when I met him I could definitely see a resemblance. Jackie piqued my interest because she is someone I would classify as straight-up gay. She is a masculine-identified woman who says she has always desired feminine women; she had her first lesbian relationship at age fourteen. She sees her sexuality as an essential part of herself. Based on my observations of other lesbian mothers in the study, I would not have expected straight-up gay women like Jackie who came out as lesbian at such an early age to have borne a child through heterosexual intercourse—and in fact she had not. Jackie, it turned out, is the adoptive mother of one of her sister's biological children.

Before I interviewed Jackie, I expected her story to be primarily about her experiences as a mother who is masculine-identified. I found, however, that the most salient obstacles for her as a parent concern the day-to-day survival of herself and her immediate and extended family. Jackie's story resonates with the experiences of thousands of other women of color living in the poor urban neighborhoods of yesterday and today. Children raised in harsh urban environments encounter drugs, crime, and violence not only in their neighborhoods but also in their households, and these conditions threaten their survival. The story of Jackie's route to motherhood is a story of her struggle to foster the survival of her family and community by ensuring the survival of her family's children—behavior that Collins identifies as a "fundamental dimension of racial ethnic women's motherwork" (2004b, 49).

Jackie was born into chaotic circumstances in 1962. She has lived her entire life in West Harlem, and during the 1960s and 1970s that area of New York was in many respects characterized by poverty, crime, and drug trafficking. Jackie reports that her mother was "in and out of the house" in violent relationships with men and engaged in drug and alcohol abuse; her grandmother raised Jackie, her brother, and her sister "from birth." Of her three siblings, Jackie is the only one who has managed to live an economically independent adult life. Her brother left home at age thirteen and returned periodically to visit the family until he died in 1993 from complications relating to AIDS. Her sister, Latrice, had her first child at age twenty-one, a second child at age twenty-three, and a third child at age twenty-five. Around the time she had her second child, Latrice fell madly in love with the father of this child, who was a drug dealer. He introduced Latrice to crack cocaine. Latrice now has a total of five children and remains addicted to drugs.[14] Her other four children live with various family members or have been adopted by non-kin through the court system.

Despite the chaos of her family life, Jackie managed to graduate from college with a bachelor's degree. She currently works as an officer in the New York City Department of Corrections. Leaving home to attend school gave her a legitimate excuse for not having to assume any major responsibilities in her family, particularly the care of her sister and her sister's children. She says:

> I went away to college. I just did not want to stay in that household and try to go to school at the same time, because my grandmother was working, so she expected me to take care of my sister and keep an eye on her, and go to school, and help her with the household and everything. And I couldn't see myself doing that because there were too many distractions for me as far as the streets were concerned. . . . I went to SUNY New Paltz, and when I told my grandmother, she begged me not to go. She was like, "What am I gonna do without you?" I was the oldest, I was her right hand. And at that point it became, "You know what? If I stay here, I am not going anywhere in my life." That was a decision that I had to make and stick to, and that's what I did. I went away to college, and my grandmother would call me and say, "Oh your sister—" [and I would tell her,] "I am not interested in hearing it. I didn't have a child—call her mother."

Jackie's remarks suggest that myriad "pull factors" attempting to keep her in a poor economic and family situation might have prevented her from completing college and creating a stable life for herself. They also foreshadow her constant struggle to distance herself from the mothering needs of her family members in order to live an independent life. As the oldest, Jackie was responsible for caring for her brother and sister "for the majority of the time that [they] were growing up," and Latrice still looks to her as a mother figure. When she returned home from college, Jackie felt intense pressure to help her family and to relieve some of the many responsibilities her grandmother had taken on. At the same time, she could feel the pull of the streets and the temptation of drugs, as well as other contextual conditions that threatened to keep her from meeting her goal of attaining stability and independence. This was particularly the case after her grandmother's death. Jackie thinks of her grandmother as the glue that bound the family together, and she says her grandmother raised her to take over that role. Jackie did not want the job, but she wound up taking it on anyway.

Jackie became mother to her son, Andrew, when he was two weeks old. This was not her first experience parenting a child, however. In addition to taking on a parenting role for her siblings, Jackie took in her sister Latrice's first child for a short time while living in her grandmother's apartment in Harlem, though she eventually turned over the parenting of this child to her grandmother. By the time Jackie was thirty-two, Latrice had become the mother of two more children. When Latrice attempted suicide and was taken to the hospital, Jackie was awarded temporary custody of her two nieces. After her sister was released from the hospital, she returned to drugs, and Jackie felt pressure to continue the custody arrangement. She kept the children and parented them for about a month, but she says a combination of factors resulted in a traumatic outcome for the children and for herself:

> The apartment above me was a friend of my sister's, and she [Latrice] would be upstairs partying with this girl . . . and everybody is partying all night long, and I'm working and I got two kids. And of course because they were raised in a household where there was no structure, they was 'buck wild!' . . . The one-year-old was constantly crying and whining and wanting to stay up all night. The three-year-old would curse me out. . . . So I told my sister, this was like a month afterwards, and I am like, "This is crazy." I told her, "If you don't take your kids back, you are going to go into the system and get them, because I don't want no kids."
>
> And she didn't come get them. And the hardest thing I think I've had to do in my whole life was give up those two girls. And I took them down to DCW [Department of Child Welfare]. . . . The scene there, the oldest one was pulling on my legs and she's screaming, "Don't leave me." And the baby, because she sees her screaming, she's screaming, and I'm crying. When I came home, the only thing I wanted to do was kill my sister. Why should I have to be subjected to that? Well, she never went and got them. So they were adopted [into the foster care system].
>
> And at one point, the foster mother was like, "Oh, I'll let you stay in contact with them." But the social worker didn't like me, so she was telling this woman all kinds of stuff [about me], and . . . the next time I went to visit my nieces, the social worker was like, "She doesn't want you to have any contact with the girls anymore." I had sent a money order for my niece's birthday because any birthday, Christmas, or whatever, I always make sure that they have [something]. Well, they sent me the check back and told me that she wanted no contact with me. And that was something that I had to deal with and accept.

After that experience, Jackie was overcome with a range of emotions, including guilt for not wanting to care for her nieces and being denied any further contact with them once they were in the child protective services system, anger at her sister and mother for not having the capacity to care for the children, and remorse for not being able to be the pillar of strength her family needed. After she gave up the children, Jackie became what she calls a "functional addict." She says, "I came from a family of alcoholics and addicts, and that's what I fell right into, even though I had completed college—I was the first one in my family to get my GED, the first person to graduate from college. But besides all of that, I used drugs." At some point, she says, she realized, "I was losing track of who Jackie was, and that for me was more devastating than anything else." When I asked for the signs that she was losing herself, she replied: "It wasn't something that was very overt. One day I got up after getting high, I looked into the mirror and I didn't know who was looking back at me. I just didn't recognize *me*. I felt like it was a demon looking at me back out of the mirror, and . . . at that point, I went to work and I told my boss, 'I need some help.' I went to rehab, and I came out and I started going to AA meetings." Jackie says she realized she had to make a change to avoid going down the same path as her mother and sister. About one year after she stopped using drugs, she got the call about Andrew.

Andrew is Latrice's fourth biological child. When Andrew was born, Jackie would visit him in the hospital, sit with him, and feed him. Soon after one of her visits, she received a call from the hospital saying a urine test revealed cocaine in his system and asking whether she was interested in taking custody of the baby. A number of emotions flooded through her. Even though she told the hospital she needed time to think it over, she said she knew immediately that she would take him, in part to make up for relinquishing her nieces to the child welfare system—an act she still felt guilty about. At this point, she was at a different stage in her life: assuming responsibility for Andrew was, she says, "something that I have chosen to do, not something that was put upon me." She explains: "That's my nephew. That's my blood. I fed him when I went to the hospital, and he had big, big eyes, and he looked at me like, 'Don't let her [Latrice] keep me. You have to help me. Think about your nieces. Think about my sisters.'"

Adopting a child born to a drug-addicted mother has created more stress than Jackie had ever imagined it would, despite her previous experiences with parenting. The difficulties have included the typical financial worries that single mothers often have, among them finding affordable, adequate daycare; battling unexpected ear infections and other illnesses; and sleep deprivation. She also describes having many of the same concerns that other working parents face: feeling that there is not enough time in the day to spend with her son, or trying to figure out how to get him to go to bed at a reasonable hour and to sleep in his own bed.

But Jackie also talks about the joys of having a son. According to Jackie, Andrew has her "wrapped around his little finger. . . . I'm just a sucker for him. He gets me each and every time." She does not consider herself a nurturing person, but she is very affectionate with Andrew. She explains: "I feel that children are supposed to be hugged and kissed. I mean, if Andrew doesn't know anything else, even though I know sometimes he thinks I am the meanest person in the whole world, he also knows that I love him. And I feel that when you have a child, you have to give him that. . . . I buy him—he has everything in the world that he can [have.] . . . I grew up in a household where I couldn't have certain things because my grandmother couldn't afford to give them to me. What did I do? I went in the street. He doesn't have to do that because I give him [everything]. And working for parole, I see so many young Black men come through parole where it is like, 'What went wrong? What happened?' So with Andrew, I look at Andrew and I know that right now it is on me to mold who he is."

Andrew's life with Jackie involves a weekday routine of school, afternoon child care, homework, dinner, bath, and bedtime. His biological mother, paternal grandmother and other paternal relatives, and three siblings (two of Latrice's children and a brother through Andrew's father) also remain in his life. Jackie skillfully navigates herself and Andrew through this intricate web of familial relationships. Andrew has a biological sister living in a foster home in Brooklyn who Jackie regularly checks in on through phone calls and pictures, sometimes taking Andrew and his fourteen-year-old brother, Samuel, to visit. Samuel is Andrew's oldest brother who was first raised by Jackie's grandmother; after her passing, he went to live with his biological father. From time to time, Samuel comes for sleepovers at Jackie and Andrew's home. During one such visit, Samuel told Andrew that Jackie was their aunt and that they shared the same biological mother. When Andrew asked Jackie about it, Jackie told him: "Well, Latrice did give birth to you, yes, that is true. But I'm the mommy, okay. I'm that one that when you don't feel good, I'm there. When you want something from the store, you come to me. Regardless of whatever, Andrew, I'm your aunt, but I'm your mother, and I love you as much as anyone's mother could. So I don't care what Samuel told you, I am your mommy." Andrew replied, "So that means I have two mommies." Jackie replied, "Yes, that's exactly what it means." In reply, Andrew said "Okay," and, as Jackie remembers, "that was the end of that."

Not everyone accepted Jackie's status as Andrew's mother so easily. "With Andrew, they gave me *hell* to get him because of my sexuality"; this comment is Jackie's summary of her experiences navigating the child adoption agency. Jackie was assigned a social worker as part of the process of adopting her nephew. He was a West Indian man, and Jackie thinks his ethnicity had something to do with his negative reaction to her once he discovered her sexuality. Although Jackie was living alone at the time she adopted Andrew, she had a girlfriend who was very feminine looking. Jackie has a transgressive gender presentation, but is also slim, with light skin and soft, long, dreadlocked hair. Men often find her attractive. During the social worker's first visit, he looked at her and suggestively remarked, "Oh, I think you'll make a lovely parent."

During his second visit, however, he noticed a photo of Jackie and her girlfriend sitting on the coffee table. He looked at the picture, turned around and looked at Jackie, returned his gaze to the picture, and then began criticizing the home and suggesting that Jackie would not be a fit parent. He questioned why she had not installed window guards. He asked how she knew she would not put Andrew back in the system, since she had given up her two nieces after saying she would care for them. At the end of this meeting, he said, "Well, I don't know. I don't think this [the adoption] would be a very good idea." At this point, Jackie was working as a parole officer and knew how to navigate the complicated bureaucracy of the New York child welfare system. She began making phone calls to agencies to learn her rights. When the social worker returned for a third visit, he said something that was offensive to Jackie, and she confronted him head-on, saying, "You know what? Right now, I really don't like the way that you are speaking to me, and I'm telling you that I'm feeling uncomfortable, and that does not happen where I pay rent. So I'm asking you to leave."

Jackie made an appointment to meet with her social worker's supervisor. During that interview, she told the supervisor (whom she describes as a Black American woman): "This is my nephew. This is my blood. Not you, not this man, not anyone in this world that's of a mortal nature can tell me that I can't have this child." The supervisor looked at her and told her, "You know what? I think you'll be an excellent mother!" When the social worker returned to Jackie's house with Andrew in tow, she says: "Oh, he was heated. He literally, literally threw him in my arms! I looked at him and said, 'See, I told you—you can't stop what's meant to be.'" He replied, "You know what you are doing is wrong' [referring to Jackie's sexuality]." Jackie responded, "Let me tell you something: If I had a tape recorder, your agency would be paying me for that remark. Trust what I am saying to you." And he stomped out the door.

The series of confrontations Jackie had with both social workers concerned judgments about whether her sexuality, and specifically her gender presentation, made her unfit to be a mother. Her impassioned plea at the supervisor's office, however, was taken as evidence of her fitness for motherhood. Other factors that might have also helped deflect the potentially negative impact of her gender presentation have to do with Latrice's absence, drug addiction, and the number of times she had borne children and put them into the child welfare system. Jackie's economic self-sufficiency, combined with her fierce interest in and love for Andrew, outweighed any negative impact of having a lesbian identity in the agency's final decision-making process. The problems of Andrew's biological mother had lessened the stigma of Jackie's openly gay sexuality.

In describing the relationship African American women have historically had with portrayals of their own sexuality, Black feminist scholars identify themes of Black womanhood that may be enacted differently according to social class. While poor, working-class, and middle-class Black women share a narration of having always to defend their sexuality and morality as women, as partners, and as mothers, they may have different experiences around the expression of sexual agency. Middle-class Black women have a long history of resisting dominant and hegemonic constructions of Black sexuality as licentious with a "politics of silence" around their sexual behavior, as I elaborated on earlier (see Introduction). They perceive a need to "protect the sanctity of inner aspects of Black women's lives" with an image of super-morality.[15] In contrast, Brown (1994) and others note that while some working-class Black women also conform to the politics of respectability with a silence around issues relating to sexuality, others resist losing their sexual agency or an articulation of their sexuality. Davis (1998) argues that Black working-class women's model of womanhood emphasizes strength, resilience, and autonomy in all areas of their lives. She identifies Black working-class music as a site that reveals these women's capability of exercising agency in choosing their partners, and shows their rejection of sexual passivity as a defining characteristic of womanhood. Jackie's refusal to closet her sexuality, even in the face of authority figures that have a heightened interest in her sexuality as it relates to motherhood, supports this alternative notion of Black womanhood that articulates a sense of sexual autonomy.[16]

When Jackie is with her son, she says, she cannot and does not want to separate her status as lesbian from her sense of herself as a parent. She sees herself as being both a mother and a father to her child. Most single parents, regardless of their sexuality, feel that the absence of a partner means they have to fulfill the traditional roles of both mother and father. But there was some suggestion in Jackie's interview that she thinks more concretely than most single parents about how to accomplish this in her relationship with Andrew. On the one hand, she describes behaviors with her son that might be construed as female-gendered. She laughingly remarks, "Andrew is like my husband." She prides herself on being very affectionate with Andrew and admits to acquiescing to his requests for extra toys and games. Interactions of this type are typically associated with mothers: she is emotionally responsive and concerned about Andrew's immediate well-being, stresses the emotional security she brings to their relationship, and works at maintaining Andrew's ties with his biological siblings and other relatives.

On the other hand, Jackie also feels responsible for molding Andrew into a good man, and she attempts to do this through behaviors associated in the developmental psychology literature with father-child interaction. Some of the actions I observed Jackie and Andrew engaging in, along with her description of the activities they participate in on a typical weekend, suggest she is a strong disciplinarian and is physical in her play with him. When I asked Jackie if seven year-old Andrew knows she is gay, she replied, "Andrew knows I'm something! I don't think he fully understands, but yeah." She says she does not hide her sexuality from him, but she is also very careful about bringing home dates—not because she is reluctant to expose her lesbian sexuality to Andrew but because she wants to model responsible sexual behavior. Jackie is concerned about how she may influence Andrew's attitudes toward women as he grows up (she assumes he will be heterosexual). She explained:

> When he was younger, women have spent the night at my house. I don't let that happen when Andrew is home now, because my thing is if I have different women sleeping at my house, in my bed, Andrew is going to think it's okay to do that. You know, I'm single. It's no way for me to—I am not going to even try to justify my behavior, but I know that I don't necessarily want him to have the type of attitude that it is okay to sleep with 50 million different women. That's why I don't show him that. . . . I don't have women jumping in and out of my bed because for me at this particular point in my life . . . I know what [sex] is about. So, for him, if it's going to be about him respecting women when he grows up, then I have to also show respect towards women. I can't make it seem like, "Oh, yeah well I had this one, I had that one" and then expect him to think that it's wrong to do that.

Jackie sees her task as a parent who dates women as one that involves modeling healthy, respectful relationships with women, and her remarks indicate that her sense of sexual agency and approach to modeling respectable womanhood differ from the politics of silence expressed by middle- and upper-middle-class Black women. Jackie's actions are also consistent with studies of father-child relationships that show that fathers contribute to children's development often by acting as "advisors, social guides, and rule providers," and these types of interactions enhance children's self-esteem.[17] Jackie thinks it is important to teach her son how to interact in a positive way with women, and she wants to present behaviors in her dating relationships that reflect this ideal to him. While she is not exactly socializing her son to understand "maleness," this aspect of her parenting style implies that there may be opportunities for children to experience both maternal and paternal interactive styles in lesbian-headed households. Certainly, the gender socialization of children in lesbian-headed households warrants further exploration.[18]

That lesbians like Jackie choose motherhood despite difficult family and environmental circumstances and against societal odds reveals the strong intentionality of motherhood for these women. Contextual factors, as well as a tradition of kinship care and tightly woven interfamilial relationships, have dictated their course toward parenthood more strongly than innate or intense personal desires to mother. These women perceive a *social responsibility* to mother based on other callings from relationships and familial obligations, and these are crucial to consider when defining and explaining lesbian motherhood. The experiences of women like Jackie are not captured in research that limits the study of lesbian motherhood to biological mothers.

Upbringing and personal history also strongly influence experiences of lesbian motherhood. One strong motivating factor behind Jackie's decision to assume responsibility for Andrew was her wish that he not have to experience childhood with an unstable mother as she and her siblings did. In Andrew's case, there was no grandmother to take on the parental role. As the eldest grandchild, Jackie was used to helping her grandmother as an additional stabilizing force in the family, and this was a position she reluctantly assumed more fully once her grandmother passed away. This suggests that sometimes the relationships and connections individuals have built with their family members serve as the impetus for motherhood. Thus far Jackie's sexuality has presented only a minor challenge to her parenting. Her challenges, rather, have involved the important contexts of race, family structure, and the social ills associated with poverty.

Intentional Mothering as Biological Moms and Co-mothers

It was a crisp afternoon in November when I arrived at the home of Nyla Ransom, Zora Hammond, and their three sons. The childhood poverty experiences of both women in this household represent the family backgrounds of two-thirds of the African American women I studied. Zora was born in 1961, and grew up in West Harlem in a low-income, multigenerational household. She entered into a gay sexuality through the straight-up gay pathway described in Chapter 1 and has a gender presentation that hovers between gender-blender and transgressive. Nyla, also born in 1961, was raised in housing projects in a different northeastern city with her alcoholic mother and a father who was in and out of the family. She fits into the conformist pathway of lesbian sexuality, having experienced same-sex attraction in her teenage years but initially not believing that she could or should act on those desires. Nyla's feminine gender presentation complements Zora's less feminine display. But in important ways this couple's present-day lives also resemble many middle-class White lesbian-headed families: both attended elite private colleges and have high-status occupations, and both had a child (or, in Zora's case, twins) in the context of their relationship using alternative insemination techniques. This family shares a large brownstone in Brooklyn, and the house has lots of character, with tall windows, narrow hallways, and steep staircases. It has the lived-in feel often found in households with several kids, two working parents, and no paid housekeeper.

Zora's and Nyla's route to lesbian motherhood involved an intricate web of overlapping paths. The two first met in college in the early 1980s and dated secretly for three years while remaining integrated into various aspects of Black heterosexual life on their predominantly White college campus. Zora even pledged a historically Black sorority. They were inseparable as lovers ("best friends" to the outside world) until senior year, when Zora says that they both felt about their relationship, "This is like a college thing, I can't be doing this at home, you know. Can't take this out of here, can't take this off campus!" After this realization, they each went their separate ways, Nyla to a heterosexual cohabiting relationship with a Black middle-class businessman and Zora to a life of casually dating women. They continued to see each other as "friends," occasionally getting together for intimate liaisons. After three years, they renewed their romantic relationship and decided to make it a permanent one; they have been together ever since.

Nyla and Zora have been moms for many years, in many ways, to several children. Earlier in their relationship, they spent seven years as full-time parents to Nyla's two godsons when the children's biological mother was having difficulties and could not care for them. Nyla says that the experience of raising children was pretty stressful at times, but it also confirmed for them that they wanted to have children of their own. They are currently raising three sons: twin six-year-olds birthed by Zora and a ten-month-old whom Nyla bore. All three of their children were conceived through the in vitro insemination process using sperm from an anonymous Black donor.[19] Their upper-middle-class occupations have afforded them great health insurance plans, as well as additional savings to help pay for these procedures. Their options for donors were rather limited because they wanted Black sperm, and banks have limited numbers of African American donors.[20] They knew of another African American lesbian couple also looking for a Black sperm donor, and this further reduced the pool of potential donors since they did not want their children to have the same biological father as their friends' children.

Zora has always wanted to be a mother. She says: "I just think that for me it just all makes sense for who I am. I don't have an ideology or philosophy about what lesbians do, like there's a handbook, the lesbian handbook—okay, page 1, section 23, can't have children, or you should have children. . . . I just live my life in the way that best suits me and my family. And for me, my life was incomplete without children. . . . Children are not for everybody. There are heterosexual couples that choose to be childless, and that's fine. But I don't think that I should have to forgo that because I happen to be a lesbian."

Though Zora mentioned several times in her interview that she has always wanted children, she still felt some apprehension about having a child as an openly gay woman. She remarked: "I think for me the decision to have biological children was a tough one. The reason I had children so late was because I really wasn't sure if wanted to do it, because I knew it would be a difficult situation for the children more so than me. I didn't want my children to be ostracized or treated a certain way because of me and the choices that I made. But the truth of the matter is that there's always going to be something. . . . You can look at any group of people and say why they shouldn't have children."

Zora's remarks highlight the complex negotiation that lesbians who become mothers make between convention, personal desire, and selfless regard for their children. Lewin (1994) notes that for women who decide to become mothers once their identification as lesbians is firm, the process of becoming a mother demands agency. At the same time, to the degree that wanting to be a mother is perceived as a natural desire, one unmediated by culture or politics, becoming a mother permits a lesbian to move into a more natural or normal status than she otherwise has. In this sense, becoming a mother represents a step toward conformity with conventional gender expectations. But to the extent that it means overcoming the equation of homosexuality with unnaturalness, this transformation allows the lesbian mother to resist gendered constructions of sexuality. Lewin says this act of resistance is paradoxically achieved through compliance with conventional expectations for women, so it may also be construed as a gesture of accommodation (1994, 349).

Both Nyla and Zora wanted to experience conceiving, carrying to term, and giving birth to a child. Each woman adopted the other's biological child shortly after birth, so together they are the legal parents of all three children. The boys call them both "mommy" or, if they need to distinguish between them, by their names. Even though Nyla and Zora both consider themselves full and complete parents of all three children, they also agree that the experience of giving birth to a child produced a qualitatively different feeling than they initially had toward the child or children whom they adopted. When I asked Nyla, the biological mom of the ten-month-old baby, if she feels different with the baby than she did with the twins, she replied: "Yes, oh yes. I didn't think I would, but Zora kept telling me, 'Nyla, it's different.' I would say, 'No—those are my babies, those are my boys.' She would say, 'No, it's going to be different.' . . . And I feel bad, but it's the reality. I thought that I would be able to do more parenting of [the twins] after the baby was born, but he [the baby] is really very demanding. . . . It's very different when you have your own."

Her feeling that "it's very different when you have your own" child as opposed to adopting a partner's child suggests that there is a more intense set of feelings and connection for the biological mother to the child, as other work on this topic has found.[21] As Nyla described how the new baby fits into the family, however, it became clear that the bonding that occurs between biological mother and child, and between adoptive mother and child, is affected by the renegotiation that must take place when a new child enters the home. Nyla's comments about the "difference" in having this baby are also about the adjustments that have had to be made to everyone's schedules and the reduced time available to focus solely on the twins: "So, it's very different when you have your own. But I try, you know I just try to give them [the twins] time too, but I see that it's different because I used to be up there with them just doing things and now it's like, 'Oh—I have to see about the baby.' And then they [the twins] cry." When I asked, "Do you think that that's because he is the one that you conceived, or is it because he's younger?" Nyla replied: "I think it's more so because he is younger, because if I had him first, and then they [the twins] came along, I know that I would probably be catering more to the babies because they just need more. I really have made a conscious effort to try to treat them all the same because they're my children."

While Nyla and Zora have different gender presentations, there seems to be little or no gender distinction in the way they parent the children. When I asked how much the children know about their gay identities, Nyla said: "You know what? I don't think they would say, 'Our moms are gay.' I think they would say, 'We have two moms.' So that's how we put it out there. I can't say that I am a hundred percent sure that they're equating it as being gay or just having two moms." The daily lives of both parents seem to be organized around the well-being of the children. Zora used to work as a corporate attorney at a top law firm. After they had the twins, she left her job to spend more time at home, and she now works as a teacher at a public elementary school. Nyla works full-time as a hospital administrator. Their lives are intertwined in a complex web of school, sports, and various enrichment activities. When asked about some of the positive aspects of her life, Nyla pointed to the "normalcy" of her everyday life and the opportunity to have that experience as a lesbian woman: "I think having a family, seeing them . . . grow to be these great kids. Just the cohesiveness that we have and just being a unit is very nice. And knowing that we are all here for each other. It's upsetting when I hear people say, 'Gay people shouldn't have kids,' because we love our kids just like anybody else. We do the same things with our kids. We probably don't play football, you know, we'll try some basketball. For the most part, we are doing all the same things."

The two primary concerns both mothers have about their family life have to do with one known experience with inequality and one unknown experience. Both women were born in 1961 and came of age in the late 1970s. They were among the first cohorts of African Americans to be admitted to the nation's top predominantly White colleges and universities, and both of them participated in the ABC—A Better Chance program, which was designed to help racial minority high school students prepare for selective colleges by admitting and funding their enrollment at elite prep schools around the country, particularly in the northeast. In this way, they were socialized into a particular type of upper-middle-class life, and they are used to being "the only" or one of very few Blacks in educational, work, and social settings. While they are open to having their sons participate in these types of environments for their schooling, Nyla and Zora also look for social activities for their boys that promote positive, uplifting representations of African Americans. Zora explained:

> Actually we're in this group. I get the e-mail and never go to any of the events—"Park Slope Queer Parents" or something. But the group is predominantly White, and the issue I have with that is my children already go to a predominantly White school, and they're surrounded by White people constantly. And I don't have anything against White people, but at the same time I want them to have a basic understanding and awareness and level of comfort within their own culture. It's like they spend enough time around people who are not like them racially. So those are the times when they do things like their African dance or when they go to karate, that's predominately people of color. And I don't want to take away from that, because we have so many different areas to cover with them, so many different things to make sure that they get, and that [placing the children in environments with other children of gay parents] kind of takes a back seat to some extent.

Zora's comments suggest the importance of race and of promoting healthy racial awareness and development as part of parenting. The twins attend karate classes with other Black children, and all three children have Swahili names. For these upper-middle-class parents, the parenting focus is on how to achieve as balanced and fulfilling a life as possible for the boys—one free from the potential stigma that might be associated with the various identity statuses the family occupies. What remains an unknown but potential threat for them as co-mothers is how society will respond to the boys for having gay mothers. Nyla says she is concerned that her and Zora's gay identities will become a problem for their sons, both in society at large and within the Black community: "That's a very big concern. We want them to be proud and know that this is our choice. It's not their issue. We're concerned about other people making it their issue and trying to hurt them. We don't want them hurt."[22]

In this study, lesbians who become mothers have a particular commitment to learning how to navigate parenthood as lesbians and how to parent in a way that helps all members of the family remain connected to the racial group. They are aware of potential problems or feelings of discomfort for themselves and for their children, but the solution to these concerns rarely involves distancing themselves from their own gay sexuality. This stands in contrast to mothers who become lesbians, who are more likely to express ambivalence about maintaining an openly gay identity in the face of their child's opposition or potential disapproval from society. This is one way that the timing of identity statuses matters for self-definition.

Situational Mothering and Hierarchies of Motherhood in Lesbian Stepfamilies

The final entry to lesbian motherhood that I observed is that of the lesbian stepparent. While both partners in lesbian stepfamilies undergo a series of transitions as they unite to share a household, the partner of the biological mother has often already undertaken a series of transitions that may be different than those faced by the biological mom.[23] None of the women acting as stepparents in their relationships—a total of thirteen—have been heterosexually married, and all of them have a nonfeminine gender presentation. They came out as gay at early ages (eighteen years old on average) and have achieved a level of comfort with and acceptance of their gay sexuality. They experience their homosexuality as part of an identity status that is integrated with a strong racial and/ or ethnic identity, and most have achieved a satisfactory resolution with their kin and racial community regarding their sexuality. These women have sustained connections with the larger African American LGBT community, and they use this community as a primary source of social and emotional support.

Coda Mackey's experiences are similar to many of the lesbian stepparents I interviewed. Coda, a West Indian woman born in 1974, came into her sexuality through the straight-up gay pathway and has a transgressive gender presentation, though large breasts, a small waist, and a bright, pretty smile together confirm she is female. She was attracted to girls and had intimate relationships with young women in high school. Currently, Coda works two jobs and attends college part-time. She has been in a committed relationship with her partner, Daphne, for three years. Daphne, a Puerto Rican woman (b. 1969) did not go to college and operates a child care service from their home. Throughout their relationship, they have shared an apartment in the Bronx with Daphne's biological son Paulie and Daphne's nephew Samuel, for whom they are both foster parents. Despite the legal relationship Coda has with Samuel, she does not consider herself a mother to either of the children, and she is not sure exactly how to define her place in the family aside from being a partner to Daphne. In choosing to be in a relationship with Daphne, she has also taken on the additional responsibility of building a stepparent relationship with Paulie and a less-defined parenting relationship with foster child Samuel.

One of the more pressing issues for this stepfamily concerns the role of Coda, the stepparent, in relation to Daphne, the biological mother, and Jorge, the biological father of the oldest child Paulie. Daphne's pregnancy with Paulie was the result of a casual romantic relationship with Jorge, and it wasn't until the past year that circumstances led to his becoming aware of Paulie's existence. Since that time, Jorge has become involved in Paulie's life by giving Daphne money for Paulie's care and having Paulie visit him and his extended family. Jorge's recent entry into the family has resulted in an even more ambivalent position for Coda. While Coda respects Jorge as the father of Paulie, she also sees his involvement as one more factor that decreases her status in the household. Coda says, "I was a big part of Paulie's life before and now all of a sudden I'm on the bottom of the scale with him. And I just have to realize I'm really not important anymore." For example, Daphne and Jorge decided together that Paulie would spend part of the Christmas holiday with Jorge's family, and Coda did not become aware of this until it was time for Jorge to pick up Paulie on Christmas day.

Coda's status as a parent is very much defined by her lesbian sexuality: she is only a parent to the extent that she partners with a lesbian mother. She has no intention of ever dating men and no desire to physically bear a child, so unless she adopts a child at some point in her life, her status as a parent is tied to her relationships with women. Her experiences with parenting are not intentional but rather situational, and affect the status she is able to garner within the family unit. The issues that impact lesbian stepfamily functioning are explored more fully in Chapter 5.

DISCOURSES OF RESPECTABILITY AND CONTEXTUAL INFLUENCES ON THE ENACTMENT OF LESBIAN MOTHERHOOD

Claiming a lesbian identity makes the mothers in my study particularly sensitive to whether they are being seen as "good mothers" by others. Collins (2000) once argued that feminist theorizing about motherhood at times distorts and omits large categories of human experience. I find that focusing on Black women within the study of lesbian motherhood draws attention to ways in which the pursuit of self-definition can be mediated by membership in different racial and social class groups, and it reveals how issues of identity are crucial to all "motherwork." The social locations of Black women born in the 1960s and 1970s not only shape the ideologies they bring to the experience of parenting as lesbian women, but also shape the parenting experience itself. The contexts in which these processes of and decisions around mothering are taking place are what distinguish the lesbian mothers I interviewed from the White middle-class lesbian mothers whose experiences have previously drawn the attention of researchers.

More than twenty years ago DiLapi (1989) argued that lesbian motherhood is "inappropriate motherhood," relegated to the bottom of the parenting hierarchy because lesbian-headed families do not include a father, the women are not primarily supported by a husband, both parents tend to be engaged in full-time paid work and are therefore not completely devoted to home life, and the adults' enactment of same-sex desire suggests they pursue self-fulfillment over self-sacrifice. While one might question the legitimacy of this sentiment today, we need only look at the various state laws that continue to ban openly gay people from adopting children to recognize its continued relevance in certain parts of the country. The primary consideration many courts continue to ponder regarding the legality of same-sex marriage, moreover, concerns whether a child raised by two partners of the same sex faces an undue disadvantage relative to children raised by heterosexually married parents.[24]

In contrast, the motherhood hierarchy in Black communities has never relied as heavily on these traditional constructions and behavioral expectations of motherhood. To be a good mother has required one to provide for one's children, to retain custody or keep children out of child protective services even during hard times, and to do the best that one can to work and give children the things they need. Until very recently, it was rare to see Black mothers raising their children in openly lesbian co-habiting relationships, so Black communities did not need to define gay motherhood as "inappropriate motherhood" in any consistent manner. Instead, inappropriate mothers were those who suffered from drug addictions or who left their children unattended and in harm's way. Jackie Roberts suggested this point many times during the course of her interview when she described her addicted sister's poor parenting and her own mother's violent relationships with men. Despite Jackie's openly gay sexuality (and transgressive gender presentation), she sees herself as a better mother than her own heterosexual mother and sister.

Unlike lesbian mothers examined in past research, my respondents are not strong proponents of actively altering existing systems of motherhood, because they have been socialized in contexts that allow for a wider range of nontraditional parenting, such as parenting outside of marriage or parenting with limited financial means. Instead, the women in this work attempt to adopt a practice of *assimilationism*, which Hequembourg defines as "a constellation of discursive practices aimed at emphasizing similarity as a strategy to attain equality" (2007, 4). As Blacks and as gays, they seek social change that will facilitate their integration into existing social structures. Even when they oppose structures of domination, they see their success as rooted in how well they are able to conform to the expectations created by those structures. The twist, however, is that their efforts to assimilate are carried out in ways that are in opposition to how we understand assimilation. They are not merely attempting to reproduce the Black communities that they are in. I see their choices, rather, as attempts to enact an identity in which race and sexual orientation inform and therefore modify one another. Choosing to enact a gay sexuality in the context of a previous heterosexual identity as mother and a racial and gender identity as Black woman is a political act that is communal and collective as well as psychological or individual. Black lesbian motherhood has the potential to confront sexual stigma and dismantle some of the key frameworks of Black women's character that find Black women internalizing stigma (self- and other-directed), shame, silence, secrecy, and self-protection at any cost.[25] Making a choice to confront stigma in the context of Black lesbian motherhood might mean challenging the emptiness and stifled sense of self that Althea Payne and others evoke in their stories.

TIMING OF MOTHERHOOD AND LESBIAN IDENTITY

In different, sometimes conflicting ways, lesbian sexuality as an identity status is important to how the mothers in this study define themselves. One finding that stands out is that mothers who became lesbians and lesbians who became mothers involve their children in lesbian community life very differently. Women who had children before coming out as gay tend to compartmentalize their lesbian sexuality and their children. The statuses of "lesbian" and "mother" are largely separate and distinct for them. They must figure out how a gay sexuality fits into their self-definition and whether and how to incorporate it into other components of both their own and their children's lives, including self-identities at work, the social roles they have typically played in their broader kinship networks, and relationships with their children's biological fathers. Some of these mothers have not yet come out to the children and do not want the children or the children's fathers to know about their sexuality, while others are open with their older children about their sexuality. These mothers are also less likely to involve their children in lesbian social events and may understand their lesbian practice as part of "adult social activities" they participate in, or behavior that does not have to be carried out in private but nevertheless should not be visible to the child. They are cautious about inviting friends over when the child is at home and are not likely to be demonstrative with their mates when the children are present. They see themselves as moms first when they are with the child and want their lesbian sexuality to take a backseat or become less visible. For mothers who become lesbians, motherhood does not represent a larger share of their identities relative to lesbians who become mothers, it just represents a separate realm, a more distinctive component that exists in addition to, rather than together with, a gay sexuality.

In contrast, lesbians who become mothers are more likely to involve their children in the gay community.[26] They incorporate the statuses of mother and lesbian into their sense of self in more complete and multidimensional ways than do women who become mothers before they identify as lesbian. They show a strong commitment to lesbian sexuality as an identity status that is a visible part of their lives, and they seek ways to blend their lesbian identity with their new status as mothers. They and their families have strong connections to the lesbian community, and invite others to celebrate their status as mothers with them. They rely more significantly on other lesbian-led families for validation and social support. In turn, their success at becoming parents serves as positive encouragement to other gay people who wish to become parents. These women also bring their status as lesbian mothers into the heterosexual world, inviting work colleagues, neighbors, and others to unify these aspects of their identity that they have woven together.

Social class is important to this group's success in blending their lesbian and mothering identities. Because women who come out as gay before having children have been able to devote more time to schooling and career advancement, they tend to have higher levels of education, higher incomes, and higher-status jobs than mothers who subsequently become lesbians. These processes may have all taken place before childbearing, such that when these women enter into motherhood they have already learned how to negotiate their sexuality and may have had to invest a greater amount of time and effort into the process of having a child. They are more likely to have a concrete, firmly entrenched lesbian identity, seeing gay sexuality as a way of life rather than an activity they may partake of during their leisure.

Lesbians who enter parenthood through a stepfamily relationship with a woman who already has a child are the most detached in their parenting. Unlike co-parents who have the child together in the context of a lesbian relationship, these stepparents tend not to define themselves primarily in relation to the children in the home. They tend to compartmentalize the children and do not discuss them much within the lesbian community. Indeed, in the case of Coda Mackey, I had known her for over a year before she ever mentioned the parenting conflicts in her household. Parenthood represents a small share of the lesbian stepmother's self-identity—if any share at all. Lesbian stepparents often lack a legal place in the family unit, and this makes the stepparent and her partner less certain about how she fits into the household.

Harlem couple on their
wedding day, 2006.
Photo by Pickers
Studios, Brooklyn, NY.

Top: Sunday afternoon in the park. Photo by author.

Bottom: Family day in Prospect Park, Brooklyn, NY. Photo by author.

Top: Three brothers. Photo by author.

Bottom: Mom sees her daughter off to join Naval Sea Cadets. Photo by Esther Holmes.

Brooklyn couple
and their two daughters.
Photo by author.

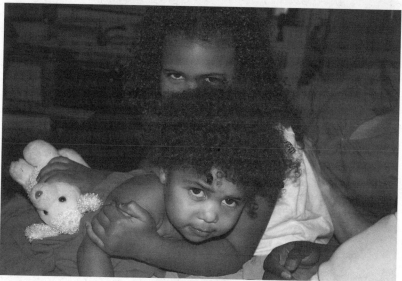

Top: Holding the littlest one. Photo by author.

Bottom: Two sisters. Photo by author.

Mom with her preteen
in Harlem, NY. Photo by
Norma Moreno.

Jamaican couple in Greenwich Village, NY. Photo by Elaine Harley.

Enjoying a Sunday afternoon
in the backyard. Photo
by Elaine Harley.

Harlem mom with her sons. Photos by Elaine Harley.

Couple in downtown Brooklyn, NY. Photo by author.

Top: Moms with their children. Photo by author.

Bottom: Off to Disney World! Photo by author.

CHAPTER 5

Family Life and Gendered
Relations between Women

Shelly Jackson, a thirty-eight-year-old city bus driver, lives with her three children in a high-rise housing project in East New York. Her partner, Shaunte Austin, moved in with the family two years ago. Commenting on how she and her partner divide the household finances, Shelly says that regardless of sexuality, each person should bring her or his own resources to a relationship: "I don't give a damn who you're with, you always need to be able to be independent and take care of yourself." I heard echoes of Shelly's remark from the overwhelming majority of the lesbian couples to whom I spoke about finances and the division of household labor.

Studies of heterosexual family life tell us that, with few exceptions, power dynamics and gender stratification in these families are defined by men's greater earning power, in combination with gender ideologies. Even when husbands earn less than their wives, a norm of greater male power and decision-making authority is the dominant organizing principle.[1] Since the 1970s, feminist research on the division of labor in families has strongly discouraged the gender specialization model of husband as primary wage earner and wife as primary caretaker of the home, instead favoring a particular egalitarian division of labor whereby partners have joint responsibility for both breadwinning and homemaking aspects of cohabiting life (Walby 1990).[2] This model encourages both individuals to have equal concern for and commitment to the lower-status work of household organizing that has historically been relegated to women. Feminist perspectives that originated in the 1970s women's liberation movement saw women's economic contributions through work as insufficient to raise their status within the family unit; men's equal responsibility for home life would also be necessary.[3]

In lesbian relationships, however, there is no sex difference between partners, and since most households have two earners, partners tend to be on a more even financial footing (Peplau and Fingerhut 2007). Indeed, Shelly's remark and others like it suggest that some Black lesbian couples may place a premium on one aspect of egalitarianism: financial independence. Given this context, should we also expect to find a more equal distribution of housework and child care in these households, or might different aspects of egalitarianism be more important to the well-being of these relationships? We know from contemporary research into same-sex parenthood that in lesbian families where one partner has become pregnant through alternative insemination, the lack of sex distinctions between partners tends to result in relationships wherein couples divide paid work, housework, and child care in a relatively equal way. Many of today's educated lesbians organize their family lives using the feminist egalitarian framework, meaning they seek to equalize the balance of marital power by distributing housework and child care duties across the couple using an "ethic of equality." They create relationships that reject the specialization of family roles, linking such specialization to gender inequality in heterosexual unions. While the division of tasks in lesbian-headed households is not always as equal as subjects portray their families to be, and while the biological parents in these households tend to spend more time on child care, particularly during the months immediately after birth, such lesbian couples do tend to actively discourage hierarchical relationships between partners, and they believe that neither partner should have greater authority because she has greater resources.[4]

One limitation to existing research on lesbian family formation, however, is that it is almost entirely based on the experiences of college-educated White lesbians who share an ideological commitment to having an egalitarian relationship—a commitment that originated in 1970s second-wave feminism. We do not know whether the tendency toward more egalitarian relationships exists generally among lesbian couples. It may be the case that previous studies have overrepresented families that follow these principles. Important processes around mothering may also have been obscured by data drawn disproportionately from White middle-class women with particular feminist leanings. The scholarly focus on couples who use alternative insemination to bring children into same-sex unions tends to overlook the reality that for the majority of today's lesbian families, and particularly for Black women, children primarily enter the family through their mothers' prior heterosexual relationships, making most lesbian-headed households similar in structure to heterosexual stepfamilies.[5] Women who bear children in heterosexual unions may experience particularly gendered understandings of mothering that they take with them as they begin to parent in lesbian relationships—understandings that could have consequences for expectations of household organization and divisions of labor.

Likewise, it is worth considering how race might influence the ways in which Black lesbians approach the division of financial responsibility and household labor with their partners. Noted Black feminist Cheryl Clarke made a similar point when she argued that Black lesbians are conditioned to be self-sufficient because of their experiences of being raised in Black families so poor that they "did not have the luxury to cultivate dependence among the members of their families" (1995, 247). If we look carefully at the tenets of Black feminist thought, we see that self-reliance, autonomy, and self-actualization are key to Black women's advancement and self-liberation.[6] However, not much has been written about the equal distribution of housework and child care as avenues of Black women's liberation. This does not suggest that the equal division of household chores is not important to this population or that Black heterosexual women want to do more of the housework in their families. Rather, it suggests that other areas of inequality have been more salient for Black women, and that what is particularly important in organizing their households is the joint contribution of finances—perhaps more important than spending equal amounts of time on family chores.

We also know that historically, labor, whether paid or unpaid, voluntary or coerced, has been a distinctive characteristic of Black women's experiences in families.[7] Nevertheless, Blacks in heterosexual marriages are more likely than are White couples to bank separately and less likely to use the egalitarian money-management system of jointly controlled financial accounts.[8] The greater employment experience of Black heterosexual women and their greater use of "separate pots" rather than joint pooling systems emphasize the economic aspect of egalitarianism in Black heterosexual households. A comparison of Black and White heterosexual couples in the National Survey of Family and Households found, for example, that Black women hold more favorable attitudes toward women's labor force participation even while holding less egalitarian attitudes toward female-typed domestic work in families (Kamo and Cohen 1998).

At the same time, women and mothers have an authoritative status in the organization of African American family life. This is partially due to the higher rates of single parenthood and greater responsibilities for child rearing among Black women, but certain aspects of African American culture also emphasize motherhood as a revered status. Gilkes (2001) illuminates the power held by women in mainline Black Christian denominations. The title of "church mother" is bestowed upon older women who have been long-standing congregants and have shown leadership and faithfulness over time. Along with this title comes a particular type of power and authority. Special seats are reserved for church mothers in Sunday services, and they are given the authority to discipline parishioners and provide guidance to worshipers. Pastors often consult with the church mothers before making important decisions because church mothers maintain such a powerful influence over key congregants.[9] The status of "mother" in Black family life, therefore, might influence decision making in households headed by lesbians raised in predominantly Black contexts. If African American lesbians organize family life in ways that are consistent with Black heterosexual households, we should expect to see high levels of economic independence between both partners, but we should not necessarily expect this financial independence to be accompanied by an expectation to equally distribute all of the household chores and child care.

All of these perspectives on the organization of Black family labor suggest a need to reevaluate the social organization of Black lesbian households. Family process, household organization, and the division of labor are analyzed in this chapter to determine the way this population of Black same-sex couples structures bargaining and decision making in the home. I focus on the seventy-four respondents who were living in couple households at the time of my fieldwork. Thirty-two are in stepfamilies, eight had children together using alternative insemination, and thirty-four are cohabiting with no children in the home. Drawing from field notes wherein I observed the interactions among these couples inside their homes and in various social settings, their responses to questions on the survey, their responses to questions during the in-person individual interviews, and the perspectives shared in the focus group on family and relationship dynamics, I show that Shelly's comment that "You always need to be independent and take care of yourself" has great resonance in Black lesbian-headed households. Economic independence, rather than the egalitarian distribution of household chores, is the primary feminist organizing mechanism in these families, and the different emphasis of Black lesbians relative to the White middle-class gay women represented in most previous studies can be traced to the different goals of lesbian-feminism and Black feminist ideologies. I also point to the importance of the status of "mother" as an alternative mechanism creating hierarchies in stepfamily households where partners are not differentiated by sex (see also Moore 2008). Finally, I argue that gendered presentations of self in Black lesbian relationships are associated with some of the household tasks partners take on in the home.

MEASURING EGALITARIAN IDEOLOGIES AND BEHAVIOR

To measure egalitarian ideologies and behavior, I first considered whether the women in this work expect both partners to co-provide, which would be consistent with the literature on lesbian-headed families, or if one partner tends to possess the greater economic responsibility to the family, as we see in heterosexual couples. The data show that both partners are likely to be employed: 84 percent of women in cohabiting relationships are working or in school full-time. Dual employment was important to the women I studied. When asked what characteristics she looks for in a partner, Ro Gaul (b. 1966) gave a response that was typical of the working-class women in the study: "They have to be working because I'm extremely independent, and I believe everybody should work. I grew up as a young child working, and I am still working. So I believe that you must have a job. If it means that the job is paying you enough for you to maintain yourself or your own independence, you have to be working." Carlie Lewis is a hairstylist who lives with her partner of three years, Berit Fontaine. They have no children. When asked how they divide the bills and deal with household finances, Carlie answered bluntly: "I love her to death and trust her more than any female I've ever known. [But] she ain't getting' my check. You know what I'm saying? And I don't want her check. You work for your money. As long as you take care of responsibilities we got in the house, I don't care what you do with your money."

Class backgrounds and experiences growing up provide different explanations for why self-sufficiency is so important to the women in my study.[10] Women raised in working-class families encourage economic independence because they tend to see everyone in the household as having an equal responsibility to bring in financial resources to help the family get ahead; they also want to have the income necessary to escape unstable or unhealthy relationships. Middle-class lesbians tend to view economic independence as important in their relationships because they have seen how the presence or absence of their own mother's employment facilitated or hindered her personal growth and self-actualization. For example, Dr. Renee Martin, a high-ranking physician at a major metropolitan hospital, discusses the importance of financial independence for her partner Naja Rhodes, a social worker, in terms of how to help Naja achieve greater independence and fulfillment in her own career. Renee was born in 1967 and raised with her younger sister in a Black middle-class neighborhood in New Orleans. Her father was one of the first African Americans to receive a doctorate in Chemical Engineering. After having two children, Renee's mother continued to work as a college professor, recently retiring after achieving the rank of associate dean. Although Renee's father earned more than her mother, throughout her childhood she witnessed her mother in a middle-class occupation that she found personally fulfilling.

Renee's discussion of financial independence does not mention economic survival or a worry about being able to provide for herself in the absence of an employed partner. These issues are not part of how she envisions her life nor are they part of her past experiences. Coming from a socioeconomically secure background and having a high status and lucrative occupation precludes Renee from many of the same worries expressed by working-class women. She could easily take on the traditional provider role in her relationship, relieving Naja from any obligation to contribute financially to the household. Instead, Renee's discussion of egalitarianism in her relationship involves helping her partner achieve greater independence and fulfillment in her career. Renee encourages Naja to own her own property and has shown her how to build wealth. Renee's interest in financial independence for herself and her mate is motivated by middle- and upper-middle-class outlooks and experiences.

While all of the couples reported sharing responsibility for household bills, just 57 percent of them actually shared a bank account. Partners value self-sufficiency and autonomy, and these values get transmitted in the relationship through the maintenance of separate financial accounts. Control over their own finances allows both partners to claim a co-provider role even when their incomes are not equal. It also makes it easier for the partners to exit the relationship in case of dissolution.

Consider the experience of Marilyn Richards, president of a national nonprofit organization. When asked whether partners should pool all of their assets in a relationship, she emphatically disagreed, saying: "We have our own money, our own accounts, and we have household funds that we use to do the lawn, the snow removal. . . . We met as fully-formed adults with other obligations in our lives. I think that we should pool the assets [for things] that we want to do together like [buy] a home, a car, which we do, a savings together for things. She is my beneficiary along with my son, and I am hers along with her children, so that is pooling out in the afterlife, so to speak. But she doesn't ask me how I spend my money, and I don't ask her how she spends hers. She has a job—and a very responsible one—and we have our own discretionary income."

Marilyn's comment mentions a notion of "pooling to build up," or combining income to reach a common goal, such as the purchase of a home. But it also demonstrates a strong interest in preserving financial independence—an emphasis that the survey data also reflect, particularly among women who are the biological mothers of children. This interest persists even when they contribute fewer financial assets than their partners and would receive the greater economic benefit from comingling funds. Relative to their partners, biological mothers (bio-moms) in stepfamilies were less likely to agree with the statement, "The two mates should pool all their property and financial assets." Responses in the in-depth interviews suggest that this hesitancy stems in part from many bio-moms' having navigated a history of relationship transitions and cohabiting partners while raising their children. The majority of the bio-moms bore children in past heterosexual relationships, spending time as single mothers and sole economic providers for their children prior to cohabiting in their lesbian relationships. Their past experiences influence how those who have created lesbian stepfamilies organize the household finances.

For example, Adina Montany, an artist, shares a very comfortable home in a New Jersey suburb with her partner, Dr. Beverly Howard, a physician, and Beverly's one-year-old daughter. Adina has been in other cohabiting relationships and has adopted a philosophy toward comingling assets that reveals both a belief that couples should jointly participate in building assets and a wariness of the difficulties of disentangling comingled resources in the event of a breakup. Even though Adina brings considerably fewer assets to the relationship than Beverly, she believes it is in her best interest to maintain her financial autonomy. She says: "If you are really in love with the person that you're with, and you're really willing to share, then you can share out of your own account. You know, there are things that you can do that don't require you to get all that paperwork that makes it hard to get out of when you separate or if you separate."

Not only do the majority of Black lesbians in this study value economic independence for themselves, they also find it an important characteristic in their mates. While they accept as reasonable their partners' taking time off from work for a career change or additional schooling, they feel that work instability or the prolonged absence of employment causes problems in a relationship and constitutes a "deal breaker." When asked how happy she is with the way she and her partner, Shaunte, divide household responsibilities, Shelly comments that she is happier in the relationship now that her partner has found a job: "Don't get me wrong. She has always been so good to me as far as helping me out with the kids, 'cause my hours is crazy and Shaunte is somebody I could depend on. But it was hard when she wasn't working. She wasn't having no income coming in, and I was like, 'I'm not your sugar mama!'" This final comment emphasizes Shelly's expectation that Shaunte will contribute economically to the home at the same time that it draws on negative images of women's dependence on a male "sugar daddy." Shelly later said that when Shaunte was unemployed, she would have dinner ready for Shelly, would help the children with their homework when Shelly was at work, and would put the children to bed when Shelly worked late hours. While Shelly acknowledged and appreciated Shaunte's work around the home, it did not compensate for her lack of financial resources.

Previous studies have not analyzed well the feminist principle of economic independence in lesbian relationships, emphasizing instead those ideologies related to the division of housework and child care. My survey asked three opinion questions to measure the strength of egalitarian attitudes among partnered women in the study: "Both mates in a relationship should divide evenly the household tasks (washing dishes, preparing meals, doing laundry, etc.)," "If both mates work full-time, both of their career plans should be considered equally in determining where they will live," and "It is better if one person in the relationship takes the major financial responsibility and the other person takes the major responsibility of caring for the home." Each respondent was also asked how often she, relative to her partner, was responsible for thirteen different household chores, and she was also asked to report how many hours per week she and her partner each spent on household chores.

Responses to these questions show that the majority of respondents profess views that are consistent with feminist measures of equality or egalitarianism in relationships. Eight-four percent agreed or strongly agreed that both mates should divide household tasks evenly, 89 percent agreed or strongly agreed that both partners' career plans should be equally considered when making decisions about where to live, and 84 percent disagreed or strongly disagreed with the specialization model of one person taking on the major financial responsibility and the other person primarily caring for the home. In face-to-face interviews, I asked respondents how they divided housework and finances and how satisfied they were with their current arrangements. I also spent afternoons at the homes of some respondents, observing them as they prepared for birthdays or dinner parties, taking notes on the actual work each person performed, how they talked about the work they each put into the events, how they felt about the work their partners performed, and how satisfied they were with these arrangements.

Despite their ideological agreement with feminist egalitarian principles, when it came to carrying out the daily chores, the respondents did not actually behave in egalitarian ways.[11] The data show clear indications of specialization, particularly in households with children: the biological mothers in these families tend to perform more of the household organizing tasks, assume responsibility for making sure various chores and activities are implemented smoothly, and see the household and the efficiency with which it is run as a representation of themselves as good partners to their mates and as good mothers. In families with children, one person tends to spend much more time performing household chores. While this is sometimes a source of frustration for the partner who does more housework, it is not the primary source of conflict in their relationships and it is not the primary measure of whether they believe their relationships to be fair. Self-sufficiency and autonomy are highly valued, and respondents place a premium on economic independence rather than the division of family labor as a value and behavior that is critical for relationship satisfaction.

In lesbian stepfamilies, the bio-mom assumes more of the responsibility for household chores. Bio-moms in these households tend to perform the time-consuming and female-stereotyped chores more often than their partners. Thirty-two percent of survey respondents reported spending equal amounts of time washing dishes, while 48 percent said that bio-moms spent more time on this task and only 20 percent said that

TABLE 1. DIVISION OF LABOR IN LESBIAN STEPFAMILIES: CERTAIN HOUSEHOLD TASKS ARE NECESSARY TO KEEP THINGS RUNNING SMOOTHLY. WHO DOES EACH OF THESE TASKS MORE OFTEN?[1]

Household Chores	We Do This Equally (%)	Bio-Mom Does This More (%)	Partner Does This More (%)
Washes dishes	32	48	20
Does laundry	36	52	13
Cleans bathroom	16	64	16
Cleans floors	6	73	21
Arranges daily meals	23	39	32
Straightens family room	16	67	15
Dusts furniture	16	75	8
Grocery shopping	34	24	42
Mixes drinks for company	30	52	18
Takes out trash	25	18	56
Repairs things around house	14	48	37
Cares for pets	20	32	48
Performs yard work	18	32	54

[1] These questions are modified from those in Blumstein and Schwartz (1983) and Cowan and Cowan's "Who Does What" scales (1990). It contains five possible responses ranging from 1 (*She does this much more*) to 5 (*I do this much more*). In my data analysis, the measure was collapsed into three categories: 1 (*She does this more*); 2 (*We do this equally*); and 3 (*I do this more*).

the bio-mom's partner spent more time washing dishes (see Table 1 for detailed responses regarding the division of household tasks). When asked how much time each person spent on household chores, on separate surveys respondents from the same households tended to agree that the bio-mom spent much more time each week on chores than did her partner, at an average of 11.4 hours per week versus the partner's 5.2 hours. Partners on average reported spending 4.4 hours per week on chores relative to the bio-mom's 12.1 hours per week.[12] In research on two-earner heterosexual couples, husbands have tended to undercount the amount of time their wives spend on housework (Ferree 1991). In this study, however, lesbian partners perceived bio-moms as spending *more* time each week on housework than bio-moms reported for themselves, suggesting a greater acknowledgment of or respect for work around the home that has traditionally been defined as women's work.

The bio-moms who take care of the daily cleaning needs of the home (i.e., cooking, dishes, general cleaning, and straightening of rooms) complained about the imbalance and criticized the way their partners completed the tasks they have usually assigned to them. The response of

Dana Russell, the bio-mom of seventeen-year-old Marina, in reference to her partner, Angie Russell, is typical: "Am I happy with it? She don't do nothing! [laughs] But it wasn't an issue. She'll do the laundry or she'll go to the grocery store or take me, which is important, because I can't carry things because I hurt my back. We've always done the laundry together, pretty much. We've always done the food shopping together. Anything around the house, I've got to kind of bitch to get her to do stuff." There is some evidence here that bio-moms, as household organizers, can delegate to their partners the chores they want them to perform. Dana acknowledges that her partner, Angie, performs less housework, and her comments suggest this is both a problem ("I've got to kind of bitch to get her to do stuff") and something she accepts about the relationship ("She don't do nothing! [laughs] But it wasn't an issue").

I repeatedly found this inconsistency both in the interview data and in my observational notes. Bio-moms expressed frustration about the unequal amounts of time partners were allotting to household chores, but they also expressed an acceptance, often accompanied by a modest boasting about their superior cleaning and organizational skills, which called for them to continue to have the final say over those areas of family life. Consider this exchange that I had with Jocelyn Barnum in reference to her partner, Joi Jamison:

I: *Are you happy with the way you and your partner divide household responsibilities? How does that work in your relationship?*

Jocelyn: I mean, she steps up to the plate. I'm the domestic person, I do the cooking, I do the laundry. She does the cleaning, we both do the cleaning. I think I do more of the household stuff though, and sometimes I just want her to probably do more without me having to ask her. Let me just say this in her defense though, she will say to me, "Oh, I'll do the dishes," and I'll say, "Oh no, I've got it," because sometimes I just think I wash dishes faster than her. So instead of her standing over the sink for an hour, we can have more quality time. So she does volunteer to do it, and I'll say, "Oh no, I'll do it."

I: *Are you happy with the way the household is run?*

Jocelyn: Yes. (pauses) Yes.

Jocelyn is a professional woman who owns her own educational consulting firm and is the bio-mom of Issim, her seventeen-year-old son. Despite her professional identity, she identifies herself as "the domestic person" in her relationship with Joi. On separate surveys, both Jocelyn and Joi reported that Joi spends eight hours per week on housework. Jocelyn says she spends seventeen hours on chores, while Joi says Jocelyn devotes forty hours each week to chores. Looking more closely at the meaning behind the division of labor in these stepfamilies, I found that bio-moms accept the greater responsibility for various aspects of household organization not because they like washing dishes or cleaning the living room but because having control over those areas allows them to also have a strong say, and sometimes the deciding voice, in other aspects of the family that are important to them, particularly money management and child rearing.

MONEY MANAGEMENT, CHILD-REARING CONFLICTS, AND THE STRENGTH OF THE HOUSEHOLD ORGANIZER POSITION

Sonjee Montag, the mother of two teenage boys, recalls the financial powerlessness she felt many years ago after leaving the father of her children, who had been the family's sole economic provider. She granted temporary custody of her sons to their grandmother until she was able to get back on her feet and re-enter the labor force. While her current partner, Corey James, gets along well with her children, Sonjee is emphatic about being the money manager for the household. When asked if she is happy with the way she and Corey divide financial responsibilities, Sonjee said: "I can tell you right now, Corey cannot financially manage money. I manage the money in this household, only simply because Corey knows my first priority is my sons, but my next after that is my damn bills. I do not play when it comes to the bills. Corey knows if I'm down to my last, I will pay a bill."

Sonjee's comment suggests the critical importance that money management can take on for women in lesbian stepfamilies. Pahl's (1983) research on the allocation of money makes a distinction among the control, management, and budgeting of money as three distinct points in the flow of financial resources through the household. I find that at the point where money first enters the family, both partners in lesbian stepfamilies *negotiate* how the money will be allocated, meaning they decide together how much money will be needed to pay the bills each month and how much of their own funds each person will contribute toward these expenses. But biological mothers usually take the lead in *managing*, or putting into operation, the allocative system the couple has adopted. This includes the more detailed work of deciding how much money will be apportioned for each expenditure (e.g., how much they will spend on groceries or how much will go toward credit card debt). The bio-mom makes sure bills are actually paid and that there is enough money to fuel the car or to pay for new shoes for the child. The bio-mom is also usually in charge of *budgeting*, or the more time-consuming work of deciding which foods to buy, whether the children need new clothes for the first day of school, whether the family should have the premium or standard cable TV package, and the like.

Consider the Adams family. Anita and Trina Adams share a small two-bedroom apartment in Harlem with Anita's two daughters. Anita did not finish college, while Trina is a college graduate and earns about $12,000 more per year than Anita. Anita and Trina pool their money for household expenses, but Anita writes out the checks and makes sure the bills are paid. Anita primarily draws from her own income to support her daughters and from time to time will divert household money to school clothes or holiday gifts, instructing Trina to assume more financial responsibility for the monthly bills. Anita is more likely to factor the needs of the children into the family's financial decisions and is more outwardly concerned with how the distribution of finances will affect the girls.

When I asked Trina how she and Anita divide household chores, she said, "Well, I do the laundry. I cook, I clean up, but it's like I'm very sporadic. Anita will kick my boots or something, or she'll go [makes a sound like she's clearing her throat] and she'll look at the living room, and I'll start cleaning it. But she definitely does the chores way more than I do." On separate surveys, both Anita and Trina reported that Anita performs more of the daily tasks like washing dishes, straightening the rooms, and emptying the trash, while Trina participates more equally in tasks that are less frequent, like the grocery shopping and laundry. They both report that Anita spends twice as much time per week on household chores.

Relying on the survey data alone might lead one to the conclusion that Trina has more authority in the relationship: she has more education and a higher salary than Anita, carries fewer family responsibilities, and gets away with doing less work around the home. Because Anita is the bio-mom and was a single mother prior to meeting Trina, she might be thought of as the person bringing more baggage into the relationship. The qualitative data, however, suggest that the decisions Anita makes actually carry more weight in the family. Trina moved into a household that was already established by Anita, so in this sense Trina is the new addition and must adapt to a structure that already has Anita as the leader and organizer. Anita is the money manager and makes the decisions about how to allocate family finances, including Trina's own personal wants and needs. Anita enjoys having this type of authority: in her interview, she proudly told me, "I'm the bill keeper. She [Trina] gives the finances, I stay on the bills. I'm like 'Look, this is due.' And it works out pretty good. We have a good little system going on with the bills."

Anita's position in the family does impose more constraints on her time, and she expresses frustration over the additional hours she spends on household chores. But while Anita may want her partner to do more work around the house, she does not want Trina to assume more child-rearing responsibilities or more influence over how their money is spent. Anita's control over the family's finances allows her to decide how much of their funds each month will go to bills, the children's needs, and her and Trina's own personal wants and needs. Because the allocation of money toward family expenditures is not done jointly but rather is primarily performed by Anita, Anita's decisions play a significant role in determining the proportion of Trina's paycheck that Trina has left over for her own leisure activities. Anita has a full-time job, and her family was functioning before she met Trina, so while Trina is an important co-provider (her income enabled the family to move out of their apartment into a house that Trina and Anita eventually purchased together), the utility of her economic contributions is tempered by the knowledge that the family can survive without her.

The lesbian family literature says couples jointly make decisions about how money will be spent because control in this arena is a sign of a more fundamental power that neither person thinks one partner should assume on her own. The literature on heterosexual family life says that having the responsibility for the daily task of money management is the lower-status position, and that the person with the greater economic resources is able to "buy" his way out of having to do this work and has the power to challenge and even "veto" his wife's decisions. Note that here we see a difference in the literatures in how this position is conceptualized, with lesbian partners acknowledging control over household decisions as a sign of authority in their relationships, while in the literature on heterosexual couples the job of money manager is perceived more as an undesired task or responsibility that the male partner gets to "hand off" to his wife, only to take up again whenever he feels it necessary. I would argue that the difference in how lesbian and heterosexual couples interpret the position of money manager is linked to women's greater attention to and interest in what Kranichfeld (1987) defines as "family power." Kranichfeld conceives of family power not as the acquisition of resources and status outside of the family but as skills that facilitate or advance an individual's ability to relate to others within the family. This type of power is "complex, enduring and significant" (42), and it is structured around the parent-child relationship rather than the partner dyad.

Unlike in heterosexual households, where husbands are often granted the opportunity to pass family decision making over to their wives, in lesbian relationships bio-moms are largely not assigned the task of household organizer. Instead, bio-moms want and take control over this activity because it more directly involves the needs and considerations of the children, and they have the greater motivation to make sure the children are properly cared for. While doing more housework is not evidence of greater authority or status in the home, in lesbian stepfamilies the returns from doing more housework include a greater say over how money should be allocated in other areas of family life.

MOTHERHOOD IDENTITY AND GENDER CONSTRUCTION

When Jocelyn and Anita each speak of their own identities, they place great importance on being mothers. They see their status as mother as being more salient and a greater part of their identities than their status as gay. Both say that even though they felt same-sex desire at an earlier point in time, they waited until after they had children to act on that attraction. Their intentions to be a "good mother" mean that they are willing—that they even expect—to control household activities, because taking care of work around the home is part of how one constructs an identity as a good mother. A good mother should not have a house that is messy, her kids should be fed and look presentable, and she should create a schedule to coordinate these activities.

How a woman views her own identity as a mother and as a lesbian depends in part on the timing of her transition into these statuses. As I argued in Chapter 4, women who have clearly established lesbian identities and have formed unions with other women before making the transition to motherhood may begin their parenting with particular understandings or belief systems about their own and their partners' responsibilities toward their children. That they bore the children in unions with women instead of with men may influence how they interpret each adult's relationship to the others in the home. In contrast, many women who had children before coming out as gay tend to identify first and foremost as mothers, ranking their status as lesbians lower in their personal identity construction.[13] In the lesbian stepfamilies they create, one partner has a more clearly defined identity as the mother and primary childrearer. Her ownership of that status creates a context that facilitates the repeated production of a particular gendered identity performance in her relations with her partner. She might assert control over certain family tasks as a way to remain consistent with societal expectations of what it means to be a good wife/female partner and mother, especially when those tasks relate to the well-being of the child.

Bio-moms in lesbian relationships may find that their identity as mothers is less salient to others than it was when they were partnered with men, and some may feel correspondingly compelled to show others and themselves that they have constructed their gender in a way that is appropriate for mothers and that reflects "gendered norms of accountability" (Erickson 2005).[14] Essentialist views of biological motherhood might be particularly salient for women who began parenting in a heterosexual context or who did not initially share parenting responsibilities with a female partner. If to be a good mother means that one has the greater responsibility for the implementation of child-rearing decisions or the final say in evaluating the ways household chores are carried out, the performance of this work will remain central to how women—even women with same-sex desire—construct a gendered sense of self.

Kranichfeld (1987) argues that mothers use social power to control their families, to shape the lives of their children, and to maintain family cohesion. If this is true, the power that mothers derive from within their families is a gender-related factor that complicates the lives of stepmothers (Coleman, Troilo, and Jamison 2008). The enduring power of biological mothers has consequences for stepmothers' authority. In lesbian stepfamilies, the partners of bio-moms often want more say over child rearing and expect to have some parenting authority because they are partners, because they are women, and because they are adults living in the household. But even when a couple decides at the onset of the relationship what each person's responsibility to the children will be (i.e., whether the partner will fulfill a parenting role or merely act as an adult friend toward the children), biological mothers always have the option of overriding prior contracts and having the final word. The bio-mom also has more say because in the event of a split in the relationship she has the authority to decide whether and how much visitation her partner can have with the children.

One summer during the early stages of my field work, I attended a surprise birthday party for Ro Gaul hosted by her partner, Sifa Brody. The party was held at the Vulcan Society in Brooklyn, which is part of the Black Firefighter's Association of New York City. The people at the party were predominantly West Indian, with a few Black Americans in attendance. (Both Ro and Sifa are Jamaican.) The people there were gay men and lesbians; I do not know who Ro worked with to host her event at this venue, since she is not a firefighter. At the party, I ran into Laverne Taylor, whom I thought lived with her partner and their four children. When I approached Laverne about participating in the survey component of the study, she said she was not eligible because she and her partner had ended their relationship. I asked why, and she said it was because her partner "spoils" her children, and sometimes Laverne disagreed with how she handled the discipline. She said this was a problem that kept coming up. I asked, "So you broke up because she spoils her children?" And Laverne responded, "Well, we broke up because she wouldn't let me make any of the decisions in the house when it came to the kids." At the time, I did not make much of her comments. It was not until I conducted a focus group on household decision making and all of the couples with children repeatedly focused on this area of home life as the major source of conflict in their families that I began to recognize the seriousness of this issue and the potential influence gendered ideologies about motherhood might have in the structure of lesbian-headed families.

When I compared the behaviors of the lesbian stepfamilies in this study to the research on heterosexual stepfamilies, I observed interesting parallels. Relative to wives in first marriages, women in heterosexual stepfamilies were more likely to be employed and more likely to have separate financial accounts (Coleman and Ganong 1989). O'Connor and Insabella's (1999) study of mother-stepfather families showed that biological mothers assumed greater child-rearing responsibilities than their partners and had more authority over decisions regarding children living in the home. Relative to biological mothers, stepfathers in remarried households were more likely to show a disengaged parenting style characterized by low levels of involvement, control over stepchildren's behavior, parental monitoring, and discipline (Hetherington and Clingempeel 1992). Men's family roles are narrower, and the cultural conceptualization of good fathers allows for more distant involvement with children. The parameters around child rearing that biological mothers set for stepfathers can produce strain in the marital relationship, but relative to women who are stepparenting, men expect to have less active involvement in day-to-day, minute child-rearing activities.

Biological fathers in father-stepmother households tend not to provide the same high levels of caregiving as do biological mothers in stepfamilies. Instead, child care tends to be gendered, with stepmothers experiencing more pressure to have primary responsibility for child rearing and other time-consuming activities normally undertaken by the biological mother (Cherlin and Furstenburg 1994).[15] Stepmothers spend more time in close proximity to stepchildren, participate more often in the day-to-day aspects of parenting, and become more involved in specific dilemmas around housework and caregiving compared to stepfathers (Ambert 1986; Nielsen 1999). Particularly when stepfamilies are first formed, parenting from the nonbiological parent is best received when performed at a distance, especially in relationships with adolescents (Bray and Kelly 1998). This arrangement may work better for men who as father-figures have a more acceptable place as the less involved parent. But for the female stepparent, being asked to take on a more emotionally distant parental identity can lead to conflict because even though parents may have gendered expectations around parenting, the children often do not accept parenting from the stepmother. This produces discrepancies between the father's gendered expectations of the stepmother and what the children in the household will accept.

In the case of Anita and Trina, Trina does not have an identity as a mother. Yet as the adult partner to Anita, she expects to have a greater say in the area of parenting than Anita will grant her. Trina says: "I look at it like [this]: I'm your significant other, and I'm not going anywhere, and I'm going to be here until you die. Now I have some say because I'm here, you know I pay bills, I help with everything, I'm a mentor to her, to her daughter. . . . Don't get offended if I say something, it is out of care and concern." Trina's interest in being involved with the parenting is more like that of a stepmother than that of a stepfather, but what Anita seems to expect of her is more of a stepfather's role. This creates conflict over the duties each adult presumes she will perform because the bio-moms are looking for their partners to interact with their children with a disengaged parenting style that is typical of stepfathers, whereas the partners are attempting to fulfill more of a stepmother role, and research has shown that the two positions function quite differently.

In a dispute between Trina and Anita's oldest daughter, Kiyana, Anita was called on to decide who was right and who was wrong. Anita did not come down firmly on either person's side, and this caused a heated argument with Trina, who believed Anita should have supported her because she is the adult. Anita said she would take Kiyana aside and tell her the things she did right and the things she did wrong. According to Anita, Trina would rather Anita "start yelling and screaming in front of Kiyana," but Anita said she could not do that. She believes that a good mother should "defend her child," and she has a difficult time doing this while simultaneously letting the child know when she is behaving inappropriately. Referring back to how the dispute between Trina and Kiyana was settled, Anita said: "Even if Trina is rebellious and she don't want to hear it, it'll come to a head where she'll say, 'O.K., now I understand what you're saying.' And the same thing with Kiyana, she rebels, after awhile she will see, and it will come to a head." Even the language Anita uses ("Trina is rebellious") suggests that her partner and her daughter have the same lower status relative to her.

In considering how a similar scenario might play out in a heterosexual stepfamily, one might imagine analogous efforts by the biological mother to "protect" her child from the stepparent's wrath. However, stepfathers often compensate for the bio-mom's greater authority in child rearing by contributing the greater financial resources. Studies show that on average, stepfathers work more hours and have higher incomes than their wives.[16] Stepfathers also receive social rewards for assuming financial responsibility for another man's biological children, and they can enter a legally sanctioned union with the mother that also provides a legal relationship with the child. In lesbian stepfamilies, however, the bio-mom's partner rarely has a legal parental role, and she therefore has a harder time establishing her authority in the family or gaining status from her attempts to care for the child. Lesbian partners also do not gain any gender advantage in the labor market and experience more difficulty compensating for their secondary parenting role through greater economic contributions to the family.

Conflict is to be expected in stepfamilies, and it can be productive or destructive, depending on how it is managed. Loyalty conflicts, in which children attempt to create divisions between their custodial parent and the stepparent, are particularly common (Coleman et al. 2001). Experts say the best way to combat this type of conflict is for the adults to communicate the importance and permanence of the marital bond to the children (Kelley 1995). However, the majority of lesbian relationships lack the security and permanence of the marital bond.

Consider the Russells. For the past four and a half years, Angie and Dana Russell have shared a life together with Dana's daughter, Marina, in a Black middle-class neighborhood in Queens. In Angie's interview, she presented the reality of raising the child of a lesbian partner: "As a non-biological, it's not your child. When it comes down to the bottom line, if anything happens to this biological parent, the grandparents get first dibs. You see plenty cases of that. Even when women raise children from newborns, Grandma comes in and says [to the biological mother's part-ner] 'No, no, I loved you and we was cool at Thanksgiving, but no, this is my daughter's child, and I want to raise her. Yeah, I know she called you mommy too, but *no*.' And that's the bottom line. That's the reality of it, that's the disadvantage of it I guess."

That at the "bottom line" there is no legal relationship between the partner and the stepchild makes the partner's position in the family less certain and less permanent. In separate interviews, both Angie and Dana described Angie's deteriorating relationship with Marina. Dana stated that she is reluctant to allow Angie significant authority in par-enting despite the fact that Marina's biological father is deceased: "I tried to make it comfortable for both of them so Angie could feel she's a part of Marina's life. . . . We took family vacations, we'd do family things. But she [Marina] was raised already, so someone really can't come in and have a lot of input. *I didn't even allow it.*"[17] Research has shown that when biological mothers identify strongly with possessive, exclusive notions of motherhood, stepmothers have little chance of developing close relationships with their stepchildren (Nielsen 1999). Jones (2004) describes the parenting experiences of stepmothers as "caregiving without authority," because in her study of heterosexual stepmothers the women reported that their authority as parents was of-ten undermined by the children's biological mother. Stepfamilies that are successful in making the transition to "family" are able to develop and maintain flexible boundaries as they merge together. Households that are unable to successfully negotiate their family ties have boundaries that "become extremely rigid and impermeable, demarcating blood-lines" (Braithwaite et al. 2001, 241). In these situations, parents and children from one family align with one another, creating distance from their new stepfamily members.

Angie said she participated in some of the child care responsibilities when Marina was younger, but this changed as Marina got older. After a time, Angie said, she just stopped offering advice, asking questions, and generally involving herself in Marina's parenting. She says she felt "cut off" from this aspect of family life and powerless to do anything to change her position. Not only did the relationship between Angie and Marina suffer from this distancing, but the relationship between Angie and Dana suffered as well. The opinions of biological mothers are likely to carry more weight in lesbian relationships because of the way these families are often formed. In this study, two-thirds of the lesbian stepfamilies were created when the mother's partner moved into an existing single-parent household that had the bio-mom as family head. The bio-moms often continue parenting as though they are single mothers, deciding when to give authority to the new cohabiting partner and how much to give. The partner's place in the family hierarchy is less clear, and the uncertainty surrounding her position gives her an initial status that is lower than that of her partner.

The pattern of behavior that emerges in many lesbian stepfamilies is one in which the child resists the authority of her mother's partner, and the biological mother also resists, undermines, or challenges her partner's parenting attempts, aligning herself with her child even when she may agree with her partner's parenting recommendations. When Anita Adams talks about the dynamics of her partner's relationship with her older daughter, she says she sees herself as caught in the middle of two people whom she loves and who each expect her to take their side. She describes this tension as "a conflict of love." Marilyn Richards says that the role of the biological mother is "to defend your child and be a peacemaker with your partner." Richards acknowledges, "It is a very difficult balance to maintain the love you have for your children and the love you have for your partner and trying to keep them getting along and limit the child's resentment or the partner's resentment for the kid."

One interesting question that these results invite is what happens in families in which both partners bring biological children from prior relationships to live together in the home. Unfortunately, my surveys and interviews did not capture any families of this type. This may attest to the difficulties of forming cohabiting relationships when both partners are parenting children. Single mothers who were dating other single mothers tended to retain their own separate residences. During my three years of field work, however, I came across two cohabiting couples wherein both women were parenting children from prior heterosexual relationships. In these households, both adults were working, and each parent retained authority over decisions regarding her own children. There was still some task specialization, in that one partner had the greater responsibility for the allocation of finances and the housework. Other factors determined who would take on the job of household organizer in these cases, however, such as flexibility of work schedule and the age and needs of each person's biological child.

Lesbian stepfamilies in which there is a severe discrepancy in income or in which one partner is not economically self-sufficient may also operate in a different way than the dominant model discussed in this chapter. In this study, the personal incomes of both partners in the majority of families was fairly matched, so even when one person had a greater income, her additional earnings did not translate into more authority in the relationship.[18] In two households, however, the bio-mom's partner had an income more than three times higher than hers.[19] In both of these families, the mother's partner had accumulated significantly more assets prior to union formation, and the biological mother had a weak attachment to the labor force. The bio-moms and their children lived in their partners' homes, whereas in most of the stepfamilies I studied, the partner joined the mother and child in the bio-mom's previously established home. These two cases suggest that in families where the bio-mom has significantly fewer material assets and resources, including a lower or unsteady income, her status as the biological mother still gives her greater authority over child rearing, but her opinions do not carry as much weight in the area of family finances. In relationships in which one partner earns much more than the other or one partner is not self-sufficient, the more economically advantaged person has greater overall say in the household despite her lesser influence over the children.

DIVISION OF LABOR IN OTHER
COHABITING HOUSEHOLDS

Two other types of cohabiting unions are represented in my study—couples who have had children together using alternative insemination methods and couples who do not have children living with them in the home—and it is useful to compare the pattern of household decision making in lesbian stepfamilies to them. In my sample, eight women (four couples) conceived children together through alternative insemination methods. These families were middle and upper middle class. They supported the ideology of equal financial contributions and equal housework and child care but did not practice an equal division of household labor. Similar to the lesbian stepfamilies, partners who did less housework tended to make jokes and laugh uncomfortably when asked about the division of chores. This, for instance, is what Zora Hammond had to say in reference to her partner, Nyla Ransom:

I: *So you're pretty happy with it [the division of housework] the way you've described it?*

Zora: Well, it's not fair. Nyla does most of the work, and I don't do a lot of it.

I: *And she allows that?*

Zora: She does! Since I've known Nyla, she has always cleaned. People used to say in college, "Why are you cleaning up Zora's messy room, let her clean up her own room." And it's like she set this wheel in motion, so it's her fault, isn't it? Thank you, I no longer feel guilty!" [laughter]

In two of these families, the bio-moms performed more of the housework and managed the money. In a third couple, both partners were bio-moms, but one took on a much larger share of the household chores. In the fourth, the co-mother performed more of the housework than the bio-mom. In all of these families, the bio-mom's partner was either the legal adoptive parent of the children or in the process of adopting the child.

Unlike in lesbian stepfamilies, mothers in three of the four households where children were conceived through alternative insemination co-parented and shared in authority and decision making.[20] Rather than undermining their partners' efforts, bio-moms found it important to validate them as legitimate co-mothers of the children. Marissa Dillard and Josephine Owens, for example, are both attorneys who jointly own an apartment in an upper-middle-class neighborhood in Brooklyn. They have a six-year-old son named Jonathan whom Marissa conceived through alternative insemination. When I interviewed her, Marissa was six months pregnant with their second child. Josephine is the legal parent of Jonathan and planned to adopt the new baby as well. In neither of their interviews did they speak of Jonathan as "mine" or "my child." Instead, they both used words and phrases like "ours," "the kids," and "We provide for them." When asked whether they ever disagreed on how to parent Jonathan, Marissa said that in the past they had "eventually come to a consensus" despite their different disciplinary styles by "talk[ing] about it and tr[ying] to find some sort of middle ground that we both feel comfortable with."

In these families, when one partner had a greater say in a decision regarding the child, it was not always the biological mother. One reason the biological tie does not confer a higher status for partners who conceive through alternative insemination is that they have made the decision before having the child that the role of each partner in parenting will be equal. They enter motherhood with this arrangement, and the way they frame their thinking about the responsibilities of each person is more similar to the decision making involved in two-biological-parent families. They are both involved in the insemination process, from selecting the sperm donor to finding a medical professional to assist with the procedure. They have a similarly vested interest in the child. The biological mother in these families wants her partner to be legitimated in larger society as the parent, she wants their child to see her partner in that way, and in order for the household to run smoothly, she herself wants to see her partner in that way.[21]

Thirty-four of my respondents were partnered and cohabiting but did not have children living with them in the home. Eighty-five percent, or twenty-nine respondents, agreed or strongly agreed that "both mates in a relationship should divide evenly the household tasks." Just as in the stepfamilies and alternative insemination families, there was a gap between their theoretical support for an egalitarian division of housework and their actual daily behavior. There is some suggestion, however, that these partners organized at least some of the family labor according to gendered presentations of self. Women with a self-defined feminine gender presentation reported spending an average of 5.2 hours per week on chores and said their partners spent about 1.5 hours less per week, or an average of 3.7 hours, on household tasks. Women with a less feminine gender presentation reported spending an average of 5.9 hours per week on chores and said their partners spent a similar amount of time on chores, 5.7 hours per week. We see here that in households with no children present, the more feminine-looking partner perceived herself to be spending more time on household chores, while the less feminine partner perceived them to be spending equal amounts of time on housework.

When respondents with no children were asked how often they performed certain household tasks, about one-third of them reported spending similar amounts of time as their partners on many chores, including washing dishes, arranging daily meals, and straightening the living room. When tasks were not performed equally by partners, there was no consistent relationship between gender presentation and the *daily* housework partners performed. The less feminine partner, however, was

TABLE 2. DIVISION OF LABOR IN LESBIAN COUPLES WITH NO CHILDREN: CERTAIN
HOUSEHOLD TASKS ARE NECESSARY TO KEEP THINGS RUNNING SMOOTHLY. WHO
DOES EACH OF THESE TASKS MORE OFTEN?

Household Chores	We Do This Equally (%)	More Feminine Partner Does This More (%)	Less Feminine Partner Does This More (%)
Washes dishes	33	38	30
Does laundry	26	33	52
Cleans bathroom	19	35	46
Cleans floors	26	32	42
Arranges daily meals	30	42	27
Straightens family room	31	32	36
Dusts furniture	27	40	33
Grocery shopping	59	15	23
Mixes drinks for company	27	40	32
Takes out trash	27	24	48
Repairs things around house	12	36	52
Cares for pets	36	31	32
Performs yard work	0	27	56

more likely to perform certain *infrequent* tasks that are male stereotyped,
like taking out the trash, making household repairs, and performing yard
work (these patterns are shown in Table 2).

CONCLUSION

The very creation of and participation in what we have defined as "family" encourages pre-established gendered patterns of interaction, even
in same-sex unions. The institutional characteristics of structures we
identify as family are so steeped in gendered relations that efforts to
construct and participate in them result in scripts of actions that more
often than not carry established gendered meanings. Addressing how
housework, paid work, money management, and child rearing are nego-
tiated among same-sex couples—couples who have developed a lesbian
identity outside of the feminist egalitarian framework—sheds important
light on gender construction, gendered interaction, power, and hierarchy
within familial relationships. These findings have important implications, and not just for same-sex partners. Rather, if resources beyond
income have the potential to influence authority and interactions within
families headed by same-sex couples, they likely have this potential in
heterosexual unions as well.

Control over domestic labor can be associated with greater family power for lesbians actively engaged in creating structures identified as families. Even in same-sex unions, gender profoundly influences the construction of family life, motivating the greater involvement of bio-logical mothers in housework and child care in exchange for greater decision making in the household. The construction of "appropriate" gender norms may be particularly important for lesbian mothers who bore their children in heterosexual contexts, because they have willingly moved from validated relationships with men to sanctioned, often stig-matized, same-sex unions. Social demands produce or offer an incentive to enact behaviors that signal they are good mothers, and lesbians seek-ing to minimize stigma have an additional motivation to promote them-selves as good mothers to family members, society, and to themselves.

Without the gender structure of male privilege, and absent the mate-rial advantage of high income differentials, the management of household activities in lesbian relationships can be a source of power. Biological mothers want more influence over the household since such control is typically seen as quite consequential to the well-being of children—children whom biological mothers see as primarily theirs and not their partners'. They use the "doing" of housework and authority over child rearing as a trade-off for significant control of household finances and organization. This has implications for how we think about the creation of hierarchies and the enactment of power in lesbian couples, of course—but arguably in heterosexual couples as well. If family relationships dic-tate that mothers be highly involved in the supervision and monitoring of children, as well as in the daily decision making that affects children's lives, we should expect similar pressures to conform to these gendered expectations among all women who are mothers, regardless of the sex of their partners. Bio-moms in heterosexual families likely see their greater family power in home life as important. The authority to schedule tasks, regulate activities, and keep the house running smoothly may go unno-ticed or be underappreciated. Women's greater management over these areas, however, is consistent with self and societal definitions of what it means to be a "good mother." It is also possible that the ideological power of male privilege or male comparative income advantage may lessen the status women (and men) attribute to family power. Both possi-bilities are deserving of further consideration in research on family forms of all types. Future work should more closely analyze how women and men feel about women's greater family power in heterosexual households and the extent to which either person interprets the wife's authority in this domain as a type of power in their households.

This chapter has also shown that bio-moms in lesbian relationships often cast their partners in traditional stepparent roles, complete with less child-rearing power, and put themselves in the middle between their children and their partners. Unlike stepfathers in heterosexual households, however, lesbian partners have less access to economic providership to leverage their position in the household, and lack a legal tie to the children in the home, which makes them less powerful actors. This relationship appears to be different relative to lesbian households wherein the children are conceived or adopted into the existing relationship, although in times of family instability or relationship dissolution the biological mother in these families may also try to exert control over her partner vis-à-vis visitation rights and other areas of the co-mother's relationship to the children.

A related insight is that the conventional model in which individuals in families exchange domestic services for financial support may not hold in certain contexts. At the greatest income disparities between partners, the economic advantages of a very high wage earner may award that person more authority in decisions over family finances. In most cases, however, the earnings differential between female partners is not so large (Peplau and Huppin 2008), and this is different from what Hofferth and Anderson (2003) find among heterosexual partners in their study of (mostly White) stepfamily and cohabiting households. The threshold at which relative differences in income influence authority in lesbian relationships remains unclear. However, there may exist an alternative kind of power in relations between women: the ability to have the final say over decisions in domestic life. More generally, it suggests the presence of power differentials that are not centered around income but instead around other expectations and identities that reveal themselves in the context of attempts to create something defined as "family."

CHAPTER 6

Openly Gay Families and the Negotiation of Black Community and Religious Life

Black neighborhoods have always been a central location for gay African American social life. Nevertheless, prior to the 1980s, gay sexuality in racial minority communities was rarely shared or articulated openly in public settings, it was not recognized as part of the larger community narrative of discrimination and struggle, and gay Blacks tended not to openly create families together.[1] Recent social and political changes, however, including the rapid spread of HIV/AIDS among Black heterosexual women, Black political and religious leaders openly addressing issues related to gay sexuality, and amplified public debates about the legal status of same-sex marriage, have moved the enactment of same-sex desire from the private into the public sphere: relationships once hidden from family and community are gradually being exposed and celebrated publically as gay women and men openly form unions and raise families together.[2]

According to Census data, the majority of Black same-sex couples reside in cities, towns, and rural areas that are predominantly African American. They are more likely to live with other Blacks in minority communities than to live with White homosexuals in cities and neighborhoods with high percentages of same-sex couples (Dang and Frazer 2004; Gates unpublished analyses of the 2008 American Community Survey; National Gay and Lesbian Task Force 2004). While residents in racial minority neighborhoods have always been aware of the presence of lesbians and gay men in their families and social environs, the recent more public visibility of lesbian- and gay-headed family life has made it difficult for Black heterosexual communities to avoid acknowledging the homosexuality of family members, neighbors, and acquaintances. However, the persistent sense of disapproval among Black heterosexuals of the open enactment of same-sex desire creates what Cohen (1999) calls a "cross-cutting issue" within the Black community. Cohen defines cross-cutting issues as concerns "rooted in or built on the often hidden differences, cleavages, or fault lines of marginal communities" and "perceived as being contained to identifiable subgroups in Black communities, especially those segments of Black communities which are the least empowered" (9). The cross-cutting issue that open Black gay sexuality poses in Black communities affects the lives of sexual minorities who also define themselves by their membership in the racial category "Black" and who are increasingly insisting that others in their communities recognize and respect the gay component of their identities.

Historians define a "modern gay identity" as one whose subject incorporates homosexual behavior into everyday experiences and encourages others to acknowledge this sexuality.[3] In this chapter I investigate the lives of gay Black women who have embraced a modern gay identity within Black communities, emphasizing the ways in which they manage the discomfort of their families and neighbors, and how well this identity status coheres with their spiritual selves. I first consider the experiences of Black lesbians as they move from viewing their homosexuality as a discrete part of their lives toward seeing it as something around which they have constructed an open self-identification. Many Black lesbians—particularly Caribbean and African women—encounter both familial and cultural resistance in this process. The women in this study learn to live with a degree of contradiction and ambiguity as they seek ways to maintain their family relationships and at the same time embrace an identity as gay women.

In the central section of the chapter I analyze the different ways Black lesbians forming families experience tolerance but not acceptance within the racial group, whose cultural norms they must negotiate. I use Goffman's (1963) analyses of stigma and covering to show the conditions under which those with stigmatized identities choose to reveal information about themselves to others. I argue that gay women have an easier time fitting into Black environments when they adhere to particular definitions of a middle-class politics of respectability and maintain their community connections through strong racial group solidarity. Everyone does not adhere to all of these conditions all of the time, however, and the conflict and reconciliation that ensue are part of the progression forward toward acceptance.

Finally, I explore how the move from private to more public presentations of gay sexuality has affected the relationships Black lesbians have with their religious communities. African American religious institutions are not just locations of spiritual guidance; they also act as agents or conduits of Black culture through their involvement in and control over secular civic, political, and economic organizations and activities.[4] The historic sacred and secular participation of religious organizations in Black community life, combined with their general ideologies that do not support homosexuality, influence the rhetoric racial group members use to criticize homosexuality, such that even those with no strong religious faith or church involvement draw on religious teachings as the first line of critique against lesbian and gay identities (Cohen 1999; Moore 2010b). Most of the subjects in this study were raised with religious faiths that are disapproving and sometimes condemning of the open practice of homosexuality. Despite the homophobia in these institutions, however, the majority of the women I studied continue to maintain a belief in God, as well as affiliations with religious organizations. While the Black heterosexual community uses religion to constrain gay behavior through an often candid denouncement of homosexuality, some in the Black gay community use religion to validate their identities as same-gender-loving people. Finally, this chapter discusses ways Black gay women negotiate and manage a group affiliation and "insider" status around one self-understanding based on race when cross-cutting issues around the public enactment of homosexuality threaten to separate them from strong and positive affiliations with the racial group.

UP CLOSE AND PERSONAL: MOVING FROM PRIVATE TO PUBLIC EXPRESSIONS OF GAY SEXUALITY AND FAMILY FORMATION

One morning, I called Marisol Sampson, a petite, feminine, highly successful thirty-two-year-old Black Puerto Rican entrepreneur with huge brown eyes, dramatic braids that hang down her back, and a biting wit. Marisol's *abuelita* (grandmother), who played a pivotal role in raising her and her brother, had recently passed away at the age of ninety. Prior to her grandmother's death, she and Marisol would have dinner on Sunday evenings at the nursing home where her *abuelita* lived. Marisol told me it was worth the extra money she spent out of pocket each month for her grandmother to live in the Jewish facility on the Upper East Side of Manhattan instead of the less expensive, lower-quality facility in East Harlem that Medicaid was willing to cover. The two were extremely close, and Marisol would use these visits to talk about various things, including her *abuelita*'s memories of their family's history, particularly the life of Marisol's mother, who passed away when Marisol was much younger.

I called Marisol to follow up on a conversation we had had many months earlier. At that time, Marisol mentioned that years after she had come out to her grandmother, she remembered a close relationship between her mother and her mother's friend and suspected that it might not have been platonic. The woman had lived for a time in her mother's house; she had also lived with her mother's sister Ruby. One evening, Marisol came right out and asked her grandmother, "Did my mother have relationships with women?" She was not prepared for her grandmother's matter-of-fact response: "Oh please—We all did!" When Marisol asked her to clarify, her grandmother told her, "You all seem to think that you women just started this whole thing, or that we don't know about such things. This has been going on for a long time. It was just not in the open like it is now." During the late 1970s and early 1980s, Marisol's mother, her mother's friend, and her Aunt Ruby had all "carried on" with a woman known as Hondura. Marisol's grandmother said that Hondura kept going back and forth in love relationships between her mother and her aunt, and it caused many an argument between the two of them.

They continued the conversation during a subsequent visit, and Marisol's grandmother told her about a relationship that she herself had during the late 1940s and early 1950s with someone she described as a "best, best kind of friend." She and the other woman were both married with children and living next door to each other. Marisol's grandmother said they were "inseparable," and while most people thought they were just best friends, people who "did that kind of thing" knew it was more than that. Eventually, her friend's husband moved her friend away. Marisol's grandmother believed the husband did this to separate the two of them because of their intense relationship. She said that back then, "Those types of relationships were not okay, and people did not discuss them," but many were aware that they existed.

The history of intimate relationships that Marisol's grandmother reports having occurred among several generations of women in their family—and the different contexts in which these relationships were enacted—attests to the changing climates in which same-sex relationships among women have been understood and practiced. While we cannot know from her grandmother's utterances whether these relationships were of a sexual nature, we can tell from the context in which her grandmother introduced the relationships to Marisol that they were on a continuum with the type of openly lesbian relationship Marisol was involved in. Her grandmother had a "best, best kind of friend" in the 1950s while she was heterosexually married, and the intimacy of their relationship was not socially acceptable and not openly discussed. Marisol's mother "carried on" with a woman called Hondura and argued with her sister over this woman. Marisol's grandmother's description suggests that Marisol's mother and aunt had a series of relatively open same-sex liaisons that took place simultaneously with her mother's heterosexual marriage to Marisol's father.

In a different example, we have Dr. Marilyn Richards. Marilyn was born in 1942 and raised on Chicago's South Side. When she first began to act on her same-sex desires in the early 1960s she knew she would have to maintain a heterosexual façade. Unlike the previous generations of women in Marisol's family, however, Marilyn chose a different path. Marilyn had her first same-sex relationship with her best friend while living in Chicago after each had divorced their husbands and moved in together with their children. Because they had been previously married and were already known in the community to have a close friendship, they were able to keep private the romantic nature of their union. Their past histories as heterosexuals provided the cloak necessary to safely pursue a more intimate relationship, and Goffman (1963) would describe the experience of keeping this relationship hidden or invisible as "passing." Marilyn marks this relationship as her entry into a lesbian identity. She sees these early experiences as part of a gay sense of self she had, and that is what allows us to link her behavior to Goffman's definition of passing. Unlike Marisol's grandmother, who never used the terms *lesbian* or *gay* to describe the experiences in her life, Marilyn defines her sexual orientation as lesbian and labeled her first same-sex relationship a lesbian one. Moreover, Marilyn and her partner, unlike Marisol's grandmother, were divorced at the time of this relationship. They did not have to maintain the relationship in the context of one person's marriage to someone else. Instead, they were able to make the relationship between themselves the primary union.

In 1960s Chicago, Black lesbians met other lesbians and socialized at private parties at women's homes that one could only learn about by falling into particular networks of women. A gay cousin was Marilyn's primary gateway into this social scene; she describes this relative as "a real sort of way out weird woman, but someone that we liked." There were also a few neighborhood bars on the South Side of Chicago that catered to a Black lesbian and gay clientele, and Marilyn and her partner would go to these places and seek out friendships with young women who shared their interests. This lesbian community that Marilyn participated in during the 1960s was racially homogeneous: she lived in an African American neighborhood and joined a network of lesbians that was also predominantly Black. These social contexts were an important backdrop and foundational aspect of Black lesbian and gay identities.

Marilyn's relationship with her best friend ended in 1971 when they were both twenty-seven, and although she continued to have lesbian relationships, she never revealed the nature of this very special union to any other family or community member outside of the lesbian social group she and her partner had been a part of. Marilyn refers to her experiences in the social groups as "her secret life." Looking back on it, she concludes that one of the most positive aspects of her first gay relationship was that it was able to safely take place within her existing racial community. She was able to keep her gay relationship a secret and still participate with her partner in family life, albeit in a closeted way. She did not have to conceal her partner—only to hide the full nature of their relationship—and she says this provided her with an easier transition to a lesbian life than she might have had in other circumstances.

As Marilyn's and Marisol's remarks emphasize, there is nothing new about Black women having a lesbian sexuality: rather, it is same-sex couples openly living and raising children together in African American communities that is a distinct departure from past understandings of lesbian and gay behavior. In the past, lesbian/gay practice was overshadowed by public identities that emphasized racial group membership and deemphasized sexuality. Participation in the private social world of Black lesbian life was accompanied by a public presentation of self that was presumed to be heterosexual; many times, women remained in marriages or other visible heterosexual relationships while fulfilling their same-sex desires. The relationships they had with women were often unstable and of a short duration.

We can attribute the preference for invisible gay sexuality in Black communities to two forces: the primacy of racial identity over other identification categories and the politics of respectability. Both of these concepts have been historically important to how people with same-sex desire chose to express that desire in heterosexual contexts. Cohen argues that Blackness as an identity status has historically been perceived to be a unifier, because as a group, African Americans share a history and current existence framed by opposition and marginalization (1999, 91). This was particularly the case during the 1960s and 1970s in the aftermath of the civil rights and Black Power movements. These movements occurred simultaneously with, and contributed to, increasing economic stratification in Black communities. In this period, members of the racial group were expected to prioritize their racial identity over other identification categories.

Black gay people sought to remain integrated into African American communities because these environments served as a buffer to the very real threat of racism and discrimination. The presence of a unifying racial identity meant they were willing to accept a "conditional membership" that required them to deemphasize or deny their gay sexuality. In return, they were able to rely on the racial community as a system of social support. Today, Black lesbians and gays are likely to express multiple identities. Yet the families of many gay Black people, especially their parents, would prefer to keep their sexuality under wraps.

Consider how Caroline Tate, a thirty-seven-year-old femme and "southern belle" born and raised in Florence, South Carolina, came out to her mother. She proudly told her: "Look at it this way, just to keep your sanity. At least I'm not shaving my head, I'm not wearing men's clothing. You can take me anywhere now, and no one would know that your daughter's a lesbian. So that should make you happy." Caroline explains: "I remember promising her I would never be that person, and she didn't have to worry about anything like that. And people wouldn't know that I'm gay unless we told them, because I'm not a dyke." Caroline meant to assuage what she perceived to be her mother's main concern about her daughter's gay identity: its visibility to others. She contrasted herself to a "dyke" in order to convey that even though she is gay, she would continue to conform to traditional expectations of a feminine gender presentation. Caroline's use of this language in coming out to her mother addressed the unspoken assumption that her mother would want to keep her daughter's gay sexuality invisible.

Later in our discussion, Caroline admitted that she had felt obligated to come out to her mother because her girlfriend at the time had a gender presentation that was very boyish and masculine, and her presence in Caroline's life was causing rumors about her among her family members. Caroline surmised that had her partner been more feminine, she probably would not have openly acknowledged the nature of that relationship to her mother. Prior to being in this gay relationship, Caroline had only been with men, and she was raising a daughter from a former cohabiting union. She allowed and even encouraged her mother to use her past experiences with men to maintain a pretense with others that Caroline was heterosexual. Caroline knew that the relationship with her lover at that time would not last. She did not see herself as creating a family with her, and she had no desire for her relatives and close friends to accept this person as an integral part of her life. In this context, it did not matter to Caroline that her mother fully accept her gay sexuality.

Many of the women I spoke to described a period of time in their lives when their family members suspected they were engaged in same-sex relationships but they did not present their partners to family members as their mates. They may have brought these individuals to family gatherings or have even cohabited with them. Both partners and their kin, however, allowed for the nature of these same-sex relationships to remain unspoken. This "don't ask, don't tell" policy enabled the women to remain on good terms with family and old friends rather than cause a breach for a relationship their families did not want to fully acknowledge.

Respondents and other lesbians I met who were from countries in Africa and the Caribbean were particularly likely to take a don't ask, don't tell approach to their early lesbian relationships. They saw this strategy as necessary because of the way their families viewed the open practice of gay sexuality: they reported that their relatives expected same-sex desire to only be enacted in the private sphere of their personal lives. This expectation for how to engage in same-sex desire was consistent with the information I learned during the course of several conversations I had with an Afro-Caribbean woman about same-sex romantic expression among African women in Paris. In late spring of 2003 I happened to visit Paris, France, during the time of a music festival that enraptured the entire city. I actively sought out spaces that were inhabited by Blacks, and found a Creole restaurant the Blacks in Paris website said was Black-owned. The restaurant was located in le Marais, the gay district. There I met a woman from Martinique named Karen. I spoke very little French and she spoke very little English, so we communicated in Spanish, a language we were both conversant but not fluent in. I told Karen I wanted to learn more about the nightlife for Blacks in Paris, and since we were in le Marais, I felt bold enough to ask if there were any places that were frequented by Black people who were gay. She told me that she was bisexual, that the two women who owned the restaurant we were in were longtime lovers, and she promised to take me to several parties that were going on that weekend, including one at the restaurant the next evening.

Karen was a gracious tour guide that weekend. I accompanied her to African restaurants, after hours night spots, as well as three different parties all organized by African Parisians. Some of these were clearly gay spaces and others were not. The largest of these parties took place on a Saturday night at a venue that had two levels. While women and men waited on line to enter the venue, once inside the men went upstairs and the women downstairs. The space for women was dark and cavernous, and women sat together in intimate groups talking, laughing, and drinking. Some of the pairs looked like they were on dates because they sat close to one another, sometimes with one person's arm around the other. They wore blouses and slacks or skirts, blue jeans and t-shirts, but I did not see any overtly masculine displays of gender in their clothing. They danced in pairs or small groups to different types of African and Afro-Caribbean music. Karen tried to explain the origins of the different sounds, but difficulties in translation kept me from fully understanding. What I could definitely understand, however, were the similarities between this party, the men's party, and the Black gay pride parties I had attended in the United States. When I went to take a peak upstairs, the men's party had more energy, the music was louder (but similar in style to the types of music played downstairs), and several men had taken off their shirts to reveal well-toned bodies. The men were also dancing in pairs with one another. There were a few White men at that event, while there were only Black women downstairs.

I asked Karen what lesbian relationships were like for African and Afro-Caribbean women in Paris, and she told me most women were married to or in relationships with men and that it was extremely rare to find two women living together openly as lesbians. She said there was no room for that sort of thing, and that their Afro-Caribbean cultures did not support or even understand what it would mean for two women to live together as a family. Sometimes their husbands or boyfriends had an inclination that their wives or girlfriends might be romantically involved with women, but so long as she continued to live out a heterosexual identity in her daily life, any same-sex liaisons were not usually openly acknowledged by her male partner. I found a version of this expectation for how to practice same-sex desire in the stories Caribbean lesbians living in the U.S. shared about their parent's and other kin's response to their sexuality.

The don't ask, don't tell solution of ignoring an individual's lesbian practice becomes problematic in contexts in which people want to publicly declare an intimate partner as "family." When Nadine Burroughs, a thirty-eight-year-old obstetrics and gynecological nurse, divorced her husband and told her Jamaican-born mother that she would now only be dating women, she recalls her mother responding that her same-sex desire "was neither new nor interesting" and that plenty of people have "indulged in that sort of thing." The problem for Nadine's mother was not that her daughter was interested in intimacy with other women; rather, she thought it was absolutely shameful for her daughter to *reveal* her engagement in those types of relationships to the outside world. While she did not object to Nadine's having sexual relationships with women, she thought Nadine should do "what is proper" and "be respectable" and "marry well." For Nadine's mother, the problem was that her daughter's open expression of homosexuality through a wedding ceremony meant she could no longer present her daughter to others as heterosexual.

Many foreign-born lesbians and women whose parents were born outside of the United States tend to view the out, visible performance of gay identity as antithetical to the values of their own cultures. In 2001, Simone Augustine and Natalie DuBois, two second-generation Haitian women, decided to affirm their five-year partnership with a wedding in the Brooklyn Botanic Gardens. Despite the close relationships each had built with the other's family, both of their mothers expressed reservations about this public event. Would they invite relatives from Haiti to the ceremony, thus bringing shame on the family in an open celebration of their disgraceful behavior? Would they embarrass themselves and their families by asking the elder from the Seventh-Day Adventist church that Natalie was raised in to officiate? Natalie's mother was particularly outraged, disappointed, and disgusted by the prospect of a lesbian wedding. She told her daughter that she did not understand how she could be so "American" in her unrestricted proclamation of the relationship. Over and over, and in tears, she asked her in Haitian Creole, "*Kòman ou fè pote kalite wont sa-a nan fanmi-an? Poukisa ou oblige agi tankou Ameriken, epi fè tout moun wè bagay sa-a?!*" [How can you bring such shame on our family? Why would you behave like an American and bring this out for everyone to see?!] Natalie's mother felt offended in part because her daughter's interest in having a lesbian wedding—even one between two Haitian people—was a sign of her assimilation into what she viewed as the negative aspects of American culture. Other foreign-born parents expressed similar sentiments about their children's "American" behavior in acknowledging their same-sex desire through something as public as a gay wedding.

The public expression of a modern gay identity through weddings or commitment ceremonies is also problematic because these types of celebrations imply the equality of gay and heterosexual unions. Shanice Benson, a Jamaican-born woman, said, "The whole idea of two women being in a relationship is really far-fetched" for her parents. While U.S. born Blacks certainly have family and racial group members who see the public expression of gay sexuality as an abomination, Blacks who were born and socialized outside of the United States particularly find there is very little room for same-sex desire and behavior in their conceptions of identity. Their ethnic identity calls for a public image of heterosexuality, and openly gay behavior is used to create boundaries between themselves and U.S. born and other Westernized groups.

Kinship and Community Ties: Learning to Live with Contradictions and Ambiguities

The move from unspoken gay sexuality to the public presentation of gay relationships and family formation forces parents and other relatives of lesbian women to acknowledge their daughters' lesbian practice more directly than they once would have. In prior generations, everyone at the dinner table may have been aware that an uncle was gay, but because he called his lover his "friend," never brought him to the family reunion, and never adopted his mate's child nor asked that the child call his own mother "Grandma," family members could reserve their negative opinions and speculation for private conversations outside of his presence. National public debates over the legalization of same-sex marriage and related issues, however, have brought the topic of gay sexuality more directly into homes and into the pulpits of community churches, creating the space for family members to be more up front in their feelings and opinions about a relative's same-sex desire.[5]

Some women have found that family members liken their sexuality to a problem behavior worse than drug addiction, adultery, or nonmarital childbearing. Thirty-seven-year-old Corey James says that Blacks will excuse negative behavior of all types but are quick to judge people who are gay. She articulates the situation in the following way: "Uncle Brian might be a crackhead, but that don't even matter to them. What matters is that, 'Oh my goodness, Mary is gay!' You know what I'm saying? And I always tell people that you can be anything in a Black household but gay and come back home. I know it for a fact that you could have robbed your mother blind and come home to live, and she'll just be like, 'Oh, my baby got a problem.' But if you come out to your family and they're strong against that, there's no going home. They'll forgive you for robbing them blind. [If you're on drugs,] they'll say you was 'a little sick,' and they'll take you in the house over and over and over and over again, but not when you're gay."

Corey's comments reflect the weight of having lived through the 1980s and 1990s drug epidemics that ravaged urban communities like the ones she has lived in. She grew up in a low-income housing project in the Bronx, and although the grandmother who raised her was tolerant when she came out as gay, she experienced some difficulty with other relatives accepting her lesbian sexuality. Corey's comments also reflect years of experience counseling people at the LGBT nonprofit agencies where she has worked. There, she has met many people who were beaten or disowned by their parents and kin because they were open about their gay identities. Some of the harshest experiences of homophobia were felt by teenagers and transgendered people who were particularly economically vulnerable and in need of social services.

Forty-one-year-old Jackie Roberts says that older Black people are particularly hypocritical and self-righteous when it comes to their opinions about gay people: "They think, 'Oh, you're going to hell. You are going to burn.' Forget the fact that you've got ten illegitimate kids running around, [or] you're messing with this lady's husband. They've broken all of your 'Big Ten' [Ten Commandments], and guess what? There's nothing in the Big Ten that says 'Thou shall not be gay.' But that adultery piece? If I go [to Hell], you're going to be burning right next to me."

Jackie never explicitly came out to her grandmother, who had raised her from birth and was an important mother figure in her life, but she was certain that her sexuality had been known to the rest of her family for some time when Jackie's grandmother found her in pajamas in the apartment of a downstairs neighbor. The openness of the situation forced a direct response from her grandmother, who had no choice but to acknowledge the situation and express her feelings against lesbian practice. Jackie's grandmother's negative response made Jackie angry, in part because Jackie had become a pillar of strength in a family mired in drug addiction, domestic violence, child abandonment, and poverty. Until her untimely death, Jackie's mother had suffered a life of abuse and violence from a husband whom the family continued to embrace. Recall from Chapter 4 that Jackie's sister has a drug addiction, so Jackie had to adopt one of her nephews and has also spent time as a foster mother to two nieces. Nevertheless, her grandmother never relented in her condemnation of Jackie's sexuality, and though they were able to repair their relationship, she never accepted Jackie's lesbian identity.

The initial occurrence of coming out to family was a difficult one for many women. Many described the pain they experienced as they revealed their intention to live an openly gay life to parents and siblings. However, by the time they were interviewed for this research, they were firmly established in their gay identities and were forming their own families. Much of the harsh, unforgiving homophobia of the earlier years had given way to a begrudging tolerance and uneasy, uncertain management of their relationships with kin. Almost all report that over time they have been able to develop stable relationships with parents and siblings. But despite their overall sense that their interacations with relatives are positive, they report a persistent tendency for their mothers, in particular, to continue to express disapproval of or discomfort with their gay sexuality. At the same time, their mothers actively seek to remain involved in their daily activities and lives. Santasha Andrews offers one example. Santasha is a hetero-identified lesbian who did not grow up having same-sex desires. Her first gay relationship occurred well after adulthood and after she had borne two children in a nonmarital heterosexual union. When she told her mother about her new girlfriend, her mother disapproved and told her: "I think it's wrong. A man should be with a woman." Santasha found, however, that "she said this with her mouth and yet still kind of embraced" the relationship: despite her feelings of disapproval, Santasha's mother would regularly invite Santasha and her former partner, Denise, to her home out at the tip of Long Island during the summer.

One year, Santasha and Denise threw a big Mother's Day celebration for both of their moms. Santasha remembers: "My mother came and met her mother. . . . After a while, she was like 'Where's Denise?' She started to embrace her. She was like 'How's Denise doing?' Even though she still, you know, made it clear that she doesn't like it." Santasha's mother's appearance of acceptance and embracement of Denise encouraged Santasha to continue to pursue a close relationship with her mother, but the negative offhand remarks her mother made about Santasha's sexuality resulted in her never being fully comfortable in that relationship. While she appreciates and is even grateful for her mother's interest in continuing their mother-daughter relationship, she knows that when it boils down to it, her mother would rather she not be gay. That unspoken (or sometimes indirectly spoken) homophobia, and the corresponding heterosexist belief that unions between women and men are the better choice, puts a strain on how close she can actually be with her mother.

When Dr. Nilda Flores, a licensed psychotherapist, returned home to South America in 1999 to attend her brother's wedding, her experiences with her family made her realize that although they said they were accepting of her gay sexuality, they were actually very uncomfortable with it. Nilda is from a small country that she says has a history of being "very progressive." Unlike nearby Buenos Aires, where she says gay sexuality is "hidden" and "under cover," in her country people are "out and about." During her trip, Nilda elaborates, "We even saw this man dressed in a tutu in the middle of the street. So it's there [openly gay expressions of sexuality], not like New York, but it's pretty open."

Nilda surmises that her parents, and particularly her mother, were hostile about Nilda's presence at the wedding because of how she portrayed her relationship with her partner, a Black middle-class woman named Adrienne Taylor: "I think what really bothered her was the public aspect of it, that everybody in the family found out." Nilda thought her mom had told her family that she would be bringing her partner to the wedding, so she was taken aback when an aunt approached her during the reception and asked when she would be getting married (to a man). She explained that she is gay and that Adrienne is her partner. Her aunt said she was very surprised, because Nilda's mother had never said anything to anybody about their relationship. After that, Nilda says, while she was in South America, "I wasn't hiding it. I went everywhere with Adrienne. I wasn't putting it in anyone's face, but if they asked me, I introduced her as *mi compañera*. It's an ambiguous term. It's the term they use for gay partnerships. It can also be used as 'my comrade,' but everybody kind of knew, and my mom was freaked out that I was introducing her that way. So I think the public aspect really bothered her."

But even though no one in her family directly told Nilda that her openness about her sexuality was problematic for them, the day after the wedding her mother responded by letting the family dog out of a fenced area to scare Adrienne. They were both afraid for their safety and left Nilda's parents' house to finish their stay in a hotel. For the remainder of the visit, nobody from the family called on or spent time with them save her father, who called once. After that experience, Nilda says she and Adrienne were traumatized. She felt horrible and particularly disappointed in her brothers and sisters, because in the past she had always been quick to stand up for them in conflicts with their parents, while in this instance no one came to her defense.

Nilda also found her mother's behavior peculiar because years before the wedding, her mother and siblings had visited Nilda in New York, and were well aware of her lesbian sexuality. They had met her friends and a woman (also Black) whom she was dating at the time. During that visit, her family was very nice to her friends and supportive of Nilda. Reflecting back on both experiences, Nilda believes that her mother responded in such a harsh way at the wedding because they were "down where the people she knew could see it, and I think she wanted to keep it under wraps."

In order to avoid this sort of behavior from disappointed family members, some of the women I spoke to decided not to be so direct in outing themselves to family. These people were mostly born right around 1970 or earlier and say they are not in the closet, in the sense that they do not hide their sexuality, but they choose not to name their relationships as gay to family members. Tammy Lindsay, for instance, is a transgressive woman who has never told her mother she is gay; instead, she just starts bringing the person she is dating with her to family functions, and people quickly catch on. She limits her displays of affection at these events in an attempt to be respectful. After all, she was raised in a Holiness-denomination church, which is so conservative that even heterosexual couples who are not married limit their expressions of affection around their elders. Tammy told me: "My mother's a churchgoing woman, so you know, I grew up in the church, in the Holiness church, and you don't need to talk to your mother about some things. Plus, you know at that age and being a church woman and all, they don't want to talk to you about sex and stuff like that. I think you should just bring her [your partner] around the family, you know, to Sunday dinner or family cookouts; she'll know what's up—she's not dumb. Plus, she probably already knows [the nature of the relationship]."

Rather than passing as heterosexual, Tammy's behavior is consistent with Goffman's (1963) and Yoshino's (2006) description of "covering." Covering is an attempt to prevent a stigma from looming large by keeping public expression of the stigma to a minimum. According to Goffman, "The individual's object is to reduce tension, that is, to make it easier for himself and the others to withdraw covert attention from the stigma"

(102). During the three years of my field work, I saw Tammy in two committed relationships, and throughout both of them she remained very involved with her immediate and extended family. One year, for Tammy's birthday, her mom and other relatives joined Tammy at her girlfriend's house for a special dinner. At the party, they played secular music and Tammy danced with her girlfriend in front of her mother.[6] She did not kiss or otherwise show outward affection, however, and neither did any of the guests, most of whom were lesbian.

Shelly Jackson is relatively new to what many gay people call "the life." Before partnering with Shaunte Austin, she was heterosexually married and had four children. When asked how her parents responded when she finally told them she was in the life, she says, "I didn't even tell them. They seen Shaunte with me, and my sister said something to somebody, and that's how it got to my father. But they know that that's my Girl." She takes as confirmation the fact that her father chastised her during a visit when she was speaking in a disrespectful way to Shaunte. He told Shelly, "Don't you talk to her like that. Don't talk to *your Girl* like that." Another time, when her family was invited to spend the night at her father's house, Shelly offered to sleep with her children in one bedroom and have Shaunte sleep in a separate room. Instead, her father told her, "No, you and Shaunte are going to sleep here together, and the boys are going to sleep there."

Shaunte says she downplays her relationship in the presence of those who are uncomfortable in order to show respect. Because Shelly's mother is aware of their relationship but does not want to talk about it, the issue is not ever raised directly. She says, "It's like they think, 'I know it's there, but I just don't want to hear about it.' And that's how some people are." She and Shelly are not affectionate in front of Shelly's mother because, she says, "I don't want anybody to make me feel uncomfortable, so I do the same thing for them. I want everybody to feel comfortable, and I don't see the point of doing something that somebody's not comfortable with."

Whether it be the blatant disregard of close family members, the more subtle offhanded comments of a disapproving mother, the polite distancing and judgment of older relatives, or the passive-aggressive behaviors of family members who are embarrassed by their daughter's obvious sexuality, all are part of the experiences that many Black women who retain connections to their families must negotiate after they have come out as gay. That the women themselves work to smooth over their parents' discomfort by downplaying their sexuality through indirect language or by limiting their displays of affection attest to the lengths they will go to maintain relations with family members. They compromise by covering or downplaying their status as lesbian. However, my research adds to the understanding of covering by showing agency in these women's decisions of how to de-emphasize their sexuality but not pass as heterosexual. While they act in a limited way around family, they frame this behavior using a narrative of respect rather than a feeling that they do not have the freedom to be gay, and in other ways reveal the importance of significant others in their lives. So while they may choose to downplay their gay identities during social interactions, they nonetheless remain clear in their refusal to give up or deny their gay sexuality. They may not kiss their partners during Thanksgiving dinner, but they will have them sitting right with them at the family table.

OPENLY GAY FAMILIES IN BLACK COMMUNITY LIFE

Anita Adams, introduced earlier, lives with her two children and her partner, Trina Adams, in Harlem, New York, a community that anthropologist John L. Jackson rightfully calls "a symbolic center for African American culture, a key reference point for Blacks who seek to define themselves in relation to a certain canonized version of African American tradition and history." Jackson notes, "People from all over the country (and even the world) link their identities to Harlem and the notable landmarks within it" (2001, 9). Neighborhoods like Harlem in Manhattan and Bedford-Stuyvesant in Brooklyn are key reference points for African Americans who define themselves in relation to a particular version of what it means to be Black and to be part of Black cultural, social, political, and economic communities.

Anita's experiences of raising her two children in a community like Harlem have made her reflect on what living an openly gay life has meant for her children, her relationship with her mate, and the neighbors around her as people come to understand the nature of their family life. While she finds that in some Black communities you have to hide the fact that you are gay because "people are not open to the lifestyle," she has learned that in Harlem, "it's become more open." She elaborates: "You're starting to see a lot of gay couples together, so people are starting to come along. But it just takes them some time. They've got to get to know the person. . . . It's like living in a development and you've been there for years. The tenants have got to get to know who this new person is, and [once] they find out this person is a nice person, it's like, 'Come over, have some tea!' And that's how it's been for us." Pretending to be exasperated, Anita tells me, "[Trina] knows everybody in the neighborhood, people that I don't even frigging know! I'm like, 'Where do you know these people from?' I'm living here all my life and *I* don't even know these people. She made friends."

Anita brings Trina to parent-teacher night at her older daughter's junior high school and to parent planning sessions at her younger daughter's elementary school. She says that even though in a general sense she is not particularly open about her sexuality with strangers, she, Trina, and the children are indeed a family. While as a single mother Anita was a little more reluctant to share with strangers her lesbian identity, as part of a same-sex union she wants Trina to take an active role in creating and developing relationships not just with Anita's kin but also with various outsiders who come into contact with the family, including neighbors, coworkers, and the parents of her children's friends. Anita was happy when Trina initiated a more active role in her daughters' school programs by volunteering for graduation committees and attending parent-themed events, because those activities help them relate to the outside world as a family. She says that the "normal," routine behaviors of her everyday life are allowing the Black community to slowly learn "who we are and how we're living" today.

The presence of openly gay families in Black communities is forcing neighbors, teachers, leaders of community organizations, and various others to acknowledge gay sexuality in a way not seen in previous generations. Many of the families in this study see their presence in Black social environments as their opportunity to show what their lives represent: a fusion of cultural identity and lesbian practice. These families express a sense, however, that most people in their communities have not quite accepted their presence, leaving them with a variety of experiences ranging from unsettlement or uncertainty to rejection and a reluctance to enact a gay sexuality in public spaces.

Marissa Dillard, a corporate attorney, was born and raised in Harlem with her mother and grandmother. Although she and her partner, Josephine Owens, are out to family and friends, she says that living an openly gay life continues to have its challenges: "It's not so easy to be out. I think we still, even now all these years later, being out for over twenty years now, I still think that there's a lot of homophobia out there. So I certainly understand for the sisters who are not out that it's not an easy thing. But I guess it's a part of dealing with our sexuality and trying to educate people in our community by letting them know it could be any of us that identify as lesbian." As visible lesbians in African American spaces, Marissa, Josephine, and their children are "new pioneers" in the struggle for gay awareness, acceptance, and equality. In her comment, Marissa refers to Black lesbians who are not out as "sisters," implying that she sees herself as part of a group of others who have a similar goal in choosing to remain in predominantly Black neighborhoods while living openly as lesbians. She also sees herself as an educator to heterosexual Blacks whom she thinks know little about the actual lives of lesbian and gay people. She believes she has a responsibility to increase the visibility of gay people in the communities where she lives and has lived. So for women like Marissa, being openly gay is not just about fulfilling same-sex desire: it also involves teaching and increasing awareness among Black people of what Black homosexuality can mean.

As discussed in Chapter 4, couples with children have to operate in various settings—school recitals, parent-teacher meetings, extracurricular sports—that directly or indirectly call for them to name their relationships to others. In these situations, the racial environment and the openness of the institutional setting affect the level of comfort Black lesbians feel about revealing a gay sexuality. Because of the Black community's collective discomfort around sexuality, Black gays and lesbians have not gained enough political and social traction to be able to create as many gay-friendly spaces *within* Black environments relative to the spaces gay Whites in urban areas occupy. Rather, Black gays and lesbians are largely subject to the cultural norms of their communities. Anita says she has felt more comfortable engaging with officials at her younger daughter Kacey's school because it is in Greenwich Village, where she estimates that 95 percent of the administrators and parents are White and there are other children with two moms or two dads. This predominantly White, gay-friendly environment is new to her and is something she clearly likes. She says: "It's interesting. I mean it's just so cool. I think there's more peace. When you see a closed type of school there's a lot of pressure, but when you go to a school where everyone's open about whatever, it's so different. I went to a potluck at Kacey's school a couple of Sundays ago, and some of the parents were gay. It was men and women [who were gay], and it was just so interesting. And it was peaceful! You didn't have to be ashamed—not ashamed, just hiding. It was just so interesting."

Anita's older daughter, Kiyana, on the other hand, attends a "closed type of school" that is less inviting for Anita and Trina as openly gay parents. When Trina has tried to interact with teachers and administrators as a parent to Kiyana, she has been met with discomfort and resistance. During a parent-teacher conference, for example, awkward silences followed her and Anita's explanation of how Trina fit into the family. They were determined not to take the easy way out by saying Trina was Kiyana's aunt or godmother. They have faced other uncomfortable moments at the school, but Anita likens the resistance they encounter to the fact that Black people are still "coming along and learning what the lifestyle is all about." Nevertheless, there was a noticeable difference in Anita's tone when she talked about the greater comfort she has experienced at Kacey's school in Greenwich Village. She moved from a "buck up and tough it out" way of talking about how to survive as gay parents at Kiyana's predominantly Black school to a wistfulness over being able to let down her guard in the predominantly White, overtly gay-friendly setting. She mused that she was glad that at the school in Greenwich Village, she and Trina "didn't have to be ashamed." She immediately corrected herself by saying, "not ashamed, just hiding." But the slip of her tongue spoke volumes: Anita's comments, and the comments of others suggest that for Black lesbians, interacting in Black communities invites a struggle to avoid portraying to others—and perceiving within themselves—that their sexuality is something for which they should be ashamed or sorry.

In other contexts, the concern is not about rejection or feelings of shame but about how to negotiate relationships with outsiders who seem to accept these women's gay sexuality but who suggest through their interactions that they are reluctant to acknowledge the nature of these unions out loud. Trina says: "At my office, it is a known fact that I am a lesbian, it is a known fact that Anita is my spouse, but it's just never talked about. When she comes to the office, it is like all smiles, and they genuinely love her. When she comes into my office, everyone is trying to grab her into their office. So it is like, 'We know, but we don't want to talk about it. We love you guys, but we don't want to talk about it.'" Other people report similar experiences. Neighbors will behave in a friendly way to a gay couple but become uncomfortable when they have to use language that acknowledges the relationship the individuals have to one another. They will refer to a woman's partner as "the young lady who lives with you" or "your friend." Coworkers will ask how a partner is doing by referring to the partner by name rather than using a label of "girlfriend" or "partner."

Many of the lesbians in my study say they are not closeted in Black communities. They wear engagement- or wedding-type rings to signal their commitment (even when they have not married and have not registered for a domestic partnership) and will let heterosexual people know they are engaged to or partnered with a woman. They dress with gender complementarity when going out with their mates, which particularly makes lesbian couples visible to one another and to the public.[7] Biological mothers list their partner as their child's guardian on school forms. While these behaviors let others know they are part of a couple, they remain careful in how they directly represent themselves to outsiders because they say they are never certain how people will respond to their relationship, and are cautious about avoiding the potential for homophobic violence. They tend not to post rainbow flags or other symbols of gay/lesbian identity on their cars or clothing, and at events like a funeral service or church function they will introduce a partner by name instead of using a title like "lover," "girlfriend," or "wife."[8] They tend to be indirect when acknowledging the nature of their relationship to those with whom they do not interact on a daily basis.

Nilda Flores says people in the Latino community of Washington Heights, where she works and lives, tolerate her gay sexuality as long as she looks and behaves like "an acceptable gay person" and as long as she does not try to equate it with heterosexual marriage. She finds that their definition of an "acceptable gay person" is someone who does not show public affection or impose their sexuality on others. She concludes, "They want us to be a little apologetic, like 'Oh, let me not offend you.' They want you to treat their [heterosexual] relationship as more important or more legitimate. That's the sense I get."

For some women, it is less important that family or the larger community agree with their choices or support them as gay people than that they tolerate them and allow them to live their lives without overt conflict. Venus Giles, an army veteran born in 1965, said: "I just want to live in an environment where people don't necessarily have to agree, but they accept it and move on. Don't be concerned about what we doing. It ain't your business! I ain't worried about what you doing. I don't care what you doing, you know? So I just would like for it to be someday, somewhere, where we can go and we can just live in harmony and just live our lives and just be who we gonna be, whatever that might be." Venus concluded that one of the costs of being gay is giving up the open expression of her self, saying, "I have given up the freedom to be able to express myself affectionately in the street, you know, to be able to announce my love like everybody else has the right to do. So you give up some things." She did not follow this statement with a wish that she could change the way people think or the environment to make it more tolerant. Instead, she said: "You give and take, you know? But hey, it's part of the way you have to live these days." To her, this is the cost of being gay, and she has decided to take on that cost as the price of her own self-fulfillment.

The Ambiguity of "Tolerant" Attitudes and Patterns of Integrative Marginalization

The November 2008 national election had on the ballot a Black candidate who was a serious contender for the office of President of the United States. That year, African Americans across the country paid particular attention to national politics, including a measure on the California ballot to repeal the rights of same-sex couples in that state to marry. The measure passed and sparked public interest because of the large percentages of racial minorities and Blacks in particular who supported the measure. I happened to be in New York that November to follow up on some of the families in this study and to initiate some new research. I spoke with a group of older Black lesbians and gay men, and the topic of the Black community and same-sex marriage legislation was on many of their minds. They agreed that there is widespread ideological disapproval among Blacks of the open practice of homosexuality, and hypothesized myriad reasons why this is the case.[9] Jackie Roberts told me: "I think Black people overall have a problem with sexuality as a whole, so when you start breaking it down in different categories, it just becomes more pronounced. . . . What we do is that we internalize those things that we feel or we think will make them [Whites] more accepting of us."

Cohen (1999) lays out a theoretical framework for understanding how gay and lesbian people experience life in Black communities. She argues that "integrative strategies provide control by unequivocally regulating the *majority* of marginal community members while allowing *a chosen few* to have limited access to dominant institutions and resources" (58, emphasis in original). A limited number of individuals within marginal communities have special resources or relationships with dominant group members that give them access to a privileged status in the larger society. Cohen says they hold a unique position both inside and outside of the community, and they are expected to live out a "double status" of allegiance and group membership. In my own work, I find that middle-class lesbians are most likely to experience the integrative marginalization Cohen describes. Their income, education, and occupational status compensates for the negative status their gay identity imposes. Katrice Webster works for one of the top three corporate law firms in New York, Dr. Renee Martin is the head resident in emergency room medicine at a large metropolitan hospital, Ro Gaul is a licensed electrician, and Angie Russell is one of only a handful of female African American sergeants in the New York City Police Department. People in the racial community admire and respect these women because of their professional accomplishments. Their parents brag about their occupational achievements, and this acceptance partially makes up for the disapproval of their openly gay sexuality. Twenty-nine percent of the women in this study completed their education with a four-year college degree, and an additional 33 percent have advanced degrees. Among the 38 percent who did not complete college, all but four have some education beyond high school, usually technical training or mastery of a trade. Forty-seven percent report an annual individual income greater than $50,000 (in 2004 dollars). Their education, income, and occupational status, when taken together, bestow on them a measure of self-determination and authority over their own lives.

Middle- and upper-middle-class lesbians also select into the more socially organized, economically stable and safer Black and Latino communities, which lessens the threat of being a victim of crime more generally, and of hate crimes in particular. Couples like Katrice and Caroline or Marissa and Josephine live in sections of Harlem and Brooklyn that have more services and resources, a greater presence of working people, and that are currently undergoing or have recently undergone gentrification by middle-class Blacks, Whites, and other racial groups. In contrast, working-class women like Corey, Jackie, and Venus live in parts of Brooklyn, Queens, and the Bronx where revitalization is slow and where there is more disadvantage and higher crime rates. There is a more cautious atmosphere in these neighborhoods. Strangers in these contexts may be more menacing, and safety in these communities is a sobering concern—not just around sexuality but around any visible identity that targets one as an easy mark. In less stable neighborhoods the greater concerns over physical safety make it difficult for lesbians who do not conform to traditional expectations of femininity to live open lives.

According to Cohen, integrative marginalization also "alters dominant ideological practices previously used to justify the total exclusion of marginal group members in order to account for the limited integration of some oppressed group members. . . . The adjustments made in the ideological explanations of exclusion stress the ability of certain oppressed group members to take on dominant group characteristics and values. The success of their assimilation is rationalized as being facilitated by biological, social, or material characteristics differentiating them from the majority of marginal group members" (1999, 59–60). Integrative marginalization, in other words, allows lesbians with high-status occupations and high incomes who practice gender conformity or who assimilate in other ways to suffer less social distance. Sometimes, they are given special status among heterosexuals. While social class affords them an advantaged position inside and outside the lesbian community, the racial community, and larger society, they may still be understood as inferior because of one or more of their marginalized statuses (race, gender, and/or sexuality).

Having a pleasing appearance can similarly mitigate against the larger racial community's disapproving attitudes toward homosexuality. An attractive style may encourage the larger racial group to overlook its negative perception of homosexuality in this specific case, and excuse homosexual behavior or reinterpret it in ways that allow the individuals to participate undisturbed in the larger life of the community. Karen Jabar, a forty-two-year-old law enforcement officer, for example, says she notices that when a woman has a "so-called butch image or dyke image" or "clothing like a guy," being gay "seems to be something that people sneer up about. But when you happen to be cute, or . . . when your speech can be viewed as being a bit more intelligent and not that ghetto slang," being gay "seems to be a little more tolerated." She describes her unease on the one or two occasions when she has gone out with women who "are dressed like boys: I don't feel comfortable. I just don't feel comfortable because it's like all eyes are on us. We're the focus of attention on the subway or something. But I've noticed when I go out with a very feminine woman, or a woman like myself, it's just viewed as a cute thing." She does not believe people are viewing herself and the feminine woman as straight. Instead, she comments, "they think perhaps that there's something going on, but it's cute."

Jackie says the inherent traits she has (fair skin and soft hair texture from her father's Portuguese heritage; a slight yet athletic physique maintained with regular visits to the gym) are valued by others and protect her from the harassment that often accompanies women with a nonfeminine gender presentation. She proudly tells me that her gender presentation is specifically "not urban ghetto": she does not like to wear jerseys, fitted caps, baggy jeans, or sneakers. Instead, she wears men's dress boots, slim jeans, and men's button-down shirts. Her clothes are neither feminine nor representative of a traditionally urban masculine style typically associated with today's young Black males. Both women and men find her appealing, and this limits the negative comments in the neighborhoods she frequents.

Overall, the more positive responses that economically successful lesbians and lesbian women who are perceived as attractive receive suggest a bifurcation in how gay identities are accepted in families and in communities, with greater acceptance for women who are able and willing to conform in other ways that uphold a positive, respectable image of Black people. This partial acceptance of a select few sexual minorities by the Black community as a whole according to their possession of valued traits that promote Black respectability is consistent with Cohen's concept of integrative marginalization. The exceptions described above exemplify the ways in which Black gay people negotiate a sexuality that is based in racial group membership. Heterosexuals are most likely to include gays and lesbians as part of the racial group when gays and lesbians remain connected to their racialized communities by living in Black neighborhoods and contributing to racial group uplift.[10] The larger community is also most accepting when an individual's expression of gay identity is consistent with the dominant expressions of Black culture in terms of music, dress, hair, residence, racial political ideologies, and so forth.[11] Black gays want to show to heterosexuals that their racial identity remains important to their sense of self (Moore 2010a; 2010b).

For lesbians who interact in predominantly Black social networks, this is not a problem. In my study, their primary relationships are with other Blacks—even their gay social groups are predominantly Black or Black and Latino. There are times, however, when they feel forced to choose between identities based in race and sexuality or when an alignment with race comes at a cost to one of their other identities. Certain issues, such as the legalization of same-sex marriage or the repeal of the ban against openly gay soldiers serving in the military, may call for them to demonstrate allegiances based in sexuality. Commitment to these issues offers the potential for racial distancing, particularly when race leaders argue that there are more pressing issues like poverty and employment that Blacks should rally around.

Even though the open expression of homosexuality is a cross-cutting issue in Black communities, other characteristics of the newly visible Black lesbian and gay population make their homosexuality more palatable to the racial group. They are openly gay and remain involved in their families of origin, hosting barbecues and fish fries that make other gay people of color visible in the community. They are walking their dogs together, going into car dealerships to purchase cars, opening joint bank accounts, and in various ways interweaving themselves into the social fabric of Black community life with multiple identity statuses that are observable to the rest of society. The strong racialized contexts of lesbian and gay life in New York allow for gay and lesbian issues to be seen as issues that are important for Black people.

BLACK RELIGION AS SIMULTANEOUS SOURCE OF CONDEMNATION AND STRENGTH

Most of the women I spoke with have a history of membership and belonging in Black religious communities. In many cases, their choice to openly express their lesbian sexuality threatened to put them on the outside of religious and sometimes racial group membership. In African American communities, religious structures provide direction for the language, rituals, and behaviors individuals incorporate in their lives. People participate in churches and mosques not just for spiritual guidance but also to find a sense of community, and they use the teachings of these religious groups as a set of practices or blueprints by which to organize their lives, however loosely or stringently. Many Black religious institutions participate in public rule enforcement and policing of parishioners' lives, and they openly condemn behaviors deemed to fall outside of religious teachings. Ministers, elders, even church mothers have the authority to approach individual congregants whom they suspect of violating the rules of the church (i.e., wearing clothes that are inappropriate, engaging in nonmarital sex) to confront or sanction them. Leaders frame this disciplinary action around their interest in saving souls or helping people (usually young people) resist temptation.

According to Reverend Horace Griffin, a former Baptist minister, there are few arenas where the dread and condemnation of homosexuality is more noticeable than in Black church settings (2006, chapter 1). Because of the involvement of the church across so many different community institutions and social groups, many researchers suggest that in Black communities, the philosophies and beliefs of religious organizations significantly impact the philosophies and views residents have on other issues, including homosexuality. Herek and Capitanio (1995) have found that religiosity, measured through organizational religious involvement (i.e., church attendance) and a conservative religious orientation, is associated with negative attitudes toward lesbians and gays and lack of support for civil rights for homosexuals. And those who have internalized religious teachings, particularly conservative teachings, are more likely to practice heterosexism (VanderStoep and Green 1988).

The move from private to public expressions of gay sexuality have highlighted a contradiction between Black churches' use of religion to constrain gay behavior and the use of religion and spirituality by many gay people to support and validate their gay identities. Lesbians who express a personal or ideological conflict between their sexuality and their religious beliefs tend to have been raised in conservative faiths where negative attitudes toward the enactment of sexual desire more generally, and of same-sex desire in particular, produce feelings of guilt and shame. Both the disapproval of homosexuality as a sin and the cultural leadership that religious organizations have historically had in Black communities make many—even those who are not particularly religious—wonder within themselves if their behavior is wrong.

Nyla Ransom is a very "out" lesbian. She and her partner have conceived three children together during their ten-year relationship. She references her mate in conversations at work and at the children's school, and when people are unclear about what she means by "partner," she tells them she is in a gay relationship. Yet when she is around religious people, it causes her to retreat into invisibility with regard to her family life. She has tried different churches but has never felt satisfied with organized religion. She says: "I get very uncomfortable around people who are religious. I haven't had conversations with them, but I think that they think it's [homosexuality is] something wrong. That's the group that I really just get very uncomfortable [around], and I don't really, like, stand up and say, 'I'm gay' kind of thing. I notice that about myself: there is something about religion that just, I don't know, maybe I feel like maybe it's wrong, but I haven't delved into religion again because it kind of turns me off." When she gets into a conversation about how religion ties into her gay identity, Nyla is filled with questions and uncertainties that she has not been able to resolve within herself. As a consequence, she says she "steers clear" of religion.

Althea Payne says being born in Jamaica, West Indies, and raised in the Pentecostal faith has caused her to struggle with how to maintain a connection to religious institutions as a gay woman. She says:

> I've had to do a lot of soul-searching with that, because the church that my family goes to, I have also been going to for thirty years, so I don't know anything else. But over the years, I've felt myself just kind of pulling away,

because their teachings are totally against my lifestyle, so it's very difficult for me to sit in the congregation and be comfortable and feel like I'm being blessed or any of those things. I've had to kind of just find my own spirituality away from the church, even if [that means] just on a Sunday, listening to some gospel [music] and reading my Bible and praying, because I felt that I just couldn't commune with Him in church. So I go [to church] once in a while on special occasions—Easter, Christmas, and in between—but for the most part I just do that communing with Him on a one-on-one.

Althea says she kept asking herself, "Why do the people that I worship with seem to preach that God doesn't love me because of my sexuality? . . . I do believe that God loves me, and even though they may not agree with what I am, I think that this is between me and God, and they are pretty much out of their mind to try to teach me that I'm not loveable." Notice that she does not say that God is accepting of her sexuality, only that her sexuality is not going to prevent God from loving her.

I convened a focus group to discuss how religion fit into the lives of Black lesbians. Yolanda Carmichael was in that group, and shared that she grew up in the Baptist church where she was taught that "homosexuality, same-sex gender relationships were wrong." Today, she maintains many of the spiritual beliefs she was raised with, but is ambivalent about whether the community in which she was brought up is accepting of homosexuality. She says that Blacks "as a people are very religious people," and this has consequences for how they respond to same-sex relationships: "You know, people go back to the Bible, and they take what they want from the Bible, and they add what they want to the Bible. But because we are who we are in terms of our religion and our spirituality, that [pause] I don't know, I see it both ways. I see that people are accepting because no matter what, we are children of God, and those without sin—if this is considered sin—cast the first stone. But on the flip side of that, I see for the most part people saying, 'Do what you want to do.'"

Yolanda does not completely disagree with the desire of the community that gay people be less visible, because she sees their disapproval as rooted in Black Christianity, "our religion and our spirituality." She says people are accepting because we are all God's children, regardless of our sin, adding the caveat "if this is considered sin"—meaning if being gay or living a gay life is a sin. She seems uncertain whether lesbian practice is a sin, and she does not come down firmly on either side. We can see a cloud of uncertainty over her thinking about whether she is participating in a life that is sinful. When asked whether she felt any condemnation or guilt about being gay, given her Baptist faith, she paused and said that guilt and condemnation "were projected" onto her by family and the church. In response, she "went through a lot of spiritual stuff" because it mattered to her what her family thought, and it "really, *really* mattered what God thought." She asked God for help in dealing with her feelings of attraction to a particular woman. When I asked her, "What did God say?" she laughed and replied, "Well, I'm still a lesbian today, and I'm a happy lesbian today!" She says that after all of her talks with God, the bottom line is that "I'm His child, regardless." Her comments do not suggest a complete feeling of acceptance from God or a complete resolution that her life fits with her spirituality, but rather that she has come to a place where she can be happy in her sexuality without renouncing her religious faith.

Saidiya Muhammad came to a similar place of compromise after struggling to find a place for her same-sex desire within Islam:

> I just threw caution to the wind and did what I had to do. In the beginning it was hard because I felt like a hypocrite, you know, praying, socializing, pretending that I'm straight. And then finally I spoke to the Imam. I said, "I need a break you know, I desire women now." He's like "What?!" I said I just need to be by myself to see if I could cope with the whole issue with Islam and Allah and my sexuality. He said, "Just keep it to yourself." So . . . I stayed away from [religious] activities. I just wanted to build [a romantic] relationship with this person without pressures. . . . I had just broken down—no praying, no fasting. Nothing. I went out naked. When I say naked, I mean I showed my arms, shorter skirts, going to the club, you know, just doing the wild and crazy carefree stuff! I had to do it, because this was something that I hadn't done in years. . . . And after some time, I realized I could do this—I could incorporate both of them in my life and have my fun, in a way. And after six years, I am stronger than ever [in my faith], and I'm still with my desires.

Yolanda and Saidiya both struggled to reconcile their feelings about their different religious commitments, and both managed to find peace in their relationships with God without abandoning an identity as openly gay women.

Love the Sinner, Hate the Sin

Gay people have always participated in the church. Althea told me, "When I went to my dad's church, there were always gays in the choir. [About] the choirmaster, my dad used to say 'Oh, we have a fairy,' but he was always embraced. I've never heard anyone say anything other than, 'Oh, he was a fairy.'" Leading an openly gay life, however, forces the individual and the church to confront homosexuality more directly and invites a "Love the sinner, hate the sin" approach to dealing with gay people. Dr. Frank M. Reid III, senior pastor of Bethel AME Church in Baltimore, offered the following commentary on homosexuality and the church: "The Black church does not have a history of gay-bashing and homophobia. Even those churches that hold to the conservative approach on sexual issues have loved the homosexual while disliking the practice of homosexuality. While our pews hold people who have committed adultery and fornication, and may have had children outside of marriage, the Black church at its best has managed to love this sinner without loving the sin" (Reid 1991).

The frameworks of "love the sinner, hate the sin" or "don't ask, don't tell" imply that gay people can and should occupy a lesser status in the community. Bishop Carl Bean, an openly gay minister and head of the Unity Fellowship Church of Christ, says that the love the sinner but not the sin approach to dealing with homosexuality in Black churches relegates lesbians and gays to a lower social class and translates into "We love you, but not who you really are" (Brown 1994). When gay sexuality is closeted, everyone can know about it and rationalize it merely as a bad behavior that a fellow congregant may need forgiveness for, just as one might need forgiveness for adultery or theft. But to be openly gay means that one is asking for that behavior to be condoned. It forces a confrontation of the assumption that homosexuality is morally wrong.

There are lesbians who feel they gain a spiritual connection to God in churches that are publicly and vocally gay-friendly, even when the church does not preach the exact same doctrine as the one they were raised in. Ellasteen Johnson left the church when she was twenty years old because she felt there was no place for her there as a gay woman. She returned almost fifty years later, after the death of her lesbian partner of thirty years, to a church that is considerably more liberal than the Apostolic faith she grew up in because being in the church gave her "a sense of being an authentic person." Ellasteen joined this new church despite its having a different doctrine than the one she was raised with because, she said, she wanted to worship in a place where she could "feel a sense of myself as a spiritual person connected to a higher order of belief." Although the satisfaction she now experiences in church is "nothing like when I was a child," she stays because of a need to have this connection for her "spiritual self." Ellasteen attends Riverside Church[12] and says she and other gay parishioners have made it a priority to connect with each other and to have a visible presence. She chose Riverside as a place of worship because of its active support and embracing of lesbian and gay people. She calls her church "very gay-friendly" and says that the church has an LGBTQ ministry for homeless sexual minority youths.

Many who grew up in strict religious sects are wary of churches that are very open in their acceptance of homosexuals or that have outwardly gay leadership, however, because these places of worship often deviate in substantive ways from the more conservative religious ideologies they were raised with. Many also perceive these churches to overemphasize and call attention to homosexuality. Those from more conservative denominations often say they are unwilling to completely depart from the traditions they were taught to believe. While they will allow for modifications of church "rules" about the type of clothing they can wear or adornments of jewelry and make-up that may be frowned upon, to renounce the tenets of the faith—baptism rituals, rules that allow successful entry into heaven—can feel sacrilegious.

Ruthie Erickson has a mother and older brother who are saved and attend church services several times a week. Even though Ruthie was not raised with any particular religious beliefs, her brother will often "go head-to-head" with her about "living her life right" for herself and her three-year-old son Lawrence by going to church. She says she doesn't listen to him "at all," but she does send Lawrence over to her mother's house to attend church from time to time. Last year, Ruthie decided that she wanted her son to have the experience of belonging to a church, and she visited several different congregations trying to find one where she felt comfortable. So even though she says her mother's churchgoing behaviors and her brother's arguments about the importance of going to church have no effect on her, she has made efforts to introduce more formal religion into her own and her son's lives.

A friend introduced Ruthie to a church created by and for openly gay Christians, but Ruthie did not like it because "it was all about [being] gay." She says the church was too focused on being gay, and the behaviors of the parishioners made her feel like she "was going to the club" because the members seemed less interested in the Word of God and more interested in meeting other gay people. Ruthie is interested in finding a church where gay people can feel comfortable worshipping but that is also focused on "the Bible" and the "teachings of Christ." She says of some gay-oriented churches, "They, you can't change the whole Word, the Bible and everything to suit you. It is written one way to be conceived in that way and you can't just change it because you're gay and make it all about gays. It's not. But at the same token, you can't be throwing stones at them and all that, either. So it should be open and you should feel comfortable, [but] I haven't found that comfort yet." In contrast to Ellasteen, Ruthie and others believe it important that a church retain the conservative doctrine and teachings that are the foundation of its spiritual beliefs. They want a church that is accepting of gay people but that still retains the principal doctrine of that faith.

Church Membership as Representation of Racial Group Consciousness

Because religious organizations are the moral, social, and political authority in Black communities, some of the women I interviewed keep trying to find a way to participate in them despite their feelings of ambivalence and uncertainty toward much of Black religion. This helps to explain why Van Green, who knew she felt a strong attraction to women and a very weak attraction to men during all of her teenage years, married a man at age eighteen, only to divorce him and return exclusively to women six months later. She says her marriage was part of an effort to fulfill the wishes of society, her family, and her religious faith.

Adrienne Witherspoon says even though she did not attend church regularly while growing up, "It was a very big part of my life culturally because my family and my extended family was in it, and my parents talked to me about the Bible all the time, and so it really did impact my psyche even though I wasn't physically going to church every Sunday. But I had a lot of conflict from very young about God and what that meant, because I did have a very independent personality and it didn't seem like it was congruent to a lot of the values that my parents were espousing and things that they wanted me to do. So it was always a huge struggle for me." Adrienne's current concerns do not lie in her family's acceptance or condemnation; her mother is deceased, and she does not worry about what the rest of her family thinks. She was estranged from her family prior to coming out as gay, and this did not change once her family members became aware of her sexuality. Instead, her concerns lie in how to retain connections to the Black community and how to develop a spirituality that can strengthen her and contribute to her personal growth. For the past year, Adrienne has been attending Riverside Church, the same church as Ellasteen. At Riverside, she has found a group of people among whom she can be herself, and this has helped her retain a connection to the Black community. Past homophobic experiences with community leaders combined with her emotional distance from family members and involvement in an interethnic relationship with a woman from South America could in combination create distance between herself and Black people. She uses her involvement in the church to mediate this potential distance. In sum, Black religious organizations hold the potential to bind Blacks together as a cultural group, despite differences across class or other constructed categories.

Strategies of Resistance and Accommodation

How do gay people negotiate the limitations religion imposes? Most people go through a period in which they try to acquiesce to the church's expectations and their family's hopes that they live their lives as heterosexual. Even those who say they have always been drawn to women or who have had same-sex desire from a very young age usually try heterosexuality through relationships, marriage, and/or childbearing. Those committed to practicing a gay sexuality who still desire a connection to religious institutions seek out organizations that are either tolerant of or silent on the issue of homosexuality. Davina Brown characterizes the Black community as "traditional," "conservative," "homophobic," and "not very accepting" of lesbian and gay people. She also identifies as Baptist and attends what she defines as a "traditional Black" church in Brooklyn. She says that its leaders and congregation rarely mention homosexuality, however, and when they do, it is not discussed in a negative way. She is happy about that, because she would not feel comfortable worshipping in a church where the pastor was "denigrating homosexuals or saying negative things." She has identified "quite a few" other gays and lesbians in the congregation, and she often attends services with her Trinidadian partner, Rochelle. Nevertheless, they do not identify themselves as partners to the other parishioners, and she is not "out" at church. Thus any perceived judgments or homophobia that might exist in the ideology of religious institutions toward homosexuality can be mediated when those values are not openly or publicly stated, but rather are left as an understood or uncertain position of the church.

The process of searching for God can lead to self-acceptance of a gay sexuality, even when individuals reach no firm conclusion of support or acceptance from a religious institution. Marisol Sampson has gone through a process of searching for a church, and in the process, she says, "I really kind of found myself, where I fit, regardless of the church."

While she would like to find a church that uplifts all of who she is, she's no longer actively searching for it:

> I've found my relationship with God, and I'm really happy, and it's [the search has] kind of made me much stronger. Now I'm not concerned at all about what anybody thinks. I'm just kind of like, "This is me and so be it," and sometimes people are like, "Well, you know this church believes this, and you know Catholics believe that and this and that," and I'm just like, "That's what *they* believe, but I know that God wants me to be happy, and He wants me to do the right thing, and He wants me to live my life properly, and that's what I'm concerned with, not your version of what it is that I should or should not be doing." So I can sit in church and enjoy, you know, the whole kind of, like, the energy of what's going on and the spirituality without really kind of getting up in the minutiae of what everybody else is saying about what I should and should not do.

CONCLUSION

When their public enactment of homosexuality threatens to separate them from strong and positive affiliations with their racial group, Black gay women must negotiate and manage their group affiliate and insider status based on race. Several strategies that these women use for dealing with disapproving attitudes and religious condemnation have been discussed in this chapter.[13] The majority of the women in this study remain in predominantly Black neighborhoods and social contexts and negotiate regularly with family and community. Those who remain, particularly those with the resources to leave if they choose, say the support of and membership in the larger Black community is important to them. They remain because they trust in racial solidarity and racial group membership. They also remain because they have less confidence that they will ever be fully accepted as members of other identity groups, such as those based in sexuality.

In the past decade, Black gay people have been increasingly willing to test that trust by making their gay identities more public and asserting their interest in being involved and taking on leadership roles in the Black community. The move from gay sexuality as a primarily private enactment to the open expression of it and insistence on acknowledgment of it from family, community residents, and even church parishioners comes at a price: openly gay people often have to give up full acceptance from family and friends. But this is a price Black lesbians who remain in African American communities are willing to pay in order to maintain a racial group affiliation. In Pattillo's (2007) study of class tensions within the rapidly gentrifying Chicago neighborhood of North Kenwood, she identifies the various disputes between Black residents as the working- and middle-class struggle for ownership of the community. She shows that these ongoing debates are part of the contestations of what it means to be Black, and she concludes that participation in the Black community requires the periodic engagement in debate and the negotiation and reconciliation that follow. Those committed to the group choose "participation over abdication and involvement over withdrawal, even and especially when the disagreements get heated and sometimes vicious" (5).

Patillo's argument suggests that the women I have studied remain involved in Black community life despite the conflicts over acceptance of their sexuality because those conflicts are part and parcel of their sense of community and belonging. The struggle over power and having one's voice heard are all part of the social organization of Black communities. Group membership is not about sameness or having one voice, but about having a commonality, a perceived link that connects its members regardless of other differences that might also exist. This chapter offers insight into how Black lesbians embark on the maintenance of group affiliation and insider status around one identity based on race when cross-cutting issues around the public enactment of homosexuality threaten to separate them from strong and positive affiliations with the racial group.

Intersections, Extensions, and Implications

Throughout this book I have examined the ways race and class influence how Black women who are gay understand their sexual orientation, find partners, and form families, thus challenging a number of generalizations about lesbian family patterns that have been drawn from research almost exclusively focused on White, middle-class, feminist women. This effort bridges work in the lesbian and gay studies field that has not paid enough attention to issues of race and class with the literature on Black families that has remained silent on issues of sexual orientation. The population I study has also largely remained invisible in the debates on same-sex marriage and portraits of gay and lesbian parenting. This work offers its audience a more comprehensive and nuanced picture of racialized sexual minorities and their families than has previously existed.

Invisible Families shows how identities formed early on in life, like those based in race and gender, influence how individuals perceive and enact later group memberships, like those based in sexuality. It does this through the analysis of a group of women who, because of their year of birth, geographic location, social class, and other characteristics, came of age during periods of heavy racial segregation and entered into their gay sexualities with firmly entrenched racial identities. It finds that initial self-understandings based on race and gender influence subsequent practices of same-sex desire, processes of family formation, routes to motherhood, and the ways gender is expressed in households headed by two women. This study also explores the practice of lesbian sexuality in the context of racial group membership and involvement in racially similar communities. Some of these subjects have not been elucidated in past empirical research. Others have been identified but primarily understood from the perspectives of lesbian-feminists or women who experience their gay sexualities through academic or political interpretations of gender inequality.

One unique feature of *Invisible Families* is that it analyzes the identity and structural contexts of lesbian sexuality and family formation through the study of women who not only lie at the intersection of the single dimensions of race, gender, and sexuality, but whose experiences as a group have been systematically neglected because of their very position at the boundaries of those categories. Writing about such mainstream topics as family, class, and gender through the specific case of Black-identified gay women offers a coherent way to understand how intersectionality as a paradigm operates. It reveals the complex social relations that intersectionality embodies, and it substantively analyzes those relationships in ways that challenge the "singularity, separateness, and wholeness" of each of these social categories (McCall 2005, 1778). Moreover, it reveals diversity, variation, and heterogeneity where researchers might have assumed singularity, sameness, and homogeneity. In so doing, this work provides insights that challenge basic—sometimes false—understandings of how gender, sexuality, and race-ethnicity shape individuals' lives.

Gay sexuality is an arena in which questions of identity, authenticity, and self-representation intersect with race in vivid ways. One thread that runs through this book concerns how the exploration of family formation in the context of Black lesbian experience highlights for some women the fine line between maintaining images of respectability that shield Black women's sexuality from criticism, and revealing and affirming their autonomy through the expression of sexual freedom. In previous generations of Black life, the families in this study would have largely remained absent from the narratives of Black community activity, and indeed many families like these are not part of the written record, nor are their lives spoken about in much of lesbian oral history or the history of women of color more generally.

Wolcott's (2001) historical analysis of the relationships between working-class and middle-class Black women in Detroit emphasizes the gendered nature of the language of respectability, as well as the ways discourses of respectability have been used and transformed by Black women over time. In my study, Black lesbian mothers seek to embody a definition of respectability in their dress, parenting, and management of home life. This definition removes the deviant assumption of a lesbian sexuality, finding ways to encompass a lesbian sexual self within the larger set of discourses around respectability. Whereas in the past the expression of sexuality might have been submerged into private spaces, the women in this book reclaim sexuality as a component of their public, "respectable" selves. This study's analysis of Black women's sexual agency has consequences for the strict and rarely questioned definitions of acceptable Black cultural expression and behavior. It also reveals the ways popular culture images, political representations of gay life and group membership, Black life and group membership, and everyday discourse structure understandings of multiple and intersecting statuses.

The distinctiveness of the group under study—racial minority women with same-sex practice—is neither accidental nor trivial. More general processes of group formation and identity development occur in a variety of contexts but are most salient in a group whose race and sexuality are hypervisible. The social construction of gender might be difficult to recognize in a heterosexual couple, for example, but it really stands out when same-sex partners are wearing clothing that suggests gender complementarity. Moreover, studying parenthood from the behaviors of women in same-sex unions offers a new vantage point from which to analyze more general processes of mothering. Exploring these and other issues in a sample in which biological sex is held constant, individuals have similar self-understandings of racial identification, and individuals live and socialize in similar racial contexts offers new insights not just to family sociologists or gender or race specialists but to all scholars interested in the importance of ideology and identity.

Another thread in this work is the revision it makes to what we have assumed about the sources of power in marital and marriage-like relationships, particularly stepfamilies. Holding sex constant allows us to see more intricately how gender, rather than sex, operates in families, and through this we learn that control over domestic labor can be an important source of power for individuals in the larger process of creating and maintaining family life. This finding has implications for how we think about the creation of hierarchies in familial relationships and makes us consider the possibility that control over household labor and child rearing can be a type of power in marriages and other types of unions. Power differentials in relationships may not be solely or predominantly centered around income or economic activity, but may also center around areas of decision making in home life that reveal themselves in the process of creating "family."

SAME-SEX RELATIONSHIPS IN THE TWENTY-FIRST CENTURY

Although Black lesbians may at first appear to be a relatively homogeneous and particular group, the findings of this book have implications for other populations. *Invisible Families* simultaneously articulates a distinctive experience of Black lesbians and shows how their experiences have applicability and generalizeability to other raced, socioeconomic, and sexual groups. One thing it reveals is the varied and changing nature of family formation for gay people. This research, when combined with current media reports and studies of LGBT youth, suggests that people are claiming gay identities at earlier ages than in previous generations. Another important discovery of this work is that the timing of identity statuses and when people choose to take them on importantly affects the route they take to enter parenthood. For lesbians, this process plays out differently by social class. Middle- and upper-middle-class women have greater access to more costly alternative insemination procedures and can better afford to use formal adoption services to have children. Working-class and poor lesbians are left with fewer strategies for becoming parents that do not include heterosexual intercourse.

State laws around the status of same-sex partners and the legal relationships openly gay people may form with children through adoption are continually changing. Advances and setbacks will persist as the world moves forward, but increasing diversity in family forms and routes to family creation are a reality. In 1996, noted sociologist Judith Stacey argued that important social forces were reshaping American families and that we must either acknowledge the reorganization of families or remain in denial about the changes that are taking place. *Invisible Families*, by revealing the complexity of changes that are taking place in families through the lens of race and lesbian sexuality, makes it much harder to do the latter.

One of the ongoing battles around sexuality at the start of the twenty-first century involves the federal recognition of same-sex marriage. This issue is both a cause for gay people to rally around and a representation of a moral problem some in the Black middle class feel they must fight against. Legal questions around same-sex marriage brings in gay rights issues as relevant to Black communities. At the time of data collection for this study, for example, the particular visibility and public pronouncement a wedding entails made many Black lesbians reluctant to celebrate their unions in this way. As time moves on and gay sexuality becomes increasingly recognized as a public identity, however, more Black lesbians are taking part in these rituals as a way to affirm the multiplicity of their identities and to validate their relationships to others.

In analyzing lesbian sexuality outside the contexts of lesbian feminism and the political ideologies and discourses that have previously been used to frame this literature, *Invisible Families* reveals new interpretations and discussions of female desire and eroticism. Cultural norms dictated by gender, race, and class structure lesbian sexuality and family formation, and this work attempts to authentically capture other distinctions that characterize larger Black communities. I have found that important aspects of lesbian and gay culture persist across generations to structure the social norms of community life because lesbian and gay social spaces are *racially segregated* and *class integrated*. Black lesbians' social segregation from White lesbian feminists, combined with the mixing of more closeted middle-class women with more performative working-class women, results in the persistence of gender presentation as a means of structuring relationships and community life, as this work shows. Black lesbians' community life has a history of autonomy. Their social activities primarily took place in their own neighborhoods and private residences, and these were racially segregated events. Understanding the basis of the gender complementarity that persists in Black lesbian relationships, and the sexual freedom that this public representation of women's sexuality produces, adds an important dimension to the majority of research on homosexual desire that has as its focus male homoeroticism. It also brings into our understandings cultural elements of sexual orientation, cultural elements of LGBT communities, and the culture gay people bring to their multiple identities. Black lesbians who are not part of Black gay life, meaning those who rarely participate in the social activities of these communities, and those who identify with aspects of lesbian feminism that eschew gender presentation as a means of structuring lesbian relationships and lesbian life, are less likely to portray gender complementarity in their relationships. Black lesbians who spend the majority of their social time in predominantly White spaces are also less likely to be aware of and participate in other social norms that structure Black lesbian communities.

Identity within the statuses of race, gender, class, and sexuality is experienced as a lived, continuous project shaped by structural forces, culture, historical position, and individual daily life experiences. Because of the historical experience of racial inequality and gender inequality, Black women's lives have been structured around social categories. I show here that the majority of Black lesbians in this study do not consciously seek to dismantle these categories, but rather strategically employ categories in different ways to explain who they are and how they fit in the world. The significance of age cohort in these self-understandings of race cannot be overstated. Eighty-seven percent of my sample was born between 1960 and 1975, and the rest were born between 1942 and 1960. The social locations of Black American and Afro-Caribbean women born in the 1960s and 1970s, and the historical experiences of their mothers and others in their racial communities, shape the ways they approach a lesbian sexuality and the processes of family life and parenting. The racial inequality experienced by their parents, who came of age in the Civil Rights and Black Power era, set the foundation for their own self-understandings of race. The experiences of Black women growing up during the particular political climates of the 1960s and 1970s also importantly shaped their self-understandings around these statuses.

Higginbotham (1992) has argued that gender is embedded within the context of race. She defines *race* as a highly contested representation of power relations between groups or social categories that individuals use to identify themselves and others. Furthermore, she writes, "In societies where racial demarcation is endemic to their sociocultural fabric and heritage – to their laws and economy, to their institutionalized structures and discourses, and to their epistemologies and everyday customs – gender identity is inextricably linked to and even determined by racial identity" (254). Higginbotham contends that race has been so overdetermined in Western culture, and specifically in the United States, that it has come to function as a metalanguage in its discursive representation and in the way it has constructed social relationships. A close scrutiny of the ways that Black lesbians in my study experience their multiple identification statuses suggests something similar. Although social identities are complex and dynamic, particularly for those with multiple marginalized social statuses, the racial hierarchies in society experienced by women in this age cohort and region of the country work together to produce a cognizance of gender and sexuality through race. Race is the foundation of a persistently salient and powerful collective relationship they have with others, as well as a structural location that has served to order groups in society. Gender and sexuality both take on meaning in the context of race. The differences in reception by the outside world, the ways Black lesbians portray a lesbian sexuality and experience motherhood, and even the motivations behind the decisions they make when looking for a partner are consistently mediated by race and socioeconomic position.

Cohorts of Blacks, and particularly Black Americans born in the United States in the 1970s and earlier, filter their experiences through race. This is not to say that other statuses based in class, gender, sexuality or other categories are less important. But the history of race and the persistent structural inequalities that continue to exist across racial groups has resulted in their greater use of a racial lens to interpret their relationships with the world. Race is also the category around which they cohere with others as a group, though it is not always the most important status for individual self-definition. Different social contexts allow them the possibility of perceiving one identity category as primary for their self-definition and a different identity category as a status around which to join together with others. This has important consequences for how we think about identification statuses as sites for the construction of self-definition versus group membership.

Younger age cohorts have a greater social distance from the inequalities of the past. The "new racism" Bonilla-Silva (2010) identifies can disguise racial inequalities, and the reduction in overt racial injustice (relative to previous generations) allows younger people to frame their social worlds using multiple or alternative lenses. In the twenty-first century, I believe, younger cohorts of Blacks, Blacks who do not maintain close links and cultural connections to the racial group, Blacks who do not perceive a strong sense of linked fate, and Blacks with weaker racial group commitments through claims on multiracial identities, ethnic identities, and other experiences will be less likely to turn first to the lens of race to comprehend their experiences in the world.

The implications of this research point to particular political struggles on the horizon for lesbians and other gay people whose identities are firmly based in race/ethnicity. They are taking on an openly gay sexuality at earlier ages and asking that this identity be thought of as primary alongside a racial identity and racial group membership. In my recent research on the characteristics of Black LGBT protest, I argue that the tactics of Black gays may appear to be assimilationist when used by Whites to advocate for mainstream acceptance, but the particular context of Black LGBT protest and its appeal to the racial community for acceptance and full integration make the actions of Black activists read as radical to those they want to address: other Black people (Moore

2010a). The radicalism of their actions is not driven by acceptance from the broader mainstream society or from White LGBT activists, although these are goals for some individuals. Rather, their overriding concern is how to maintain and build relationships with their racial community and how to openly express a gay identity that is simultaneous with a racial identity. In the present study, I have shown how privileges based on occupational status, income, and even good looks advantage some openly gay women in their racial communities. This extends Cohen's (1999) concept of integrative marginalization, because in these intraracial contexts the dominant group is composed of heterosexual middle-class Blacks who subjectively extend limited access to resources and legitimacy to a chosen few sexual minority members, allowing other statuses to compensate for their less-favored sexual minority status.

Black gay people will continue to make and remake their sexual selves as they infuse cultural elements of family and style with gay sexuality, expressed through such things as gender presentation and performance; the ball scenes that are a continued staple of gay life in major cities like New York and Chicago; Black gay pride events that incorporate stepping, Reggae music, and lip-syncing by cross-dressers to contemporary gospel music; and versions of gay Caribana, the Caribbean music festival celebrated in cities like New York, Miami, and Toronto. The interweaving of culture into expressions of gay sexuality and identity shows us that the changes continually taking place in larger society regarding the legality, recognition, and legitimacy of same-sex relationships will influence the ways outsiders come to understand lesbians and gay men. Nevertheless, everyday practices within the family lives and social groupings of gay people will continue to shape their understandings of themselves as sexual and full beings.

A Roadmap for the Study of Marginalized and Invisible Populations

I had not planned to study Black lesbian families. My dissertation research examined the relationship between early sexual debut and pregnancy among disadvantaged, African American adolescents living in high-poverty Chicago neighborhoods. I published a series of articles from this work, but at the start of the twenty-first century, rates of teenage childbearing had begun to decrease, which changed the interest of policy makers in this area of study. Rather than continue this line of research, I thought I might explore other avenues of family sociology. I am a native New Yorker and had returned to New York in 2001 to teach at Columbia University after being away for graduate school and a postdoctoral fellowship. One snowy night in January of 2002, I met some people who would become gatekeepers to the community that is the subject of this book.

While at a family event, I met a Black, working-class lesbian couple (a billing receptionist and an administrative assistant) who invited me to their home for a game of cards; I accepted their invitation. At that point I knew very few openly gay African Americans, and did not know any Black gay women in New York. The following week I walked into their large, pre-war apartment in an area on the Grand Concourse near Yankee Stadium in the South Bronx and was introduced to a group of eight to ten Black lesbians who were cordial, though not in a middle class, obligingly polite sort of way. They offered me something to drink, a bite to eat, and I sat in the living room to play a friendly game of spades. In the back bedroom there were three children—two of whom lived in the home with the host couple (the third was a child of one of the other guests).

That night was noteworthy for several reasons. First, the hosting couple was raising two children from one partner's prior heterosexual relationship with an incarcerated drug dealer. As a family sociologist and urban poverty researcher, I was interested in how this couple came to have children, what the children thought of their mother and her partner, and how this lesbian family fit into the larger community of Black and Latino people in that historic neighborhood.

Also noteworthy was the way everyone was dressed. At first some of the styles did not look particularly "gay" to me, and after thinking about it, I realized it was because the images of lesbian sexuality that immediately came to mind were of White lesbians who wear tattoos and leather jackets, political activists who identify as queer, and what some have labeled "crunchy-granola" women—vegetarians who wear Birkenstock sandals, plaid shirts, no make-up, and short, androgynous hairstyles. I had no reference point in the lesbian world from which to understand these Bronx lesbians. Instead, I connected them to heterosexual people I have met and seen over the years in African American communities: the families on my auntie's block in Queens, New York; the people I came across in the shopping mall or various other spaces where Black people lived and socialized. I noticed that the party guests were dressed either in tight jeans, high-heeled boots, sweaters and tank tops (it was very cold outside and very warm inside, so sweaters were removed after people came in), or Dickies[1] shirts on top of thermals, long athletic jerseys, and Timberland work boots that were consistent with the styles Black and Latino men in New York were wearing at the time. While I could identify and connect their styles of dress with what I have seen women and men in Black communities wear, I had not really seen the stark differences in gender presentation among lesbians before. Although I identify as gay, I had not spent any time in predominantly Black gay social settings and had not been around large groups of gay people.

These settings were, however, sociologically interesting, and over the coming year they became increasingly so. As I continued to publish from my dissertation, the women I'd met in the Bronx stayed on my mind. Although I never became a close, integral part of their social group, from time to time they would invite me to dinners and birthday parties at other people's homes and nightclub events, and sometimes I accepted these invitations. Over the next twelve months I began to spend time in Black gay spaces in Manhattan, which were more class integrated than the working-class house parties and club parties in the Bronx. I met women across the spectrum of age, gender presentation, social class, and motherhood status, and after about eight months of observation, in the fall of 2002, I began to take a more organized, purposeful approach to studying Black lesbian sexuality. I began writing field notes describing how these social activities were organized, the clothing women wore, and other such representations of this life.

The people I met at these new venues were very friendly and quick to invite me to various activities that were almost always Black or Black and Latina. The events were class integrated but segregated by gender. They were also culturally Black—the hip hop, reggae and reggaeton music, hairstyles, dress, language, mannerisms, types of dancing, physical and verbal expressions used by the people were all anchored in Black American, West Indian, Puerto Rican, and Dominican cultural traditions. As I accumulated observations, I began to wonder how race and other statuses including gender, class, and motherhood affected the ways these women understood and practiced a lesbian sexuality. I was particularly interested in the intersections of race and sexuality as they related to family formation and family process.

I turned to the family literature, gender studies, lesbian studies, and the research in African American studies to see what social scientists who had published on race and lesbian identity had to say about racial/ethnic minority lesbians. I wanted to know what had been written about the ways identity statuses and structural experiences around race, gender, and sexuality influence the types of families Black women and other gay women of color might form, and how they understand themselves and their place in the world. Research on lesbian relationships and motherhood by Beverly Greene and Anne Peplau in counseling and psychology, the anthropologist Ellen Lewin, and sociologists like Phillip Blumstein and Pepper Schwartz reflect some of my earliest inquiries into this topic. Studies such as Barbara Ponse's *Identities in the Lesbian World* (1978), Arlene Stein's *Sense and Sensibility: Stories of a Lesbian Generation* (1997), and Paula Rust's papers on lesbian and bisexual identities (1992; 1993) were insightful in helping me develop as a scholar of lesbian sexuality. Historical work like Elizabeth Kennedy and Madeline Davis's *Boots of Leather, Slippers of Gold* (1993); Rochella Thorpe's essay "A House Where Queers Go: African-American Lesbian Nightlife in Detroit, 1940–1975" (1996); *The Persistent Desire* (1992) edited by Joan Nestle; Anita Cornwell's *Black Lesbian in White America* (1983); and Audre Lorde's essay "Tar Beach" (1995) which I first read in *Home Girls: A Black Feminist Anthology* made visible the pre-Stonewall experiences of Black lesbians in their own communities, and offered starting points from which I could trace the contemporary behaviors of Black gay women in the twenty-first century. Over a period of time there has been an ongoing exchange in the Black feminist literature between Evelyn Brooks Higginbotham, Darlene Clark Hine, Patricia Hill Collins, and others on the politics of respectability, and Evelynn Hammonds, Angela Davis, and Cathy Cohen on the silencing of Black women's sexual agency as a result of that defense of Black womanhood. When taken together, both perspectives offered key blueprints from which to understand the dilemmas faced by the Black women in my study.

These and other readings were critical sites of knowledge, and while I learned a great deal in my review of the research, I realized that important interventions were still needed in these literatures. I found very few sociological studies on contemporary gay identity among women of color, and very little on family formation and family processes in households that were not White and middle class. As I continued to read and conduct fieldwork, many more questions than answers began to form. There was a persistent invisibility of the experiences of gay women of color in the Black feminist literature, the research on family processes, in sexuality studies and in sociohistorical analyses of gay life. But my observations in the field were suggesting profound things about the way gender operates in settings where biological sex is held constant; about how people understand themselves as gay when they already have a firm group identification around race; and about what happens when Black female sexuality reveals itself in homosexual contexts. The women who would become my respondents grew up in high-poverty urban neighborhoods, in Black middle-class families, in small towns, and in rural areas in the Caribbean. All of these experiences were reflected in their expression of lesbian identity and in the decisions they were making about family life, but with very little research on the intersections of race, class, and lesbian sexuality, there was no framework for how to understand these relationships. I began to challenge the implied neutrality of the existing scholarship on lesbian sexuality, family formation, and gender ideologies. After about eight months of fieldwork and literature review, I began to frame the research questions this book seeks to answer: How do race, gender, class, and sexuality interact to shape contemporary identities for individuals with multiple, hyper-visible social statuses? What does it mean to "become" a lesbian and to publicly negotiate a lesbian identity and family in Black communities? What can we learn about family processes and about gay sexuality more generally from the study of Black gay people?

STUDY DESIGN

My next step was to decide how to more concretely pursue this line of research. I wanted to understand lesbian identification in the context of racial identification, and I wanted to know how these women made decisions about partnering, about motherhood, and about living openly gay lives. This would be one of the very first book-length, sociological studies of lesbian parenting in racial minority contexts, and I wanted to be as thorough as possible in collecting data. I had some reservations about a study of Black lesbian families. Would mainstream social scientists interested in race, gender, intersectionality, sexuality, social class, identity, and/or family be open to understanding these areas of inquiry in the context of this population? Would I become marginalized as a scholar for having a focus that some might frame as too narrow? Despite these concerns, I knew that what I was observing was sociologically relevant to many areas of the discipline and should not be ignored. I had been able to gain access to a social group and to settings that other researchers had not been able to enter, and it would be a disservice to the research community to not pursue such a study.

In the spring of 2003 I began to design a research plan. I wanted to be more rigorous in organizing my fieldwork, and supplement my notes with other, more formalized sources of data. Because several of my observations thus far were counterintuitive to some of the theoretical arguments in the literature on the current experiences of lesbians and lesbian-headed families, while other observations had not been written about by researchers in any consistent way, I wanted to be as conservative as possible in my strategies. By using more than one research method I would be able to better test hypotheses and verify my observations and findings. I decided to supplement the ethnographic field notes with a survey, focus group interviews, and in-depth, in-person interviews.

The Invisible Families Study targeted women currently living in New York and the surrounding metropolitan area who identify as lesbian, gay, bisexual, "In the Life," same-gender-loving, or women loving women, and who are forming families. I realized that conducting a study of Black lesbian families would have to mean expanding the definition of *family* to go beyond cohabiting couples with children conceived through alternative insemination. This type of family structure is one small representation of the range of family environments that lesbians create, and in the course of my fieldwork I came across very few women who had created families using this method. This narrow definition of lesbian-headed family excluded households where one partner had children through a prior heterosexual relationship, the most common experience I had been finding in my field work. While I could not capture every type of lesbian family household in this study, I incorporated into this research cohabiting couples with children of any kind, cohabiting couples with no children living in the home, and single mothers who were part of this community. I did not include lesbians living as roommates with no romantic attachment because these people did not define themselves as "family," even when they acknowledged the close, interdependency of their relationships. I did not meet any women living with two romantic partners, or raising children with gay men, although people in these types of households might also consider themselves a family unit. While my field notes include interactions with Black and Latina lesbians who are not creating families, the focus of the book is on Black women who are creating families.

To be eligible for the study, only one person in the relationship had to self-identify as Black. This includes multiracial, Caribbean, African, and Black-identified Latina women. Five of their partners identify as White. I kept these interracial couples in the study because they represent a portion of Black community life and have households co-headed by Black lesbians, and the goal of the study was to understand the range of experiences of Black lesbian-headed families.

Locating Research Subjects

In Bell, Weinberg, and Hammersmith's (1981) study of predictors and correlates of homosexual behaviors, no women were recruited from public places or private bars. More lesbians were obtained through personal contacts than through any other source. Also, no Blacks were recruited in gay baths, and very few Blacks were on the mailing lists used for recruitment. This says something specific about their methods of recruitment for lesbians and Blacks as well as the influence of researchers' networks in the respondents of studies of gay life. Blacks in that study were also more difficult than Whites to recruit—they were harder for researchers to locate and less likely to give consent to participate in the research. This pattern has persisted throughout time, with the most current research studies continuing to report difficulty recruiting non-White lesbian subjects.

In the field of lesbian and gay studies, methods of sample gathering have typically recruited individuals who are significantly involved in the most visible segments of gay communities that are predominantly White. The newspapers and magazines used by researchers to announce their studies have little non-White content in the articles, notices, and advertisements they publish (McBride 2005b). Consequently, they have few non-White gays as part of their consistent readership. The difficulty in recruiting non-White gays in predominantly White organizations and publications suggests the continuing significance of race even in communities where sexuality is the organizing identity. Advertisements to

recruit research participants placed in gay newspapers as well as notices or flyers posted at lesbian nightclubs or LGBT community centers largely go unno-
ticed or unanswered by gay populations of color, and studies that use these
methods are not successful in recruiting significant numbers of non-Whites in
their samples (Blumstein & Schwartz 1983). This is because when potential respondents see these advertisements, they usually do not know the organizations
sponsoring the research and are unfamiliar with the names of the researchers.
These factors make them reluctant to participate.

As with other areas of social life, gay and lesbian communities are often racially segregated, but the majority of researchers have not sufficiently utilized
organizations and social groups that serve non-White gays and lesbians in their
recruitment efforts. Most social science studies of lesbian life have been conducted
by individuals who are not part of predominantly Black social activities. They may
not know such activities exist, may not know where such groups meet, and may
not have anyone in those groups who can vouch for their legitimacy.

I began this research by spending time (2–5 days each week) at a variety of
public social events and private house parties that had a largely Black lesbian
attendance, including after-work networking cocktail hours, karaoke sing-
alongs, book clubs, art salons, religious meetings, shared meals, poetry readings, lesbian bars, and dance parties. I also attended gay pride or Black gay
pride events in Brooklyn, Manhattan, Washington, D.C., Atlanta, and Orlando,
all of which draw large crowds of Black women from New York. When I began
spending time in these spaces, individuals knew that I was a professor at Columbia University. They saw me attending these social activities. However, I did
not begin approaching women about participating in the study until the spring
of 2003, after they had seen me in the community for about one year. At that
point I was new enough to not have made any close friends, but people recognized my face and knew enough about me to have some level of trust.

I began distributing flyers at lesbian bars and nightclubs, and at private events
in people's homes. Rather than merely posting the flyer on an announcement
board or leaving it on a table, I gave them out to people and talked one-to-one
with them about the research. This was easy to do because the women at these
events liked to meet people. Even at dimly lit nightclubs, there were always lots
of talking, picture-taking, and chit chatting between friends, acquaintances, and
strangers. I was surprised at how many of the women, upon hearing that I
wanted to write a book on lesbian families, had children. They rarely talked
about their kids at these events, but now eagerly showed me their photos, sharing the names and ages of their children. The pride they had for their families
was clear, and their status as mothers became visible in a way that was new to
me. Motherhood was not a topic regularly discussed in these social settings, or
at least not in the conversations I overheard or was part of.

I also asked people who knew me to introduce me to the promoters, organizers, and hosts of these social activities. These individuals played a critical role in
my recruiting efforts. They would allow me to make announcements about my
study at their events, but more importantly they were key figures that helped
establish my legitimacy as a member of the community. They would introduce

me to their regular party goers, people who were very popular and could direct me to others, and people whom they knew were in committed relationships or who had children. When I found people who were eligible for the study, I made sure they received an informational flyer, wrote down their phone number and address, and mailed them a survey. Once they received the survey at home, they completed it and returned it to me by mail or occasionally in person if they happened to have it in their car at a social event. I did not hand out any surveys directly to individuals.

Most of the women in the study (71%) were recruited through this outreach: 60% through one-on-one interactions and 11% through announcements and presentations I made at special events like a woman's power brunch or a Valentine's weekend ski trip for women. Twenty-four percent of the sample were recruited through referrals from participants who received a survey or heard about the study and told others in their networks about the project. These people did not go out as frequently to public social events, and I would have had a difficult time reaching them on my own. The remaining 5% of the survey sample were recruited through referrals from non-gay people who learned about the study. In total, 131 surveys were mailed and 100 were returned, giving the survey a response rate of 76%. People who did not return the survey included people who told me they or their partner did not want to participate (eleven people), people who moved away from New York during the time the survey was distributed (two people), and others whom I never consciously came into contact with again and who for unknown reasons did not return the survey (eighteen people).

The mail-in survey consisted of fourteen pages of questions that ask about the methods the respondent has used or considered to obtain children, relationship quality, demographic and family background information, distribution of household chores, changes in sexuality over time, physical representations of gender, past experiences with female and male partners, and the extent of friendship groups and social interactions in Black communities, gay communities, and predominantly White communities. Some of the questions on the survey were taken from Blumstein and Schwartz's (1983) survey of American couples, and some were taken from Carrington's (1999) study of lesbian and gay couples. I created a modified version of Cowan and Cowan's (1990) Who Does What? scale, which measures family decision making, household tasks, and child care. Other questions were original constructs. Each survey had a number in the top left corner. Respondents were not asked to give their names, but were asked to provide their first and last initials. I was able to use these numbers, in combination with the study participants' initials, to link the survey back to the original informant. In this way I was able to tell who had and had not returned a survey. Respondents who were in partnered relationships received a survey that was slightly different than the survey for unpartnered women. Descriptive statistics from the survey are provided in Table A1. See Appendix B for the partnered women's survey.

TABLE A1. DESCRIPTIVE STATISTICS ON INVISIBLE FAMILIES
SAMPLE ($N = 100$)

	Frequencies
Age in Years (*SD*)	36.7 (7.2)
Age Range in Years	24–61
Race/Ethnicity	
Black American	64%
West Indian/Caribbean	20%
Latina/Hispanic	10%
White	4%
Other (African)	1%
Foreign Born	22%
Neighborhood Racial Composition	
Predominantly Black or Latino	27%
Racially Mixed (White and Other)	66%
Predominantly White	7%
Highest Level of Education Attained	
Less than high school	1%
High school or equivalent	37%
B.A. degree or equivalent	29%
Master's degree	20%
J.D., M.D., or other doctorate	13%
Occupational Status	
Working class	45%
Middle class	42%
Upper middle class	13%
Annual Income (n=96)	
$0–15,000	6%
$15,001–30,000	8%
$30,001–50,000	39%
$50,001–75,000	30%
$75,001–100,000	10%
$100,000–150,000	2%
$150,001 +	5%
Household Status	
Partnered with children	40%
Partnered no children	34%
Unpartnered with children	26%
Relationship Status	
In committed relationship	74%
Mean length of relationship in years (*SD*)	3.7 (3.1)
Parenting Status	
Parenting or Co-parenting at least one child	66%
Biological mother (% of total sample)	44%
Biological mother (% of parenting sample)	73%

Focus Group Interviews

Throughout the period of data collection, I used focus group interviews to inform the structure of the other study protocols, and to gain more information about topics that seemed important in the surveys, individual interviews, and field notes. My first two focus groups were held after the surveys were distributed and before I conducted in-person interviews. The first focus group included ten women and their general experiences as lesbians was discussed—what they found fulfilling about being with women, their past experiences with men, how those experiences were similar to or different from their relationships with women, how they felt about participating in Black gay social activities, and their experiences participating in other more general areas of Black community life. The second focus group involved twelve women, and focused specifically on relationships in their home lives, what their relationships were like with the fathers of their children, and the quality of their partner's relationship with their children. Only one of the participants had children with her partner using alternative insemination methods. The others had children through prior marital, cohabiting, or other heterosexual relationships, or were the partners of these women.

Midway into the data collection, I was receiving conflicting information in the surveys, the individual interviews, and in my field notes on the topic of gender presentation. I was noticing very consistent patterns of gender presentation in Black lesbian couples—one partner was always more feminine than the other. However, many of the middle-class women were disparaging about non-feminine gender display, particularly those women who were the less feminine partner in their own relationships. They were usually gender-blenders and not overtly masculine in their presentation of self. They gave themselves a higher score on the survey's gender presentation scale relative to the score they gave their partner, indicating that their partners had a gender presentation that was more feminine than themselves. I convened a focus group, (my third), consisting of ten women to help inform this component of the study. I began by showing *Butch Mystique*, a documentary film released in 2003 by award-winning filmmaker Debra A. Wilson. *Butch Mystique* profiles the lives of African American masculine-identified women. The film was a springboard for a discussion about gender display in Black lesbian communities.

I convened a fourth focus group after the interviews and surveys were completed. There were nine participants, and we discussed the role of religion in the lives of Black lesbians. The participants discussed the religious beliefs they were raised in, whether they currently practiced a faith, and the relationship between living an openly gay life and participating in Christian and Muslim faiths.

In-depth, In-person Interviews

Approximately three months after the surveys were distributed, I began conducting individual, in-person interviews with more than half ($n = 58$) of the survey respondents. The interviews garnered information about the respondent's racial group affinity, gender expression, parenting experiences, and whether/how they see their future lives as gay people. This structure allowed me to follow up on some of the responses on the survey. So, for example, when a person gave themselves a score on the gender presentation scale, I could use the in-depth interview to ask why they assigned themselves that score and what it meant to them. The interview protocol also asked in-depth questions about their experiences in their families of origin and what their neighborhoods were like while growing up, providing the opportunity to share their coming out stories in a way that could not be expressed in a survey. The interviews lasted from forty-five minutes to two hours, with most interviews lasting an average of seventy-five minutes. Partners were interviewed separately in their homes or in my home or office by Black female interviewers, including myself and one of four research assistants.

Ethnographic Field Work—Creating a Physical Space to Collect Data on Invisible Populations

The field notes I collected during the study period include observations and conversations with informants in the larger women's community who did not participate in the survey or in-depth interviews. Some of these were more private women who did not share their lesbian sexuality with people outside of the gay community, women who were not forming families but could offer insights into other aspects of Black lesbian life, and women who were not currently in relationships but had previously cohabited with women who had children.

Once the surveys were distributed and almost all of the interviews had been completed, I wanted a way to be able to keep track of the women who completed the survey because they were at the center of this research. While I continued to attend various social activities in the Black lesbian community, I did not know if and when I would see my study participants. I began to host a weekly social event that catered to the specific interests of lesbians of color. I collaborated with three other people to host "Persuasion: A Monday Night Lounge Party for Women." For the next eighteen months, I hosted this event every Monday from 9pm—2am at a lounge in the West Village,[2] and it drew a mixture of middle-class and working-class, mostly Black and Latina women (including graduate students and artists) between the ages of twenty-one and forty. We charged a nominal entry fee ($3–$5) to pay the DJ and cover other promotional costs. I sat at the front door to greet the guests. People came by after work, met up with friends and partners, celebrated birthdays, and had a good time. They came consistently, and I kept a record of the number in attendance. The event averaged about eighty-five guests each week, with more patrons in the warmer months and fewer when it rained or snowed. The numbers ranged from a low of twenty-eight during a snowstorm to more than two hundred when Halloween fell on a Monday night.

This weekly activity was critical to my fieldwork. It allowed me to have regular, sustained contact with the community. Every week some of my patrons were part of the one hundred women who completed the survey so I could observe not only my study participants, but their friends and other women in the community. I could observe their gender presentation over time to assess the consistency with which they presented as femme, gender-blender, or transgressive. I was able to notice class and cultural differences in the styles of gender presentation, comparing, for example, Jamaican working-class and middle-class feminine display, or observing differences in a transgressive style worn by a twenty-five-year-old compared to a forty-year-old woman.

I also used these lounge parties to remain visible in the minds of my study participants. I could remind people who had not returned their surveys to do so. Because I was the greeter and sat at the door each week, people got to know me. Many felt comfortable sitting next to me to share the things that were going on in their lives. I would meet new people entering the community and hear their accounts of leaving their husbands or dealing with parents who did not accept their gay identities. Others would share problems they were having with their girlfriends or dilemmas they faced with their children. People who were not part of the formal study got to know me as well, and their stories became part of my field notes. If someone shared an experience that was particularly personal, I would ask if I could include our discussion in my field notes. They usually said yes, as long as I did not use their real names. In the rare cases when they did not give consent, I did not include them in this work. Most people knew I was a professor at Columbia, and that I was writing a book about Black lesbian families. After awhile, instead of me checking to see whether they had returned their surveys, people began checking up on me, asking "How's the book coming along? When are you going to be finished?"

I recommend this approach to data collection. When trying to locate populations that lack geographic boundaries or that have particularly porous boundaries, it can be helpful to create an event that brings potential research subjects together. My reasons for hosting this weekly event were not only based in creating a space to gather data. I did not have funds to offer an honorarium to my study participants, so this was one way I could give back to this community for their time and insights. I became known as the host for this weekly event, and became part of a group of women who promote social activities for the lesbian community. Near the end of my fieldwork I received a "Women Promoters Leadership Award" plaque from a few of the other party promoters for hosting this event and helping to create a sense of community. I moved away from New York in September 2006 to accept a position at the University of California at Los Angeles. This was a neat way to cease data collection, and my weekly parties in the West Village came to an end. I continue to keep in touch with many members of the New York Women's community through an online social networking site. Through social networking and old phone numbers and addresses, in 2010, six years after I completed my in-depth interviews and four years after I left the field, I was able to locate the whereabouts of seventy my original study participants.

DATA LIMITATIONS
New York Region

While the state of California reports the greatest total number of same-sex couples reported on the 2000 U.S. Census, New York ranks number one for the largest number of Black same-sex couples (Dang and Frazer 2004), and New York City contains the highest proportion of same-sex households reporting on the U.S. Census (Bradford, Barrett, and Honnold 2002). The particular culture of New York and the increased opportunities for contact with other gay people, relative to other cities and locations, make the experience of conducting research on Black gay populations distinctive. New York is also distinctive relative to most other places in its visible presence of LGBT people in the city. One can go to Greenwich Village, the East Village, and the Chelsea neighborhoods of Manhattan and see openly gay people of various ages, ethnicities, and genders. The LGBT Community Center is located near this area of Manhattan and is open twenty-four hours a day. There are other organizations that also cater to specific groups of LGBT people. For example, African Ancestral Lesbians United for Societal Change (formerly known as Salsa Soul Sisters) is the oldest Black lesbian political organization in the country, and holds its meetings at the LGBT Center. There are social and political groups for Muslim lesbians, Asian American lesbians, Latina lesbians, immigrant African lesbians, transgendered youth, and homeless youth that one can learn about and join. The presence of these types of formal and informal groups distinguish this city, and make the experience of collecting data on Black gay populations different here than trying to do this work in Durham, NC, for example, where there is a sizable Black population but a less visible gay population and few public spaces where you can observe openly gay Blacks socializing. Likewise, San Francisco has the largest population of White same-sex couples of any city in the country, but the Black gay population is less visible there and might make the experience of gay Blacks in that city different.

New York contains many distinct, well-developed lesbian communities, and one consequence of these varied social groups is that women can enter into a gay identity or form friendships with other gay people who are not lesbian-feminists. They become socialized into gay communities that are not based on specific feminist principles, as might be the case if the primary gay, public organizations in the community were political groups. Moreover, many of these groups are segregated by race as well as gender, facilitating a coming out process or development of a gay identity in the context of a racially homogeneous environment. As a result, being gay may not be experienced as an identity that creates social distance from one's racial group or that is associated with a particular political ideology, as might be the case for women in other cities where public gay environs are predominantly White and have a feminist orientation.

The specific culture of New York City may shape the experiences of lesbians in a way that cannot be generalized to that of women in other geographical locations. For example, I have found some of the more persistent boundaries around gender presentation in New York, compared to the lesbian social life in the southern region of the United States. The women in New York seem less apologetic about consistently presenting as femme or transgressive. Meeting Black gay women at gay pride events in other parts of the country, I was relatively more likely than I was in New York to come across a woman who dressed in a transgressive way but who also wore a French pedicure or women's sandals with her masculine attire. I have also heard of transgressive Black lesbians living in other places who partner together, but I have not directly met and interacted with these types of couples.

Certain groups of Black women with same-sex desire who are forming families may be disproportionately represented in this work. For example, it is possible that younger women and younger relationships are overrepresented, though the upper- and lower-age limits and relationship duration for lesbians are not known. The median age of the women in the study is 37 years. Dang and Frazer (2004) report that the median age of Black women in same-sex unmarried partner households in the 2000 Census is 39, while respondents in the National Survey of Black Lesbians report an average age of 33 (Mays and Cochran 1988). The modal age category for respondents in the National Black Lesbian Needs Assessment is 40–49 (30% of their sample) (Ramsey, Hill, and Kellam 2010).[3] The women in the present study spend at least some amount of time in predominantly Black social settings and may have qualitatively different experiences and ideologies with regards to racial identity and race consciousness when compared to Blacks who are well-integrated into predominantly White social networks or spend very little time socializing in predominantly Black settings.

Other groups of lesbians may not well-represented in this study, including the very poor, the very closeted, and the very private. For example, while visiting my parents in Long Island, I ran into a Caribbean-born, former neighbor. She worked for the department of Social and Human Services in a nearby town. When I told her about my research, she told me that she was "in the life" and that she had been living with "her Girl" in Queens for the past four years. I mentioned some of the places I had been visiting to conduct my research. She said they did not go to night clubs and parties, but instead liked to "chill" at home or go over to their friends' houses for dinner or to play cards and hang out. I became excited and asked if she and her girlfriend would be interested in being interviewed for my study. She physically backed away, put her hand up and said, "Oh no. We wouldn't want to do something like that." I told her their identities would not be revealed to anyone, and that I would personally conduct the interviews. I told her about my own partner so that she would know I was gay. She politely but adamantly said she was not interested. When I asked why not, she said, "We just don't get down like that. We don't want our business out there." I took her comments to mean that she and her partner did not want to openly discuss their sexuality or their relationship with me, and perhaps with people outside of their social group. It was also possible that they did not discuss their sexuality with their family members or with friends outside of their social group.

Insider-Outsider Status

McCorkel and Myers (2003) write about the ways in which the multiple dimensions of the researcher's identity take shape when relating to subjects in the field. They and other feminist ethnographers argue that the researcher's status as both an outsider and an insider shifts throughout her time in the field as she negotiates and renegotiates relationships. I write from the perspective of someone who was an insider by virtue of my race, gender and sexuality, but also as an outsider, having no prior knowledge of the norms and practices of Black lesbians as a group. I spent all of my twenties in graduate school and very rarely went out to gay-themed events. I only knew of one lesbian bar in the city where I was living, and it was predominantly White. I did not actively look for gay social spaces because I was too busy in school and more generally did not tend to spend time at dances or in bars. Even after I completed graduate school I still did not spend late nights at parties or spend time with groups of gay people. As a result, when I began attending the card parties and nightclubs, many of the norms and behaviors of the group were foreign to me. I was observing them as an outsider because I had not seen the group interact before, and I had not formed my own family or spent time around other lesbian couples and families.

Yet, people are always entering (and exiting) the gay community. People come out as gay and come into the different social scenes of gay life, developing friendships and joining organizations to feel part of a community and to find a mate. People move to and away from the city, so there are always new faces in the community. When women find a partner, they often "nest" at home and reduce the amount of time they spend "out" in the social scene. When they dissolve their relationships they may return to the public gay life to spend time with friends they have ignored and to meet new people to date. The constant entries and exits allow for new people, that is, for "outsiders" to come in and quickly be seen as "insiders" because of their sexuality. This routine also makes room for these new insiders to learn about the norms and expectations of the group. Those who have been in the life for a long period of time still remember what is was like the first time they walked into a lesbian bar or party, and are willing and interested to help others become comfortable and acclimated. The nature of the social group allowed me to gain access to the population, and race definitely played an important role in increasing the level of comfort others had with me as the researcher.

The shifting contexts where my fieldwork took place at times made some of my identity statuses less visible and at other times heightened their visibility. I do not have children, which sometimes put me in the position of student when women would describe issues related to parenting. I am a Black American, and some Caribbean-born women saw me as culturally different from themselves. This may have affected how comfortable they felt discussing their ideologies about Black American lesbian communities. For example, during the in-depth interview I ask questions about the respondent's racial and ethnic identities. Some Caribbean women may not have been willing to express the extent of difference they felt toward Black American women. They may not have been as comfortable talking about the negative or homophobic aspects of their countries of origin with someone who was born in the United States. There were times during my interviews with foreign-born women where I felt their responses to certain questions about intraracial dynamics were particularly measured because of the difference in our ethnic identities.

I was a professor at Columbia University while conducting this research, and my social class made middle- and upper-class women feel connected to me and willing to share their lives. It also made them feel particularly welcome at the weekly social event I used to host. I do not know the extent to which working-class or poor lesbians may have felt discomfort in interacting with me, or how that may have influenced their level of participation in the study. I do know that many working-class women opened their homes to me and allowed me to study their relationships and families. They also attended my weekly lounge parties, introduced me to their friends, and invited me to learn about their lives.

APPENDIX B

Selected Questions from Invisible Families Survey

For each item, state whether you and your mate have done these things, if you have plans to do them in the future, or if you have no plans to do them in the future.

	Yes, we do this now	No, but plan to do this in the future	No, no plans to do this in the future	Does not apply
Share an apartment or house together	3	2	1	99
Wear a ring to signal you are in a committed relationship	3	2	1	99
Purchase a car together	3	2	1	99
Purchase a home together	3	2	1	99
Share a bank account or other finances	3	2	1	99
List your mate or your mate's children on your health insurance	3	2	1	99
List your mate as a beneficiary on financial documents, in a will, on a life insurance policy, or something similar	3	2	1	99
Share the same last name or hyphenate your last name to include both of your names	3	2	1	99

	Yes, we do this now	No, but plan to do this in the future	No, no plans to do this in the future	Does not apply
Have a marriage or special ceremony to publicly announce your commitment to one another	3	2	1	99
Register your relationship with the government, your employer, or other institution as a civil union	3	2	1	99
Bear, adopt, or foster children together	3	2	1	99
Legally adopt your mate's children	3	2	1	99

Certain household tasks are necessary to keep things running smoothly. Who does each of these tasks more often?

	I do this much more	I do this a little more	We do this equally	She does this a little more	She does this much more	Neither of us does this
Repairing things around the house	5	4	3	2	1	99
Doing the dishes	5	4	3	2	1	99
Arranging for daily meals (deciding what/when to eat)	5	4	3	2	1	99
Cleaning the bathroom	5	4	3	2	1	99
Caring for pets	5	4	3	2	1	99
Cleaning the floors	5	4	3	2	1	99
Taking out the trash	5	4	3	2	1	99
Performing yard work	5	4	3	2	1	99
Dusting furniture.	5	4	3	2	1	99
Mixing drinks for company	5	4	3	2	1	99

	I do this much more	I do this a little more	We do this equally	She does this a little more	She does this much more	Neither of us does this
Straightening/cleaning the living/family room	5	4	3	2	1	99
Doing the laundry	5	4	3	2	1	99
Grocery shopping	5	4	3	2	1	99

Thinking about all of the work you do around the house, about how many hours per week do you think you spend on these chores?

I SPEND ABOUT _____ HOURS /WEEK.

About how many hours per week would you say your mate spends on household chores?

_____ HOURS/WEEK

On average, how many hours per week are household chores done by <u>other adults or children</u> living with you?

None	1
1–2 hours	2
3–5 hours	3
6–10 hours	4
More than 10 hours	5

How many hours per week do you or your partner pay for someone else to do the household chores?

None	1
1–2 hours	2
3–5 hours	3
6–10 hours	4
More than 10 hours	5

Considering the amount of chores in your household and the time it takes to perform them, would you say your mate does her "fair share"?

She does much less than her fair share	1
She does a little less than her fair share	2
She does exactly her fair share	3
She does a little more than her fair share	4
She does much more than her fair share	5

What makes you say your mate does "much more" or "much less" than her fair share of the chores?

The following are general statements about couples but not necessarily about your relationship. How much do you agree or disagree with each statement?

	Strongly Agree	Agree	Strongly Disagree	Disagree
Both mates in a relationship should divide evenly the household tasks (washing dishes, preparing meals, doing laundry, etc.)	4	3	2	1
The two mates should pool all their property & financial assets	4	3	2	1
If both mates work full-time, both of their career plans should be considered *equally* in determining where they will live	4	3	2	1
If both mates work full-time, the needs of the mate who earns the most should have the greatest consideration when determining where they will live	4	3	2	1
Couples should try to make their relationship last a lifetime	4	3	2	1
It is better if one person in the relationship takes the major financial responsibility and the other person takes the major responsibility of caring for the home	4	3	2	1

If you had to select only one, which of these definitions would describe your sexuality? (SELECT ONE)

Exclusively lesbian	1
Predominantly lesbian, only slightly heterosexual	2

Predominantly lesbian, but significantly heterosexual	3
Equally lesbian and heterosexual	4
Predominantly heterosexual, but significantly lesbian	5
Predominantly heterosexual, only slightly lesbian	6
Exclusively heterosexual	7

Which of these definitions would have described your sexuality when you were 15 years old?

Exclusively lesbian	1
Predominantly lesbian, only slightly heterosexual	2
Predominantly lesbian, but significantly heterosexual	3
Equally lesbian and heterosexual	4
Predominantly heterosexual, but significantly lesbian	5
Predominantly heterosexual, only slightly lesbian	6
Exclusively heterosexual	7

Which of these definitions would have described your sexuality when you were 21 years old?

Exclusively lesbian	1
Predominantly lesbian, only slightly heterosexual	2
Predominantly lesbian, but significantly heterosexual	3
Equally lesbian and heterosexual	4
Predominantly heterosexual, but significantly lesbian	5
Predominantly heterosexual, only slightly lesbian	6
Exclusively heterosexual	7

At what age did you begin to feel romantically attracted to women? _____ YEARS OLD

At what age did you first act on your feelings of romantic attraction to women? _____
YEARS OLD

If you consider yourself exclusively or predominantly lesbian, at what age did you first
decide you were definitely lesbian? ___ YEARS OLD ___I DO NOT CONSIDER MYSELF
EXCLUSIVELY OR PREDOMINANTLY LESBIAN

Is there a term other than "lesbian" that better describes your sexuality? YES   NO

If yes, what is that term and why do you prefer it?_____

How much do you agree or disagree with each of these statements:

	Strongly Agree	Agree	Strongly Disagree	Disagree	No Opinion
Being gay is something that is completely beyond one's control	4	3	2	1	97
I would not give up my homosexuality even if I could	4	3	2	1	97
I feel my life would be much easier if I were heterosexual	4	3	2	1	97
Being gay is a conscious choice I have made	4	3	2	1	97
One can be gay and never act on those feelings	4	3	2	1	97
One can be gay at one period of time and then be heterosexual at another point in time	4	3	2	1	97
There should be laws to protect lesbians and gay people from discrimination in employment and housing	4	3	2	1	97
Lesbians and gay people are entitled to all of the rights and privileges as other Americans, including legal marriage	4	3	2	1	97

	Strongly Agree	Agree	Strongly Disagree	Disagree	No Opinion
Public schools should present positive portrayals of lesbians and gay people	4	3	2	1	97
The government should permit lesbians and gay people to marry someone of the same sex	4	3	2	1	97

GENDER PRESENTATION SCALE

On a scale of 1–10, with "1" being a person whose PHYSICAL ATTRIBUTES including clothing, hair, style of dress, way of walking, or way of talking are "very feminine" and consistent with those stereotypically assigned to women, and "10" being a person whose clothing, hair, style of dress, way of walking, and way of talking are "very masculine" or most like those stereotypically assigned to men, which number best represents YOUR OWN physical attributes?

1	2	3	4	5	6	7	8	9	10

very feminine	*somewhere in between feminine and masculine*	*very masculine*

Using this same scale, where "1" is someone who is very feminine and "10" is someone who is very masculine, which number best represents the physical attributes of YOUR MATE?

1	2	3	4	5	6	7	8	9	10

very feminine	*somewhere in between feminine and masculine*	*very masculine*

Using this same scale, which number best represents the IDEAL physical attributes of someone you would be attracted to?

1	2	3	4	5	6	7	8	9	10

very feminine	*somewhere in-between feminine and masculine*	*very masculine*

PERSONALITY STYLE SCALE

Now, on a different scale of 1-10, with "1" representing someone whose PERSONALITY and interaction style with others would be considered laid back, quiet, or introverted, and "10" representing someone who might be thought of as outgoing, expressive, or extroverted in social interactions with others, which number best represents YOUR OWN interaction style?

1	2	3	4	5	6	7	8	9	10

laid back/   somewhere in   outgoing/
introverted   between   extroverted
     laid back and
     outspoken

Using this same scale, which number best represents the interaction style of YOUR MATE?

1	2	3	4	5	6	7	8	9	10

laid back/   somewhere in   outgoing/
introverted   between   extroverted
     laid back and
     outspoken

Using this same scale, which number best represents the IDEAL interaction style of someone you would be attracted to?

1	2	3	4	5	6	7	8	9	10

laid back/   somewhere in   outgoing/
introverted   between   extroverted
     laid back and
     outspoken

How are the following activities for your child or children divided between you and your mate WHEN BOTH OF YOU ARE PRESENT?

	Biological mom does this more	We do this equally	Other mate does this more	Neither of us does this
Engages in "quiet" activities like reading, homework, drawing	1	2	3	99
Engages in "active" activities like playing ball, video games, etc.	1	2	3	99
Changes diapers, gives a bath, dresses child(ren)	1	2	3	99
Gets up at night when child(ren) need attention	1	2	3	99
Who do the child(ren) go to when upset/can't sleep/need advice	1	2	3	99
Takes child(ren) to doctor, dentist, other appointments	1	2	3	99
Takes child(ren) shopping, for haircuts, etc.	1	2	3	99
Takes/picks up child(ren) to/from school, play activities	1	2	3	99
Attends parent meetings at school	1	2	3	99
Makes sure child(ren) are fed	1	2	3	99
Gets child(ren) ready for bed/Puts child(ren) to bed	1	2	3	99
Buys clothes and other things the child(ren) need	1	2	3	99
Buys toys and gifts for child(ren)	1	2	3	99
Who has the most influence regarding child(ren)'s appearance	1	2	3	99
Who has the most influence on decisions regarding child(ren)'s school	1	2	3	99
Who takes the most initiative and makes the most decisions about the child(ren)'s hobbies/after-school activities	1	2	3	99
Who has the most responsibility for disciplining the child(ren)	1	2	3	99

APPENDIX C

Questions from In-Depth Interview on Self-Definitions of Sexuality

If you had to define your sexuality, how would you define it?

On your survey, when asked to define your sexuality, you said you were

_____.

What is it about your experiences with women and men that made you answer the question in that way?

Have you ever had a serious relationship with a man?

How was it different from your experiences with women?

Is being gay for you a political identity?

Do you associate it with feminism—how much is it tied to the idea of equal rights for women?

How did you come into the Life? What were those first experiences like for you?

What kind of person were you interested in attracting?

Did the kind of person you were looking for influence the way you dressed? How did you decide on a style that is comfortable for you?

How do you feel about labels like "femme" or "aggressive" or "butch?" Where do you think you would fit in if you had to choose a label? What is it about your style of dress or personality that makes you say that?

How important is it to you that someone you're interested in dating is seriously "out" to others? Are you "out" to your family? Friends? Yourself?

How have your parents or parental figures responded to your being in the Life?

Notes

1. Pseudonyms are used to protect respondents' anonymity. Following Weston's model (2004), I assign surnames to this study's participants to convey a sense of respect and adult status not always afforded sexual or racial minority group members.

2. See appendices for more detail on study criteria and other methodological questions.

3. This work draws from a long tradition of intersectional approaches to the study of how race, class, and gender structure Black women's experiences in social institutions such as the law (Crenshaw 1989, 1991), labor market (Dill 1979; Glenn 1985; Higginbotham and Romero 1997; Shaw 1996), and family life (Allen 1978; Burton and Tucker 2009; Collins 2000; Dill 1983), and how these statuses structure health outcomes for Black lesbians (Bowleg 2008; Bowleg et al. 2003; Greene 1996; Mays and Cochran 1988).

4. See McCall (2005, 1783).

5. Mays and Cochran's 1988 psychological study focusing on Black lesbians' mental health is one important exception. Social science research on the experiences of male racial minority gays is less sparse, with publications like Crichlow (2004a, 2004b), Hawkeswood (1996), and Johnson's (2008) oral histories of Black gay men in the South.

6. See, for example, the controversy over the 1965 Moynihan Report as analyzed by Franklin (1997). Jenkins (2007) argues a similar point through an analysis of African American literature. See also Ferguson (2004); Lorde (2007).

7. Clarke (1995) argues that Black lesbians, and most Black women more generally, are conditioned to be self-sufficient because of their experiences of being raised in Black families that were so poor they "did not have the luxury to cultivate dependence among the members of their families" (247). She says

that the conditioning to be self-sufficient and the predominance of female role models in her life are at the roots of her own lesbian sexuality.

8. See Higginbotham (1993) and Lincoln and Mamiya (1990). Griffin (2006) provides an historical overview and critical analysis of the stance of Black mainline churches on the immorality of homosexuality and its consequences for lesbian and gay Christians.

9. For research on historical representations of Black women that employ analyses of the politics of respectability, see Giddings (1994); Higginbotham (1992, 1993); Hine (1994); Shaw (1996); White (1999); and Wolcott (2001).

10. Ferguson (2004) writes more explicitly about the vulnerability of Black sexuality and the regulatory nature of sociology as a discipline in its pathologization of African American culture.

11. On Black women's respectability in the Caribbean, see Besson (1993); Freeman (2000); and Ulysse (1999). Ulysse argues that the dichotomy of "lady" and "woman" is a Victorian taxonomy that was reinforced by British colonials to facilitate hegemonic rule. White females were considered "ladies," and Black females were "women" or "girls." Skin color and ancestry were important markers of social class among Black women, and lighter-skinned multiracial women sought to define and redefine their identities to reconstruct themselves as "ladies" rather than "women."

12. I sometimes use the language of *enact* or *enacting* when describing people who have revealed to others a gay identity; who call themselves lesbian, gay, or same-gender-loving; or who take on a gay sexuality. Others have used the term *come out* to reference a similar set of phenomena. The language of enactment suggests not that one is choosing to "be" gay or choosing to have same-sex attraction and desire but instead that one is choosing to display those desires to others by naming their sexuality or by forming relationships with others of the same sex and asking that those relationships be publicly recognized by family, friends, and members of society at large. Throughout this book, but most directly in Chapter 1, I make a distinction between people who have same-sex desire and act on it (openly or in secret) while not specifically seeing themselves or wishing others to understand them as lesbian, and those who declare themselves to others as lesbian and express a commitment to living an openly gay life. In Chapter 1, I show how some routes to an openly gay sexuality are preceded by same-sex attraction that is not revealed to others so as not to disrupt images of heterosexuality. To "enact" a gay sexuality suggests that the individual recognizes her attraction to other women and is willing to act on that attraction in a way that signals to others that this is her preference.

13. The 2000 Census allowed researchers to identify Black same-sex couples in various census tracts across the country. The cities with the greatest number of Black same-sex unmarried partner households in those data were New York, Washington, DC, Baltimore, Chicago, Atlanta, and Los Angeles. Between 2002 and 2006, I spoke with Black organization leaders and party promoters in these cities about the types of social activities that attract Black lesbians. Compared to New York, none of the other cities had more public social events that were predominantly Black. For details on the particular context of New York and its influence on the findings of this work, see appendix A.

14. I also attended a Black gay pride event in Toronto, Canada, where the majority of Blacks are of West Indian descent (Ornstein 2000, 12, table 1).

15. For other feminist ethnography that engages with assumptions of insider/outsider status and questions of power between the researcher and the researched, see Abu-Lughod 1991; Harding 1991; Naples 1996; and Zinn 1979.

16. Mezey (2008) writes about this problem in trying to recruit Black and Latina lesbians for her research. Other studies of lesbians that have underrepresented women of color include Blumstein and Schwartz 1983; Stein 1997; Sullivan 2004; and Weston 1991.

17. Each partner was interviewed separately by a Black female researcher. I was the primary interviewer, but in cases where both partners were interviewed simultaneously, I employed one of four Black female graduate research assistants, and one Black female who was not a student but who was familiar with Black lesbian culture. I trained all five interviewers in face-to-face interview procedures.

CHAPTER ONE

1. See D' Emilio (1983); Phelan (1993).

2. This process and its variants are primarily identified in psychological research on gay men (Cass 1979; Harry 1993; Martin 1991) and adolescents (Dempsey 1994; Savin-Williams 1998). Some studies on lesbian identities find gay women to experience a similar coming out process (Bell, Weinberg, and Hammersmith 1981; Chapman and Brannock 1987; Ponse 1978; Sophie 1985–86), though research over the past fifteen years suggests women's sexuality may be more fluid than that of men and that women may more often follow a nonlinear pattern of experiencing and acting on same-sex desire (Diamond 2008; Diamond and Savin-Williams 2000; Rust 1993). Fukuyama and Ferguson (2000), Greene (1997), and Smith (1997) among others, critique the psychological coming out model and its applicability for gay people of color in the context of therapy-oriented research.

3. Findings on the nonlinear development of lesbian and bisexuality, as well as the sexual fluidity and social construction of sexual orientation, are in the work of Baumgardner (2007); Diamond (2008); Esterberg (1997); Garber (1995); Kitzinger (1987); Kitzinger and Wilkinson (1995); Peplau and Huppin (2008); Rust (1992); and Stein (1997), among others.

4. See, for example, Cohen (1999); Ferguson (2003); Johnson (2003); Johnson and Henderson (2005); and McBride (2005a) .

5. The other person in this category referred to her sexuality as "predominantly lesbian, only slightly heterosexual." See Appendix B for exact wording of this question.

6. For studies on groups of lesbians who say they have always felt "different" from other women and later linked these feelings of difference to a lesbian identity, see Esterberg (1997); Lewin (1993); Ponse (1978); and Stein (1997).

7. For a review of this work, see Bailey and Zucker (1995).

8. Historical work on White middle-class lesbians suggests a similar concern for White women in previous generations, particularly in their reluctance to use

lesbian-identified social spaces to create community. Gilmartin (1996, 18) uses a case study of one White, middle-class, masculine-identified lesbian to show the ways remaining in the closet during the 1940s and 1950s helped shape a sense of respectability. She argues that the women in her subject's social group did not seek any kind of public recognition of their sexuality, and maneuvered the relationship between sexuality and public space in ways that were different from their working-class peers.

9. Bérubé (1990) makes a similar point, writing that in the 1930s and 1940s, young women and men who felt homosexual and joined the military found that the distance from family and neighbors enabled them to more fully express their same-sex desires. Rosenfeld's (2007) work emphasizes the importance of geographic mobility for people in same-sex unions today, finding that people in gay or lesbian partnerships are significantly more likely to live in communities away from the family members of one or both partners.

10. African Ancestral Lesbians United for Societal Change is the oldest known African American lesbian group in the United States. It was founded in 1974 under the name Salsa Soul Sisters as an alternative to the bar-oriented lesbian community to address the needs of "third world" Black and Latina gay women (Carbado, McBride, and Weise 2002, 123).

11. For example, see research on gay and lesbian people in rural America (Gray 2009; Oswald 2002), and on African American gay men in the southeastern United States (Johnson 2008). For international work on pressures women in same-sex relationships experience to live an ambiguously lesbian life, see Chalmers (2002); Engebretsen (2009); Herrera (2009); Swarr and Nagar (2003). For interdisciplinary writings on the experiences of Trinidadian lesbians and gay men, see Crichlow (2004b) and Mootoo (2008). For more general work on Black female same-sex relations and practices outside of the United States, see Blackwood and Wieringa (1999); Morgan and Wieringa (2005); Potgieter (2003); and Wekker (2006).

12. Schomburg rare manuscripts collection, letter to Cheryl Clarke dated 11/19/1975, housed in C. Clarke box 1.

13. A 2009 analysis of three large-scale surveys examining social class in same-sex partner households found that African Americans in same-sex coupled households have poverty rates that are three times higher than those of White people in same-sex couples, and are also more likely than Black heterosexual couples to be poor. Furthermore, Black lesbian couples were more likely than Black gay male couples to be living in poverty (Albelda et al. 2009).

14. Research on White women supports the particular experience of the Black hetero-identified lesbians in my work. In Kitzinger and Wilkinson's 1995 study of the construction of lesbian sexuality, a portion of their sample said they were not attracted to girls as children or adolescents; it was not until adulthood when they met a particular woman or experienced a specific incident that they found themselves emotionally attracted to someone of the same gender. Cassingham and O'Neil (1999) report a similar, alternate path for women in their research.

15. See, for example, Diamond (2008); Esterberg (1997); Phelan (1993); Rust (1992); and Stein (1997).

16. "Bisexual" as an identity has historically been problematic and stigmatized. See, for example, Ponse's (1978) study of White lesbians in a large southern city; Kennedy and Davis' (1993) study of a working-class lesbian in upstate New York, and Esterberg's (1997) study of lesbians in a small eastern city.

17. Morris and Balsam (2003) analyze data from a national sample of lesbian and bisexual women, comparing women who report having been sexually abused in childhood with women who do not report such abuse. Thirty-nine percent of their sample report being sexually abused before the age of 16 and this percentage, according to the researchers, falls towards the high end of the ranges generally reported in large-scale surveys of women. The study also reported significantly higher rates of childhood sexual assault for Black lesbian and bisexual women relative to White women, and significantly lower rates of childhood sexual assault for Black relative to Latina women. Morris and Balsam did not compare lesbian and bisexual women on their experiences with sexual assault, but they did find that lesbian and bisexual women who experienced sexual abuse in childhood first self-identified as gay, lesbian, or bisexual about ten months earlier than women who did not experience childhood sexual abuse.

18. See Herek and Capitanio (1995) for data on differential acceptance of Black male and female homosexuals by Black heterosexuals.

CHAPTER TWO

1. Although the word *aggressive* ordinarily describes personality traits or behavior, many Black lesbians in New York use the term as a descriptor of a lesbian who has a nonfeminine or masculine presentation of self. Tripp (1975) used the term *aggressive woman* to explain the behavioral inversion of expected gender roles in early lesbian relationships. Women were stereotypically understood to be submissive in the aggressive-submissive binary, and the aggressive homosexual woman was thought to represent "a reversal of the commonly expected gender-role of the individual" (22). From this we can conclude that the term *aggressor* in lesbian relationships came to represent the individual thought to inaugurate and manage the sexual component of the interaction. Rubin (1992) tells us that, historically, it was the masculine-identified person in the lesbian relationship who was thought to seduce, arouse, and sexually satisfy her partner. The partner was expected to have a feminine gender display and to be sexually passive or to be the primary receiver of sexual pleasure in the interaction. These beliefs were consistent with what were also expected of men in heterosexual relationships. The work of Lisagor (1980) extends this interpretation of one person as the direct initiator, not just in sexual relations but in other less personal interactions that take place in lesbian social spaces.

Although the "aggressive" label was not race-specific in its earlier use, when my data were collected in the first decade of the twenty-first century, it continued to be used, along with its variants "AG" and "aggressor," primarily by Black and Latina younger, working-class women (under age 40) in New York. The "aggressive" category of gender presentation is similar in meaning to "stud" or "butch," but many nonfeminine Black lesbians report being uncomfortable defining themselves as "butch" and see the "stud" label as representing older Black masculine women. The use of the label "aggressive" is class biased, and many middle-class or upwardly mobile lesbians strongly dislike it. For other work on gender or sexual inversion in women, see Ellis (1921, cited in Weeks 1990); Gagnon and Simon (2005); and Wolff (1971).

2. The gender presentation categories of "butch" and "femme" are important historical categories within the lesbian experience. In Kennedy and Davis's (1989) historical account of a lesbian community in New York, they delineate the dimensions of butch and femme roles for Black and White working-class women of that era. The roles had two dimensions: "First, they constituted a code of personal behavior, particularly in the areas of image and sexuality. Butches affected a masculine style, while fems appeared characteristically female. Butch and fem also complemented one another in an erotic system in which the butch was expected to be both the doer and the giver; the fem's passion was the butch's fulfillment. Second, butch-fem roles were what we call a social imperative. They were the organizing principle for this community's relation to the outside world and for its members' relationships to one another" (244). Laporte (1992) says butch and femme are "merely a shorthand way of labeling. The qualities of femininity and masculinity are distributed in varying proportions in all lesbians. . . . A butch is simply a lesbian who finds herself attracted to and complemented by a lesbian more feminine than she, whether this butch be very or only slightly more masculine than feminine" (211).

3. Crawley's (2001) empirical analyses of lesbian gender presentation in the 1990s found that middle-class lesbians were less likely than working-class lesbians to use specific labels to describe their own gender presentation, but were no less likely to use labels like "butch" and "fem" to describe the type of partner they were seeking. Her findings suggest class differences in how open lesbians are to using labels for self-definition, but consistency across classes in the use of categories to define erotic desire.

4. For 1990s research on changes over time in the way gender presentation and butch/femme relationships are portrayed in lesbian communities, see Blackman and Perry (1990); Morgan (1993): and Stein (1997).

5. Global analyses of gender presentation in contemporary lesbian communities includes work by Engebretsen (2009) in China, Essig (1999) in Russia, and Morgan and Wieringa's (2005) research on female same-sex practice in African countries.

6. White lesbians, particularly women born after 1970, are less likely than in previous years to identify as lesbian-feminists, instead preferring "queer" identities (Warner 1993). Research on women in lesbian-headed families continues to find that these women organize their relationships around the general feminist principle of an egalitarian distribution of paid labor and unpaid housework that allows partners to exercise "similar degrees of influence in family decision making" (Sullivan 2004).

7. Most previous studies of lesbian communities have drawn their samples from organizations and social groups of lesbians bound by politics. Some examples include Ponse (1978); Stein (1997); and Wolf (1979).

8. Several sociological and historical studies of Black gay life have shown how race and culture are incorporated into the expression of gay sexuality. See, for example, Garber's (1990) accounts of Harlem's gay world in the 1920s; Beemyn's (1997) research on after-hours restaurants, bars, and house party circuits in 1940s Washington, DC; Drexel's (1997) analyses of the ball scene on the South Side of Chicago before 1960; Hawkeswood's (1996) study of Harlem gay men in the 1980s; and Johnson's more recent (2008) oral histories of Black gay men in the South. There are fewer comprehensive studies of race and culture in Black lesbian life, though important exceptions include depictions by Lorde (1995) of house parties organized by women in New York City in the late 1950s; an examination of Black lesbian nightlife in Detroit between 1940 and 1975 by Thorpe (1996); and analyses of 1940s and 1950s public lesbian life for Black and White women in Buffalo, New York (Kennedy and Davis 1993). More recently, Batista's (2006) autobiographical novel offers a look at her experiences growing up gay in 1980s New York, her involvement in the Black lesbian social scene, and what she refers to as the "lesbian underground" of Manhattan.

9. The categories in each of these items do not round to 100 because of the way these questions are worded.

10. See Blackman and Perry (1990); Hawkeswood (1996) and Moore (2006). Jackson (2005) writes about the meanings of style in Black communities, though his work does not specifically reference style in gay social worlds.

11. JoAnn Loulan (1990) reminds us that lesbians have long used versions of this scale in informal ways to evaluate the gender presentations of themselves and others in gay communities.

12. Hawkeswood also discusses the meanings of style in the Black gay world. He writes that differences between gay men and other men in Harlem are expressed through a distinctive style "that draws on both black and gay cultures and finds its expression on the streets of Harlem and in the bars and clubs of the gay social scene. This fusion of black and gay cultures offers a rare glimpse at the social construction of a new cultural identity" (187).

13. "Fem-aggressive" conveys a different meaning that "aggressive fem," in that it suggests a combination of feminine and masculine gender display. "Aggressive fem" is meant to describe the personality of an assertive woman who has a feminine gender display. The term aggressive fem is meant to distance Black feminine women from the passivity that has traditionally coincided with understandings of the femininity of White middle- and upper-class women.

14. See Kennedy and Davis (1993); Ponse (1978); and Stein (1997).

15. I developed the term *transgressive* as a category of gender presentation with sociologist France Winddance Twine during a conversation over lunch.

16. In 2003–2006 when these data were collected, working-class lesbians were more likely to share the same surname of the less feminine partner, although without having made a legal name change.

17. See, for example, Kennedy and Davis (1993) and Nestle (1992). A masculine-identified lesbian in Ponse's (1978) study comments that butch women in her time (1970s) would be embarrassed to have a femme explore their bodies sexually.

18. See Breines (2002). While Black women could in some ways relate to gender oppression as defined by the women's movement, other issues that were a platform for the movement were not as relevant to them, and many were not convinced that the type of feminism it championed served their best interests (Morrison 1971). During the 1960s and 1970s, Black lesbians were concerned with issues such as police brutality and the availability of jobs that would facilitate Black socioeconomic mobility—issues that had a direct impact on the racially segregated communities in which they lived (Combahee River Collective 1982). They could not disentangle their needs from those in larger Black communities. But many leaders in the larger movement felt these issues did not belong on the women's liberation platform (Bennett and Gibbs 1980). King (1988, 55) argues that Black women were reluctant to publicly articulate a feminist consciousness because they saw an alignment with something labeled "feminism" as antithetical to an exclusive commitment to racial interests.

White patriarchy also competed with other oppressions based on race, which left many Black lesbians outside the boundaries and influence of 1970s lesbian-feminism. During this time, for instance, Black women were employed in significant numbers as private household workers and in related jobs controlled by White middle- and upper-class women (Mullings 1997). This type of racial and class hierarchy among women made it difficult for Blacks and Whites to see all, or even most, of their interests as mutual (Breines 2002). In addition to patriarchal domination by White men in the larger society, Black women also had to combat gender discrimination in Black liberation movements that fell outside of the experiences of White women.

Many White women in the women's movement believed their perspectives and concerns were not heard by Black women and felt that Black women refused to validate the gendered oppression they were experiencing in society (Weindling 1980). Reports from White women said that Black women wanted their own issues at the forefront of the movement and wanted to blame White women for their subjugation instead of directing that anger toward men (Calderone and Charoula 1980). This difference in perspective and opinion has never been fully resolved and continues to cause distance and feelings of mistrust between the two groups.

19. Thorpe (1996), for example, documents the characteristics of the types lesbian house parties that dominated lesbian life in Black Detroit from 1940 through 1975. While the history of the gay African American experience has been poorly documented, we know that an extensive, private, racially homogeneous social life has existed for Black lesbians outside of public bars, restaurants, and nightclubs since at least as early as the 1920s in Harlem (Garber 1990); the 1930s in Detroit (Welbon 1999); the 1940s in Washington, DC (Beemyn 1997) and Buffalo (Kennedy and Davis 1993); the 1950s in Queens, NY (Lorde 1983); and the 1980s for West Indian lesbians and gays in Kingston, Jamaica (unpublished author interview with Sifa Brody, Brooklyn, NY, October 25, 2003).

20. For work on raced notions of femininity and interpretations of Black sexuality as pathological, deviant, or masculine, see Cahn (1994); Collins (2004a): Hammonds (1997); and Somerville (2000).

21. Spending time in lesbian social spaces has been shown to influence aspects of women's physical appearance. Krakauer and Rose (2002) report that most of their study participants made significant, though modest changes to their physical appearance after spending time in lesbian social groups. They linked these changes to the norms of other lesbians around styles of dress, respondents' desire to signal prospective partners, and respondents becoming more comfortable with themselves.

22. This contrasts with the White couple portrayed on the cover of Sullivan's *The Family of Women* (2004), both of whom look similarly nonfeminine. The phenomenon of two similarly transgressive Black lesbians partnering is more prevalent (though still infrequent) in other regions of the U.S. See Appendix A for more information on the particular nature of New York's Black lesbian communities.

23. Couples with two feminine partners were more common outside of New York in places where Black gay life is more closeted, like parts of Los Angeles and some cities in the Southeast, including Biloxi, MS, and Birmingham, AL.

24. See Chapter 6, "Now You Get this Spot Right Here": Butch-Fem Sexuality During the 1940s and 1950s," in Kennedy and Davis (1993).

25. For other research on class differences in the acceptability of visible Black female sexuality of any kind in Black social spaces, see Carby (1992); Cornwell (1983); and "Hamilton Lodge Ball Draws 7,000" in Heap (2009 chap. 6, note 51).

26. See Hammonds (1997); Higginbotham (1992); and Hine (1989). For the argument suggesting class distinctions among Black women in their propensity to construct a "wall of silence" around their sexuality, see Davis (1998) and Wolcott (2001).

27. Debra Wilson presents transgressive lesbians' experiences with this image in her award-winning 2003 documentary *Butch Mystique*, and her film's subjects discuss the consequences of representing Black masculinity, such as seeing women holding their purses close when they walk down the street.

28. See, for example, Rubin's (1992) reflections on conceptions and misconceptions of butch and other masculine-woman identities. She centers the White female subject in her definitions and explanations with little analysis of how such coded identities and behaviors are manifested, and the consequences of such manifestations, in other raced subjects.

29. See, for example, Royster (2003).

30. This finding supports a larger trend toward less identification with feminism across racial groups and women's sexual orientations.

31. In one of the first studies of public lesbian spaces, Lisagor found that lesbian bars are an important location for socialization into lesbian life. They provide an "introduction, induction, and integration into the gay community, and ultimately, an identity as a gay person" (1980, 141). Since the majority of my respondents came into an understanding of their gay sexuality in Black spaces like bars, parties and other social gatherings, they are apt to perpetuate the particular culture of Black lesbian communities, including the use of gender presentation to organize relationships between gay women.

CHAPTER THREE

1. Although the question is posed in the singular, the responses indicate the subject's relative sense of collective identity with the larger group represented by the singular case (i.e., "Black straight woman" represents Black straight women as a group).

2. For more on the racial integration of White ethnic neighborhoods in New York, and Canarsie in particular, see Rieder (1985).

3. For readings on the experience of children and young adults integrating all-White establishments, see LaNier (2009) and Tyson (2011).

4. For a historical discussion of problems related to race and gender experienced by Black female medical students and doctors, see Hine (1994, pt. 3).

5. See Lacy (2007); Laureau (2003); and Young (2004).

6. This finding is consistent with historical research on class differences in lesbian identification among White women. In these studies, middle-class women were less interested than working-class women in making their gay relationships visible to outside society and shielded them by having similar gender presentations as their partners. See, for example, Gilmartin (1996). Faderman (1991) reports that professional women in the 1940s and 1950s practiced discretion and were particularly concerned about people in their workplaces finding out they were lesbians because they feared that exposure would cost them their jobs. Kennedy and Davis (1993) say middle-class White lesbians made a clear separation between their lesbian social lives and work and family; they felt this was something their work required because dress and moral reputation were considered part of the employee's job performance, and lesbian identity and culture were at odds with both.

CHAPTER FOUR

1. There are noteworthy exceptions, including Hequembourg (2007), Lewin (1993), and Nelson (1996). However, the discourse in the literature on lesbian motherhood, and analyses of lesbian-headed families, tend to define lesbian mothers as women who identify as gay prior to entering motherhood who are biological or adoptive mothers, or who are co-parents with a partner who bears a child in the context of their lesbian relationship. See Gartrell et al. (2000); Mezey (2008); Patterson (1995); and Sullivan (2004).

2. Studies in psychology like those by Patterson (1995) and Gartrell and colleagues (1999, 2000) have taken this approach.

3. See Rosenfeld (2010). He finds that same-sex couple parents in the 2000 Census tend to be mostly working class.

4. For research on parenting issues in multigenerational households, see Harvey (1993) and Wakschlag, Chase-Lansdale, and Brooks-Gunn (1996). This research suggests significant levels of conflict over authority between grandmother and mother in the arenas of child rearing. For research on parenting issues between co-mothers and biological mothers in lesbian families, see Ciano-Boyce and Shelley-Sireci (2002) and Pelka (2009). This body of work suggests

some areas of family life where maternal jealously serves as a stressor to parent-child and co-mother relationships.

5. Age when the respondent first became a mother was established through survey questions asking respondent's year of birth and age of respondent's children. Age respondent took on a lesbian identity is taken from the respondent's response to two survey questions. One asks, "If you had to select only one, which of these definitions would describe your sexuality?" Responses range from 1 (*Exclusively lesbian*) to 7 (*Exclusively heterosexual*). Respondents who gave themselves a score of 1 or 2 (*Predominantly lesbian, only slightly heterosexual*) are considered gay/lesbian. The second question used in this measure asks, "If you consider yourself exclusively or predominantly lesbian, at what age did you first decide you were definitely lesbian?" Respondents could write in an age or select "I do not consider myself exclusively or predominantly lesbian."

6. I use *discourse* in the sense that Hequemborg defines it, as not merely a language but also a "historically, socially, and institutionally specific structure of statements, terms, categories and beliefs" (2007, 5–6). Discourses are practices, rather than structures, that are lived, acted out, and spoken by individuals.

7. For past work on negative images and interpretations of Black woman-hood and Black mothers, see Collins (2004a, 2004b); Jenkins (2007); Landry (2000); and Rainwater and Yancy (1967). For other work on stereotypes of "bad" mothers, see Ladd-Taylor and Umansky (1998).

8. For example, Silvera, writing about lesbian motherhood for Jamaican women, says it is the "sexual mother" that frightens the community and forces family members to close their eyes. She recalls one of the biggest criticisms she experienced from family and friends was that in openly raising her daughters as a Black lesbian, some in the racial community felt she was flaunting her sexuality "like a red rag, a flag on a pole." She says they could tolerate her as a lesbian and as a mother, but not as a lesbian sexual mother living with a woman lover. This was "counter-culture, counter-Black, counter-mother" (1992, 316).

9. The "numbers game" or "playing the numbers" is an illegal lottery played in mostly poor Black, Latino, and Italian neighborhoods in U.S. cities, wherein the gambler places a bet with a bookie at a bar or other private place. A "runner" carries the money and betting slips between the betting parlors and the headquarters (Ianni 1974). A number runner comes into contact with many different groups of people, and Jocelyn's father would have come across openly homosexual women and men who were part of the nightlife in the Bronx. It is interesting to note his involvement in this aspect of New York life as well as his involvement in the church as a Baptist minister; historian Victoria Wolcott links some denominations of Black churches with their operation of the numbers business (2001, 121).

10. In her study examining the relationships lesbians and gay men have with their families, Weston found that besides AIDS, no other topic generated as strong an emotional response than the coming out experiences of people to their biological families. She says "claiming a gay identity in the presence of parents or siblings frequently involved an anxiety-filled struggle to bring speech about sexual identity . . . into the cultural domain of 'the family.' . . . It puts to the test

the unconditional love and enduring solidarity commonly understood in the United States to characterize blood ties" (1991, 43–44).

11. For other work on the particular nature of rejection some Caribbean lesbians and gay men experience from church leaders and Christian religions, see Klonaris (2008).

12. Although Hays's argument implicitly refers to the experiences of working heterosexual mothers, as a category lesbian mothers are also perceived as "individuals engaged in the self-interested pursuit of gain" (1996, 157). In her work, mothers struggle with whether to stay at home or go out to work for pay. For lesbians who first begin to mother in a heterosexual context, the question is whether to come out by establishing a household with a partner or in other ways make visible and show a commitment to a homosexual identity. They must also decide whether and how to incorporate their children into this new sense of self.

13. For Black feminist frameworks on motherhood, see Collins (2000); Giddings (1984); and Higginbotham (1992). For research on marginalized mothers and standards of "good" mothering, see Glenn, Chang, and Forcey (1994) and Ladd-Taylor and Umansky (1998).

14. In conducting research on Black women coming of age in a major urban city during the 1970s and 1980s, one unanticipated finding in my work was the tremendous disruption crack cocaine and other drugs had on their families of origin. The trajectory of so many women's lives was changed when parents and/ or siblings became addicted to drugs, and in assuming the care of family members, many women in my study were prevented from reaching their full intellectual and social potential. Because of their parents' addictions, some faced poverty, neglect, eviction, and homelessness, and had to take on early parenting roles to help raise their siblings. These experiences caused them to delay or forego college and other forms of education. The effect of the 1980s drug epidemic on the life course trajectories and patterns of family formation for women and men growing up in major cities during this time needs to be more carefully studied.

15. Hine (1989, 915). Also see Giddings (1984); Hammonds (1997); and Higginbotham (1982).

16. For research on Black working-class women's conceptions of womanhood, see Brown (1994); Carby (1992); Davis (1998); Giddings (1984); and Higginbotham (1992).

17. For research on father-child relationships and qualities fathers bring to parenting, see Belsky (1998, 279); Lamb and Lewis (2004); and Parke et al. (2004, 311).

18. A study of lesbian motherhood in the United Kingdom also provides evidence of gendered interaction styles in lesbian families with children. Gabb (2005) analyzes the ways children in these households describe the "other mother" and her role within the family, and her work reveals the ways same-sex parent families can be important sites of gender contestation.

19. Increasing numbers of lesbian couples have been using in vitro fertilization (IVF) to biologically co-mother, using the eggs of one partner and the womb of the other. Zora and Nyla conceived using their own eggs through IVF. IVF is a very expensive procedure that can easily exceed $10,000 and is not always covered by medical insurance. Other insemination procedures also fall

outside of the budget of many working-class and middle-class families. In 2006, the cost for a single vial for one insemination at the Sperm Bank of New York was $465.00, and this did not include any physicians' fees, which can vary from $300 to more than $3,000 depending on the medical treatment the recipient may require.

20. See "Sperm Donors from America's Most Selective Universities: Limited Choices for Black Women" (1999). In Almeling's (2011) study of how staff at egg and sperm donor agencies recruit, screen, market, and compensate women and men donors, she found that these programs have difficulty recruiting African American, Hispanic, and Asian donors. In my own research for the current study, Albert Anouna, director and CEO of the Sperm Bank of New York, revealed that African Americans represent about 5% of individuals presenting themselves for evaluation as sperm donors, and less than 10% of their current released donors are African American (phone interview 01/26/6). A follow-up inquiry reveals these proportions are accurate for this and other sperm banks as of March 2011.

21. See, for example, Pelka (2009).

22. Some of these latter concerns are shared by other co-parenting lesbians. See, for example, Lewin (1993) and Sullivan (2004).

23. For other work on lesbian stepfamilies, see Fleming (1995); Lynch (2000, 2004); and Wright (1998).

24. Dissenting opinion of Justice Cordy in *Goodridge v. Dep't of Public Health,* 798 N.E.2d 941 (MA 2003). Justice Cordy's comments suggest the continued concern of the courts with whether children can receive optimal parenting in households headed by couples who are both members of the same sex: "We turn to [the question] of whether a conceivable rational basis exists on which the Legislature could conclude that continuing to limit the institution of civil marriage to members of the opposite sex furthers the legitimate purpose of ensuring, promoting, and supporting an optimal social structure for the bearing and raising of children. In considering whether such a rational basis exists, we defer to the decision-making process of the Legislature, and must make deferential assumptions about the information that it might consider and on which it may rely." A second example of this concern of the courts can be found in *Hernandez v. Robles,* 855 N.E.2d 1 (NY 2006). The justice writes: "To support their argument, plaintiffs and amici supporting them refer to social science literature reporting studies of same-sex parents and their children. Some opponents of same-sex marriage criticize these studies, but we need not consider the criticism, for the studies on their face do not establish beyond doubt that children fare equally well in same-sex and opposite-sex households. What they show, at most, is that rather limited observation has detected no marked differences. More definitive results could hardly be expected, for until recently few children have been raised in same-sex households, and there has not been enough time to study the long-term results of such child-rearing." The most recent research, however, has continued to support the finding of no significant differences in the well-being of children raised by same-sex, compared to opposite sex, partners.

25. I thank Tiffany Willoughby-Herard for helping me think through this argument. Berger's book *Workable Sisterhood: The Political Journey of Stigma-*

tized Women with HIV/AIDS (2004) describes the politics of intersectional stigma for women with HIV/AIDS, and I draw from her conceptualization here and in the Introduction. For historical work on stigma and notions of transformation as they relate to Black women's sexuality, see Carby (1987) and Hammonds (1997).

26. Gartrell and colleagues (1999) similarly find that lesbians who became mothers are more satisfied with their identities as mothers when their families are actively involved in larger communities of other lesbians.

CHAPTER FIVE

1. An exception to these norms is seen in studies of peer marriages (Schwartz 1994) and postgender heterosexual couples (Blaisure and Allen 1995; Risman and Johnson-Sumerford 1998), suggesting that when both heterosexual partners enter a union with a commitment to equitably distribute labor, they actively create marriages that are more equal in the division of housework and market work relative to those of married couples in the larger population.

2. I say "particular" here because scholars have defined egalitarian relationships in different ways. For example, Hunter and Sellers (1998) measure attitudes toward the division of housework and employment status of husbands and wives, but do not, in their analysis of egalitarianism, look at time spent on childcare.

3. For research on gender stratification in heterosexual married couple families, see Berk and Berk (1979); Coltrane (2000); Ferree and Hess (1985); Kenney (2006); South and Spitze (1994); and Tichenor (2005).

4. For research on notions of equality in the distribution of household tasks and child care in lesbian- and gay-couple families, see Carrington (1999); Gartrell et al. (2000); Kurdek (1993); Patterson (1995): and Sullivan (2004).

5. Baumle, Compton, and Poston (2009) and Gates (2006) reveal this point in separate analyses of the same-sex unmarried partner data in the 2000 U.S. Census. A national study of lesbian mothers and nonmothers by Morris, Balsam, and Rothblum (2002) also finds that the majority of lesbian households with children have structures that are similar to stepfamilies.

6. For the central tenets of Black feminism, see Collins (1989, 2000); Combahee River Collective (1982); James and Busia (1993); and King (1988).

7. For research on labor force participation of Black wives, see Giddings (1984); Jones (1985); and Landry (2000).

8. Treas (1993) found that married African American couples were more likely than non-Blacks to bank separately. Kenney (2006) analyzed the financial allocative systems of Black and White heterosexual couples and showed that Black couples were less likely to use a jointly pooled household financial system and more likely to have separate financial accounts that were maintained by women.

9. Lincoln and Mamiya find that the role of "church mother" originates from the kinship network found within Black churches and communities and has no identified parallel in predominantly White churches (1990, 275).

10. See Moore (2009) for an analysis of how social class influences the importance of economic independence for Black lesbians.

11. This is consistent with Caldwell and Peplau (1984), who showed that lesbians reported on surveys that they believed in egalitarian relationships even when their relationships did not reflect this ideal.

12. Bittman et al. (2003) report the median number of hours per week American married couples spend on housework and say wives do an average of fourteen hours per week, while husbands do seven hours.

13. In Lewin's (1993) classic anthropological study of lesbian mothers, she finds that for some, motherhood is their central identity. They understand motherhood as a state that is generally disapproved of or as contradictory to lesbianism and emphasize their status as mothers, sometimes hiding their status as lesbians, to protect themselves and their children from stigma. Lewin argues that for these women, "being a mother eclipses and overshadows all other roles" (110–11). They see other mothers, regardless of their sexual orientation, as the people with whom they have the most in common.

14. Erickson (2005) draws attention to the symbolic importance of family work for how people "do" or portray gender, as well as the emotional components of family work. In explaining gendered norms of accountability, she states: "As long as women are held (and hold themselves) accountable for family work in ways that men are (and do) not, the performance of this work will remain more central to how women construct a gendered sense of self and, in so doing, their behavior will continue to reflect such (self-) expectations" (340).

15. Thompson, McLanahan, and Curtin (1992) analyzed the National Survey of Families and Households to compare levels of parental involvement in several family structures including mother-stepfather and father-stepmother households. They found women in both of these family forms had more active participation than men in a range of parental responsibilities.

16. Hofferth and Anderson, analyzing the Child Development Supplement to the Panel Study of Income Dynamics, report significantly higher incomes and hours worked among stepfathers relative to biological mothers in remarried and unmarried cohabiting families (2003, table 2, p. 222). Also see Snoeckx, De-, hertogh, and Mortelmans (2008).

17. Emphasis in original.

18. Other research confirms greater discrepancies in income and occupational prestige between heterosexual compared to lesbian partners. See, for example, Patterson, Sutfin, and Fulcher (2004). Peplau, Cochran, and Mays (1997) examined the demographic characteristics of respondents in their national survey of African American lesbians and gay men and found a fair degree of demographic similarity between partners. This stood in marked contrast to similar studies of White gay men and lesbians, suggesting, perhaps, that Black couples were more evenly matched on education and income than their White peers.

19. In one family the bio-mom was a part-time sales clerk and her partner was an attorney. In the other household there was an artist and a physician.

20. In the fourth family, the couple was in the process of breaking up when I interviewed them, and the bio-mom had more say over the child. Two years later they were each re-partnered but continued to share joint custody of their son in an amicable relationship.

21. Other studies of this type of parenting report similar efforts by partners to be equal co-mothers, particularly during the early years of co-parenting. See, for example, Dalton (2001); Gartrell et al. (1999); and Sullivan (2004).

CHAPTER SIX

1. For studies of gay and lesbian life in Black communities, see Beemyn (1997); Carbado, McBride, and Weise (2002); Cohen 1999; Hawkeswood (1996); Thorpe (1996); and Silvera (2008).

2. On rates of HIV and AIDS transmission for Black women, see Berger (2004); Gilbert and Wright (2003); and Watkins-Hayes (2008). Since the start of the 21st century, prominent African American elected officials and religious leaders have begun to publicly denounce discrimination against lesbians and gay men. They appeal to their constituents and other Black clergy to confront and challenge the homophobia in Black communities and to support legislation that assures civil rights for all groups. Many of these public decrees and debates have taken place within the realm of New York politics and religious environments, although with the 2008 debates over the legality of same-sex marriage in California, these types of conversations are increasingly occurring in Black communities across the country (Jackson 2003; J. Lewis 2003; Moore 2010a, 2010b; Watson 2005).

3. For definitions and elaborations of "modern gay identity" or "modern homosexual identity," see Chauncey (1994) and D'Emilio (1983).

4. The term *Black religions* encompasses any predominantly Black religious congregation, even if it is part of a predominantly White denomination. A 2003 Gallup Poll shows that while 61 percent of U.S. citizens say religion is "very important to them in their own lives," 88 percent of Blacks respond to this same question in this way (Winseman 2005). On measures of the intense religiosity among African Americans, see Gallup and Castelli (1989) and Taylor, Mattis, and Chatters (1999). On the conservative nature of Black religions, see Carter (1976); Lincoln and Mamiya (1990); and VanderStoep and Green (1988). On assumptions of greater negative attitudes toward homosexuality among African Americans compared to the society at large, see Egan and Sherrill (2009); Herek and Capitanio (1995); G. Lewis (2003); and Newport (2008).

5. Smith (1999) provides a concrete example of this conflict in her hometown of Cleveland, Ohio, back in 1993 as what she calls the "pseudo-Christian right" engaged in a divisive strategy of enlisting the Black community's support for a homophobic campaign. In 2008 a similar scenario played out in California, where the Mormon church waged a successful campaign to repeal the state ban on same-sex marriage by presenting religious arguments about the family that would appeal to racial minority groups with high levels of religiosity.

6. I found this somewhat surprising—not just that she danced with her girlfriend but that she would dance at all in front of her mother, given that their religious beliefs explicitly forbid listening to secular music. Moreover, it was also noteworthy that her mother did not seem to take offense.

7. Kennedy and Davis (1993, 152).

8. This is the case when in heterosexual contexts. In lesbian and gay contexts, I have noticed an increase from 2001 to 2007 in women using the title "wife" to introduce a partner to other gay people. Earlier in the decade, before the legalization of same-sex marriage in Massachusetts, Black and Latina women used "wife" to denote a serious committed relationship; if the person was known to be seen dating other women from time to time, her labeling of her partner as wife signaled that this person had the higher status, while the others were just dalliances. There was also a class difference in the use of the term, with working-class women more likely to refer to a partner as wife. Since 2005, however, as public discussions of same-sex marriage have taken shape and lesbians and gay men have gained access to legal marriage in five countries, I have seen more middle-class and upper-middle-class women of color introducing and referring to their partners as their wives or spouses. These women have either had civil ceremonies, often going to Canada, Mexico, and even South Africa to legalize their unions, or have registered in New York and other U.S. cities as domestic partners. Regardless of either partner's gender presentation, I have only heard women use the terms *wife* and *spouse* but not *husband* to describe the person in their marriage or domestic partner relationship.

9. In published research, several factors have been shown to correlate with disapproval of homosexual behavior, including religiosity, lower levels of education, being older, having no interpersonal contact with someone who is gay, having a politically conservative ideology, and not being registered to vote.

10. For a discussion of the concept of linked fate in Black communities, see Dawson (1994). Also see Battle and Bennett (2005); Hunter (2010); and Moore (2010a; 2010b) for contemporary work examining the relationships Black lesbians and gay men have with their racial and religious communities.

11. One important exception is the disapproval often expressed among Black middle-class heterosexuals as well as many Black middle-class lesbians for hip hop expressions of gender nonconformity. Women wearing oversized jerseys, baggy jeans, and fitted baseball hats receive the most negative responses from both groups.

12. Riverside Church has had a long history of activism and political debate. It has been called "the premier model of Protestant liberalism in the United States" and "a multiracial and multiethnic church that has been at the vanguard of social justice advocacy" (Paris et al. 2004). From 1988 until 2007, the church was led by Reverend Doctor James A. Forbes Jr., its first African American senior minister. Under his leadership, the church hosted such political leaders as Nelson Mandela and Fidel Castro and held memorial services for Betty Shabazz, the widow of Malcolm X. Reverend Forbes has spoken out publicly in support of equal rights for lesbian and gay people, and continues to influence the church's ministry in his role as Senior Minister Emeritus (Barron 2006).

13. One that is not common in this study but that also exists is the physical distancing of some Black lesbian and gay people from racial communities. Some people also leave a gay life and retreat to a primary heterosexual identity while continuing to have same-sex intimate relationships in secret.

APPENDIX A

1. Dickies is a brand of American work apparel. The company makes a variety of work pants, jackets, shorts, medical scrubs, and so forth. In the early 2000s in New York, many transgressive lesbians wore Dickies pants accompanied by Timberland boots, thermal tops underneath Dickies work shirts, and other such clothing to reveal a working-class gender presentation.

2. Over the course of the eighteen months, we stayed in the West Village but changed venues three times because each venue went out of business. We were able to secure these venues without cost, possibly because they were financially struggling. Our event also took place on Monday nights, when most lounges are closed because business is so slow. We were able to keep a crowd large enough to satisfy the business owners.

3. All of these studies capture women who fall outside of the target population for the current study. The Dang and Frazer (2004) report does not include lesbians who are single mothers, and the Mays and Cochran (1988) sample and Ramsey et al. (2010) sample include Black lesbians who are not forming families.

References

Abu-Lughod, Lila. 1991. "Writing against Culture." In *Recapturing Anthropology*, edited by R. Fox, 137–62. Santa Fe, NM: School of American Research Press.

Acosta, Katie L. 2008. "Lesbians in the Borderlands: Shifting Identities and Imagined Communities." *Gender & Society* 22(5): 639–59.

Albelda, Randy, M. V. Lee Badgett, Alyssa Schneebaum, and Gary Gates. 2009. "Poverty in the Lesbian, Gay and Bisexual Community." California Center for Population Research On-Line Working Paper Series, CCPR-2009-007. Accessed August 20, 2010, from http://escholarship.org/uc/item/17r6mo1h #page-2.

Alexander, M. Jacqui, and Chandra Talpade Mohanty, eds. 1997. *Feminist Genealogies, Colonial Legacies, Democratic Futures*. New York: Routledge.

Allen, Walter. 1978. "The Search for Applicable Theories of Black Family Life." *Journal of Marriage and Family* 40(1): 117–21.

Almeling, Rene. 2011. *Sex Cells: The Medical Market for Eggs and Sperm*. Berkeley, CA: University of California Press.

Ambert, Anne-Marie. 1986. "Being a Stepparent: Live-in and Visiting Stepchildren." *Journal of Marriage and the Family* 48:795–804.

Bailey, J. Michael, and Ken J. Zucker. 1995. "Childhood Sex-Typed Behavior and Sexual Orientation: A Conceptual Analysis and Quantitative Review." *Developmental Psychology* 31: 43–55.

Barron, James. 2006. "Minister of Riverside Church to Step Down." *New York Times*, September 18. Accessed August 17, 2007, http://www.nytimes.com.

Barth, Fredrik. 1969. "Introduction." In *Ethnic Groups and Boundaries: The Social Organization of Culture Difference*, edited by F. Barth, 9–38. Boston: Little, Brown.

Batista, Christina. 2006. *Hersband*. BookSurge Publishing.

Battle, Juan J., and Natalie D. A. Bennett. 2005. "Striving for Place: Black Lesbian, Gay, Bisexual, and Transgender (LGBT) People in History and Society." In *A Companion to African American History*, edited by Alton Hornsby, 412–45. New York: Blackwell.

Baumgardner, Jennifer. 2007. *Look Both Ways: Bisexual Politics*. New York: Farrar, Straus and Giroux.

Baumle, Amanda K., D'Lane Compton, and Dudley L. Poston Jr. 2009. *Same-Sex Partners: The Social Demography of Sexual Orientation*. Albany: State University of New York Press.

Beemyn, Brett. 1997. "A Queer Capital: Race, Class, Gender, and the Changing Social Landscape of Washington's Gay Communities, 1940–1955." In *Creating a Place for Ourselves: Lesbian, Gay, and Bisexual Community Histories*, edited by Brett Beemyn, 183–210. New York: Routledge.

Bell, Alan P., Martin S. Weinberg, and Sue Kiefer Hammersmith. 1981. *Sexual Preference: Its Development in Men and Women*. Bloomington: Indiana University Press.

Belsky, Jay. 1998. "Paternal Influences and Children's Well-Being: Limits of, and New Directions for, Understanding." In *Men in Families: When Do They Get Involved? What Difference Does It Make?*, edited by Alan Booth and Ann C. Crouter. Mahwah, NJ: Lawrence Erlbaum Associates.

Bennett, Sara, and Joan Gibbs. 1980. "Racism and Classism in the Lesbian Community: Towards the Building of a Radical, Autonomous Lesbian Movement." In *Top Ranking: A Collection of Articles on Racism and Classism in the Lesbian Community*, edited by Joan Gibbs and Sara Bennett, 1–30. New York: February 3rd Press.

Berger, Michele. 2004. *Workable Sisterhood: The Political Journey of Stigmatized Women with HIV/AIDS*. Princeton, NJ: Princeton University Press.

Berk, Richard, and Sara Fenstermaker Berk. 1979. *Labor and Leisure at Home: Content and Organization of the Household Day*. Beverly Hills, CA: Sage.

Bérubé, Allan. 1990. *Coming Out Under Fire: The History of Gay Men and Women in World War Two*. New York: Penguin.

Besson, Jean. 1993. "Reputation and Respectability Reconsidered: A New Perspective on Afro-Caribbean Peasant Women." In *Women and Change in the Caribbean: A Pan-Caribbean Perspective*, edited by Janet Momsen, 15–37. Bloomington: Indiana University Press.

Bittman, Michael, Paula England, Nancy Folbre, Liana Sayer, and George Matheson. 2003. "When Does Gender Trump Money? Bargaining and Time in Household Work." *American Journal of Sociology* 109(1): 186–214.

Blackman, Inge, and Kathryn Perry. 1990. "Skirting the Issue: Lesbian Fashion for the 1990s." *Feminist Review* 34: 67–78.

Blackwood, Evelyn, and Saskia Wieringa, eds. 1999. *Female Desires: Same-Sex Relations and Transgender Practices Across Cultures*. New York: Columbia University Press.

Blaisure, Karen R., and Katherine R. Allen. 1995. "Feminists and the Ideology and Practice of Marital Equality." *Journal of Marriage and the Family* 57(1): 5–19.

Blumstein, Phillip, and Pepper Schwartz. 1983. *American Couples: Money, Work and Sex.* New York: Morrow.

Bonilla-Silva, Eduardo. 2010. *Racism Without Racists: Color-Blind Racism and the Persistence of Racial Inequality in the United States.* 3rd ed. Lanham: Rowman & Littlefield Publishers.

Bowleg, Lisa. 2008. "When Black + Lesbian + Woman ≠ Black Lesbian Woman: The Methodological Challenges of Qualitative and Quantitative Intersectionality Research." *Sex Roles: A Journal of Research* 59: 312–25.

Bowleg, Lisa, Jennifer Huang, Kelly Brooks, Amy Black, and Gary Burkholder. 2003. "Triple Jeopardy and Beyond: Multiple Minority Stress and Resilience among Black Lesbians." *Journal of Lesbian Studies* 7(4): 87–108.

Bradford, Judith, Kirsten Barrett, and Julie A. Honnold. 2002. *The 2000 Census and Same-Sex Households: A User's Guide.* New York: The National Gay and Lesbian Task Force Policy Institute, the Survey and Evaluation Research Laboratory, and The Fenway Institute. Accessed October 1, 2007, http://thetaskforce.org/reports_and_research/census_full.

Braithwaite, Dawn, Loreen Olsen, Tamara Golish, Charles Soukup, and Paul Truman. 2001. "'Becoming a Family': Developmental Processes Represented in Blended Family Discourse." *Journal of Applied Communication Research* 29(3): 221–47.

Bray, James H. 1999. "From Marriage to Remarriage and Beyond: Findings from the Developmental Issues in Stepfamilies Research Project." In *Coping with Divorce, Single Parenting and Remarriage: A Risk and Resiliency Perspective,* edited by E. Mavis Hetherington, 253–73. Hillsdale, NJ: Erlbaum.

Bray, James H., and John Kelly. 1998. *Stepfamilies: Love, Marriage and Parenting in the First Decade.* New York: Broadway.

Breines, Wini. 2002. "What's Love Got to Do With It? White Women, Black Women, and Feminism in the Movement Years." *Signs* 27(4): 1095–1133.

Brekhus, Wayne H. 2003. *Peacocks, Chameleons, Centaurs: Gay Suburbia and the Grammar of Social Identity.* Chicago: University of Chicago Press.

Brown, Elsa Barkley. 1994. "Negotiating and Transforming the Public Sphere: African American Political Life in the Transition from Slavery to Freedom." *Public Culture* 7(1): 107–46.

Brown, Malaika. 1994. "Holy Dilemma: The Church and AIDS." *Los Angeles Sentinel,* Sept. 1.

Brown, Rita Mae. 1972. "The Woman-Identified Woman." *The Ladder* (Winter): 13.

Brubaker, Rogers, and Frederick Cooper. 2000. *Theory and Society* 29(1): 1–47.

Bullough, Vern L. 2008. "Childhood Gender Nonconformity and Adult Homosexuality: A Historical View." *Journal of Gay and Lesbian Mental Health* 12(1/2): 7–15.

Burton, Linda, and M. Belinda Tucker. 2009. "Romantic Unions in an Era of Uncertainty: A Post-Moynihan Perspective on African American Women and Marriage." *The Annals of the American Academy of Political and Social Science* 62: 132–48.

Butler, Judith. 1999. *Gender Trouble: Feminism and the Subversion of Identity.* New York: Routledge.

Cahn, Susan K. 1994. *Coming on Strong: Gender and Sexuality in Twentieth-Century Women's Sport.* New York: Free Press.

Calderone, Laura, and Charoula. 1980. "The Personal Is Political Revisited: An Exploration of Racism in the Lesbian Community." In *Top Ranking: A Collection of Articles on Racism and Classism in the Lesbian Community*, edited by Joan Gibbs and Sara Bennett, 1–30. New York: February 3rd Press.

Caldwell, Mayta A., and L. Anne Peplau. 1984. "The Balance of Power in Lesbian Relationships." *Sex Roles* 10: 587–600.

Cantú, Lionel. 2001. "A Place Called Home: A Queer Political Economy of Mexican Immigrant Men's Family Experiences." In *Queer Families Queer Politics: Challenging Culture and the State*, edited by Mary Bernstein and Renate Reimann, 112–36. New York: Columbia University Press.

Carbado, Devon, Dwight McBride, and Donald Weise, eds. 2002. *Black Like Us: A Century of Lesbian, Gay, and Bisexual African-American Fiction.* San Francisco: Cleis Press.

Carby, Hazel V. 1986. "It Jus Be's Dat Way Sometime: The Sexual Politics of Women's Blues." *Radical America* 20(4): 9–22.

———. 1987. *Reconstructing Womanhood: The Emergence of the Afro-American Woman Novelist.* New York: Oxford University Press.

———. 1992. "Policing the Black Woman's Body in an Urban Context." *Critical Inquiry* 18(4): 738–55.

Carlson, Shirley. 1992. "Black Ideals of Womanhood in the Late Victorian Era." *Journal of Negro History* 77(2): 61–73.

Carrington, Christopher. 1999. *No Place Like Home: Relationships and Family Life among Lesbians and Gay Men.* Chicago: University of Chicago Press.

Carter, Harold. 1976. *The Prayer Tradition of Black People.* Valley Forge, PA: Judson.

Cass, Vivienne C. 1979. "Homosexual Identity Formation: A Theoretical Model." *Journal of Homosexuality* 4(3): 219–35.

Cassingham, Barbee J., and Sally M. O'Neil. 1999. *And Then I Met this Woman.* Freeland, WA: Soaring Eagle.

Chalmers, S. 2002. *Emerging Lesbian Voices from Japan.* New York: Routledge.

Chapman, B. E., and J. C. Brannock. 1987. "Proposed Model of Lesbian Identity Development: An Empirical Examination." *Journal of Homosexuality*, 14(3–4): 69–80.

Chauncey, George. 1994. *Gay New York: Gender, Urban Culture, and the Making of the Gay Male World, 1890–1940.* New York: Basic.

Cherlin, Andrew J., and Frank F. Furstenberg. 1994. "Stepfamilies in the United States: A Reconsideration." *Annual Review of Sociology* 20: 359–81.

Chin, Staceyann. 2009. *The Other Side of Paradise: A Memoir.* New York: Simon & Schuster.

Ciano-Boyce, Claudia, and Lynn Shelley-Sireci. 2002. "Who Is Mommy Tonight? Lesbian Parenting Issues." *Journal of Homosexuality* 43:1–13.

Clarke, Cheryl. 1983. "The Failure to Transform: Homophobia in the Black Community." In *Home Girls: A Black Feminist Anthology*, edited by Barbara Smith, 197–208. New York: Kitchen Table/Women of Color Press.

———. 1995. "Lesbianism: An Act of Resistance." In *Words of Fire: An Anthology of African-American Feminist Thought,* edited by Beverly Guy-Sheftall, 242–51. New York: The New Press.

Cohen, Cathy. 1999. *The Boundaries of Blackness: AIDS and the Breakdown of Black Politics.* Chicago: University of Chicago Press.

Coleman, Marilyn, and Lawrence H. Ganong. 1989. "Financial Management in Stepfamilies." *Journal of Family and Economic Issues* 10: 217–32.

Coleman, Marilyn, Lawrence H. Ganong and Shannon Weaver. 2001. "Relationship Maintenance and Enhancement in Remarried Families." In *Close Romantic Relationships: Maintenance and Enhancement,* edited by John Harvey and Amy Wenzel, 255-276. Mahwah, NJ: Erlbaum.

Coleman, Marilyn, Jessica Troilo, and Tyler Jamison. 2008. "The Diversity of Stepmothers: The Influences of Stigma, Gender, and Context on Stepmother Identities." In *The International Handbook of Stepfamilies: Policy and Practice in Legal, Research, and Clinical Environments,* edited by Jan Pryor, 369–93. Hoboken, NJ: Wiley.

Collins, Patricia Hill. 1989. "The Social Construction of Black Feminist Thought." *Signs* 14: 745–73.

———. 2000. *Black Feminist Thought: Knowledge, Consciousness, and the Politics of Empowerment.* 2nd ed. New York: Routledge.

———. 2004a. *Black Sexual Politics: African Americans, Gender, and the New Racism.* New York: Routledge.

———. 2004b. "Shifting the Center: Race, Class, and Feminist Theorizing about Motherhood." In *Mothering: Ideology, Experience and Agency,* edited by E. N. Glenn, G. Chang, and L. Forcey, 45–65. New York: Routledge.

Coltrane, Scott. 2000. "Research on Household Labor: Modeling and Measuring the Social Embeddedness of Routine Family Work." *Journal of Marriage and the Family* 62(4): 1208–33.

Combahee River Collective. 1982. "A Black Feminist Statement." In *All the Women Are White, All the Blacks Are Men, But Some of Us Are Brave: Black Women's Studies,* edited by Gloria Hull, Patricia Bell-Scott, and Barbara Smith, 13–22. Old Westbury, NY: Feminist Press.

Cornell, Stephen, and Douglas Hartmann. 2007. *Ethnicity and Race: Making Identities in a Changing World.* 2nd ed. Thousand Oaks, CA: Pine Forge Press.

Cornwell, Anita. 1983. *Black Lesbian in White America.* Tallahassee, FL: Naiad.

Cowan, Carolyn Pape, and Philip A. Cowan. 1990. "Who Does What?" In *Handbook of Family Measurement Techniques,* edited by John Touliatos, Barry F. Perlmutter, and Murray A. Straus, 447–48. Beverly Hills, CA: Sage.

Crawley, Sara L. 2001. "Are Butch and Fem Working-Class and Antifeminist?" *Gender and Society* 15(2): 175–96.

Crenshaw, Kimberlé. 1989. "Demarginalizing the Intersection of Race and Sex: A Black Feminist Critique of Antidiscrimination Doctrine, Feminist Theory, and Antiracist Politics." *University of Chicago Legal Forum* 1989: 139–67.

———. 1991. "Mapping the Margins: Intersectionality, Identity Politics, and Violence against Women of Color." *Stanford Law Review* 43:1241–99.

Crichlow, Wesley. 2004a. *Buller Men and Batty Bwoys: Hidden Men in Toronto and Halifax Black Communities*. Toronto: University of Toronto Press.

———. 2004b. "History, (Re)Memory, Testimony and Biomythography: Charting a Buller Man's Trinidadian Past." In *Interrogating Caribbean Masculinities*, edited by R. E. Reddock, 185–222. Kingston, Jamaica: University Press of the West Indies.

Dalton, Susan E. 2001. "Protecting our Parent-Child Relationships: Understanding the Strengths and Weaknesses of Second-Parent Adoption." In *Queer Families Queer Politics: Challenging Culture and the State*, edited by Mary Bernstein and Renate Reimann, 201–20. New York: Columbia University Press.

Dang, Alain, and Somjen Frazer. 2004. *Black Same-Sex Households in the United States: A Report from the 2000 Census*. New York: National Gay and Lesbian Task Force Policy Institute and the National Black Justice Coalition.

Davis, Angela Y. 1998. *Blues Legacies and Black Feminism*. New York: Pantheon.

Dawson, Michael C. 1994. *Behind the Mule: Race and Class in African-American Politics*. Princeton: Princeton University Press.

———. 2001. *Black Visions: The Roots of Contemporary African-American Political Ideologies*. Chicago: University of Chicago Press.

D'Emilio, John. 1983. *Sexual Politics, Sexual Communities: The Making of a Homosexual Minority in the United States, 1940–70*. Chicago: University of Chicago Press.

Dempsey, Cleta L. 1994. "Health and Social Issues of Gay, Lesbian, and Bisexual Adolescents." *Families in Society* 75(3): 160–67.

Diamond, Lisa M. 2008. *Sexual Fluidity: Understanding Women's Love and Desire*. Cambridge: Harvard University Press.

Diamond, Lisa M., and Rich C. Savin-Williams. 2000. "Explaining Diversity in the Development of Same-Sex Sexuality among Young Women." *Journal of Social Issues* 56: 297–313.

DiLapi, Elena M. 1989. "Lesbian Mothers and the Motherhood Hierarchy." *Journal of Homosexuality* 18(1–2): 101–21.

Dill, Bonnie Thornton. 1979. "The Dialectics of Black Womanhood." *Signs: Journal of Women in Culture and Society* 4(3): 543–55.

———. 1983. "Race, Class and Gender: Prospects for an All-Inclusive Sisterhood." *Feminist Studies* 9(1): 131–50.

Drexel, Allen. 1997. "Before Paris Burned: Race, Class, and Male Homosexuality on the Chicago South Side, 1935–1960." In *Creating a Place for Ourselves: Lesbian, Gay and Bisexual Community Histories*, edited by Brett Beemyn. New York: Routledge.

Edin, Kathryn, and Maria Kefalas. 2006. *Promises I Can Keep: Why Poor Women Put Motherhood before Marriage*. Berkeley: University of California Press.

Egan, Patrick J., and Kenneth Sherrill. 2009. "California's Proposition 8: What Happened, and What Does the Future Hold?" Unpublished paper commissioned by the Eveyln and Walter Haas Jr. Fund in San Francisco and released under the auspices of the National Gay and Lesbian Task Force Policy Institute.

Ellingson, Stephen, Nelson Tebbe, Martha Van Haitsma, and Edward O. Laumann. 2001. "Religion and the Politics of Sexuality." *Journal of Contemporary Ethnography* 30(3): 3–55.

Ellison, Ralph. [1964] 1995. "Shadow and Act." Reprinted in *The Collected Essays of Ralph Ellison*, edited by John F. Callahan. New York: Modern Library.

Engebretsen, E. L. 2009. "Intimate Practices, Conjugal Ideals: Affective Ties and Relationship Strategies Among LaLa (Lesbian) Women in Contemporary Beijing." *Sexuality Research & Social Policy* 6: 3–14.

Erickson, Rebecca. 2005. "Why Emotion Work Matters: Sex, Gender, and the Division of Household Labor." *Journal of Marriage and the Family* 67(2): 337–51.

Essig, Laurie. 1999. *Queer in Russia: A Story of Sex, Self, and the Other*. Durham, NC: Duke University Press.

Esterberg, Kristin. 1996. "'A Certain Swagger When I Walk': Performing Lesbian Identity." In *Queer Theory/Sociology*, edited by S. Seidman, 259–79. Oxford, UK: Blackwell.

———. 1997. *Lesbian and Bisexual Identities: Constructing Communities, Constructing Selves*. Philadelphia: Temple University Press.

Eves, Alison. 2004. "Queer Theory, Butch/Femme Identities and Lesbian Space." *Sexualities* 7(4): 480–96.

Faderman, Lillian. 1991. *Odd Girls and Twilight Lovers: A History of Lesbian Life in Twentieth-Century America*. New York: Penguin.

———. 1992. "The Return of Butch and Femme: A Phenomenon in Lesbian Sexuality of the 1980s and 1990s." *Journal of the History of Sexuality* 2(4): 578–96.

Ferguson, Roderick A. 2004. *Aberrations in Black: Toward a Queer of Color Critique*. Minneapolis: University of Minnesota Press.

Ferree, Myra Marx. 1991. "The Gender Division of Labor in Two-Earner Marriages." *Journal of Family Issues* 12(2): 158–80.

Ferree, Myra Marx, and Beth B. Hess. 1985. *Controversy and Coalition: The New Feminist Movement*. Boston, MA: Twayne Publishers.

Fleming, Louise. 1995. "The 'Second Mother.'" In *Lesbian Parenting: Living with Pride & Prejudice*, 148–53. Charlottetown, P.E.I., CA: Gynergy Books.

Franklin, Donna. 1997. *Ensuring Inequality: The Structural Transformation of the African-American Family*. New York: Oxford University Press.

Freeman, Carla. 2000. *High Tech and High Heels in the Global Economy*. Durham, NC: Duke University Press.

Fukuyama, M. A., and A. D. Ferguson. 2000. "Lesbian, Gay, and Bisexual People of Color: Understanding Cultural Complexity and Managing Multiple Oppressions." In *Handbook of Counseling and Psychotherapy with Lesbian, Gay, and Bisexual Clients*, edited by R. M. Perez, K. A. DeBord, and K. J. Bieschke, 81–105. Washington, DC: American Psychological Association.

Gabb, Jacqui. 2005. "Lesbian M/Otherhood: Strategies of Familial Linguistic Management in Lesbian Parent Families." *Sociology* 39(4): 585–603.

Gagnon, John H., and William Simon. 2005. *Sexual Conduct: The Social Sources of Human Sexuality*. 2d ed. New Brunswick, NJ: Aldine Transaction.

Gallup, George, Jr., and Jim Castelli. 1989. *The People's Religion: American Faith in the 90s*. New York: Macmillan.

Garber, Eric. 1990. "A Spectacle in Color: The Lesbian and Gay Subculture of Jazz Age Harlem." In *Hidden from History: Reclaiming the Gay and Lesbian Past*, edited by Martin Duberman, Martha Vicinus, and George Chauncey, 318–31. New York: Penguin.

Garber, Marjorie. 1995. *Vice Versa: Bisexuality and the Eroticism of Everyday Life*. New York: Simon and Schuster.

Gartrell, Nanette, Amy Banks, Jean Hamilton, Nancy Reed, Holly Bishop, and Carla Rodas. 1999. "The National Lesbian Family Study 2: Interviews with Mothers of Toddlers." *American Journal of Orthopsychiatry* 69(3): 362–69.

Gartrell, Nanette, Amy Banks, Nancy Reed, Jean Hamilton, Carla Rodas, and Amalia Deck. 2000. "The National Lesbian Family Study 3: Interviews with Mothers of Five-Year-Olds." *American Journal of Orthopsychiatry* 70(4):542–48.

Gartrell, Nanette, Amalia Deck, Carla Rodas, and Heidi Peyser. 2005. "The National Lesbian Family Study 4: Interviews with the Ten-Year-Old Children." *American Journal of Orthopsychiatry* 75(4): 518–24.

Gates, Gary. 2006. "Same Sex Couples and the Gay, Lesbian, Bisexual Population: New Estimates from the American Community Survey." Research report produced for the Williams Institute on Sexual Orientation, Law and Public Policy, UCLA School of Law. Accessed March 20, 2007, http://www.law.ucla.edu/williamsinstitute/publications/.

Giddings, Paula. 1984. *When and Where I Enter: The Impact of Black Women on Race and Sex in America*. New York: HarperCollins.

Gilbert, Dorie J. and Ednita M. Wright (eds.). 2003. *African-American Women and HIV/AIDS: Critical Responses*. Westport, CT: Praeger.

Gilkes, Cheryl Townsend. 2001. *If it Wasn't for the Women . . . : Black Women's Experience and Womanist Culture in Church and Community*. New York: Orbis Books.

Gilmartin, Katie. 1996. "'We Weren't Bar People': Middle-Class Lesbian Identities and Cultural Spaces." *Gay & Lesbian Quarterly* 3: 1–51.

Glenn, Evelyn Nakano. 1985. "Racial Ethnic Women's Labor: The Intersection of Race, Gender and Class Oppression." *Review of Radical Political Economics* 17(3): 86–108.

Glenn, Evelyn Nakano, Grace Chang, and Linda Rennie Forcey, eds. 1994. *Mothering: Identity, Experience and Agency*. New York: Routledge Press.

Goffman, Erving. 1963. *Stigma: Notes on the Management of Spoiled Identity*. Englewood Cliffs, NJ: Prentice-Hall.

Gottschalk, Lorene. 2003. "Same-Sex Sexuality and Childhood Gender Non-Conformity: A Spurious Connection." *Journal of Gender Studies* 12: 5–50.

Gray, Mary L. 2009. *Youth, Media, and Queer Visibility in Rural America*. New York: New York University Press.

Greene, Beverly, ed. 1996. "Lesbian Women of Color: Triple Jeopardy." *Journal of Lesbian Studies* 1(1): 109–47.

————, ed. 1997. *Ethnic and Cultural Diversity among Lesbians and Gay Men: Psychological Perspectives on Lesbian and Gay Issues*, vol. 3. Thousand Oaks, CA: Sage.

————. 2002. "African American Lesbian and Bisexual Women." *Journal of Social Issues* 56(2): 239–49.

Griffin, Horace. 2006. *Their Own Receive Them Not: African American Lesbians and Gays in Black Churches.* Cleveland, OH: Pilgrim Press.

Halberstam, Judith. 1998. *Female Masculinity.* Durham, NC: Duke University Press.

Hammonds, Evelynn M. 1997. "Toward a Genealogy of Black Female Sexuality: The Problematic of Silence." In *Feminist Genealogies, Colonial Legacies, Democratic Futures*, edited by M. Jacqui Alexander and Chandra Talpade Mohanty, 170–82. New York: Routledge.

————. 2004. "Black (W)holes and the Geometry of Black Female Sexuality." In *The Black Studies Reader*, edited by Jacqueline Bobo, Cynthia Hudley, and Claudine Michel, 301–14. New York: Routledge.

Harding, Sandra. 1991. *Whose Science? Whose Knowledge?* Ithaca, NY: Cornell.

Harris, Laura, and Elizabeth Crocker. 1997. *Femme: Feminists, Lesbians and Bad Girls.* New York: Routledge.

Harry, Joseph. 1993. "Being Out: A General Model." *Journal of Homosexuality* 26(1): 25–39.

Harvey, David L. 1993. *Potter Addition: Poverty, Family and Kinship in a Heartland Community.* Edison, NJ: Aldine Transaction.

Hawkeswood, William. 1996. *One of the Children: Gay Black Men in Harlem.* Edited by A. W. Costley. Berkeley: University of California Press.

Hays, Sharon. 1996. *The Cultural Contradictions of Motherhood.* New Haven: Yale University Press.

Heap, Chad. 2009. *Slumming: Sexual and Racial Encounters in American Nightlife, 1885–1940.* Chicago: University of Chicago Press.

Hequembourg, Amy. 2007. *Lesbian Motherhood: Stories of Becoming.* New York: Harrington Park Press.

Herek, Gregory M., and John P. Capitanio. 1995. "Black Heterosexuals' Attitudes Toward Lesbians and Gay Men in the United States." *Journal of Sex Research* 32(2): 95–105.

Herrera, F. 2009. "Tradition and Transgression: Lesbian Motherhood in Chile." *Sexuality Research & Social Policy* 6: 35–51.

Hetherington, E. Mavis. 1989. "Coping with Family Transitions: Winners, Losers and Survivors." *Child Development* 60(1): 1–14.

Hetherington, E. Mavis, and W. G. Clingempeel. 1992. "Coping with Marital Transitions: A Family Systems Perspective." *Monographs of the Society for Research in Child Development* 57, no. 2-3, serial no. 227.

Hiestand, Katherine R., and Heidi M. Levitt. 2005. "Butch Identity Development: The Formation of an Authentic Gender." *Feminism Psychology* 15: 61–85.

Higginbotham, Elizabeth, and Mary Romero. 1997. *Women and Work: Exploring Race, Ethnicity and Class.* Thousand Oaks, CA: Sage Publications.

Higginbotham, Evelyn Brooks. 1992. "African-American Women's History and the Metalanguage of Race." *Signs* 17(2): 251–74.

———. 1993. *Righteous Discontent: The Women's Movement in the Black Baptist Church, 1880–1920.* Cambridge: Harvard University Press.

Hill, Marjorie. 1987. "Child-Rearing Attitudes of Black Lesbian Mothers." In *Lesbian Psychologies: Explanations and Challenges*, edited by the Boston Lesbian Psychologies Collective, 215–26. Urbana, IL: University of Illinois Press.

Hine, Darlene Clark. 1989. "Rape and the Inner Lives of Black Women in the Middle West: Preliminary Thoughts on the Culture of Dissemblance." *Signs* 14(4): 915–20.

———. 1994. *Hine Sight: Black Women and the Re-Construction of American History.* Brooklyn, NY: Carlson.

Hofferth, Sandra L., and Kermyt G. Anderson. 2003. "Are All Dads Equal? Biology versus Marriage as a Basis for Paternal Investment." *Journal of Marriage and Family* 65: 213–32.

Honey, Maureen, ed. 1999. *Bitter Fruit: African American Women in World War II.* Columbia: University of Missouri Press.

Hunter, Marcus Anthony. 2010. "All the Gays Are White and All the Blacks Are Straight: Black Gay Men, Identity, and Community." *Sexuality Research and Social Policy* 7(2): 81–92.

Hunter, Andrea G. and Sherrill L. Sellers. 1998. "Feminist Attitudes Among African American Women and Men." *Gender and Society* 12(1): 81–99.

Ianni, Frances A. J. 1974. *Black Mafia: Ethnic Succession in Organized Crime.* New York: Simon & Schuster.

Jackson, Jesse L., Jr. 2003. "Building a More Perfect Union through Human Rights and Equal Protection under Law." Address delivered to the Fourteenth Michigan Dinner of the Human Rights Campaign, Detroit, MI. Accessed December 11, 2003, http://www.365gay.com/opinion/Releases/Releases.htm.

Jackson, John L. 2001. *Harlemworld: Doing Race and Class in Contemporary Black America.* Chicago: University of Chicago Press.

———. 2005. *Real Black: Adventures in Racial Sincerity.* Chicago: University of Chicago Press.

James, Stanlie M., and Abena P. A. Busia. 1993. *Theorizing Black Feminisms: The Visionary Pragmatism of Black Women.* New York: Routledge.

Jenkins, Candice M. 2007. *Private Lives, Proper Relations: Regulating Black Intimacy.* Minneapolis: University of Minnesota Press.

Jenkins, Richard. 2008. *Social Identity.* 3rd ed. New York: Routledge.

Johnson, E. Patrick. 2003. *Appropriating Blackness: Performance and the Politics of Authenticity.* Durham, NC: Duke University Press.

———. 2008. *Sweet Tea: Black Gay Men of the South: An Oral History.* Chapel Hill: University of North Carolina Press.

Johnson, E. Patrick, and Mae G. Henderson, eds. 2005. *Black Queer Studies: A Critical Anthology.* Durham, NC: Duke University Press.

Jones, A. C. 2004. "Transforming the Story: Narrative Applications to a Step-mother Support Group." *Families in Society: Journal of Contemporary Social Services* 85:129–38.

Jones, Jacqueline. 1985. *Labor of Love, Labor of Sorrow: Black Women, Work and the Family from Slavery to the Present.* New York: Vintage.

Kamo, Yoshimori, and Ellen L. Cohen. 1998. "Division of Household Work between Partners: A Comparison of Black and White Couples." *Journal of Comparative Family Studies* 29(1): 131–45.

Katz, Jack. 1975. "Essences as Moral Identities: Verifiability and Responsibility in Imputations of Deviance and Charisma." *American Journal of Sociology* 80: 1369–90.

Kelley, Patricia. 1995. *Developing Healthy Stepfamilies.* New York: The Haworth Press.

Kelley, Robin D. G. 1997. "Playing for Keeps: Pleasure and Profit on the Postindustrial Playground." In *The House that Race Built*, edited by W. Lubiano, 195–231. New York: Random House.

Kennedy, Elizabeth Lapovsky, and Madeline D. Davis. 1989. "The Reproduction of Butch-Fem Roles: A Social Constructionist Approach." In *Passion and Power: Sexuality in History*, edited by K. Peiss and C. Simons, with R. A. Padug. Philadelphia, PA: Temple University Press.

———. 1993. *Boots of Leather, Slippers of Gold: The History of a Lesbian Community.* New York: Routledge.

Kenney, Catherine T. 2006. "The Power of the Purse: Allocative Systems and Inequality in Couple Households." *Gender and Society* 20(3): 354–81.

Kent, Mary Mederios. 2007. "Immigration and America's Black Population." *Population Bulletin* 62(4): 1–16.

Kessler-Harris, Alice. 2003. *Out to Work: A History of Wage-Earning Women in the United States.* New York: Oxford University Press.

King, Deborah. 1988. "Multiple Jeopardy, Multiple Consciousness: The Context of a Black Feminist Ideology." *Signs* 14(1): 42–72.

Kitzinger, Celia. 1987. *The Social Construction of Lesbianism.* Newbury Park, CA: Sage.

Kitzinger, Celia, and S. Wilkinson. 1995. "Transitions from Heterosexuality to Lesbianism: The Discursive Production of Lesbian Identities." *Developmental Psychology* 31: 95–104.

Klonaris, Helen. 2008. "Independence Day Letter." In *Our Caribbean: A Gathering of Lesbian and Gay Writing from the Antilles*, edited by Thomas Glave, 197–201. Durham, NC: Duke University Press.

Krakauer, Ilana D., and Suzanna M. Rose. 2002. "The Impact of Group Membership on Lesbians' Physical Appearance." *Journal of Lesbian Studies* 6(1): 31–43.

Kranichfeld, Marion L. 1987. "Rethinking Family Power." *Journal of Family Issues* 8: 42–56.

Kurdek, Laurence A. 1993. "The Allocation of Household Labor in Gay, Lesbian, Heterosexual and Married Couples." *Journal of Social Issues* 49(3): 127–39.

Lacy, Karyn R. 2007. *Blue-Chip Black: Race, Class and Status in the New Black Middle Class.* Berkeley: University of California Press.

Ladd-Taylor, Molly, and Lauri Umansky. 1998. *"Bad" Mothers: The Politics of Blame in Twentieth-Century America*. New York: New York University Press.

Lamb, Michael E., and Charles Lewis. 2004. "The Development and Significance of Father-Child Relationships in Two-Parent Families." In *The Role of the Father in Child Development*, 4th ed., edited by Michael E. Lamb, 272–77. New York: Wiley.

Landry, Bart. 2000. *Black Working Wives: Pioneers of the American Family Revolution*. Berkeley: University of California Press.

LaNier, Carlotta Walls. 2009. *A Mighty Long Way: My Journey to Justice at Little Rock Central High School*. New York: Ballantine.

Laporte, Rita. 1992. "The Butch-Femme Question." In *The Persistent Desire: A Femme-Butch Reader*, edited by J. Nestle, 208–19. Boston, MA: Alyson Publications.

Lareau, Annette. 2003. *Unequal Childhoods: Class, Race and Family Life*. Berkeley: University of California Press.

Lewin, Ellen. 1993. *Lesbian Mothers: Accounts of Gender in American Culture*. Ithaca, NY: Cornell University Press.

———. 1994. "Negotiating Lesbian Motherhood: The Dialectics of Resistance and Accommodation." In *Mothering: Ideology, Experience and Agency*, edited by E. N. Glenn, G. Chang, and L. Forcey, 333–53. New York: Routledge.

Lewis, Gregory B. 2003. "Black-White Differences in Attitudes Toward Homosexuality and Gay Rights." *Public Opinion Quarterly* 67:59–78.

Lewis, John. 2003. "At a Crossroads on Gay Unions." *Boston Globe*, October 25. Retrieved December 11, 2003, http://www.boston.com/news/globe/editorial_opinion/oped/articles/2003/10/25/at_a_crossroads_on_gay_unions.

Lincoln, C. Eric, and Lawrence H. Mamiya. 1990. *The Black Church in the African American Experience*. Durham, NC: Duke University Press.

Lisagor, Nancy. 1980. *Lesbian Identity in the Subculture of Women's Bars*. Ph.D. diss., University of Pennsylvania. University Microfilms International.

Lorber, Judith. 1994. *Paradoxes of Gender*. New Haven: Yale University Press.

Lorde, Audre. 1995. "Tar Beach." In *Afrekete: An Anthology of Black Lesbian Writing*, edited by Catherine McKinley and L. Joyce DeLaney, 1-18. New York: Anchor.

———. 2007. *Sister Outsider: Essays and Speeches*. Berkeley: Crossing Press.

Loulan, JoAnn. 1990. *The Lesbian Erotic Dance: Butch, Femme, Androgyny and Other Rhythms*. Minneapolis: Spinsters Ink.

Lynch, Jean M. 2000. "Considerations of Family Structure and Gender Composition: The Lesbian and Gay Stepfamily." *Journal of Homosexuality* 40(2): 81–97.

———. 2004. "The Identity Transformation of Biological Parents in Lesbian/Gay Stepfamilies." *Journal of Homosexuality* 47(2): 91–107.

Mahon, Maureen. 2004. *Right to Rock: The Black Rock Coalition and the Cultural Politics of Race*. Durham, NC: Duke University Press.

Martin, Harold P. 1991. "Coming Out Process for Homosexuals." *Hospital and Community Psychiatry* 42: 158–62.

Mays, Vickie M., and Susan D. Cochran. 1988. "The Black Women's Relationships Project: A National Survey of Black Lesbians." In *The Sourcebook on*

Lesbian/Gay Healthcare, 2nd ed., edited by M. Shernoff and W. Scott, 54–62. Washington, DC: National Lesbian/Gay Health Foundation.

McBride, Dwight A. 2005a. "Straight Black Studies: On African American Studies, James Baldwin, and Black Queer Studies." In *Black Queer Studies: A Critical Anthology*, edited by E. P. Johnson and M. G. Henderson, 68–89. Durham, NC: Duke University Press.

———. 2005b. *Why I Hate Abercrombie and Fitch: Essays on Race and Sexuality*. New York: New York University Press.

McCall, Leslie. 2005. "The Complexity of Intersectionality." *Signs: Journal of Women in Culture and Society* 30(3): 1771–1800.

McCorkel, Jill A., and Kristen Myers. 2003. "What Difference Does Difference Make? Position and Privilege in the Field." *Qualitative Sociology* 26(2): 199–231.

Mezey, Nancy J. 2008. *New Choices, New Families: How Lesbians Decide about Motherhood*. Baltimore, MD: Johns Hopkins University Press.

Moore, Mignon R. 2006. "Lipstick or Timberlands? Meanings of Gender Presentation in Black Lesbian Communities." *Signs: Journal of Women in Culture and Society* 32(1): 113–39.

———. 2008. "Gendered Power Relations among Women: A Study of Household Decision Making in Black, Lesbian Stepfamilies." *American Sociological Review* 73(2): 335–56.

———. 2009. "Independent Women: Equality in African-American Lesbian Relationships." In *Families as they Really Are*, edited by B. Risman, 214–27. New York: Norton.

———. 2010a. "Articulating a Politics of (Multiple) Identities: Sexuality and Inclusion in Black Community Life." *Du Bois Review: Social Science Research on Race* 7(2): 1–20.

———. 2010b. "Black and Gay in LA: The Relationships Lesbians and Gay Men have with their Religious and Racial Communities." In *Black Los Angeles: American Dreams and Racial Realities*, edited by D. Hunt and A. Ramon, 188–212. New York: New York University Press.

———. 2011. "Two Sides of the Same Coin: Revising Analyses of Lesbian Sexuality and Family Formation through the Study of Black Women." *Journal of Lesbian Studies* 15(1): 58–68.

Mootoo, Shani. 2008. "Out on Main Street." In *Our Caribbean: A Gathering of Lesbian and Gay Writing from the Antilles*, edited by Thomas Glave, 252–60. Durham, NC: Duke University Press.

Morgan, Cherrie. 1993. "Butch-Femme and the Politics of Identity." In *Sisters, Sexperts, Queers: Beyond the Lesbian Nation*, edited by Arlene Stein, 35–46. New York: Penguin.

Morgan, Ruth, and Saskia Wieringa. 2005. *Tommy Boys, Lesbian Men and Ancestral Wives: Female Same-Sex Practices in Africa*. Johannesburg, South Africa: Jacana Media.

Morris, Jessica F., and Kimberly F. Balsam. 2003. "Lesbian and Bisexual Women's Experiences of Victimization: Mental Health, Revictimization, and Sexual Identity Development." *Journal of Lesbian Studies* 7(4): 67–85.

Morris, Jessica F., Kimberly F. Balsam, and Esther D. Rothblum. 2002. "Lesbian and Bisexual Mothers and Nonmothers: Demographics and the Coming-Out Process." *Journal of Family Psychology* 16(2): 144–56.

Morrison, Toni. 1971. "What the Black Woman Thinks about Women's Lib." *New York Times*, August 22.

Mullings, Leith. 1997. *On Our Own Terms: Race, Class, and Gender in the Lives of African-American Women.* New York: Routledge.

Naples, Nancy A. 1996. "A Feminist Revisiting of the Insider/Outsider Debate: The 'Outsider Phenomenon' in Rural Iowa." *Qualitative Sociology* 19: 131–51.

National Gay and Lesbian Task Force. 2004. "Fact Sheet: Black Same-Sex Households in the New York City Metropolitan Area." Accessed February 1, 2005, http://www.thetaskforce.org/downloads/blackcensus/BCRNYCFact.pdf.

Nelson, Fiona. 1996. *Lesbian Motherhood: An Exploration of Canadian Lesbian Families.* Toronto: University of Toronto Press.

Nestle, Joan, ed. 1992. *The Persistent Desire: A Femme-Butch Reader.* Boston: Alyson Publications.

Newport, Frank. 2008. "Blacks as Conservative as Republicans on Some Moral Issues." *Gallup*, December 3. Accessed June 6, 2010, http://www.gallup.com/poll/112807/Blacks-Conservative-Republicans-Some-Moral-Issues.aspx.

Nicholson, Jan M., Matthew R. Sanders, W. Kim Halford, Maddy Phillips, and Sarah W. Whitton. 2008. "The Prevention and Treatment of Children's Adjustment Problems in Stepfamilies." In *The International Handbook of Stepfamilies: Policy and Practice in Legal, Research, and Clinical Environments*, edited by Jan Pryor, 495–521. Hoboken, NJ: Wiley.

Nielsen, Linda 1999. "Stepmothers: Why So Much Stress? A Review of the Research." *Journal of Divorce & Remarriage* 30 (1/2): 115–48.

O'Connor, Thomas G., and Glendessa M. Insabella. 1999. "Marital Satisfaction, Relationships, and Roles." *Monographs of the Society for Research in Child Development* 64(4): 50–78.

Ornstein, Michael. 2000. "Ethno-Racial Inequality in Toronto: Analysis of the 1996 Census." Report prepared for the Access and Equity Unit Strategic and Corporate Policy Division, Chief Administrator's Office, Toronto, Canada, May. Accessed February 5, 2010, http://www.toronto.ca/diversity/ornstein_fullreport.pdf.

Oswald, Ramona. 2002. "Who Am I in Relation to Them? Gay, Lesbian and Queer People Leave the City to Attend Rural Family Weddings." *Journal of Family Issues* 23(3): 323–48.

Pahl, Jan. 1983. "The Allocation of Money and the Structuring of Inequality within Marriage." *Sociological Review* 31(2): 237–62.

Papernow, Patricia. 2008. "A Clinician's View of 'Stepfamily Architecture.'" In *The International Handbook of Stepfamilies*, edited by J. Pryor, 423–54. Hoboken, NJ: Wiley.

Paris, Peter, John W. Cook, James Hudnut-Beumler, Lawrence Mamiya, Judith Weisenfeld, and Leonora Tisdale. 2004. *The History of the Riverside Church in the City of New York.* New York: New York University Press.

Parke, Ross D., Jessica Dennis, Mary L. Flyr, Kristie L. Morris, Colleen Killian, David J. McDowell, and Margaret Wild. 2004. "Fathering and Children's Peer Relationships." In *The Role of the Father in Child Development*, 4th ed., edited Michael D. Lamb, 307–40. New York: Wiley.

Patterson, Charlotte. 1992. "Children of Lesbian and Gay Parents." *Child Development* 63(5): 1025–42.

———. 1995. "Families of the Lesbian Baby Boom: Parents' Division of Labor and Children's Adjustment." *Developmental Psychology* 31(1): 115–23.

Patterson, Charlotte, Erin L. Sutfin, and Megan Fulcher. 2004. "Division of Labor among Lesbian and Heterosexual Parenting Couples: Correlates of Specialized Versus Shared Patterns." *Journal of Adult Development* 11(3): 179–89.

Pattillo, Mary. 2007. *Black on the Block: The Politics of Race and Class in the City*. Chicago: University of Chicago Press.

Pattillo-McCoy, Mary. 1998. "Church Culture as a Strategy of Action in the Black Community." *American Sociological Review* 63(6): 767–84.

Pelka, Suzanne. 2009. "Sharing Motherhood: Maternal Jealousy amongst Lesbian Co-Mothers." *Journal of Homosexuality* 56(2): 195–217.

Peña, Susana. 2004. "Pájaration and Transculturation: Language and Meaning in Miami's Cuban American Gay Worlds." In *Speaking in Queer Tongues: Globalization and Gay Language*, edited by William L. Leap and Tom Boellstorff, 231–50. Champaign: University of Illinois Press.

———. 2005. "Visibility and Silence: Mariel and Cuban American Gay Male Experience and Representation." In *Queer Migrations: Sexuality, U.S. Citizenship and Border Crossing*, edited by Eithne Luibheid and Lionel Cantú. Minneapolis: University of Minnesota Press.

Peplau, L. Anne, Susan D. Cochran, and Vickie M. Mays. 1997. "A National Survey of the Intimate Relationships of African-American Lesbians and Gay Men: A Look at Commitment, Satisfaction, Sexual Behavior and HIV Disease. In *Ethnic and Cultural Diversity among Lesbians and Gay Men*, edited by Beverly Greene, 11–38. Newbury Park, CA: Sage Publications.

Peplau, L. Anne, and Adam W. Fingerhut. 2007. "The Close Relationships of Lesbians and Gay Men." *Annual Review of Psychology* 58: 405–24.

Peplau, L. Anne, and Mark Huppin. 2008. Masculinity, Femininity and the Development of Sexual Orientation in Women. *Journal of Gay and Lesbian Mental Health* 12(1/2): 147–67.

Phelan, Shane. 1993. "(Be)Coming Out: Lesbian Identity and Politics." *Signs* 18:765–90.

Potgieter, C. A. 2003. "Black South African Lesbians: Discourses on Motherhood and Women's Roles." *Journal of Lesbian Studies* 7: 135–51.

Ponse, Barbara. 1978. *Identities in the Lesbian World: The Social Construction of Self*. Westport, CT: Greenwood.

Prager, Jeff. 2009. "Melancholic Identities: Post-Traumatic Loss, Memory and Identity Formation." In *Identity in Question*, edited by Anthony Elliott and Paul du Gay, 139–57. Thousand Oaks, CA: Sage.

Rainwater, Lee, and William L. Yancy. 1967. *The Moynihan Report and the Politics of Controversy*. Cambridge, MA: MIT Press.

Ramsey, Francine, Marjorie J. Hill, and Cassondra Kellam. 2010. "Black Lesbians Matter: An Examination of the Unique Experiences, Perspectives, and Priorities of the Black Lesbian Community." Report. Sacramento, CA: Zuna Institute.

Reid, Frank M. 1991. "Perspective on Aids: In the Black Church, There Is No 'Silence'; Even Though We Must, and Do, Help the Sinners, We Cannot Be Pressured into Condoning Their Sins." *Los Angeles Times*, December 27.

Rieder, Jonathan. 1985. *Canarsie: The Jews and Italians of Brooklyn against Liberalism*. Cambridge: Harvard University Press.

Risman, Barbara J., and Danette Johnson-Sumerford. 1998. "Doing It Fairly: A Study of Feminist Marriages." *Journal of Marriage and the Family* 60: 23–40.

Rosenfeld, Michael. 2007. *The Age of Independence: Interracial Unions, Same-Sex Unions, and the Changing American Family*. Cambridge: Harvard University Press.

———. 2010. "Nontraditional Families and Childhood Progress through School." *Demography* 47(3): 755–75.

Ross, Marlon. 2005. "Beyond the Closet as Raceless Paradigm." In *Black Queer Studies: A Critical Anthology*, edited by E. P. Johnson and M. G. Henderson, 161–89. Durham, NC: Duke University Press.

Royster, Deirdre. 2003. *Race and the Invisible Hand: How White Networks Exclude Black Men from Blue-Collar Jobs*. Berkeley: University of California Press.

Rubin, Gayle. 1992. "Of Catamites and Kings: Reflections on Butch, Gender, and Boundaries." In *The Persistent Desire: A Femme-Butch Reader*, edited by J. Nestle, 466–82. Boston, MA: Alyson Publications.

Rust, Paula. 1992. "The Politics of Sexual Identity: Sexual Attraction and Behavior among Lesbian and Bisexual Women." *Social Problems* 39: 366–86.

———. 1993. "Coming Out in the Age of Social Constructionism: Sexual Identify Formation among Lesbians and Bisexual Women." *Gender and Society* 7: 50–77.

Savin-Williams, Ritch C. 1998. " . . . And Then I Became Gay": Young Men's Stories. New York: Routledge.

Schwartz, Pepper. 1994. *Peer Marriage: How Love Between Equals Really Works*. New York: Free Press.

Shaw, Stephanie. 1996. *What a Woman Ought to Be and to Do: Black Professional Women Workers During the Jim Crow Era*. Chicago: University of Chicago Press.

Shockley, Ann Allen. 1983. "The Black Lesbian in American Literature: An Overview." In *Home Girls: A Black Feminist Anthology*, edited by Barbara Smith, 83–93. New York: Kitchen Table/Women of Color.

Silvera, Makeda. 1992. "Confronting the 'I' in the Eye: Black Mother, Black Daughters." In *Lesbian Parenting: Living with Pride and Prejudice*, edited by Katherine Arnup, 311–20. Charlottetown, PEI, Canada: Gynergy Books.

———. 2008. "Man Royals and Sodomites: Some Thoughts on the Invisibility of Afro-Caribbean Lesbians." In *Our Caribbean: A Gathering of Lesbian and Gay Writing from the Antilles*, edited by Thomas Glave, 344–54. Durham, NC: Duke University Press.

Simmel, Georg. 1964 [1950]. *The Sociology of Georg Simmel*. New York: Free Press.

Smith, Althea. 1997. "Cultural Diversity and the Coming-Out Process: Implications for Clinical Practice." In *Ethnic and Cultural Diversity among Lesbians and Gay Men*, Vol. 3 of *Psychological Perspectives on Lesbian and Gay Issues*, edited by Beverly Greene, 279–300. Thousand Oaks, CA: Sage.

Smith, Barbara, ed. 1983. *Home Girls: A Black Feminist Anthology*. New York: Kitchen Table/Women of Color.

———. 1999. "Blacks and Gays: Healing the Great Divide." In *Dangerous Liaisons: Blacks, Gays, and the Struggle for Equality*, edited by Eric Brandt, 15–24. New York: New Press.

Snoeckx, Laurent, Britt Dehertogh, and Dimitri Mortelmans. 2008. "The Distribution of Household Tasks in First-Marriage Families and Stepfamilies across Europe." In *The International Handbook of Stepfamilies: Policy and Practice in Legal, Research, and Clinical Environments*, edited by Jan Pryor, 277–98. Hoboken, NJ: Wiley.

Somerville, Siobhan B. 2000. *Queering the Color Line: Race and the Invention of Homosexuality in American Culture*. Durham, NC: Duke University Press.

Sophie, Joan. 1985–86. "A Critical Examination of Stage Theories of Lesbian Identity Development." *Journal of Homosexuality* 12(2): 39–51.

Sorenson, Annemette, and Sara McLanahan. 1987. "Married Women's Economic Dependency: 1940–1980." *American Journal of Sociology* 93(3): 957–87.

South, Scott J., and Glenna Spitze. 1994. "Housework in Marital and Nonmarital Households." *American Sociological Review* 59(3): 327–47.

"Sperm Donors from America's Most Selective Universities: Limited Choices for Black Women." 1999. *Journal of Blacks in Higher Education* 25: 38–39.

Stacey, Judith. 1996. *Brave New Families: Stories of Domestic Upheaval in Late-Twentieth-Century America*. Berkeley: University of California Press.

Stein, Arlene. 1992. "All Dressed Up, But No Place to Go? Style Wars and the New Lesbianism." In *The Persistent Desire: A Femme-Butch Reader*, edited by Joan Nestle, 431–39. Boston: Alyson.

———. 1997. *Sense and Sensibility: Stories of a Lesbian Generation*. Berkeley: University of California Press.

Sullivan, Maureen. 2004. *The Family of Woman: Lesbian Mothers, Their Children, and the Undoing of Gender*. Berkeley: University of California Press.

Swarr, A. L. and Nagar, R. 2003. "Dismantling Assumptions: Interrogating 'Lesbian' Struggles for Identity and Survival in India and South Africa." *Signs: Journal of Women in Culture and Society* 29: 491–516.

Taylor, Robert J., J. Mattis, and Linda M. Chatters. 1999. "Subjective Religiosity among African Americans: A Synthesis of Findings from Five National Samples." *Journal of Black Psychology* 25:524–43.

Thompson, Elizabeth, Sara McLanahan, and Roberta Braun Curtin. 1992. "Family Structure, Gender, and Parental Socialization." *Journal of Marriage and the Family* 54(2): 368–78.

Thorne, Barrie, with Marilyn Yalom, eds.1992. *Rethinking the Family: Some Feminist Questions*. Boston, MA: Northeastern University Press.

Thorpe, Rochella. 1996. "'A House Where Queers Go': African-American Lesbian Nightlife in Detroit, 1940–1975." In *Inventing Lesbian Cultures in America*, edited by Ellen Lewin, 40–61. Boston: Beacon.

Tichenor, Veronica Jaris. 2005. *Earning More and Getting Less: Why Successful Wives Can't Buy Equality*. New Brunswick, NJ: Rutgers University Press.

Treas, Judith. 1993. "Money in the Bank: Transaction Costs and the Economic Organization of Marriage." *American Sociological Review* 58:723–34.

Tripp, C. A. 1975. *The Homosexual Matrix*. New York: McGraw-Hill.

Twine, France Winddance. 1996. "Brown Skinned White Girls: Class, Culture and the Construction of White Identity in Suburban Communities." *Gender, Place and Culture* 3(2): 205–24.

Tyson, Karolyn D. 2011. *Integration Interrupted: Tracking, Black Students, and Acting White*. New York: Oxford University Press.

Ulysse, Gina. 1999. "Uptown Ladies and Downtown Women: Female Representations of Class and Color in Jamaica." In *Representations of Blackness and the Performance of Identities*, edited by Jean Rahier, 147–72. Westport, CT: Bergin and Garvey.

VanderStoep, Scott W., and Charles W. Green. 1988. "Religiosity and Homonegativism: A Path-Analytic Study." *Basic and Applied Social Psychology* 9(2): 135–47.

Wakschlag, Laura S., P. Lindsay Chase-Lansdale, and Jeanne Brooks-Gunn. 1996. "Not Just Ghosts in the Nursery: Contemporaneous Intergenerational Relationships and Parenting in Young African-American Families." *Child Development* 67: 2131–47.

Walby, Sylvia. 1990. *Theorizing Patriarchy*. New York: Oxford University Press.

Warner, Michael. 1993. *Fear of a Queer Planet: Queer Politics and Social Theory*. Minneapolis: University of Minnesota Press.

Waters, Mary C. 1999. *Black Identities: West Indian Dreams and American Realities*. Cambridge: Harvard University Press.

Watkins-Hayes, Celeste. 2008. "The Social and Economic Context of Black Women Living with HIV/AIDS in the US: Implications for Research." In *Sex, Power and Taboo: Gender and HIV in the Caribbean and Beyond*, edited by Dorothy Roberts, Rhoda Reddock, Dianne Douglas, and Sandra Reid, 33–66. Kingston, Jamaica: Ian Randle Publishers.

Watson, Jamal. 2005. "Sharpton Pledges Fight against Homophobia Among Blacks." *New York Sun*, August 3. Accessed August 30, 2007, http://www.nysun.com/pf.php?id=17991&v=4921948811.

Weaver, Shannon E., and Marilyn Coleman. 2010. "Caught in the Middle: Mothers in Stepfamilies." *Journal of Social and Personal Relationships* 27: 1–22.

Weeks, Jeffrey. 1990. *Coming Out: Homosexual Politics in Britain from the Nineteenth Century to the Present*. London: Quartet.

Weindling, Gwendolyn Naomi Rogers. 1980. "Righteous Anger in Three Parts: Racism in the Lesbian Community; One Black Lesbian's Perspective." In *Top Ranking: A Collection of Articles on Racism and Classism in the Lesbian Community*, edited by Joan Gibbs and Sara Bennett, 70–78. New York: February 3rd Press.

Wekker, Gloria. 2006. *The Politics of Passion: Women's Sexual Culture in the Afro-Surinamese Diaspora*. New York: Columbia University Press.

Welbon, Yvonne, dir. 1999. *Living with Pride: Ruth Ellis @ 100*. Chicago: Our Film Works.

Welter, Barbara. 1966. "The Cult of True Womanhood: 1820–1860." *American Quarterly* 18(2): 151–74.

Weston, Kath. 1991. *Families We Choose: Lesbians, Gays, Kinship*. New York: Columbia University Press.

———. 1993. "Do Clothes Make the Woman? Gender Performance Theory, and Lesbian Eroticism." *Genders* 17: 1–21.

———. 2004. "Fieldwork in Lesbian and Gay Communities." In *Approaches to Qualitative Research: A Reader on Theory and Practice*, edited by Sharlene Nagy Hesse-Biber and Patricia Leavy, 177–84. New York: Oxford University Press.

White, Deborah Gray. 1999. *Too Heavy a Load: Black Women in Defense of Themselves, 1894–1994*. New York: Norton.

Williams, Lawson. 2008. "On Homophobia and Gay Rights Activism in Jamaica." In *Our Caribbean: A Gathering of Lesbian and Gay Writing from the Antilles*, edited by Thomas Glave, 382–88. Durham, NC: Duke University Press.

Williams, Walter L. 1998. "Social Acceptance of Same-Sex Relationships in Families: Models from Other Cultures." In *Lesbian, Gay, and Bisexual Identities in Families: Psychological Perspectives*, edited by C. J. Patterson and A. R. D'Augelli. New York: Oxford University Press.

Wilson, Debra A., dir. 2003. *Butch Mystique*. Oakland, CA: Mojo Entertainment.

Winseman, Albert L. 2005. "Religion 'Very Important' to Most Americans." Gallup Poll Organization, December 20. Accessed August 26, 2007, http://www.galluppoll.com/content/?ci=20539.

Wolcott, Victoria W. 2001. *Remaking Respectability: African American Women in Interwar Detroit*. Chapel Hill: University of North Carolina Press.

Wolf, Deborah Goleman. 1979. *The Lesbian Community*. Berkeley: University of California Press.

Wolff, Charlotte. 1971. *Love between Women*. New York: Harper and Row.

Wright, Janet. 1998. *Lesbian Step Families: An Ethnography of Love*. Binghamton, NY: Haworth.

Yoshino, Kenji. 2006. *Covering: The Hidden Assault on Our Civil Rights*. New York: Random House.

Young, Alford A., Jr. 2004. *The Minds of Marginalized Black Men: Making Sense of Mobility, Opportunity, and Future Life Chances*. Princeton, NJ: Princeton University Press.

Zinn, Maxine Baca. 1979. "Insider Field Research in Minority Communities." *Social Problems* 27(2): 209–19.

Zucker, Kenneth J. 2004. "Gender Identity Disorder in Girls." In *Handbook of Behavioral and Emotional Problems in Girls*, edited by Debora Bell-Dolan, Sharon L. Foster, and Eric J. Mash, 285–319. New York: Plenum Publishers.

Index

Acosta, Katie L., 40
acting on lesbian desire, 23; as choice,
    42; and conformist path, 38–39,
    44–45; and hetero-identified path,
    52–53; and social constructionism,
    64; and straight-up gay path,
    29–33
African Ancestral Lesbians United for
    Societal Change, 38, 234, 254 n.10
African women, 181
Afro-Caribbean women in Paris, 187–89
aggressive fem label, 71, 257 n.13
aggressor/aggressive/AG labels, 66, 75, 76,
    255–56 n.1, 257 n.13
Alexander, M. Jacqui, 5
alternative insemination, 132, 142; and
    class privilege, 114, 119, 143, 262–63
    n.19; sperm donors, 143, 263 n.20.
    See also intentional mothering
Ambert, Anne-Marie, 170
Anderson, Kermyt G., 179, 265 n.16
androgyny, 79. See also gender-blender
    presentation; transgressive gender
    presentation
assimilationism, 150
athletics: and racial/gender/sexual
    identity relationships, 106, 107;
    and straight-up gay path, 25, 26,
    32–33
attraction to women. See experiencing
    lesbian desire

Balsam, Kimberly F., 114, 130
Barrett, Kirsten, 234
bars. See social lesbian/gay sphere
Barth, Fredrik, 107
Bean, Carl, 209
Bell, Alan P., 227
Bérubé, Allan, 254 n.9
bi-curious women, 58
bisexuality: and conformist path, 45–46;
    and hetero-identified path, 50; and
    sexually fluid path, 53, 54, 55–56, 255
    n.16; stigmatization of, 53–54, 57–58,
    255 n.16
Bittman, Michael, 265 n.12
Black community. See Black culture; Black
    religious institutions; openly gay
    families in Black community; racial
    solidarity expectations
Black culture: dual nature of, 72; and gay
    men's style, 257 n.12; and gender
    presentation, 69, 71, 72, 75–76, 88–89,
    90; and Harlem, 196; importance of
    Black religious institutions in, 9, 182,
    205, 211, 266 n.4; and openness/secrecy,
    204; as parenting priority, 146; status of
    motherhood in, 8, 149–50, 156, 157,
    168–69
Black female stigmatization: and employ-
    ment, 12–13; and gender presentation,
    81, 85; and motherhood, 116, 120,
    130–31, 139; and racial/gender/sexual

Black female stigmatization *(continued)*
    identity relationships, 104, 105; and
    respectability discourses, 10, 11–12
Black feminism: and Blues singers, 12; and
    household organization, 155, 157; and
    methodology, 3; and motherhood, 139;
    and respectability discourses, 10, 225;
    and sexual agency, 10, 225
Black lesbian invisibility, 2–3, 215, 251 n.5;
    and gender presentation, 80; and
    household organization, 114, 154–55;
    and methodology, 3, 15, 253 n.16; and
    motherhood, 113, 114, 149, 154–55;
    and racial/gender/sexual identity
    relationships, 7–8; and topic selection,
    225–26
Black men: Black lesbian identification with,
    97, 98, 106, 107–8; and masculinity
    stereotypes, 83, 86–88, 259 n.27; and
    transgressive gender presentation,
    75–76. *See also* relationships with men
Black religious institutions: challenges to
    homophobia, 180, 266 n.2; church
    mother role, 156, 264 n.9; homophobia
    in, 205–6, 209, 212; importance of, 9,
    182, 205, 211, 266 n.4; lesbian/gay
    participation in, 208–9, 212; and
    motherhood, 125; and numbers game,
    261 n.9; and openness/secrecy, 180, 190,
    209, 212, 266 n.2
"Black" term, 17
Blackman, Inge, 67, 71
Blues Legacies and Black Feminism (Davis),
    12
Blues singers, 12
Blumstein, Phillip, 162, 225, 228, 229
Bonilla-Silva, Eduardo, 221
Bradford, Judith, 234
Braithwaite, Dawn, 172
Bray, James H., 128, 170
Brekhus, Wayne, 35
Brown, Malaika, 139, 209
Brown, Rita Mae, 79
Brubaker, Rogers, 92
Bullough, Vern L., 26
Burton, Linda, 46
butch/femme labels, 66, 76, 78, 79, 83, 89,
    256 nn.2,3
Butch Mystique (Wilson), 231, 259 n.27
Butler, Judith, 67

Cahn, Susan K., 81
Caldwell, Mayta A., 265 n.11
Cantú, Lionel, 40

Capitanio, John P., 205
Carby, Hazel V., 12
Caribbean women. *See* Haitian women;
    Jamaican women; West Indian women
Carlson, Shirley, 72, 73
Carrington, Christopher, 229
Chatters, Linda M., 9
Cherlin, Andrew J., 170
childhood experiences: and coming into the
    life, 24–28, 37; and racial/gender/sexual
    identity relationships, 96–97; sexual
    abuse, 56, 255 n.17. *See also* family-of-
    origin relationships
Christianity. *See* Black religious institutions;
    religion
church. *See* Black religious institutions
church mother role, 156, 264 n.9
claiming/enacting a gay identity, 23; and
    conformist path, 36–37, 39, 40–42, 44;
    earlier timing trends, 218; and
    family-of-origin relationships, 120–21;
    and hetero-identified path, 50; and
    motherhood, 122, 151–52; and religion,
    206, 212–13; reversal of, 267 n.13; and
    sexually fluid path, 54; and social class,
    47; and social constructionism, 64; and
    straight-up gay path, 29, 35–36, 40;
    terminology, 252 n.12
Clarke, Cheryl, 40, 80, 155, 251–52 n.7
class. *See* social class
Clingempeel, W. G., 169
closeting. *See* openness/secrecy
clothing. *See* gender presentation
Cochran, Susan D., 235, 268 n.3
Cohen, Cathy, 181, 182, 186, 201–3, 222,
    225
Cohen, Ellen L., 156
Coleman, Marilyn, 128, 129, 168, 169, 171
collective consciousness. *See* racial solidarity
    expectations
college experiences, 34–35, 46–47, 53,
    133–34, 135
Collins, Patricia Hill, 8, 116, 133, 148, 225
colonialism, 252 n.11
coming into the life, 21–64; and closeness
    with women, 58–59; coming out model,
    21–22, 52, 61, 62, 253 n.2; commonali-
    ties, 58–60; data gathering, 22–23; and
    femme gender presentation, 72; and
    gender-blender presentation, 73;
    hetero-identified path, 49–53; and
    lesbian feminism, 59–60, 62; and
    motherhood, 117–18, 120–21, 122, 123,
    124, 130–31, 142, 150–51; and race as

dominant identity, 62; and racial/gender/
sexual identity relationships, 96–97; and
racial solidarity expectations, 23, 31, 36,
48; sexually fluid path, 53–58, 72; and
social class, 29–33, 46–49, 61, 101–2;
and transgressive gender presentation, 74,
76; and White lesbians, 260 n.6. *See also*
conformist path; straight-up gay path
"coming out" model, 21–22, 52, 61, 62,
253 n.2. *See also* coming into the life
conformist path, 36–49; and claiming/
enacting a gay identity, 36–37, 39,
40–42, 44; and gender presentation, 37,
72, 73, 74; and motherhood, 117–18,
142; and relationships with men, 36,
37–38, 41, 42–46, 47, 48; and
respectability discourses, 37, 41, 47–49;
and sexuality self-definitions, 38–39, 45;
and social class, 46–49
conformity. *See* conformist path; openness/
secrecy; respectability discourses
Cooper, Frederick, 92
Cordy, Robert J., 263 n.24
Cornell, Stephen, 17
Cornwell, Anita, 79–80, 225
"covering," 194–95, 196. *See also* openness/
secrecy
Cowan, Carolyn Pape, 162, 229
Cowan, Philip A., 162, 229
Crawley, Sara L., 85, 88
Crocker, Elizabeth, 72
cult of true womanhood, 10–11
Curtin, Roberta Braun, 265 n.15

Dang, Alain, 180, 234, 235, 268 n.3
Davis, Angela Y., 12, 139, 225
Davis, Madeline D., 26, 72, 82–83, 89, 225,
256 n.2, 260 n.6
desire. *See* acting on lesbian desire;
experiencing lesbian desire; sexuality
Diamond, Lisa M., 52, 56
DiLapi, Elena M., 149
Dill, Bonnie Thornton, 8
discourses of respectability. *See* respectability discourses
dress. *See* gender presentation
drug abuse: and family-of-origin relationships, 46–47, 133, 191–92, 262 n.14;
and motherhood, 135–36; and
openness/secrecy, 191

egalitarian household organization ideals:
and Black lesbian invisibility, 114; and
childless households, 176; definitions of,

264 n.2; and feminism, 153–54; in
heterosexual households, 264 n.1; and
intentional mothering, 154, 174–75,
176, 265 n.20, 266 n.21; and money
management, 166; violation of, 161,
265 n.11; and White lesbians, 256 n.6
Ellingson, Stephen, 9
Ellison, Ralph, 90
employment, 8–9; and acting on lesbian
desire, 29–31; and Black female
stigmatization, 12–13; and household
organization, 155–56; and racial/gender/
sexual identity relationships, 98, 99,
101; and respectability discourses,
10–11, 30–31
enacting a gay identity. *See* claiming/
enacting a gay identity
Erickson, Rebecca, 168, 265 n.14
essentialism, 63; and coming into the life,
35–36, 36, 42, 53; and experiencing
lesbian desire, 63–64; and motherhood,
168; and race, 36, 50
Esterberg, Kristin, 7, 59
Eves, Alison, 67
experiencing lesbian desire, 23, 60; and
conformist path, 36, 37, 38, 46; and
hetero-identified path, 49, 50, 51; and
racial/gender/sexual identity relationships, 96; and sexually fluid path, 56;
and social constructionism, 63–64; and
straight-up gay path, 24–25, 27–28

Faderman, Lillian, 66, 260 n.6
family life. *See* household organization
family-of-origin relationships, 62; and
conformist path, 48; and drug abuse,
46–47, 133, 191–92, 262 n.14;
emotional intensity of, 192, 194,
261–62 n.10; and geographic mobility,
33–35, 40, 48, 52–53, 59, 254 n.9; and
motherhood, 124, 125, 137, 141; and
openness/secrecy, 186–87, 189–94,
195–96, 266 n.6; and passing as
heterosexual, 184–85; and religion, 210;
and respectability discourses, 120–21;
and sexually fluid path, 56–57
The Family of Women (Sullivan), 259 n.22
fem-aggressive label, 73, 257 n.13
feminism: and ethnography, 14–15, 236–37;
and gender presentation, 72; and
household organization, 153–54; lack of
identification with, 88, 259 n.30. *See
also* Black feminism; gender ideologies;
lesbian feminism

femme gender presentation, 70–73; and
Black culture, 71, 72, 88–89; and gender
ideologies, 88–89; and hetero-identified
path, 50, 52, 72; and integrative
marginalization, 203; and motherhood,
123, 142; and openness/secrecy, 186;
and racial/gender/sexual identity
relationships, 94, 103, 104, 111; and
sexually fluid path, 72. See also butch/
femme labels
Ferguson, Roderick A., 252 n.10
Ferree, Myra Marx, 162
Fingerhut, Adam W., 154
Forbes, James A., Jr., 267 n.12
foreign-born women, 40, 181. See also West
Indian women
Frazer, Somjen, 180, 234, 235, 268 n.3
Furstenburg, Frank F., 170

Gabb, Jacqui, 262 n.18
Ganong, Lawrence H., 169
Gartrell, Nanette, 264 n.26
Gates, Gary, 180
gay men: and Black culture, 257 n.12; and
coming into the life, 41–42, 44, 62, 253
n.2; and sexual desire, 219
"gay" term, 17
gender. See gender ideologies; gender
presentation; racial/gender/sexual
identity relationships
gender-blender presentation, 73–74; and
gender complementarity, 82; and
hetero-identified path, 50, 52; and
motherhood, 142; and racial/gender/
sexual identity relationships, 104–5,
108; and social class, 83–84
gender complementarity, 69; and childhood
experiences, 27–28; commonness of, 82,
259 n.23; and openness/secrecy, 200;
and sexual desire, 90, 219; and shifting
presentations, 78; and social lesbian/gay
sphere, 81, 82, 89, 219; and straight-up
gay path, 36; and White lesbians, 259
n.22
gender display. See gender presentation
gender ideologies: and gender presentation,
26, 71, 72, 82–83, 88–89; and
household organization, 168, 169,
177–79, 217–18, 265 n.14; and
lesbian feminism, 59–60; and motherhood, 139–41, 145, 262 n.18; and
stepfamilies, 170–71. See also
Black feminism; feminism; lesbian
feminism

gender presentation, 65–91; aggressor/
aggressive/AG labels, 66, 75, 76, 255–56
n.1, 257 n.13; and Black culture, 69, 71,
72, 75–76, 88–89, 90; and Black female
stigmatization, 81, 85; and Black
masculinity stereotypes, 69, 83, 86–88,
259 n.27, 267 n.11; butch/femme labels,
66, 76, 78, 79, 83, 89, 256 nn.2,3;
childhood, 25–28, 97; and conformist
path, 37, 72, 73, 74; and context, 68,
74; data gathering, 69–70, 257 n.11;
gender-blenders, 50, 52, 73–74, 82,
83–84, 104–5, 108; and gender
ideologies, 26, 71, 72, 82–83, 88–89;
and hetero-identified path, 50, 52, 72;
and household organization, 88, 157,
176–77; labels for, 66–67, 70–71, 84,
255–56 nn.1–3; and lesbian feminism,
66–67, 79–80, 82, 88, 89–90; and
motherhood, 123, 132–33, 139, 142,
147; and openness/secrecy, 186–87, 200,
203–4; and racial/gender/sexual identity
relationships, 94, 97, 103, 104–5, 108,
111; and respectability discourses, 69,
84–85; and sexual agency, 82, 83, 88,
91, 219; and sexual desire, 90, 219; and
sexually fluid path, 54, 72; shifting, 78;
and social class, 69, 76, 78, 83–86, 89;
and social constructionism, 64; and
social lesbian/gay sphere, 68, 68–69,
81–82, 83, 89, 90–91, 219, 259
nn.21,31; and straight-up gay path, 24,
25–28, 35, 36, 73, 74, 76. See also
femme gender presentation; gender
complementarity; transgressive gender
presentation
geographic mobility, 59, 254 n.9; and
conformist path, 48; and hetero-
identified path, 52–53; and immigration,
40; and straight-up gay path, 33–35
Giddings, Paula, 10, 116
Gilkes, Cheryl Townsend, 156
Gilmartin, Katie, 254 n.8
Goffman, Erving, 181, 184, 194–95
Goodridge v. Dep't of Public Health, 263
n.24
Gottschalk, Lorene, 28
Green, C. W., 206
Greene, Beverly, 62
Griffin, Horace, 205

hairstyles. See gender presentation
Haitian women, 189–90
Halberstam, Judith, 67, 76

Hammersmith, Sue Kiefer, 227
Hammonds, Evelynn M., 116, 130, 225
Harlem, 6, 196
Harris, Laura, 72
Hartmann, Douglas, 17
Hawkeswood, William, 62, 257 n.12
Hays, Sharon, 130, 262 n.12
Heap, Chad, 84–85, 87
Henderson, Mae G., 60
Hequembourg, Amy, 150, 261 n.6
Herek, Gregory M., 205
Hernandez v. Robles, 263 n.24
hetero-identified path, 49–53; and femme
    gender presentation, 50, 52, 72; and
    motherhood, 117–18, 120, 123; and
    sexuality self-definitions, 50; and White
    women, 254 n.14
heterosexual household organization: and
    Black female employment, 8–9; chores/
    child care, 265 n.12; egalitarian ideals,
    264 n.1; and female employment,
    155–56; and feminism, 153–54; and
    financial independence, 264 n.8; and
    gender ideologies, 178–79; and money
    management, 166–67; stepfamilies,
    169–70, 171, 265 nn.15,16
heterosexual privilege, 57, 118, 120, 123
Hetherington, E. Mavis, 128, 169
Hiestand, Katherine R., 27
Higginbotham, Evelyn Brooks, 10, 96, 108,
    220, 225
high-status women. *See* middle/upper-
    middle class women; upwardly mobile
    women
Hill, Marjorie J., 235
Hine, Darlene Clark, 10, 225
HIV/AIDS, 180
Hofferth, Sandra L., 179, 265 n.16
homophobia: in Black community, 37,
    190–91, 201; and Black lesbian
    invisibility, 80; Black religious
    institution challenges to, 180, 266 n.2;
    in Black religious institutions, 205–6,
    209, 212; and conformist path, 37, 38,
    39, 43, 44–45, 48; correlates with,
    205–6, 267 n.9; and gender presenta-
    tion, 80; and hetero-identified path,
    52–53; and motherhood, 123, 125–26,
    129, 137–39, 149, 263 n.24; and
    straight-up gay path, 29, 30, 31, 33. *See
    also* openness/secrecy; respectability
    discourses
Honey, Maureen, 8, 9
Honnold, Julie A., 234

household organization, 153–79; and Black
    female autonomy, 8, 155, 251–52 n.7,
    264 n.8; and Black lesbian invisibility,
    114, 154–55; childless households,
    176–77; chores/child care, 160–64,
    174–75, 265 nn.11,12,14,15; data
    gathering, 161; and employment,
    155–56; financial independence, 155,
    157, 157–60, 174, 264 n.8; and gender
    ideologies, 168, 169, 177–79, 217–18,
    265 n.14; and gender presentation, 88,
    157, 176–77; money management,
    164–67; and motherhood, 145, 159,
    262 n.18; multigenerational households,
    115, 260 n.4; and racial/gender/sexual
    identity relationships, 99; and status of
    motherhood in Black culture, 8, 156,
    157, 168–69; surname sharing, 257
    n.16; White women, 256 n.6. *See also*
    egalitarian household organization
    ideals; heterosexual household
    organization; stepfamilies
Hunter, Marcus Anthony, 264 n.2
Huppin, Mark, 28, 179

identity: importance of, 5–6; individual vs.
    collective, 93, 94, 101, 105, 106–7; as
    lived project, 4, 219–20; and mother-
    hood, 167–68, 265 n.13; postmodern
    anti-categorical approach, 5–7; and
    similarity/difference, 107–8; structural
    vs. relational nature of, 97, 101, 106–7,
    108, 111–12
identity relationships. *See* racial/gender/
    sexual identity relationships
immigration. *See* foreign born-women; West
    Indian women
in vitro fertilization (IVF). *See* alternative
    insemination
Insabella, Glendessa M., 169
insider-outsider status, 14–15, 236–37
integration experiences: and motherhood,
    145–46; and racial/gender/sexual
    identity relationships, 95–96, 98, 111;
    and straight-up gay path, 30–31, 32
integrative marginalization, 201–5, 222
intentional mothering, 132, 142–44; and
    Black lesbian invisibility, 114; and
    claiming/enacting a gay identity,
    151–52; and class privilege, 119, 143;
    and egalitarian household organization
    ideals, 154, 174–75, 176, 265 n.20, 266
    n.21; and kin adoption, 133, 134–35,
    136–39, 141

Internet, 47
intersectionality, 4–5, 20, 216
Islam. *See* Black religious institutions; religion
"It Jus Be's Dat Way Sometime" (Carby), 12
IVF (in vitro fertilization). *See* alternative insemination

Jackson, John L., 196
Jamaican women: and conformist path, 44–45; and gender presentation, 75; and household organization, 157, 169; and motherhood, 123, 125–26, 129; and openness/secrecy, 189, 190, 261 n.8; and religion, 206–7; and respectability discourses, 11
Jamison, Tyler, 128, 168
Jenkins, Candice M., 10, 11, 103, 105, 107
Johnson, E. Patrick, 60, 62
Jones, A. C., 172

Kamo, Yoshimori, 156
Katz, Jack, 35
Kellam, Cassondra, 235
Kelley, Robin D. G., 26, 172
Kelly, John, 128, 170
Kennedy, Elizabeth Lapovsky, 26, 72, 82–83, 89, 225, 256 n.2, 260 n.6
Kessler-Harris, Alice, 8
Krakauer, Ilana D., 259 n.21
Kranichfeld, Marion L., 167, 168

labor. *See* employment
Lacy, Karyn, 85
Landry, Bart, 8
Laumann, Edward O., 9
lesbian feminism: and coming into the life, 59–60, 62; and gender presentation, 66–67, 79–80, 82, 88, 89–90; and household organization, 157
lesbian/gay activism, 41, 68, 221–22. *See also* social lesbian/gay sphere
lesbian/gay community groups, 38, 234, 254 n.10. *See also* social lesbian/gay sphere
"lesbian" term, 17
Levitt, Heidi M., 27
Lewin, Ellen, 129–30, 131, 143–44, 265 n.13
Lincoln, C. Eric, 9
Lisagor, Nancy, 7, 255 n.1, 259 n.31
Lorber, Judith, 67
Lorde, Audre, 15, 79, 225

Loulan, JoAnn, 79, 257 n.11
Lynch, Jean M., 118

Mahon, Maureen, 90
Mamiya, Lawrence H., 9
Mattis, J., 9
Mays, Vickie M., 235, 268 n.3
McBride, Dwight A., 227
McCall, Leslie, 216
McCorkel, Jill A., 14, 236
McLanahan, Sara, 265 n.15
methodology, 14–18; and Black lesbian invisibility, 3, 15, 253 n.16; and coming into the life, 22–23; data gathering overviews, 15–16, 231–33, 253 nn.16,17, 268 n.2; data limitations, 62–63, 234–37, 268 n.3; and gender presentation, 69–70, 257 n.11; and household organization, 161; intersectionality, 4–5, 20, 216; locations, 14, 234–35, 252 n.13, 253 n.14; and motherhood, 261 n.5; pseudonyms, 251 n.1; and racial/gender/sexual identity relationships, 93, 260 n.1; and researcher insider-outsider status, 14–15, 236–37; study design, 226–33; survey questions, 239–47, 249; topic selection, 223–26
Mexican women, 40
Mezey, Nancy J., 114, 253 n.16
middle/upper-middle class mothers: and Black culture, 146; and Black lesbian invisibility, 114, 154–55; and class privilege, 114, 118–19, 143, 218, 262–63 n.19; and intentional mothering, 132, 142, 143, 151–52, 174; and openness/secrecy, 126; and respectability discourses, 130, 131, 139
middle/upper-middle class women: and aggressor/aggressive/AG labels, 256 n.1; and Black lesbian invisibility, 2, 149, 154–55, 157; and class privilege, 99, 102, 118–19, 201–2, 203, 218, 262–63 n.19; and coming into the life, 29–31, 47–49, 101–2; and cult of true womanhood, 10; and gender presentation, 69, 78, 83–85, 89; hostility toward transgressive gender presentation, 83, 85–86, 267 n.11; household organization, 158, 174–75; and integrative marginalization, 201–3, 222; and openness/secrecy, 101, 102, 126, 260 n.6; and racial/gender/sexual identity relationships, 97, 98–102, 111; and

researcher insider-outsider status, 15, 237; and respectability discourses, 10, 13, 84–85, 139; and terms for partners, 267 n.8. *See also* middle/upper-middle class mothers

Mohanty, Chandra Talpade, 5

Moore, Mignon R., 3, 8, 9, 182, 204, 221–22

Morris, Jessica F., 114, 130

mosques. *See* Black religious institutions

motherhood, 113–52; adoption vs.
biological conception, 144–45; and assimilationism, 150; and Black female stigmatization, 116, 120, 130–31, 139; and Black feminism, 139; and coming into the life, 117–18, 120–21, 122, 123, 124, 130–31, 142, 150–51; data gathering, 261 n.5; definitions of, 113–15, 155, 260 n.1; and family-of-origin relationships, 124, 125, 137, 141; and gender ideologies, 139–41, 145, 262 n.18; and gender presentation, 123, 132–33, 139, 142, 147; and homophobia, 123, 125–26, 129, 137–39, 149, 263 n.24; and household organization, 145, 159, 262 n.18; and identity, 167–68, 265 n.13; and openness/secrecy, 124, 126–28, 129–30, 139, 197, 198–99; pathways to, 36, 115, 132, 134, 155, 218; and researcher insider-outsider status, 15, 236; and respectability discourses, 13, 116–17, 119, 217; and self-interest cultural contradiction, 130–31, 149, 262 n.12, 263 n.24; and sexual agency, 116, 117, 119, 121, 139, 141; and sexual desire, 117, 118, 261 n.8; and social class, 118–19, 260 n.3, 262–63 n.19; and social lesbian/gay sphere, 151, 264 n.26; status of in Black culture, 8, 149–50, 156, 157, 168–69; and stepfamilies, 115, 128–29, 147–48, 152. *See also* intentional mothering

Myers, Kristen, 14, 236

National Gay and Lesbian Task Force, 180

Nestle, Joan, 225

New York, 14, 63, 196, 234, 252 n.13

New York City Gay and Lesbian Community Center, 38, 234

Nicholson, Jan M., 128

Nielsen, Linda, 170, 172

nonfeminine gender presentation. *See* gender-blender presentation; transgressive gender presentation

numbers game, 261 n.9

O'Connor, Thomas G., 169

openly gay families in Black community, 196–205; as cross-cutting issue, 181, 204, 214; and distancing, 212, 267 n.13; increased visibility, 166 n.2, 180, 197–98, 205, 208–9, 213; and tolerance, 200–201. *See also* openness/secrecy

openness/secrecy, 180–214; and Black culture, 204; and Black religious institutions, 180, 190, 209, 212, 266 n.2; and conformist path, 37–38, 39, 43–44; and "covering," 194–95, 196; and employment, 31–32, 101; and family-of-origin relationships, 186–87, 189–94, 195–96, 266 n.6; and gender presentation, 186–87, 200, 203–4; historical background, 182–84; and integrative marginalization, 201–5; and motherhood, 124, 126–28, 129–30, 139, 197, 198–99; and passing as heterosexual, 184–85; and race as dominant identity, 180, 185–86, 204, 213; and respectability discourses, 131, 186, 200, 204; and same-sex marriage debates, 180, 190, 201, 204, 266 nn.2,5; and straight-up gay path, 31–33; and West Indian women, 187–90; and White lesbians, 253–54 n.8, 260 n.6. *See also* homophobia; openly gay families in Black community

Pahl, Jan, 164

Papernow, Patricia, 128

parties. *See* social lesbian/gay sphere

partners, terms for, 200, 267 n.8

passing as heterosexual, 50, 184–85. *See also* openness/secrecy

Pattillo, Mary, 110, 214

Pattillo-McCoy, Mary, 9

Peña, Susana, 62

Peplau, L. Anne, 28, 154, 179, 265 n.11

Perry, Kathryn, 67, 71

Ponse, Barbara, 25, 72, 225

poor women: and autonomy, 251–52 n.7; and coming into the life, 46–47, 48, 61; and motherhood, 133, 218; poverty rates, 254 n.13. *See also* social class; upwardly mobile women

Prager, Jeff, 99

primary lesbians. *See* straight-up gay path

public sphere. *See* social lesbian/gay sphere

queer identity, 17, 256 n.6

race: and essentialism, 36, 50; invisibility in lesbian identity literature, 7–8; and sense of difference, 26–27; and social constructionism, 96; and sperm donors, 263 n.20. *See also* integration experiences; race as dominant identity; racial/gender/sexual identity relationships; racial solidarity expectations

race as dominant identity, 93–94, 95–102, 109–11, 220–21; and coming into the life, 62; and integration experiences, 95–96, 98, 111; and intersectionality, 4–5; and openness/secrecy, 180, 185–86, 204, 213; race frame concept, 17; and racism, 95–96, 97, 186, 220; and religion, 211–12; and similarity/difference, 107–8; and social class, 99–101. *See also* racial solidarity expectations

race frame concept, 17

racial/gender/sexual identity relationships, 92–112, 220; and Black female stigmatization, 104, 105; and Black lesbian invisibility, 7–8; and coming into the life, 96–97; data gathering, 93, 260 n.1; and gender presentation, 94, 97, 103, 104–5, 108, 111; and hetero-identified path, 50; heterogeneity within categories, 93; inability to rank, 105–6; individual vs. collective identities, 93, 94, 101, 105, 106–7; and intersectionality, 4–5, 20, 216; and racism, 6–7, 95–96, 100, 220; and respectability discourses, 103, 105; and social class, 94, 99–102, 111; and straight-up gay path, 36. *See also* race as dominant identity

racial solidarity expectations: and biracial/multiracial identities, 57–58; and Black gay activism, 221–22; and Black lesbian invisibility, 3; and coming into the life, 23, 31, 36, 48; and essentialism, 36; and femme gender presentation, 72–73; and openness/secrecy, 185–86; and racial/gender/sexual identity relationships, 98, 104, 105; and respectability discourses, 11–12, 116–17, 204; and women's liberation movement, 258 n.18. *See also* race as dominant identity

racism: and race as dominant identity, 95–96, 97, 186, 220; and racial/gender/sexual identity relationships, 6–7, 95–96, 100, 220. *See also* Black female stigmatization

Rainwater, Lee, 8

Ramsey, Francine, 235

Reid, Frank M., 209

relationships with men: and conformist path, 36, 37–38, 41, 42–46, 47, 48; and feminism, 60; and hetero-identified path, 49; and motherhood, 122, 123–24; reasons for ending, 121–22; return to, 267 n.13; and sexually fluid path, 53, 54–55, 57, 58; and straight-up gay path, 28–29. *See also* heterosexual household organization

religion, 205–13; as correlate to homophobia, 205–6, 267 n.9; gay-friendly churches, 209–11, 267 n.12; lesbian ambivalence about, 206–8; and lesbian/gay self-acceptance, 206, 212–13; and race as dominant identity, 211–12. *See also* Black religious institutions

respectability discourses, 10–13, 216–17; and acting on lesbian desire, 30–31; and Black feminism, 10, 225; and colonialism, 252 n.11; and coming into the life, 23; and conformist path, 37, 41, 47–49; cult of true womanhood, 10–11; and employment, 10–11, 30–31; and family-of-origin relationships, 120–21; and gender presentation, 69, 84–85; and motherhood, 13, 116–17, 119, 217; and openness/secrecy, 131, 186, 200, 204; and racial/gender/sexual identity relationships, 103, 105; and racial solidarity expectations, 11–12, 116–17, 204; and sexual agency, 216, 217; and silence about sexual desire, 85, 139, 261 n.8; terminology, 261 n.6; and upwardly mobile women, 13, 31–32, 48–49, 120. *See also* Black female stigmatization; homophobia

Righteous Discontent (Higginbotham), 10

Riverside Church, 209–10, 211, 267 n.12

role models, lack of, 28, 30

Rose, Suzanna M., 259 n.21

Rosenfeld, Michael, 254 n.9, 260 n.3

Ross, Marlon, 62

Rothblum, Esther D., 114, 130

Rubin, Gayle, 255 n.1, 259 n.28

Rust, Paula, 55, 225

same-sex marriage debates, 218–19; and Black lesbian invisibility, 215; and openness/secrecy, 180, 190, 201, 204, 266 nn.2,5; and terms for partners, 267 n.8

Savin-Williams, Rich C., 52

Schwartz, Pepper, 162, 225, 228, 229
secrecy. *See* openness/secrecy
Sellers, Sherrill L., 264 n.2
sense of difference: and conformist path, 37; and gender presentation, 72, 85; and hetero-identified path, 50, 52; and race, 26–27; and racial/gender/sexual identity relationships, 97; and social class, 85; and straight-up gay path, 24–25, 27; and transgressive gender presentation, 76
sexual abuse, 56, 255 n.17
sexual agency: and gender presentation, 82, 83, 88, 91, 219; and hetero-identified path, 50; and motherhood, 116, 117, 119, 121, 139, 141; and respectability discourses, 216, 217; and working-class women, 12–13
sexual behaviors, 77–78, 82, 89, 255 n.1, 257 n.17
sexual desire: and gender complementarity, 90, 219; and motherhood, 117, 118, 261 n.8; and racial/gender/sexual identity relationships, 97; and respectability discourses, 85, 139, 261 n.8. *See also* acting on lesbian desire; Black female stigmatization; experiencing lesbian desire
sexuality self-definitions: and conformist path, 38–39, 45; and hetero-identified path, 50; and openness/secrecy, 184; and sexually fluid path, 53–54, 56; and straight-up gay path, 23–24, 253 n.5; terminology, 17
sexually fluid path, 53–58, 72
Shaw, Stephanie, 8, 11, 73, 98
Shockley, Ann Allen, 80
Silvera, Makeda, 80, 125, 129, 261 n.8
Simmel, Georg, 107
Smith, Barbara, 40, 79, 266 n.5
social class: and aggressor/aggressive/AG labels, 256 n.1; and Black lesbian invisibility, 2; and coming into the life, 29–33, 46–49, 61, 101–2; and gender presentation, 69, 76, 78, 83–86, 89; and intersectionality, 20; Jamaica, 126; and motherhood, 118–19, 260 n.3, 262–63 n.19; and racial/gender/sexual identity relationships, 94, 99–102, 111; and researcher insider-outsider status, 15, 237; and social lesbian/gay sphere, 86, 219; and straight-up gay path, 29–33; and in vitro fertilization, 262–63 n.19; and women's liberation movement, 258 n.18. *See also* middle/upper-middle class

women; poor women; upwardly mobile women; working-class women
social constructionism: and coming into the life, 50, 63–64; and race, 96
social lesbian/gay sphere: and Black culture, 68; and coming into the life, 33–35, 42, 43, 44, 62; and conformist path, 42, 43, 44; and data gathering, 228–29; and gender complementarity, 81, 82, 89, 219; and gender presentation, 68, 68–69, 81–82, 83, 89, 90–91, 219, 259 nn.21,31; and hetero-identified path, 51; and lesbian feminism, 79; lesbian/gay community groups, 38, 234, 254 n.10; and motherhood, 151, 264 n.26; and openness/secrecy, 185; racially segregated nature of, 34–35, 59, 62, 68, 79, 185, 219; and social class, 86, 219; and straight-up gay path, 33–35; and West Indian women, 63. *See also* lesbian/gay activism
sperm donors, 143, 263 n.20
Stacey, Judith, 218
Stein, Arlene, 35, 59, 66, 225
stepfamilies, 161–67; with children of both partners, 173–74; chores/child care in, 161–64; conflict in, 128–29, 171–73, 260–61 n.4; and economic resource disparities, 174, 179, 265 nn.18,19; and gender ideologies, 170–71; heterosexual household organization, 169–70, 171, 265 nn.15,16; invisibility in lesbian literature, 115; money management in, 164–67; and motherhood, 115, 128–29, 147–48, 152; as predominant lesbian family form, 155, 264 n.5; and status of motherhood in Black culture, 157, 168–69
stigma. *See* Black female stigmatization; homophobia
straight-up gay path, 23–36; and acting on lesbian desire, 29–33; and childhood experiences, 24–28; and claiming/enacting a gay identity, 29, 35–36, 40; and "coming out" model, 61; and essentialism, 35–36; and gender-blender presentation, 73; and gender presentation, 24, 25–28, 35, 36, 73, 74, 76; and geographic mobility, 33–35; and motherhood, 132–33, 142; and relationships with men, 28–29; and sexuality self-definitions, 23–24, 253 n.5; and transgressive gender presentation, 74, 76

"The Stranger" (Simmel), 107
stud label, 76, 79
Sullivan, Maureen, 259 n.22
surname sharing, 257 n.16

Taylor, Robert J., 9
Tebbe, Nelson, 9
terminology, 17, 252 n.12, 261 n.6
Thompson, Elizabeth, 265 n.15
Thorne, Barrie, 116
Thorpe, Rochella, 79, 225
tomboy experience. See childhood
    experiences; gender presentation
transgressive gender presentation, 74–78,
    257 n.15; and Black culture, 75–76; and
    Black masculinity stereotypes, 69, 83,
    86–88, 259 nn.27,28, 267 n.11; hostility
    toward, 80, 83, 85–86, 267 n.11; and
    integrative marginalization, 203; and
    motherhood, 132–33, 142, 147; and
    openness/secrecy, 186–87; and racial/
    gender/sexual identity relationships, 94,
    105–6, 108, 111; and sexual behaviors,
    77–78, 257 n.17; and social class, 69,
    76, 85–86, 268 n.1; and social lesbian/
    gay sphere, 83; and topic selection, 224
Tripp, C. A., 255 n.1
Troilo, Jessica, 128, 168
true womanhood, cult of. See cult of true
    womanhood
Tucker, Belinda, 46
Twine, France Winddance, 110, 257 n.15

Ulysse, Gina, 126, 252 n.11
upwardly mobile women: and acting on
    lesbian desire, 29–30, 31–32; and
    aggressor/aggressive/AG labels, 256 n.1;
    and coming into the life, 61; and
    conformist path, 48–49; and mother-
    hood, 119–20, 123, 132; and racial/
    gender/sexual identity relationships,
    99–100; and respectability discourses,
    13, 31–32, 48–49, 120; and straight-up
    gay path, 29–30. See also social class

Van Haitsma, Martha, 9
VanderStoep, S. W., 206

Walby, Sylvia, 153
Waters, Mary C., 110
Weaver, Shannon E., 129

Weinberg, Martin S., 227
Welter, Barbara, 10
West Indian women: and conformist path,
    37, 38–39, 43–45; and gender
    presentation, 75; and motherhood, 123,
    125–26; and New York, 63; and
    openness/secrecy, 187–90, 261 n.8; and
    religion, 206–7; and researcher
    insider-outsider status, 15, 236–37;
    and respectability discourses, 11, 252
    n.11
Weston, Kath, 66, 251 n.1, 261–62 n.10
White women: Black lesbian lack of
    identification with, 103–4, 106–8;
    employment, 8–9, 253–54 n.8; and
    femininity stereotypes, 72, 257 n.13;
    and gender complementarity, 259 n.22;
    and hetero-identified path, 254 n.14;
    lesbian dress, 224; and lesbian feminism,
    67, 79, 256 n.6; lesbian motherhood,
    114; and masculinity stereotypes, 87,
    259 n.28; and openness/secrecy, 253–54
    n.8, 260 n.6; and women's liberation
    movement, 258 n.18. See also Black
    lesbian invisibility
Wilson, Debra A., 231, 259 n.27
Wolcott, Victoria W., 8, 12–13, 216–17, 261
    n.9
women's liberation movement, 78–79, 258
    n.18. See also lesbian feminism
work. See employment
working-class women: and aggressor/
    aggressive/AG labels, 76; and coming
    into the life, 101–2; and cult of true
    womanhood, 10; household organiza-
    tion, 157–58; and integrative marginal-
    ization, 202; and motherhood, 114, 118,
    139, 218; and racial/gender/sexual
    identity relationships, 94, 103–5; and
    researcher insider-outsider status, 15,
    237; and sexual agency, 12–13; and
    straight-up gay path, 32–33; and
    surname sharing, 257 n.16; and terms
    for partners, 267 n.8; and transgressive
    gender presentation, 69, 76, 85, 268 n.1.
    See also upwardly mobile women

Yancy, William L., 8
Yoshino, Kenji, 194

Zucker, Kenneth J., 28

TEXT
10/13 Sabon

DISPLAY
Sabon

COMPOSITION
Westchester Book Group

INDEXER
Do Mi Stauber

PRINTING AND BINDING
Maple-Vail Book Manufacturing Group

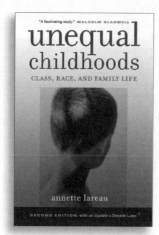

Unequal Childhoods

Class, Race, and Family Life

ANNETTE LAREAU

Second Edition with an Update a Decade Later

"A fascinating study."

—Malcolm Gladwell, author of *Outliers*

Critics Choice Award, American Educational Studies Association; Sociology of Culture Section Best Book Award, American Sociological Association; William J. Goode Best Book Length Contribution to Family Sociology Award, American Sociological Association; 2004 Distinguished Contribution to Scholarship Award, American Sociological Association Section on Children and Youth

$24.95 paper   978-0-520-27142-5

Promises I Can Keep

Why Poor Women Put Motherhood Before Marriage

KATHRYN EDIN and MARIA KEFALAS

With a New Preface

"For all the blathering about family values, few people have actually taken the time to talk to these women. Edin and Kefalas did, and the answers are startling."

—*Bitch: Feminist Response To Pop Culture*

William J. Goode Best Book Length Contribution to Family Sociology Award, American Sociological Association

$24.95 paper   978-0-520-27146-3

Dude, You're a Fag

Masculinity and Sexuality in High School

C. J. PASCOE

With a New Preface

"Pascoe's analysis is sophisticated, mapping the intricacies involved in the relationships between sexuality, gender, race, and class. Yet, her work is clean-cut and difficult to argue against."**—*Men & Masculinities***

Outstanding Book Award, American Education Research Association

$22.95 paper   978-0-520-27148-7